ALEXANDRIA

THE JOURNAL OF THE WESTERN [COSMOLOGICAL] TRADITIONS

ED[ITED BY] DAVID FIDELER

2

PHANES PRESS
1993

ALEXANDRIA

David Fideler
EDITOR AND PUBLISHER

David Fideler
Walter Bakes
Diana Barruéco
Jane Thigpen
PRODUCTION

Gillian Dennis
SUBSCRIPTIONS

The Members of
The Alexandria Society
FUNDING

PUBLISHED BY

Phanes Press
Post Office Box 6114
Grand Rapids, Michigan 49516

ISBN 0-933999-97-6

ALEXANDRIA on the Web
http://www.cosmopolis.com

Contents

Introduction:
Cosmopolis, or the New Alexandria

A MAJOR THEME of this issue of ALEXANDRIA is the ancient city of Alexandria, Egypt, the meeting place of East and West, where various philosophical, scientific, spiritual, and cosmological traditions combined to create powerful new syntheses. This process was fueled by the great university there, the Museum, and the great treasure of the Museum, the legendary Library of Alexandria, the collection of which is known to have exceeded 400,000 papyrus scrolls.

Alexandria remains the supreme archetype of the "university town," and the collection of the great Library was the largest repository of information in the ancient world. While information does not equate with true knowledge, the collection of the Library helped to fuel the brilliant work that was being undertaken in the fields of science, mathematics, literary criticism, mythology, poetry, philosophy, and theology. Later, when the Library was plundered, its collection helped to fuel the public baths.

Alexandria is named after its founder, Alexander the Great (356–323 B.C.E.), whose death marks the beginning of the Hellenistic Age. Alexander's explorations and conquests of the known world prepared the way for cultural exchange and the development of a truly cosmopolitan perspective. In the Classical period, the individual was seen as an extension of the Polis or city-state, the preeminent example of which was the city of Athens. During the fourth century B.C.E., when Plato was devising his Pythagorean models of the ideal State and Aristotle was creating political science, the city-state was already in a period of decline. With the foundation of Alexander's empire and the Hellenistic monarchies, the power of the Polis declined further.

The Hellenistic Age was a time of cultural mingling and exchange. As it became the greatest sea-port of the ancient world, Alexandria once again reveals itself as a historical and cultural archetype, as the meeting point for the collision and alchemical fusion of world cultures. In the Classical period, the individual knew where he or she stood in relation to family, state, community, and the gods. With the coming of the Hellenistic Age, however, this changed. In short, a whole new world opened up. Alexander and his troops made it to India where Greek colonizers encountered indigenous populations. Travelling merchants from the East brought their divinities and spiritual practices to the West. Clement of Alexandria, the early church father, mentions Buddha in one of his writings,[1] and it is thought that Buddhist missionaries were present in Alexandria. The Alexandrian Jews became so Hellenized that their scriptures had to be translated into Greek. In short, the Hellenistic Age marked the advent of a "new world order," one in which specific cultural forms were seen to be relative aspects of a larger world tapestry.

Historically, the dissolution of the old world order offered new opportunities, but it was an unsettling experience. In the Hellenistic Age, with the collision of cultures, the *individual* was born and life seemed far more uncertain than it had before. As individuals looked for a compass to help orient themselves within a greatly expanded universe, a wide spectrum of philosophical and religious teachings flourished in the environment. Philosophy, once the province of an intellectual elite, became an everyday, practical matter of concern for many, a source of guidance in daily life. No longer merely the extension of the Polis, the individual became a citizen of the cosmopolis, the "world city," of which the modern notion of the "global village" is only a more recent expression. The greatest living incarnation of the new cosmopolitan landscape was Alexandria; and in the spiritual and philosophical schools which flourished there, the cosmopolitan idea was taken to an even higher level: humanity, it was revealed, is not only a "world citizen," but a mediator between spirit and matter, a universal principle, a citizen of the entire *kosmos*. Only quite recently has this perspective of global and universal consciousness re-emerged in popular thought and our cultural mythology.

The Alexandrian ideal, I would like to suggest, reflects the emergence of a universal, noetic, contemplative, and cultural archetype which has been active at various points in our planetary history. Certainly an earlier incarnation of it can be seen in the Academy at Athens. But in a broader cultural sense it only becomes fully articulated in Alexandria as the tribal consciousness of the Polis gives way to the world-consciousness of the Hellenistic Age and culminates in the Universal Consciousness of Alexandria. The preeminent theme of the Alexandrian philosophic, Hermetic, and gnostic schools is the universal principle of Nous or Universal Consciousness, of which humanity is seen as the incarnation and living image. In the Polis, citizens are drawn together and encircle the pole of culture which provides for both the material and spiritual necessities of life; in the archetype of Alexandria, the Cosmopolis, scholars travel from all over the world to a universal center for the realization of their humanity through the realization of consciousness. Here, in Alexandria, the notion of "the man of letters" emerges for the first time in the history of the West. Here the study of the liberal arts is perfected, those arts which, under the tutelage of the Muses, liberate the soul and ornament one's existence with beauty and grace. Here, in the first "University" deserving of the name, the physical and intelligible universes are diligently explored against the gnostic and epistemological perspective of *homo universalis*, humanity seen as *universal* citizen and the incarnation of Consciousness (Nous) and Intelligence (Logos). In an age when our so-called universities have become vocational schools attended by students who are more interested in getting jobs than in realizing their intrinsic humanity through the liberal—and liberating—arts, the archetype of the Alexandrian University provides a reliable standard against which the aims of true education may be distinguished from the ends of modern education, falsely so-called. Much lip-service is paid these days to "raising the level of education so that we can remain globally competitive in a world economy," but what is being said here has to do with the common skills of reading, writing, and arithmetic, and nothing to do with the nature of true education. Conversely, if true education were really valued, these other concerns would take care of themselves. For once a person is truly educated and has personally realized what it means to be human, he has surely by that time learned how to learn and has become an effective agent in the world. At that point an individual is authentically empowered to do whatever he should please, in any field he may choose. It is the purpose of education—and our educators—to help each individual reach this level of personal and universal realization.

The great allure of ancient Alexandria, I think, springs from the fact that, at least for a while, this ideal became a reality; and ever since its days of glory, Alexandria, like the famous Pharos, has cast its light down the corridors of time. As a true exemplar, it has something to offer us today, and some unforgettable lessons to teach. One such lesson is that of tolerance and the value of plurality.

The Alexandrian ideal exemplifies the very highest aspirations of humanity; it reveals the true nature of humanity as a universal phenomenon and also defines the true end of education. Historically, however, the eternal vision could not be sustained in Alexandria the city, the archetype's earthly and temporal counterpart. In the same way that religious conflict and political violence have torn the earthly Jerusalem, Alexandria in Egypt, seat of universal learning, also became a deadly battleground for parochial ideologies. The most famous case is the murder of Hypatia, a beautiful, female, pagan philosopher—one of Alexandria's greatest lights—by a fanatical Christian mob, at one of Alexandria's darkest hours. At its highest, Alexandria represents the universal fusion of disparate cultures and spiritualities; at it's lowest, violence between Christians, pagans, and Jews.

Things, however, could have turned out differently. The universal, Alexandrian philosophy which underlies the work of Philo of Alexandria (a Jew), Clement of Alexandria (a Christian), and the pagan writings attributed to Hermes Trismegistus is, for all intents and purposes, identical. The Alexandrian cosmology drew upon classical Greek philosophy—especially Platonism and Pythagoreanism—and, probably in the case of the Hermetica, ancient Egyptian teachings as well. In this view, the source of the universe is the transcendental One that is even above Being. The One gives birth to, or "emanates," the first level of Being or Reality which is both Nous and Logos: the field of "Mind" and "Intelligence," not limited by space-time, which is the "image" of the One and repository of all the laws of the universe. A third level of reality, Soul, is the image of Mind, and Nature is the image of Soul. Plotinus studied in Alexandria and it is out of this intellectual matrix, and his own experience and work, that his "Neoplatonic" philosophy arose. More importantly, this universal, emanationist cosmology—which is compatible with both the highest spiritual and scientific realizations—could have provided a "common ground" between the pagan, Jewish, and emerging Christian traditions. This did, in fact, occur in ancient Alexandria, but the benefits of this vision obviously did not filter down to those in the mobs who were inciting the violence.

Christianity in Alexandria emerged on a positive note, but its subsequent history did not fulfill the initial promise. Clement of Alexandria was a learned individual and initiate who had a high regard for classical philosophy and fully understood, in accord with the Alexandrian ideal, the true end of education. As one writer notes,

> Clement would have enriched Christianity with the deep spirituality of Platonism and enthroned Christ on the highest culture of the age if the *vox populi* and the masters of ecclesiastical organization had permitted. He acclaimed Greek philosophy as inspired of God while critically sifting its propositions, and he begged Christians not to be frightened of it as of ghosts. He protests against those who would attribute the rise of philosophy to the devil; "man has been born chiefly for the knowledge of God," and Clement discovers in Greek philosophy an aid to the attainment of that knowledge, just as he represents Christianity as "the faith of knowledge" (gnostic faith). . . . He advocated a Christianity resting not on credulity but on frank inquiry: "it is impossible to find without having sought, or to have sought without examining, or to have examined without analysing and raising questions with a view to lucidity," and "one

indeed is the way of Truth, but into it, as into an ever-flowing river, streams from everywhere are confluent," and one of these main tributaries was the Greek wisdom which other apologists set in opposition to Christianity.[2]

Unfortunately, from a humanist perspective, and the perspective of *homo universalis*, the anti-intellectual contingent won out. Clement, who was an heir to the pre-Christian Pythagorean cosmological tradition, wrote that the study of science and mathematics was something that should be cultivated by Christians, and was even *necessary* for a full understanding of the early Christian allegories which appear in the New Testament, mathematical allegories like the 153 fish in the unbroken net and the feeding of the five thousand.[3] Other church fathers taught that knowledge was dangerous, that belief in preordained dogma was the only sure way to salvation; their attitude is deplorably illustrated by the words of John, Bishop of Nikiu, who describes Hypatia, a philosopher and mathematician, as being "devoted at all times to magic, astrolabes, and music," with which "she beguiled many through her Satanic wiles."[4] The danger-ous thing about Christianity, as it developed, is a tendency that it shares with other monotheistic systems: it proclaimed that it possessed the one and only truth, the *only* way to the liberation of the soul. Ironically, when Christianity started, it was essentially an apolitical or even anti-political movement, but went on to become the official state religion of the Roman Empire. Culturally, Christianity became an isolationist movement, an aspect which survives today in fundamen-talist circles. Christians refused to send their children to pagan schools and, during the fourth century and most of the fifth, classical literature and science were banned.[5] When the Christians gained political power, they passed laws prohibiting other forms of religious expres-sion. An edict issued in February of 391 C.E. outlawed all pagan worship in Rome and visits to pagan temples. On November 8, 392, an edict called for the severe punishment of anyone involved in the practice of pagan religions, including private devotions.[6] Other laws were passed which allowed for the confiscation of pagan property, prohibited pagans from passing on their estates, and prohibited the employment of those who followed the old traditions.[7] Finally, in 529, the emperor Justinian issued an edict which prohibited the teaching of classical (i.e., "pagan") philosophy; this had the effect of closing down the Platonic Academy in Athens which had stood as a cultural and educational center for nearly one thousand years. Naturally, none of this *had* to happen, and Christianity could have peacefully co-existed side-by-side with other religions in the same way that the worship of Isis could peacefully co-exist with the worship of Mithras.

* * *

The uncanny thing about ancient Alexandria is its resemblance to the world situation of today. Never since the golden age of Alexandria has the world witnessed such a period of interchange (and collision) between world cultures. For better or worse, the boundaries and distinctions between cultures are being dissolved. In some cases, this gives birth to valuable new art forms and cultural manifestations; all too often, it results in homogenization and "a McDonald's in every port." The *kosmopolis* of old is replaced with the contemporary idiom of "the global village," linked by television, telephones, and telecommunications. Eskimos in the northern reaches of Canada now receive cable television via satellite. They are not the only indigenous people for whom this phenomenon is having a pernicious effect on their oral culture, family structure, and traditional ways. A century ago, missionary activities eroded the cultural identities of native peoples; now, through technology, the process of "conversion" has taken on a life of its own.

In the spiritual sphere, a remarkable phenomenon has occurred, reminiscent of the atmosphere in ancient Alexandria. At this moment, every person has potential access to every living spiritual tradition. The Alexandrian Library, minus all of the destroyed texts, is as near as the local interlibrary loan department. As in the Hellenistic period, the specific cultural context of spiritual traditions becomes obvious. In a *world* of spiritual traditions, no one tradition can lay claim to possessing the Absolute Truth without appearing absurd. If, as Clement of Alexandria noted, the "the Truth is One," then, as he says, like a river, there are many tributaries that flow from it and to it.[8] Or, as Porphyry the Neoplatonist explained, "No doctrine has yet been established to form the teaching of a philosophical sect which offers a universal way for the liberation of the soul; no such way has been produced by any philosophy (in the truest sense of the word), nor by the moral teachings and disciplines of the Indians, nor by the magical spells of the Chaldaeans, nor in any other way."[9] Robert Wilken observes that, in the view of Porphyry, "All of the various ways to salvation were concrete and particular, suitable for one people or nation, and it is illegitimate to think that the way of one people can be imposed upon all other peoples. As Symmachus, writing in the later fourth century, puts it in his little treatise defending the Altar of Victory in the Senate House against Christian efforts to have it removed, 'We cannot attain to so great a mystery by one way.'"[10]

The very diversity of spiritual traditions in the contemporary cosmopolis demands greater responsibility and consciousness on the part of the individual than at any previous point in history. In medieval times, spiritual *praxis* meant work within *one* tradition, within *one* cultural context; today, anyone seriously interested in spirituality cannot afford to remain isolated within one tradition and ignorant of the others. In fact, because the burden of spiritual responsibility seems to be passing from the institution of Tradition to the institution of the individual, the individual is being forced to consciously compare one tradition with others in ways that were never before necessary or even possible. The contemporary collision of cultures forces us to distinguish between true spirituality as such, which reflects universal realities, and the concrete, cultural, dogmatic, and institutionalized forms that it takes in specific traditions.

I believe that out of necessity, by reference to the universal standard of human nature, the future spirituality of the West will mark a return to the Alexandrian ideal; but what form will the New Alexandria take?

While it is impossible to answer this question precisely because we are living in times of such rapid change, it might nonetheless be possible to indicate a specific direction. The question is, How will the eternal archetype of Alexandria intersect with the world culture of today and tomorrow in the matrix of space and time?

One clue is that technology is eroding the boundaries of space and time. Therefore, the New Alexandria will not be located physically in one particular place, but will be a virtual community, an Invisible College, of like-minded souls dedicated to the realization of their humanity and the transformation of nature through consciousness and art. While located nowhere, the New Alexandria will be virtually present everywhere, and its existence will be reflected in many disparate locales through that special medium of universal, human nature: the individual. Abiding in the *mundus imaginalis* but reflecting its existence in the *anima mundi* of cultural discourse, the New Alexandria will make itself felt on many levels, all reflecting a return to what it means to be human, what it means to be universal. In the community of the New Alexandria, each soul will be situated, star-like and jewel-like, at the intersection point of a multi-dimensional net, each connected with every other, each reflecting the One Light in prismatic, rainbow hues, according to its own unique cut, lucidity, and opulence. Should some type of interstellar motion set the organism in motion, I can imagine each gem radiating a distinct color and tone, reflecting as a whole the harmony of the entire universe and the music of the spheres.

—DAVID FIDELER

Notes

1. Clement of Alexandria, *Stromata* I, 15; in Roberts and Donaldson, editors, *The Ante-Nicene Fathers* (Edinburgh, 1868. Reprint. Grand Rapids: Eerdmans, 1981), volume 2.

2. S. Angus, *Religious Quests of the Graeco-Roman World: A Study in the Historical Background of Early Christianity* (London: John Murray, 1929), 112–113.

3. See my recent book, *Jesus Christ, Sun of God: Ancient Cosmology and Early Christian Symbolism* (Wheaton: Quest Books, 1993), for a study of these geometrical "story problems" and their origin in pre-Christian, Pythagorean cosmology.

4. See his account of Hypatia in this issue, pp. 61–63.

5. Walter Hyde, *Paganism to Christianity in the Roman Empire* (Philadelphia: University of Pennsylvania Press, 1946), 198.

6. M. J. Vermaseren, *Mithras: The Secret God* (London: Chatto and Windus, 1963), 191, and Hyde, *Paganism to Christianity in the Roman Empire*, chapter 7.

7. Ramsay MacMullen, *Paganism in the Roman Empire* (New Haven: Yale University Press, 1981), 135–36.

8. "The way of truth is therefore one. But into it, as into a perennial river, streams flow from all sides" (*Stromata*, I, 5).

9. Porphyry, *On the Return of the Soul*, quoted by Augustine, *City of God* 10.32; Augustine, in this chapter, makes the claim, however, that "This religion [Christianity] constitutes the single way for the liberation of all souls, for souls can be saved by no way but this."

10. Robert Wilken, *The Christians as the Romans Saw Them* (New Haven: Yale University Press, 1984), 163.

The Museum at Alexandria

EDWARD ALEXANDER PARSONS

from his work *The Alexandrian Library: Glory of the Hellenic World*
Amsterdam, London, and New York: The Elsevier Press, 1952

IN THE BRUCHEION, the Royal Greek center of the city, an amazing
pile of white marble and stone was consecrated to the Muses. Here
were statuary-halls, picture-galleries, lecture-rooms, and refectories
for resident and itinerant scholars. Perhaps a hundred scholars lived
under the generous patronage of the royal foundation: the Museum.
Here, free from want and from taxes, they studied and labored, making
researches into the history of the past and seeking to discover the
secrets of nature. In verse and prose, they produced original work in
letters and made lasting contributions to science. Above all, they
collated the manuscripts, critically studied the texts, and through this
exegesis, they issued recensions of Greek literature. And still more
humbly, they copied manuscripts which they sold to those who had the
desire and means of having books of their own. There was an
archpriest of the Muses who nominally presided over the confrater-
nity, although we believe the chief librarian of the king and of the
Alexandriana was the most important personage of the intellectual
entourage.

But the Museum, considered in its larger aspect as the University of
Hellas, or rather of the Hellenic World, did not alone consist of
sleeping-apartments, refectory or common hall for eating, or walks in
cloisters or colonnaded shelters with seats for rest and contemplation,
of theatres for lectures on philosophy or science, or for readings of the
classic poets and historians, of botanical gardens and animal-parks for
the study of flora and fauna, but above all it offered to its privileged

17

fellows, or indeed to the scholarship of the world, the incomparable resources of the first real and greatest collection of intellectual materials or data ever assembled in antiquity: the Library of Alexandria.

Writing incidentally of the Museum-Library, Gregorovius says:

> The Alexandrian school diffused a splendour over the civilized world which lasted longer than that shed by any university afterwards, whether of Paris, Bologna, or Padua. Long after the creative power of Greek genius was exhausted, encyclopaedic knowledge and Greek sophistry were to be found in the Library and Museum of Alexandria.*

---

* Ferdinand Gregorvius. *The Emperor Hadrian* (London, 1898), 238.

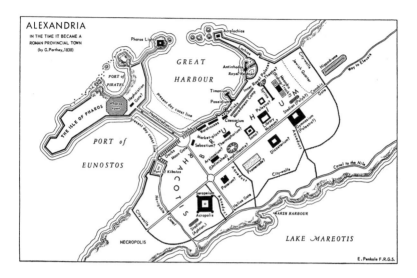

Map of Alexandria

Clio Thalia Erato Euterpe Polyhymnia Calliope Terpsichore Urania Melpomene

The Muses

A Note on the Muses

ADAM MCLEAN

THE MUSES were born as a result of the union of Zeus and *Mnemosyne* (Memory). For nine nights they lay together. After the year passed Mnemosyne gave birth to nine daughters at a place not far from the summit of Mount Olympus. They were raised there by the hunter Crotus, who was transported after death into the sky as the constellation Sagittarius. The choir of Muses made their birthplace a special dancing ground and sanctuary. They also frequented Mount Helicon, where two springs, Aganippe and Hippocrene, had the virtue of conferring poetic inspiration upon those who drank their waters. Beside these fountains the Muses would trace the graceful figures of a dance with tireless feet, while displaying the harmony of their brilliant voices.

The names and attributes of these nine sisters were as follows:

Clio (fame-giver) was the Muse of History, and her symbols were the heroic trumpet and the clepsydra, an ancient water clock. She was often depicted with a half-opened scroll or a chest of books.

Euterpe (joy-giver) presided over Lyric Poetry, and her symbol was the flute.

Thalia (the festive) was the Muse of Comedy and wore the comic mask and wreaths of ivy. She is sometimes shown as carrying a shepherd's staff.

Melpomene (the singer) was the Muse of Tragedy, and wore the tragic mask and vine leaves. She carried the club of Heracles, and was the opposite to Thalia.

Terpsichore (she who loves dancing) was the Muse of Lyric Poetry and the Dance. She also ruled choral song and carried the lyre or cithara.

Erato (awakener of desire) was the Muse of erotic verse or Love Poetry.

Polyhymnia (many hymns) was the Muse of Sacred Hymns and later of the Mimic Art and Storytelling. She was usually depicted as veiled, in an attitude of meditation, with a finger on her mouth.

Urania (heavenly) was the Muse of Astronomy and her symbols were the celestial globe and compass.

Calliope (beautiful voiced), first in rank among her sisters, was the Muse of Epic Poetry and Eloquence. Her symbols were the tablet and pencil stylus.

The Muses were represented as young women with faces smiling, grave or thoughtful according to their function, dressed in long flowing robes, covered with a mantle. At an earlier time they were worshipped in threefold form. On Mount Helicon they were originally known as *Melete* (practicing), *Mneme* (remembering), and *Aoide* (singing). There were also three Muses at Sicyon and Delphi—Nete, Mese and Hypate—personifying the three strings of the lyre.

Bibliotheca Alexandrina:
The Revival of the First Universal Library

A REPORT FROM THE UNITED NATIONS EDUCATIONAL,
SCIENTIFIC, AND CULTURAL ORGANIZATION

The First Universal Library

TRUE THOUGH it is that the city of Alexandria, founded in 332 B.C.E. by Alexander the Great, housed one of the seven wonders of the world—the lighthouse commanding access to its port—Alexandria drew its glory from its library. There, over a period of some six hundred years, a unique collection of scientific, philosophical, and literary works was built up. As a center of instruction and a research institute, it attracted countless scholars for whom it served as a haven or who came to it in search of inspiration for their work. Graeco-Roman civilization, which underlies the whole of Western culture and was also one of the richest sources of classical Arab culture, particularly in science and philosophy, blossomed there.

In about 300 B.C.E. Demetrios of Phaleron, a pupil of Aristotle, was banished from Athens which he had governed for ten years and took refuge in Alexandria. There he became an adviser to King Ptolemy I (Ptolemy Soter, "the Saviour"), who had been one of Alexander's generals and upon whom had devolved the Kingdom of Egypt at Alexander's death. A legend recorded in the twelfth century tells that Demetrios suggested that his sovereign "constitute a collection of books on kingship and the exercise of supreme authority and that he read them." The Library of Alexandria thus came into being, which was modelled on, and, according to tradition, incorporated the contents of Aristotle's library in Athens. The aim was no less than to assemble there "the books of all the peoples on earth."

Ptolemy II (Ptolemy Philadelphus, "who loves his sister") continued and added to the work of his father. Two centuries later, in a cosmopolitan city that had come to occupy second place in the Roman Empire, the library at its zenith contained, according to estimates which vary from one period to another, between 400,000 and 700,000 papyrus scrolls, representing some 30,000 works. To build up so large a collection, an army of scribes was enlisted and housed there, who spent their lives copying out manuscripts from other libraries. For, according to legend again, Ptolemy I had sent a letter "to every King and governor on earth," exhorting them to lend him the works of "poets and prose writers, orators and sophists, physicians, soothsayers and historians." Similarly, any written work brought by a ship was systematically "confiscated" for the purposes of reproduction, thus helping to build up what was known as "the ship collection."

Moreover, "from among each people scholars were recruited who not only were masters of their own languages but also were marvellously at home in Greek. Each group was assigned the appropriate texts, and thus translations were prepared from each language." At that time, however, the different peoples concerned were particularly numerous since Greek civilization held sway from the Straits of Gibraltar to the banks of the Indus, from the Danube to Upper Egypt. It was then that, as legend has it, 72 scholars—six for each of the tribes of Israel—came to Alexandria to make in 72 days a Greek translation of the Old Testament which consequently became known as the Septuagint. For the first and probably the last time in history, visitors to the library could experience the heady sensation of having before them all the books in the world.

But how was one to find one's way among them? The major innovation was the development and application of a system to classify and inventory all the documents by "key word" and by author in the "Pinakes," from the Greek word meaning "tablets," i.e. the tablets on which all the works were listed. This was the achievement of Callimachus (310–240 B.C.E.), the master of Eratosthenes, and, through the latter, of Aristarchus, two of the first directors of the library.

However, the library itself formed only part of a larger complex, the "Museum": in other words, the temple of the Muses, who were the divinities not only of the Lyric arts, but also of the sciences. Created in the image of the school founded by Aristotle in the Lyceum district in Athens, this complex contained, in addition to the library which was the source of its fame, an astronomical observatory, a zoological and botanical garden, and meeting rooms. There, for six centuries (from the third century B.C.E. to the third century C.E.), the greatest scholars lived or stayed, with the result that Alexandria became the hub of the movement of ideas throughout the Mediterranean basin and the Near East. These included Herophilus (c. 340–300 B.C.E.), who established the rules of anatomy and physiology; Euclid (330–280 B.C.E.), the inventor of geometry; Eratosthenes (284–192 B.C.E.), who calculated the circumference of the earth; Aristarchus (215–143 B.C.E.); and Dionysius Thrax (170–90 B.C.E.), who codified grammar; and Claudius Ptolemateus (90–168 C.E.), the founder of cartography.

But it has to be said, in the interests of historical truth, that this gigantic undertaking was not rooted in intellectual philanthropy. Its primary objective was to provide the rulers of Alexandria with a unique means of domination by placing at their almost exclusive disposal knowledge that could serve to buttress their authority. This knowledge was essentially that which was to be found in books, including the sacred texts of the peoples under domination, which were even translated in an attempt to get to know them better; but it was also a living form of knowledge in that the scholars, who to all intents and purposes led the lives of recluses within the precincts of the royal palace (so that the Museum became known as the "bird-coop of the Muses"), would, on request, provide the sovereigns with advice day after day.

The same concern for the historical record leads us to be very cautious regarding the real reasons for the disappearance of the library which in any case had to contend with more than its fair share of wars and invasions, not to mention their corollary, fires. It is related that in 48 B.C.E. the Egyptian boats besieging Julius Caesar entrenched in the citadel were set ablaze and that the flames spread all the way to the library, fanned by the north wind. To make up for the damage done, some years later Anthony had 200,000 scrolls transferred to Alexandria from the only rival library, in Pergamum (Asia Minor). Subsequently, the city was captured and recaptured, and often plundered at the same time, by Queen Zenobia (268 C.E.), the Roman emperors Aurelian (273 C.E.) and Diocletian (295 C.E.), the Persians (618 C.E.), and General Amr Ibn Al-As (640 C.E.).

But more prosaically, it is very possible that the library had become obsolete. The papyrus scrolls, which quickly suffered from the assaults of time, were less easy to handle than the codices, rectangular collections of manuscript sheets bound together and enclosed in wooden or leather covers, which made their appearance at the end of the third century C.E. However that may be, at the time of the arrival of the Arabs, who turned Alexandria into a military citadel, Greek manuscripts must still have existed since they have come down to us in Arabic translations.

The Project

The aim is to create a "Bibliotheca Alexandrina" which may become as renowned as the original library was two thousand years ago. And since nothing remains of that library, our present concern is not with restoration but with the revival of a temple of learning, with attention being given mainly to the history, geography, and, more generally, culture of Alexandria and the surrounding area, i.e. the Mediterranean basin and the Near East.

Endowed with the most modern facilities, it will open its doors not only to the public at large, but also to researchers in the fields of archaeology, history, architecture, philology, philosophy, Christian and Muslim theology, science, etc. In addition, it will serve as a center for the restoration and consultation of original manuscripts threatened with destruction, in particular the tens of thousands of medieval manuscripts held by Egyptian mosques, museums, monasteries and convents, for which no exhaustive catalogue so far exists.

This project, to be carried out in stages, will be completed at the beginning of the next century.

The basic collection in the fields of science and medicine housed by the present library of the University of Alexandria is to be expanded, but before that, attention will be given to the human sciences. The new library will open its doors in new buildings in 1995, with an initial collection of 200,000 volumes. Then it will gradually increase its stock (the aim being to assemble as many as four million volumes, then at a later stage eight million volumes, while reserving the possibility of enlarging the infrastructure); at the same time it will be provided with the services that have now become essential for an undertaking of this kind.

It will be managed on an entirely computerized basis and access to its catalogue will gradually be ensured through telecommunication links with universities in the region. This will be backed by a database which will store information relating in particular to Greek and Middle Eastern antiquity, the meeting of Egyptian and Greek civilizations, the birth of Coptic Christianity and the influence of Islam, with special emphasis on the history of science in the ancient world. The database will be accessible to researchers all over the world by means of a regional information retrieval service; likewise, the library will be linked to retrieval services in the rest of the world from which it will be able to obtain information on the same or related subjects.

Since it is essential that there be personnel who have been trained in all the techniques of library science, an international school of information sciences will be established on the site of the library. It will be open to students preparing an advanced diploma or specialized doctorate, not only under its own auspices but also for other institutions in Egypt and the Middle East.

Finally, all the modern communication facilities—projection, reproduction, microfiche screening, cassettes, videos, etc.—will be installed in rooms which can hold nearly 2,500 people and be used for major international congresses, so that the library may become a focal point for the exchange of advanced ideas throughout the world.

The cost of so ambitious a project is of course high, representing a total of $160 million. In addition to the price of the land ($60 million), the construction of the buildings is estimated at $60 million, and the constitution of collections and the purchase of equipment at $40 million, of which an initial amount of $12 million will be needed to assemble the first collections, $3 million for staff training and further training and $1 million for automation and access to foreign information retrieval services.

The Contribution of the Egyptian Authorities

To carry through so ambitious a project, the authorities of the Arab Republic of Egypt, which initiated it, established, by a decree dated March 25, 1987, the National High Committee of the Library of Alexandria under the patronage of the President of the Republic, Mr. Hosni Mubarak. An Executive Committee, at ministerial level, is responsible for the smooth execution of the project.

Egypt has offered to provide a plot of land of an area of four hectares, of an estimated value of $60 million, on the sea front where the Palace of Ptolemy formerly stood, together with an international conference center, forming part of the future infrastructure of the library and whose construction, practically completed, will cost $20 million. An initial allocation of 2.2 million Egyptian pounds has been included in the Egyptian five-year plan to cover the costs of the Egyptian personnel and the local project-support services, to which 15 million pounds will be added over a longer period.

The Contribution of Unesco and the
International Community

It was during a visit to Egypt undertaken by the previous Director-General, Mr. Amadou-Mahtar M'Bow, in February 1986 that the possibility of international assistance to carry out this project was officially discussed.

Accordingly, the Executive Board, which is the second decision-making body of Unesco, invited the Director-General at its 124th session (June 1986) "to co-operate, within the limits of Unesco's resources, with the Egyptian Government in the implementation and execution of this project."

A year later, after a mission of specialists had vouched for the feasibility of the undertaking, the Board at its 126th session invited the Director-General to launch an international appeal for the revival of the library, which he did on October 22, 1987:

I call on the governments of all States, international governmental and non-governmental organizations, public and private institutions, funding agencies, librarians and archivists, and last but not least, the peoples of all countries to participate, by means of voluntary contributions in cash, equipment or services, in the immense effort undertaken by the Egyptian Government to reconstruct and equip the Library of Alexandria, constitute and preserve its collections, and train the requisite personnel.

I call on all intellectuals, artists and writers, historians and sociologists, and on all those whose work it is to inform—journalists, columnists, professionals of the press, radio, television and cinema—to help to develop an awareness by the public in all countries of the universal dimension of the project for the revival of the Library of Alexandria, and to encourage them to contribute to its implementation.

Unesco's contribution to the revival of the Library of Alexandria, according to the agreements concluded to date with the Egyptian authorities, includes the following services, already provided or forthcoming:

—a feasibility study of the entire project, completed in 1987 and comprising a series of expert evaluations for the architectural program providing the basis for the international competition launched in 1988, and bearing on the acquisition of collections, the choice of data-processing systems, the establishment of the international school of information sciences and the internal organization of the library (technical requirements and choices, services, etc.);

—a mission to Europe by two Egyptian officials to study various major libraries;

—a symposium (1988) attended by some 20 experts who reviewed the feasibility study.

The estimated cost of all these services is slightly more than $100,000. But above all, Unesco has undertaken to encourage and attract foreign contributions to equip the building, to acquire collections, and to provide fellowships for the future librarians.

Office of Public Information Unesco 7, Place de Fontenoy, 75700 Paris, France. Telephone: 45.68.17.43; telex: 204379F or 200472F.

The Thothmeseion at Thebes

Aphrodite with Eros

Marble statue, second century C.E., in the
Graeco-Roman Museum at Alexandria.

Alexandria: Past, Present, and Future

ERIC MUELLER

THE VERY NAME of Alexandria has charisma. It reverberates down through the ages and conjures up ideas of intellectual greatness, cultural sophistication, and more than a touch of the exotic. When I recently walked its streets, sat in its cafes, and gazed across the wide blue bay out to sea, I wondered whether Apollonius the poet, Euclid the mathematician, Ptolemy the astronomer, or Hypatia the philosopher hadn't perhaps walked right there, sat just there, and shared the same view of the horizon.

Ancient Alexandria is no more. Yet the city today still offers the visitor hints and reminders of her ancient youth, and this in a modern setting not lacking its own charm, attraction, and power to provoke reflective thought about the tensions besetting the world and ways to really address them.

I visited modern Egypt's second largest city, al-Iskandarîyah (the Arabic name of Alexandria) in mid-April 1993. It has a population of some three million people and is a major port even today. Alexandria is a coastal city par excellence—it stretches about twenty km from east to west along the sea front, yet it only extends some two km inland.

The city's shipping and port facilities are mostly located in the western harbor, while the modern five-star hotels, resorts, and bathing beaches lie to the east of the main part of the city, along the coast and around Ma'mûrah Bay. But it is Central Alexandria, adjoining the city's eastern harbor, a spectacular semicircular bay, where almost all the sites dating back to Hellenistic times are located. This was the heart of the ancient city. It was here that I sought and found comfortable hotel accommodations—far from the tourist resorts, but conveniently close to the places that have real meaning as far as I was concerned.

My first priority was to seek out the physical remains of the ancient city. That was not hard.

Occupying a commanding position on the horizon at the northwest end of the eastern harbor is the square, fifteenth-century Qâît Bây fortress. The fort occupies the spot on what used to be Pharos island where the great lighthouse of Alexandria once stood—one of the seven wonders of the ancient world. Before that, it was here that Alexander is said to have ordered the foundations of the city of Alexandria to be laid on April 7, 331 B.C.E. I remembered the ancient writer Plutarch's account of the traditional tale:

> According to this story, after Alexander had conquered Egypt, he was anxious to found a great and populous Greek city there to be called after him. He had chosen a certain site on the advice of his architects, and was on the point of measuring and marking it out. Then as he lay asleep he dreamed that a grey-haired man of venerable appearance stood by his side and recited these lines from the *Odyssey*: "Out of the tossing sea where it breaks on the beaches of Egypt rises an isle from the waters: the name that men give it is Pharos." (*Odyssey* 4.354–5)
>
> Alexander rose the next morning and immediately visited Pharos. At that time it was still an island near the Canopic mouth of the Nile, but since then it has been joined to the mainland by a causeway. When he saw what wonderful natural advantages the place possessed—for it was a strip of land resembling a broad isthmus, which stretched between the sea and a great lagoon with a spacious harbor at the end of it—he declared that Homer, besides his other admirable qualities, was also a very far-seeing architect, and he ordered the plan of the city to be designed so that it would conform to this site.[1]

The lighthouse was built around 280 B.C.E. by Ptolemy II Philadelphos on Pharos island. Ancient writers say the lighthouse stood about 120 meters high, and they describe it as having three main "stories." The lowest was square and contained 300 rooms. A spiral staircase led up from this base through the octagonal second story and the cylindrical third story to the lantern at the top. The structure was then surmounted by a statue of Poseidon. The lighthouse was equipped with a mirror, enabling its light to shine far out to sea.

Over centuries silt built up the causeway, called in antiquity the Heptastadion (because it was seven stades or three-quarters of a mile long), between the mainland and Pharos island. The record of the Roman Civil War attributed to Julius Caesar recounts a battle between Roman and Egyptian forces on the narrow causeway.[2]

The lighthouse was largely destroyed during the Middle Ages, the final blow having been dealt by an earthquake in the fourteenth century. About 1480 C.E., the Egyptian Sultan Qâît Bây used the fallen stone blocks of the lighthouse to build the present-day fort.

A short walk from my hotel took me to the site of the Roman amphitheater. A small semicircular theater with astoundingly well-preserved seats, it is adorned with columns of Italian marble and surrounded by a complex of passages and "dressing rooms." The amphitheater was probably built in the third century C.E., but was later modified. The seats still bear carved graffiti dating to the sixth century expressing support for the "Blue" and "Green" supporters of rival charioteer teams which raced in the hippodrome.

Well below the current surface level of the land, the amphitheater was discovered in modern times by workmen digging the foundation for an apartment building. Adjacent to the theater are other areas, still under excavation, where the remains of residences, a school, and a gymnasium can be seen.

A few blocks away is the Graeco-Roman Museum which houses a brilliant collection of artifacts dating back to the Ptolemaic and Roman periods of the city. These include a striking statue of Isis, in the Hellenistic style, and a black Apis bull cult statue. Many smaller votive statues are no less attractive. Also of considerable interest are the mosaics, objects of daily use, glass vessels and much else. The museum boasts an excellent collection of ancient Ptolemaic, Roman,

Byzantine, and Islamic coins. These include several portrait coins of Cleopatra VII (the famous one), as well as striking gold and silver portrait coins of Roman emperors and occasional empresses, like Septimius Severus' Syrian wife, Julia Domna.

Also in walking distance of the bay, just south of the intersection of Shâri' an-Nabî Dâniâl ("Prophet Danial Street," which runs north-south) and Tarîq al-Hurrîyah ("Freedom Avenue," which runs east-west) is the Mosque of the Prophet Dâniâl. It is a relatively modern, nondescript building but it occupies the site which tradition holds to be the location of the still undiscovered tomb of Alexander the Great. The last recorded visit to Alexander's tomb was by the Roman Emperor Caracalla in 215 C.E. Today there's not much to be seen there: a modern building and a crowded intersection of two very busy streets. One of these, Tarîq al-Hurrîyah, is the modern name for the ancient main street of Hellenistic Alexandria: the Canopic Way. It ran from the Gate of the Sun in the city's eastern walls to the Gate of the Moon in the west.

Well south of this area are the Catacombs or Kawm al-Shuqâfah which consist of underground chambers that served as burial sites for Alexandrians in the second century C.E. They were discovered around the turn of the century when men tried to rescue a donkey that had fallen into a hole leading into the catacomb complexes.

Most of the chambers in the catacombs are undecorated. Bodies were entombed in humble niches, their names and ages marked in red on the stone slabs which covered their resting places. There is one tomb within the catacombs, however, which displays unique and extensive carving. In its central chamber are three false sarcophagi and the entire tomb exhibits a fascinating mix of ancient Egyptian and Hellenistic artistic styles. Over the entrance are uraei and faces of Medusa. Inside, figures of Anubis, Isis, and Horus, carved in high relief in a distinctly "naturalistic" style, grace the walls.

Near the entrance to the catacombs is a large room with a stone platform in the center. This evidently was a gathering place where friends and relatives of the deceased could come to hold a *klinê*—a banquet in honor of the dead. Archaeological excavations have turned up written invitations to just such occasions at several sites in Egypt.

In the same vicinity was the Tegran Tomb which has been excavated and reconstructed in a little kiosk above ground. This differs from the others in that its decoration consists entirely of wall paintings. It too is strong testimony to the intermingling of Egyptian and Hellenistic religious and artistic forms.

Not far from the catacombs is the ancient Acropolis of Alexandria, site of the the Serapeum and pillar of Diocletian (erroneously called "Pompey's Pillar" by medieval crusaders and still known by that name today). The pillar was erected by the Alexandrians in honor of the Emperor Diocletian, who opened the grain stores for them during a time of famine. In the same area, on the site of the Temple of Serapis, or Serapeum, there is an underground cistern system with very deep (now dry) wells and ancient conduits (now dry ditches). The aquaducts channeled water from a Nile canal and carried it to a bath designed for the purification of priests of the Apis bull cult, an aspect of the worship of Serapis. The Serapeum also housed a library, probably dating from Ptolemaic times, which was a branch of the famous Library of Alexandria. This place, today a dry barren hill, once witnessed some significant events in Western history.

In 391 C.E. Theophilus, patriarch of Alexandria, ordered the conversion of a temple of Dionysus in Alexandria into a Christian church. Rioting between Christians and pagans resulted, in the course of which Christian mobs occupied the Serapeum and subsequently destroyed it.

Today remains of underground halls of the library can still be seen in a long underground passageway, now partly flooded. Niches, dug out of passageway's earthen walls, used to hold papyrus scrolls.

At the same location there is, near the bottom of the Acropolis, a Nilometer, essentially a small (man-sized), undecorated arch located in a stony, depressed gully, now completely dry, but originally connected to a canal leading to a branch of the Nile. Ancient Memphis (near modern Cairo) and Aswan, far in the south of Egypt, were also equipped with Nilometers, designed to measure the level of the river.

This is far from all of interest to a visitor to Alexandria. The long street along the bay, Shâri' al-Gaysh, is lined with small restaurants affording magnificent kofteh, kebâb, rice and other delicacies, plus a spectacular view of the bay in an atmosphere refreshed by sea breezes.

Alexandria is a thriving Mediterranean city, an Arab and predominantly Muslim city. Its three million people crowd the streets and shops and work in the factories, service jobs, and offices which keep the city going.

We are accustomed to thinking of the cosmopolitan legacy of Alexandria as "Western," and that is more than justified. But in this context, the "Middle East" must be seen as "Western" too. Egypt, Mesopotamia, and Syria-Palestine were direct precursors of the Classical civilizations, and it is there that the roots of Western Civilization can be traced. In turn, Hellenism and Rome left a deep imprint throughout the Eastern Mediterranean world—even beyond the borders of the Roman Empire. Many of the great philosophers of antiquity were "Middle Easterners"—Zeno of Citium, founder of Stoicism, was a Phoenician (Lebanese) from Cyprus; Plotinus was an Egyptian; Porphyry was from South Lebanon; Iamblichus was from northern Syria; and that's only a few. Even after the rise of Islam, philosophy and Sufism sprang almost directly from the philosophical and spiritual legacy of the Hellenistic and Roman world.

As is well known, the Christian Byzantine Emperor Justinian I closed the Academy in Athens in 529 C.E. and banned the teaching of "pagan philosophy." But the teaching and writing of Platonic and Aristotelian philosophy continued unabated in Alexandria into the seventh and eighth centuries, directly transmitting this knowledge to the Islamic world after the Arab conquest of Egypt.

One of the seminal figures of philosophy in the Muslim world, Abû Nasr al-Fârâbî (who died in 950) knew Greek and studied philosophy in Harrân, now in southern Turkey. Harrân was an area that had resisted Christianization right up until the Islamic conquests and had been a center of philosophic study in late antiquity. There too a direct link between the two civilizations can be established.

So, how does modern al-Iskandarîyah relate to ancient Alexandria? How close a connection is felt? After visiting some of the antique sites we have some idea of where the city and the region have been, but where are they going now?

Sadly, the vast majority of Alexandrians do not particularly identify with the ancient legacy. In fact, this is generally true of most modern Egyptians.

The Middle East is perceived as a region where religious feeling runs very strong. In large measure, this is a testimony to the strength and persistence of literalist orthodoxy, the "official" Islam which has long served as a pillar of ruling governments. Under the strong influence of such an approach, the common, popular attitude to "pagan" Egypt is that it was a time of undifferentiated ignorance and darkness. The idea of drawing philosophical or mystical inspiration from such sources as the Book of the Dead, or the cult of Isis, would seem to most average Egyptians to be akin to some form of satanism, and would be regarded as anathema.

Egyptian Christians, the Copts (who account for up to ten or fifteen percent of the population), tend to feel somewhat closer to the ancients, since they regard themselves as "pure" Egyptians, unlike the Muslims who supposedly have Arab admixture. (In historical fact, the percentage of Arab admixture in Egypt is very small, and most Egyptians are Muslims today because their ancestors converted, not because they emigrated from the Arabian peninsula.) Yet even the Copts tend to regard the coming of Christianity to Egypt as the "salvation" of the country, and the average Copt today would not be inclined to look to ancient mythology for spiritual inspiration.

Of course there are intellectuals, poets, and others in Egypt and the rest of the Arab world who do draw at least artistic inspiration from all ages of their history and who are quite open to the notion that there are universal philosophic principles or visions of which specific religions are symbolic reflections.

The Nobel Prize winning Egyptian author, Naguib Mahfouz, in his youth wrote a number of historical novels about ancient Egypt. Tâhâ Hussein, another twentieth-century Egyptian literatus, drew on the ancient Egyptian legacy too. Elsewhere in the Arab Middle East it is very common for poets to use images drawn from ancient religion and literature. One of the leading modern Arabic poets is the Syrian (living in Paris), 'Alî Ahmad Sa'îd, better known by his pen name, Adonis (a name he chose based on Adonis' role in Mesopotamian and ancient Syrian mythology as a god of fertility, suffering, and rebirth). Many other prominent literary people draw on the mythic legacy of the region. The renowned Iraqi poet 'Abd al-Wahhâb al-Bayyâtî (who lives in Spain) comes to mind for his use of Gilgamesh and other such currents. But these are all intellectuals, people who have read and studied and seriously pondered their history. They certainly do not represent mainstream spiritual tendencies.

The late nineteenth and early twentieth centuries saw the development of "liberal" reformist Islamic and secular thought in Egypt and the rest of the Muslim world, akin, in many respects, to developments in Renaissance Europe. Today's intellectuals are beneficiaries of this development, but the intellectuals by no means represent the majority; on the level of the masses, more traditional, literalist thought predominates, and the international situation has in recent years increasingly fostered the traditional literalist and fundamentalist perspectives.

It is an indisputable fact that the international means of modern communication and the world economy are today largely dominated by the major Western nations and Japan. For a long time the military, economic, and technological power of these Western, capitalist states was to some extent balanced by the military and political power of the Soviet Union and other Communist-led states. The Third World was the object of "superpower rivalry." But this rivalry in turn allowed the Third World nations to assert a measure of independence, seeking the protection of both sides against the other.

With the fall of the Soviet Union, however, things have changed drastically. Middle Easterners now feel more seriously threatened than ever before in recent memory due to the developed West's monopoly position and its enormous power. Their cultural identity is in jeopardy due to the influx of Western music, styles, commodities, etc. Their economic livelihood is threatened by the dictates of the World Bank and International Monetary Fund coupled with the vicissitudes of the international market.

When people feel they are under attack and besieged, it is natural for them to "rally 'round the flag," to guard the trappings of their cultural identity with particular jealousy, ever watchful for attempts at subversion. From the standpoint of the Egyptian "man in the street," now that the Soviet Union and Eastern Europe have collapsed, there is no longer any Western country which can be said to oppose the prospect of Western domination of the Arab world.

A new world order is being imposed that seems neocolonialist, since it is premised on the industrialized countries' undiluted economic, political, and cultural predominance. To make matters worse, in the Third World in general, and the Arab countries in particular (including Egypt), social class differences are still severe, life-and-death matters for millions of people. Many are opting to make a sort of last stand for what they see are their rights and livelihood on the ideological basis of Islamic fundamentalism (rampant literalism), which concretely means stubbornly upholding all the outward trappings of orthodox Islam—the signposts that proclaim cultural defiance of the looming homogeneous, materialist, North American-European "world order."

From a humanist standpoint, this fundamentalist trend is very disturbing. It seeks to impose on all Muslims a literalist, exoteric version of Islam where meticulous adherence to ritual practices and orthodox attitudes is the be-all and end-all of "true faith." This not only runs counter to the increasingly cosmopolitan world of today, but it is a negation of the free inquiry and creative thought which were the glory of the medieval Islamic world. Fundamentalism potentially could spell "death" to the sincere, spiritual, humanistic, philosophical approach of Arab philosophers and Sufis which is quintessentially Islamic.

At the same time, the evident assumption by Western elites that the imposition of their shallow, materialistic, computerized cosmology is the only path to "salvation" (now frequently called "democracy") is no less pernicious. How can the indiscriminate opening of "Third World markets" to anything and everything produced in industrialized states serve to raise the level of real culture there? And what kind of "quality of life" is left without culture?

Anyone familiar with life in the industrialized countries is well aware that mass production for the mass market at best panders to mediocrity and to the homogenization of thought and practice which is the scourge of the modern world. Imposing this tyrantless tyranny on the rest of the world will only broaden the scope of our problems and make them more intractable. This is obviously a threat to all humanists, too.

While there are still social class differences in the industrialized countries, the experience of Europe and North America shows that materialistically alleviating social inequalities and achieving a high level of consumer spending is not sufficient to solve the dilemmas of humanity. In the industrial and post-industrial countries of Europe and North America, the rise of interest in spiritual philosophy of all persuasions is a reaction to the shallow, materialistic, and automated post-industrial status quo, and also to the traditional literalist or fundamentalist religious option. Neither mechanistic materialism nor fundamentalism, however, allows for knowledge of the Real, of Being, in Plato's sense.

Fundamentalism reduces cosmology and philosophical and spiritual inquiry to the dogma of one scripture and a single orthodox interpretation of it. The vast cosmic reality is ignored. In its place, half truths are absolutized.

Plato recognized that philosophy was a realm that fairly defied written formulae. Dogmatism or literalism clings to empty formulae. Clearly a bright future can not be secured by such an approach. Materialist positivism, on the other hand, denies the knowability of things in themselves. If the real can't be known, it may as well not exist. "The Good" is defined as what sells. In such an outlook, quality and value become meaningless, quantity is all. Knowledge and understanding of the organization and beauty of the universe are abandoned. This positivist materialism too is a kind of literalism in practice, where statistics take the place of reality. Ecological and social crises are the least that can be expected when this path is followed to its ultimate end.

To address the real, basic problems besetting the modern mind, the modern world—to counter both materialism and fundamentalist dogmatism—we must return to our Western cosmological philosophical-spiritual heritage. That is, if you will, a return to the spirit of ancient Alexandria which brought together a myriad of currents of thought and belief and became a beacon to all the nations of the Hellenistic and Roman world.

The cosmological, spiritual, philosophical approach of ancient Alexandria was characterized by tolerance, pluralism and abhorrence of dogma, yet at the same time it recognized the order and beauty of the universe, the *kosmos*.

This spirit of Alexandria is a healthy alternative to the materialist malaises of the industrialized world (from which the Third World suffers too). It is also a reasonable alternative to the exoteric, literalist perversion of spirituality which, precisely because of its dogmatism, is an intellectual dead end.

Ancient Alexandria is no more, to be sure. But its spirit lives on as an example for the modern world. As contemporary problems grow more and more intractable, the relevance of the "Alexandrian ideal" will become increasingly obvious. Then, more and more intelligent and concerned people will discover as they gaze out at the world that Apollonios the poet, Euclid the mathematician, Ptolemy the astronomer, and Hypatia the philosopher did indeed share with them the same view of the horizon.

Notes

1. Plutarch, "Life of Alexander," in *The Age of Alexander*, trans. Ian Scott-Kilvert (Penguin Books, 1988), 281–82.

2. Caesar, *The Civil War*, Events in Egypt, 16, 17, 18, trans. Jane F. Gardner (Penguin Books, 1967), 175–76.

Alexandria

Alexandria, pictured as a European town in the 1493 edition of the *Nuremberg Chronicle*.

Hypatia of Alexandria: Mathematician, Astronomer, and Philosopher

NANCY NIETUPSKI

ALMOST sixteen hundred years have passed since Hypatia's death, yet her story still fires the imagination. While there is no one incident that marks the definitive end of the Hellenistic, pagan culture, for many Hypatia's courageous life and death personifies the demise of that era as much as Constantine's conversion marked the advent of the Christian age for the Roman Empire.

What we know about Hypatia comes down to us through eight ancient sources; yet, even brought together, they are woefully inadequate at giving us a real portrait.[1] Her violent death so shocked the populace that it dominates almost every account and, like a shroud, it obscures our view of who she was. However, before she died two men wrote of her: Theon, her father, and Synesius, a student and friend who later became the Christian bishop of Ptolemais.

Theon is the last known teacher of the famed Museum of Alexandria, established about 300 B.C.E., which was an institution that nourished and supported advanced learning. Often described as a philosopher, his writings are in mathematics and astronomy.[2] Theon mentions his daughter in book three of his commentary on Ptolemy's *Syntaxis Mathematica* or *Almagest* in which he credits her with editing.[3] The *Almagest* was the definitive work of ancient astronomy that explained the geocentric model of the universe.

Hypatia was born *circa* 370 C.E. in Alexandria and died in 415. We know nothing about her mother or siblings. She was a pagan and it is likely that Theon was her teacher in mathematics and astronomy. It is not known with whom she studied philosophy.[4] Like most women who attained personal distinction, she followed her father's profession. Nothing is said about their personal relationship but Theon must have had lofty hopes for his daughter because he gave her the name Hypatia, derived from *hypatos*, which means "the highest."

She was an established teacher in 393 when Synesius came to Alexandria, and according to the ecclesiastical historian Socrates Scholasticus, students would come from great distances to study under her. He wrote that she succeeded to the head of the school of Plato and Plotinus.

Synesius became a friend of Hypatia's and seven letters which he wrote to her between 394 and 413 are still extant. While they are disappointing at giving us any real picture of who she was, Hypatia must have had considerable influence in Alexandria because Synesius petitioned her on the behalf of two young men saying: "You always have power, and long may you have it and make a good use of that power . . . try to get support for them from all your friends, whether private individuals or magistrates."[5]

Scholars have attempted to discover the type of philosophy Hypatia taught through a study of Synesius' writings. She is said to have expounded on all types but her emphasis was on Plato as interpreted by Plotinus, the Neoplatonist. Her student Synesius' quotation of the *Chaldaean Oracles* suggests that Hypatia was also familiar with these writings, but there is no surviving evidence to suggest that she was a practicing theurgist.[6]

One of our main sources for information about Hypatia comes from the tenth century lexicon called the *Suda*, where the author used three different sources.[7] The first paragraph of the *Suda* entry is generally attributed only to Hesychius of Miletus from his *Onomatology* or index of persons illustrious in studies. However, evidence suggests that information was also used from Philostorgius' ecclesiastical history.[8] The third is an excerpt from the book *Life of Isidorus* by Damascius (*c*.480–*c*.550 C.E.), the final head of the Platonic Academy in Athens.

The only source we have for Hypatia's works is the *Suda* lexicon which states that they were in mathematics and astronomy. She wrote a commentary on the *Arithmetica* of Diophantus and it has been suggested that it was interpolated into the surviving books of Diophantus. The *Suda* mentions the *Astronomical Canon* as her work, but this may refer to her father's commentary on Ptolemy which she edited. Her commentary on *The Conics* of Apollonius is still lost.[9]

The *Suda* states she was the wife of the philosopher Isidorus, but this is an obvious error; while we do not have the exact dates of Isidorus' birth, we do know that he could not have been more than an infant at the time of her death.[10] In fact, both Socrates and Damascius say that she remained a virgin all her life. No one has been able to determine where this error about the marriage arose, but it influenced how the author of the *Suda* edited the last portion of the entry on Hypatia; for he added a large portion of Isidorus' biography on to it which only alludes to her.

The *Life of Isidorus* by Damascius is the biography of his friend and mentor who succeeded Proclus at the Academy in Athens. Damascius was the last director of the Platonic Academy before it was closed forever by Emperor Justinian in 529. The book is lost and exists only in fragments; but with the help of a summary that was made of it around 867 by Photius a reconstruction of the book has been attempted.[11]

As R. T. Wallis notes, Damascius "digresses at incredible length to deal with most of the leading personalities of the Athenian and Alexandrian schools . . . [and] Damascius' eulogy of Isidorus contrasts amusingly with his vivid depiction of the foibles and failings of the other late Neoplatonist."[12]

There is the famous quote about Hypatia included in the summary of *Life of Isidorus* (but not in the *Suda*) attributed to Damascius: "Isidorus was superior to Hypatia, not only as a man is to a woman but as a philosopher is to a mathematician."[13] Although Damascius also states some very flattering things about her, his critical comments and omissions suggest an animosity towards women teachers and highlights the tension and rivalry that existed between the Academy in

Athens and the Alexandrian school.[14]

An example of this animosity appears in an anecdote that Damascius relates when apparently one of Hypatia's students fell madly in love with her and "was unable to control himself and openly showed her a sign of his infatuation." In response, "she gathered rags that had been stained during her period and showed them to him as a sign of her unclean descent and said, "This is what you love, young man, and it isn't beautiful!"[15] She did this to imply that he was preoccupied with sexual desire rather than his philosophical studies.

In many cultures past and present women have been kept out of the public sphere because their presence alone was considered to be sexually provocative. In Athens, respectable women did not enjoy freedom of movement but were secluded in their homes except at times of public festivals. As one writer notes in *The Oxford History of the Classical World*, "We should remember that (polygamy apart) the position of Athenian women was in most important respects the same as that of the 200,000,000 women who today live under Islam."[16] In choosing to relate this incident with the young student, Damascius is telling more than just an interesting story. He is making a comment about a woman's effect as a teacher on her male students. Although today many would see it as amusing, it is still a shocking story, with the intention of making a unfavorable impression. In fact, this anecdote has greatly affected the telling of Hypatia's story throughout the years and it was not until fairly recently that the incident was even related in English.[17]

Generally the anecdote was either completely edited out or distorted. In 1720, John Toland reported that "she took a handkerchief, of which she had been making some use of on that occasion, and throwing it in his face, said; this is what you love, young fool and not anything that's beautiful."[18] In 1721, Thomas Lewis related that she, "without attempting to reason with him like a Platoness, made use of a Stratagem to put an end to the courtship which I believe the most common Prostitute in Venice would blush at: It is so gross an Argument, and a Conviction so Obscene and Odius, that I shall . . . not stain my Paper or offend the Reader with the Translation."[19]

Another area of Hypatia's life which Damascius obscures in order to lessen her credibility is how he describes her teaching position. This is very different from how Socrates Scholasticus puts it in his ecclesiastical history. While Socrates says she succeeded to the school of Plato and Plotinus—the implication being that she headed the Neoplatonic school in Alexandria—this is not the impression that Damascius gives. In the account by Damascius, the emphasis is on Hypatia teaching in the streets or giving an audience in her home. He writes: "The woman used to put on her philosopher's cloak and walk through the middle of town and publicly interpret Plato, Aristotle, or the works of any other philosopher to those who wished to hear her."[20] While Socrates tells of Hypatia frequently appearing in public and indicates that she did not feel abashed about coming into the assembly of men, he did not imply that this was her classroom. There is no mention by Damascius of any type of formal setting, but we know that Synesius traveled from Cyrene, as did many others, to study mathematics, astronomy, and philosophy from Hypatia, and it is unlikely that the instruction took place in the streets of Alexandria.

All accounts of her death attribute the murder to a throng of murderous Alexandrians who attacked her in the street, but the various accounts give different motivations. While there is no direct evidence that Cyril, the Christian Patriarch of Alexandria, actually plotted the murder of Hypatia, historians agree that, at the very least, he set the right climate for the incident.

Socrates wrote at considerable length to place Hypatia's death within the context of the political tumult that was occurring at the time.[21] In 412, Cyril had succeeded his uncle to become the powerful Patriarch of the Roman Catholics in Alexandria through the riotous persuasion of his followers. His first action was to shut down the churches and confiscate the belongings of the Novations, the only other rival Christian sect in Alexandria. Shortly afterwards, a riot ensued between the Christians and the Jewish residents of the city. Many Christians were killed. Socrates relates that "Cyril, accompanied by an immense crowd of people, going to their synagogues . . . took them away from them, and drove the Jews out of the city, permitting the multitude to plunder their goods."[22] This added to the already strained relations between Cyril and the Augustral Prefect, Orestes, because the prefect resented Cyril interfering in his civil authority.

When Cyril attempted to make peace with Orestes and the overture was publicly rebuffed, monks from the mountains of Nitria "with very fiery dispositions" came to the city to fight for Cyril's injured honor. They stopped Orestes in the street and accused him of being a pagan. One, named Ammonious, threw a stone at his head and wounded him, whereupon Orestes arrested him and tortured him so severely that he died. Cyril, who spent five years in Nitria, may have known Ammonious and was extremely upset at his death. He brought the monk's body to a church and, in an emotional eulogy, pronounced him a martyr for his faith.

It was in this climate that a fatal rumor started: it was Hypatia, a friend of Orestes, who was the real cause of all the strife. We can hear the echoes of those rumors in the chronicles written by John of Nikiu when he wrote that Hypatia "was devoted at all times to magic, astrolabes and instruments of music, and she beguiled many people through [her] Satanic wiles. And the governor of the city honoured her exceedingly; for she had beguiled him through her magic."[23]

Shortly after the eulogy for Ammonious, a throng of lay church workers called *parabalani*, led by a lector named Peter, attacked Hypatia in the streets. They murdered her with tiles or oystershells and tore her to pieces, and then burned her body in a church.[24] Was the murder the action of a frenzied Christian mob, driven to extremes by the fasting of Lent, who wanted to defend their bishop's honor, or did Cyril incite his followers to riot to exact revenge against Orestes? Was Hypatia's death just an unfortunate result? Within the framework which Socrates builds, these are some of the implied motives.

The account given by Damascius of Hypatia's murder has, for the most part, been dismissed out of hand by scholars. He relates that

Cyril passed by her house one day and was filled with envy at the crowd which gathered to hear her speak and so plotted her murder. Yet, the notion of Cyril having designs against Hypatia and her school may not be far from the truth.

Nowhere in all the volumes written by Cyril is Hypatia ever mentioned, and nowhere in any of the accounts does it say that he had any regrets about her death. While it may not be possible to know exactly how he felt about Hypatia, we do know how he felt about the cultural perspective she represented, Hellenism, and about those Christians whose loyalties may have been divided between paganism and Christianity. Cyril saw Hellenism as a dangerous adversary; and as guardian of the faithful, it was his duty to do battle with it. Eighteen years after Hypatia's death he finished a massive apologetic work, *For the Holy Religion of the Christians Against the Books of the Impious Julian*.[25]

The apology was written in response to Emperor Julian's *Against the Galilaeans*, a scathing indictment of Christianity which, though now lost, was in wide circulation in the fifth century among the pagans. Julian was raised a Christian, but converted to a mystical form of Neoplatonism in 351, and Cyril felt that his book was exerting a dangerous influence on the Alexandrian Christians.

Hypatia's profession as an astronomer also made her very vulnerable because it was a serious offense to practice the art of divination.[26] Astronomy and astrology were closely related for those who studied the works of Ptolemy. Cyril specifically mentions his objections to astrology in his works.[27]

Given his attitude toward Julian's book and the fact that Hypatia attracted Christian students, it is hard to imagine that Cyril would simply sit quietly aside and allow Hypatia's school to exist unmolested. His past and future actions showed that he would actively defend his vision of orthodoxy against anyone who might threaten it. Whether that action would take the form of murder is the real question.

Unless further evidence surfaces, the question will remain open as to exactly how involved Cyril was in Hypatia's death, but at no other time did he resort to plotting murder. Perhaps he thought if enough pressure was put on Hypatia that she would simply flee the city. He witnessed this happen with other philosophers and teachers in 391 when his uncle destroyed the Great Temple of Serapis.[28] In later years, several Neoplatonic philosophers fled their cities when they were persecuted by the Christians, including Damascius himself.[29]

Only in Damascius' account is the idea of retribution for her murder ever mentioned, and only in this account is bribery discussed as a reason why justice was never sought. He stated, "the Emperor was angry, and he would have avenged her had not Aedesius been bribed."[30] While justice lay in the hands of the Emperor, it is unlikely that he made any decisions one way or the other about it: Theodosius II was only a boy of fourteen at the time and power lay in the hands of his sister Pulcheria, who assumed the regency. Pulcheria was an extremely devout Christian who had vowed to remain a virgin, and during this time new, repressive anti-pagan laws were passed.[31] No attempt was ever made to bring the guilty to trial; and in fact, Cyril was later canonized by the Catholic church.

The Aedesius accused of being bribed, presumably by Cyril, is only mentioned by Damascius, and so far no one has determined who he may have been. But there is another possible interpretation. Aedesius may not be an actual person at all, but a literary allusion made by Damascius, or perhaps a misunderstanding of the text by the author of the *Suda Lexicon*. The name Aedesius comes from *aedesis* which means "respect," but which can also mean, under Athenian law, "pardon."[32] According to the *Thesaurus Graecae Linguae*, under the law it was permitted to escape the charge of involuntary murder if the defendant had been able to petition someone with intimate supplication and drawn that person to the point of pardon. It is not a difficult stretch to believe that Cyril "drew the court of Pulcheria to the point of pardon" by the use of bribes because he did so in 431 when he found himself embroiled in the infamous Nestorian Controversy.[33]

When Cyril's predecessor destroyed the magnificent Temple of Serapis in 391, its destruction was seen as being symbolic of the downfall of paganism. But Hypatia dared to breath life back into the

Alexandrian School. Her life was like a watershed between the old Hellenistic world and the emerging Christian era; the high ground amid two divergent rivers. She died when the one river crashed through that high wall to swallow the other.

Some modern scholars believe that her claim to fame rests solely on her beauty and uniqueness as a female teacher and that her murder secured the posthumous glory which her work alone would never have warranted. The implication is that, since she did not publish widely, her fame is undeserved and she "won the admiration of that less professional audience."[34]

Yet in 391, when many other philosophers fled Alexandria in fear to different cities, she stayed amid much danger and continued to teach, to publish, and to inspire. At a time when religious differences tore people apart, she sought to be inclusive and teach students of all persuasions. And in a city continually torn by political strife and racial conflict, she chose to live her life openly, forthrightly, and honorably. Hypatia's life story rings with courage, and the way she lived reveals more about how to be a wise and righteous person than any book ever could.

Notes

1. The eight sources from earliest to latest are:

Theon of Alexandria: Adolphe Rome, *Commentaires de Pappus et de Theon D'Alexandrie*, in *Studi E Testi* (Rome: Biblioteca Apostolica Vaticanna, 1943), 54 and 106.807.

Synesius of Cyrene: Augustine Fitzgerald, *The Letters of Synesius of Cyrene* (London: Oxford University Press, 1926), letters 10, 15, 16, 33, 81, 124, 154.

Philostorgius: *The Ecclesiastical History of Philostorgius: As Epitomized by Photius, Patriarch of Constantinople*, trans. Edward Walford (London: Henry G. Bohn, 1853), 489.

Socrates: *Ecclesiastical Church History* 7.15. In *Nicene and Post-Nicene Fathers* (Grand Rapids: Eerdmans, 1989), II, 160.

Damascius: *Life of Isidorus*, trans. Jeremiah Reedy in this issue of *Alexandria*, "The Life of Hypatia," pp. 57–58.

John Malalas: *The Chronicle of John Malalas*, trans. E. and M. Jeffreys, R. Scott (Melbourne: Australian Association for Byzantine Studies, 1986), 196.

Hesychius of Miletus: *Onomatologi*, ed. Joannes Flach (Leipzig: Teubner, 1882), 219–20.

John of Nikiu: *The Chronicle of John, Bishop of Nikiu*, trans. Robert Henry Charles (Amsterdam: Apa-Philo Press, 1916), 100.

2. G. J. Toomer, *Dictionary of Scientific Biography* (New York: Charles Scribner's Sons, 1976), 8.321.

3. Alan Cameron, "Isidore of Miletus and Hypatia: On the Editing of Mathematical Texts," *Greek, Roman and Byzantine Studies* 31 (1990), 155.

4. Mary E. Waithe, "Hypatia of Alexandria," in *A History of Women Philosophers* (Dordrecht, Boston, Lancaster: M. Nijhoff Publishers), 169–95.

5. Fitzgerald, *The Letters of Synesius* 81.174.

6. For a discussion on the type of philosophy Hypatia may have taught see R. T. Wallis, *Neoplatonism* (London: Duckworth, 1972), 139–44, and Jay Bregman, "Synesius of Cyrene: Early Life and Conversion to Philosophy," *California Studies in Classical Antiquity* 7 (1974), 55–88.

7. *Suidae Lexicon*, ed. Ada Adler (Leipzig: B. G. Teubner, 1935), 4.644–6.

8. On Philostorgius: Adler, *Suidae Lexicon*, 20–1, and Rudolf Asmus, "Zur Rekonstruktian von Damascius' Leben des Isidorus," *Byzantinische Zeitschrift*

18 (1909), 440.

9. Thomas Heath, *A History of Greek Mathematics* (Oxford: Clarendon Press, 1921), 528, and Waithe, *A History of Women Philosophers*, 176–92.

10. Proclus was born *circa* 410 and died 485 and Isidorus succeeded him as head of the Academy upon his death.

11. Damascius, *Vitae Isidori Reliquiae*, ed. Clemens Zintzen (Hildesheim: Georg Olms Verlagsbuchhandlung, 1967).

12. Wallis, *Neoplatonism*, 8.

13. Damascius, *Vitae Isidori* 218. Translated by Dr. Kenneth Bratt, Professor of Classics at Calvin College, Grand Rapids, Michigan.

14. Wallis, *Neoplatonism*, 141.

15. Reedy, "Life of Hypatia."

16. Oswyn Murray, "Life and Society in Classical Greece," in *The Oxford History of the Classical World*, ed. J. Boardman (New York: Oxford University Press, 1986), 214.

17. J. R. Rist, "Hypatia," *Phoenix* 19 (1965), 214–25.

18. John Toland, "Hypatia: or the History," in *Tetradymas* (London: Brotherton, 1720), 123.

19. Thomas Lewis, "The History of Hypatia," in *Tetradymas* (London: Bickerton, 1721) as cited by Waithe, *A History of Women Philosophers*, 171–2.

20. Reedy, "Life of Hypatia."

21. Socrates, *Ecclesiastical History* 7.7.13.14.

22. Socrates, *Ecclesiastical History* 7.13.

23 John of Nikiu, *The Chronicle*, 100.

24. On *parabalani*: A. H. M. Jones, *The Later Roman Empire 284–602: A Social, Economic and Administrative Survey* (Oxford: Blackwell,1964), 2.906, 911.

25. William Malley, *Hellenism and Christianity: The Conflict between Hellenic and Christian Wisdom* (Rome: Universita Gregoriana Editrice, 1978), 240–2, and Cyril of Alexandria, *Patrologiae Cursus Completus*, Series Graeca, ed. J. P. Migne (Paris: Lutetiae Parisiorum, 1857–1905), 77.509–1058.

26. *The Theodosian Code and Novels*, trans. Clyde Pharr (Princeton: Princeton University Press, 1952), 9.16.12.

27. Cyril, *Patrologiae* 527.

28. Socrates, *Ecclesiastical History* 5.16, and Sozomen, *The Ecclesiastical History of Sozomen* 7.15, in *Nicene and Post-Nicene Fathers* II, trans. Chester D. Hartranft (Grand Rapids: Eerdmans, 1989), 385–6.

29. Wallis, *Neoplatonism*, 138.

30. Reedy, "Life of Hypatia."

31. Kenneth G. Holum, "Aelia Pulcheria Augusta," in *Theodosian Empresses: Women and Imperial Dominion in Late Antiquity* (Berkeley: University of California Press, 1982), and J. H. W. G. Liebeschuetz, *Barbarians and Bishops: Army, Church, and State in the Age of Arcadius and Chrysostom* (Oxford: Clarendon Press, 1990), 146–53.

32. Translated by Dr. Kenneth Bratt.

33. Jones, *Later Roman Empire*, 1.346.

34. Rist, "Hypatia," 224.

The Life of Hypatia
from The Suda

Translated by Jeremiah Reedy

Hypatia, daughter of Theon the geometer and philosopher of Alexandria, was herself a well-known philosopher. She was the wife of the philosopher Isidorus, and she flourished under the Emperor Arcadius. Author of a commentary on Diophantus, she also wrote a work called *The Astronomical Canon* and a commentary on *The Conics* of Apollonius. She was torn apart by the Alexandrians and her body was mocked and scattered through the whole city. This happened because of envy and her outstanding wisdom especially regarding astronomy. Some say Cyril was responsible for this outrage; others blame the Alexandrians' innate ferocity and violent tendencies for they dealt with many of their bishops in the same manner, for example George and Proterius.

Regarding Hypatia the Philosopher and the Sedition of the Alexandrians

Hypatia was born, reared, and educated in Alexandria. Since she had greater genius than her father, she was not satisfied with his instruction in mathematical subjects; she also devoted herself diligently to all of philosophy.

The woman used to put on her philosopher's cloak and walk through the middle of town and publicly interpret Plato, Aristotle, or the works of any other philosopher to those who wished to hear her. In addition to her expertise in teaching she rose to the pinnacle of civic virtue. She was both just and chaste and remained always a virgin. She was so beautiful and shapely that one of her students fell in love with her and was unable to control himself and openly showed her a sign of his infatuation. Uninformed reports had Hypatia curing him of his affliction with the help of music. The truth is that the story about music is corrupt. Actually, she gathered rags that had been stained during her period and showed them to him as a sign of her unclean descent and said, "This is what you love, young man, and it isn't beautiful!" He was so affected by shame and amazement at the ugly sight that he experienced a change of heart and went away a better man.

Such was Hypatia, as articulate and eloquent in speaking as she was prudent and civil in her deeds. The whole city rightly loved her and worshipped her in a remarkable way, but the rulers of the city from the first envied her, something that often happened at Athens too. For even if philosophy itself had perished, nevertheless, its name still seems magnificent and venerable to the men who exercise leadership in the state. Thus it happened one day that Cyril, bishop of the opposition sect [i.e. Christianity] was passing by Hypatia's house, and he saw a great crowd of people and horses in front of her door. Some were arriving, some departing, and others standing around. When he asked why there was a crowd there and what all the fuss was about, he was told by her followers that it was the house of Hypatia the philosopher and she was about to greet them. When Cyril learned this he was so struck with envy that he immediately began plotting her murder and the most heinous form of murder at that. For when Hypatia emerged from her house, in her accustomed manner, a throng of merciless and ferocious men who feared neither divine punishment nor human revenge attacked and cut her down, thus committing an outrageous and disgraceful deed against their fatherland. The Emperor was angry, and he would have avenged her had not Aedesius been bribed. Thus the Emperor remitted the punishment onto his own head and family for his descendant paid the price. The memory of these events is still vivid among the Alexandrians.

The Life of Hypatia
by Socrates Scholasticus,
from his Ecclesiastical History 7.13

THERE WAS a woman at Alexandria named Hypatia, daughter of the philosopher Theon, who made such attainments in literature and science, as to far surpass all the philosophers of her own time. Having succeeded to the school of Plato and Plotinus, she explained the principles of philosophy to her auditors, many of whom came from a distance to receive her instructions. On account of the self-possession and ease of manner, which she had acquired in consequence of the cultivation of her mind, she not unfrequently appeared in public in presence of the magistrates. Neither did she feel abashed in going to an assembly of men. For all men on account of her extraordinary dignity and virtue admired her the more. Yet even she fell victim to the political jealousy which at that time prevailed. For as she had frequent interviews with Orestes, it was calumniously reported among the Christian populace, that it was she who prevented Orestes from being reconciled to the bishop. Some of them, therefore, hurried away by a fierce and bigoted zeal, whose ringleader was a reader named Peter, waylaid her returning home, and dragging her from her carriage, they took her to the church called *Caesareum*, where they completely stripped her, and then murdered her with tiles.* After tearing her body in pieces, they took her mangled limbs to a place called Cinaron, and there burnt them. This affair brought not the least opprobrium, not only upon Cyril, but also upon the whole Alexandrian church. And surely nothing can be farther from the spirit of Christianity

* ὀστράκοις, literally "oystershells," but the word was also applied to brick tiles used on the roofs of houses.

than the allowance of massacres, fights, and transactions of that sort. This happened in the month of March during Lent, in the fourth year of Cyril's episcopate, under the tenth consulate of Honorius, and the sixth of Theodosius.

The Life of Hypatia
by John, Bishop of Nikiu,
from his Chronicle 84.87–103

AND IN THOSE DAYS there appeared in Alexandria a female philosopher, a pagan named Hypatia, and she was devoted at all times to magic, astrolabes and instruments of music, and she beguiled many people through (her) Satanic wiles. 88. And the governor of the city honored her exceedingly; for she had beguiled him through her magic. And he ceased attending church as had been his custom. But he went once under circumstances of danger. And he not only did this, but he drew many believers to her, and he himself received the unbelievers at his house. 89. And on a certain day when they were making merry over a theatrical exhibition connected with dancers, the governor of the city published (an edict) regarding the public exhibitions in the city of Alexandria: and all the inhabitants of the city had assembled there (in the theater). 90. Now Cyril, who had been appointed patriarch after Theophilus, was eager to gain exact intelligence regarding this edict. 91. And there was a man named Hierax, a Christian possessing understanding and intelligence who used to mock the pagans but was a devoted adherent of the illustrious Father the patriarch and was obedient to his monitions. He was also well versed in the Christian faith. 92. (Now this man attended the theater to learn the nature of this edict.) But when the Jews saw him in the theater they cried out and said: "This man has not come with any good purpose, but only to provoke an uproar." 93. And Orestes the prefect was displeased with the children of the holy church, and Hierax was seized and subjected to punishment publicly in the theater, although he was wholly guiltless. 94. And Cyril was wroth with the governor of the city for so doing, and likewise for his putting to death an illustrious monk of the convent of Pernôdj[1] named Ammonius, and other monks (also). And when the chief magistrate[2] of the city heard this, he sent word to the Jews as follows: "Cease your hostilities against the Christians." 95. But they refused to hearken to what they heard; for they gloried in the support of the prefect who was with them, and so they added outrage to outrage and plotted a massacre through a treacherous device. 96. And they posted beside them at night in all the streets of the city certain men, while others cried out and said: "The church of the apostolic Athanasius is on fire: come to its succour, all ye Christians." 97. And the Christians on hearing their cry came fourth quite ignorant of the treachery of the Jews. And when the Christians came forth, the Jews arose and wickedly massacred the Christians and shed the blood of many, guiltless though they were. 98. And in the morning, when the surviving Christians heard of the wicked deed which the Jews had wrought, they betook themselves to the patriarch. And the Christians mustered all together and went and marched in wrath to the synagogues of the Jews and took possession of them, and purified them and converted them into churches. And one of them they named after the name of St. George. 99. And as for the Jewish assassins they expelled them from the city, and pillaged all their possessions and drove them forth wholly despoiled, and Orestes the prefect was unable to render them any help. 100. And thereafter a multitude of believers in God arose under the guidance of Peter the magistrate—now this Peter was a perfect believer in all respects in Jesus Christ—and they proceeded to seek for the pagan woman who had beguiled the people of the city and the prefect through her enchantments. 101. And when they learnt the place where she was, they proceeded to her and found her seated on a (lofty) chair; and having made her descend they dragged her along till they brought her to the great church, named Caesarion. Now this was in the days of the fast. 102. And they tore off her clothing and dragged her [till they brought her] through the streets of the city till she died. And they carried her to a place named Cinaron, and they burned her body with fire. 103. And all the people surrounded the patriarch Cyril and named him "the new Theophilus"; for he had destroyed the last remains of idolatry in the city.

Notes

1. The Coptic word for the desert of Nitria.
2. This is apparently wrong. It should be "Cyril."

Demeter and Hekate

Psychedelic Effects and the Eleusinian Mysteries

Shawn Eyer

Eleusis was a small bay city approximately fifteen miles northwest of Athens. Beginning as early as the fifteenth century B.C.E., an agricultural cult of the goddess Demeter is associated with the location. It is this provincial fertility cult which grew in Hellenistic times to become the most important of the *mysteria megale*, the great mystery religions. Noted historian Walter Burkert explains that these mysteries were not religious bodies apart from the wider context of ancient paganism, but rather were tangential and supplemental for those who desired them. "Mysteries," he says, "were initiation rituals of a voluntary, personal, and secret character that aimed at a change of mind through experience of the sacred."[1] Scholars have long held considerable interest in these mysteries: of Dionysos, Orpheus, Mithras, Cybele, and Isis; but none quite so much as those of the goddess Demeter and her daughter Persephone, celebrated before thousands of initiates every fall in ancient Greece. Although we know that the Eleusinian Mysteries profoundly impressed those who experienced them, modern scholarship has struggled for well over a century to explain why the secret rites within the sanctuary were so compelling and convincing to so many people of varied background and sophistication. The curiosity with which classical scholars approach this problem has not diminished to the present day.

The Eleusinian rites were just as compelling in the pagan world and were highly respected and revered. Pausanias tells us they were held in superiority to all other religious functions "as gods are higher than heroes."[2] It was, of course, forbidden to disclose the secrets of the initiations—those who did faced exile or death[3]—and so our sources for reconstructing the events are sometimes sparse or questionable. Accepting this limitation, we may proceed to examine what facts remain available. We have as our sources not only literary testimonies, but the architectural and artistic remains from the site and elsewhere. George Mylonas, who performed a complete archaeological survey of the site four decades ago, confronted the whole of this data and was both confident and frustrated: "We cannot know, at least we still do not know, what was the full content and meaning of the Mysteries of Demeter held at Eleusis. We know the details of the ritual but not its meaning."[4] We can describe with some degree of confidence both the order of events and even—in certain limited cases—the acts performed.

The oldest and most fundamental source related to the Eleusinia is the *Homeric Hymn to Demeter*,[5] probably composed in the seventh century B.C.E., which records the sacred story or *hieros logos* of the cult. The Hymn contains the mythic kernel of the Eleusinian religion and provides important clues about the rites. In it we read of the familiar tale of Persephone, who while gathering flowers far from her mother Demeter, was captured by the nether-god Plouton and secreted away into the depths of the earth to be his queen. Demeter exiles herself from Olympus and goes wandering on the earth in search of the maiden, arriving eventually at none other than Eleusis:

> No man, no woman who saw her recognized her, until she arrived at the home of clever Keleos, who was the king of fragrant Eleusis at the time. The daughters of Keleos of Eleusis saw her as they came to draw water. . . . They did not recognize her, for gods are hard for mortals to see (95–97, 105, 110).

Demeter, disguised as an old woman named Doso, goes with the girls to Keleos' household, on pretext of becoming a wet nurse for the newly-born son of Queen Metaneira. However, once they arrive at the palace, the goddess is obviously forlorn:

She sat down, holding her veil in front with her hands. For a long time she sat there on the stool sorrowfully, without speaking; and made no contact with anyone in word or gesture. Without smiling, without touching food or drink she sat, consumed with yearning for her daughter, until Iambe understood and made plenty of jokes and jests and made the holy Lady smile with kindly heart, and ever afterward she continues to delight her spirit. Then Metaneira filled a cup of sweet wine and offered it to her, but she refused it, for she said it was not right for her to drink red wine. Instead she asked her to give her barley groats and water mixed with crusted pennyroyal to drink. She made the compound, the *kykeon*, as she commanded, and offered it to the goddess. Deo the greatly revered accepted it for the sake of the ceremony (196–211).

All goes well, and Doso is given charge of young Demophon. One evening, though, the Queen discovers the old woman passing her son through fire in a magical operation designed to render him immortal. Demeter, offended, then reveals herself. Sick with grief, she causes the earth to become barren. The gods are threatened with the end of mankind's honor for them, so Zeus sends one after another to coax Demeter back to Olympus. She refuses to leave until Persephone is returned, so Zeus sends Hermes into the netherworld to bring the maiden back. The mother and daughter are joyfully reunited, and in celebration Demeter lifts her curse on the earth and bestows the Mysteries upon the people of Eleusis:

Promptly [Demeter] sent up fruit on the rich-soiled fields, and the whole broad land was loaded with leaves and flowers. She went to the royal stewards of the right and to Triptolemos, Diokles the driver of horses, mighty Eumolpos, and Keleos the leader of the people. She showed the tendance of the holy things and explicated the rites to them all, to Triptolemos, to Polyxeinos, and to Diokles sacred rites, which it is forbidden to transgress, to inquire into, or to speak about, for great reverence of the gods constrains their voice. Blessed of earthbound men is he who has seen these things, but he who dies without fulfilling the holy things, and he who is without a share of them, has no claim ever on such blessings, even when departed down to the moldy darkness (471–483).

The rites of the Greater Mysteries, to which the *Homeric Hymn* refers, were held in the autumn every year. The day before the celebration began, the *hiera*—"holy relics"—were taken from the inner Sanctuary of Demeter in Eleusis and transported to the acropolis of Athens in sealed chests (*kistai*). There were four days of elaborate preparation during which aspirants offered piglets for sacrifice, bathed in the sea, fasted, and rested.

On the fifth day, the procession, bearing the chests containing the Hiera, started out from Athens along the fourteen-mile Sacred Way to the Telesterion in Eleusis, a gigantic hall of initiation large enough to hold well over a thousand initiates at a time. The enthusiasm and spirit of the crowd was personified in a boy-god named Iacchos, and they sang and celebrated all along the road.[6] At night the parade would arrive at the outer court in Eleusis, where it would spend the night in song and dance.[7] These conspicuous events above took place in public for any to see. What happened at Eleusis in the privacy of the Sanctuary is another matter entirely.

The Telete ("Perfection") began the evening of Boedromion 20. By every indication, the initiates continued to fast until nightfall on the 20th, when they ended the abstention with the sacred *kykeon:* the traditional brew of barley groats, water, and pennyroyal which the goddess Demeter accepts "for the sake of the ceremony" in the *Homeric Hymn*. Then, within the walls of the complex, the initiates were taken through an initiation process involving, as we have it from ancient authors, three elements: the Dromena ("Drama"), the Legomena ("Sayings"), and the Deiknymena ("Displaying").

The Dromena was certainly some enactment of the *hieros logos*. This dramatization, performed "with very few explanatory words and no dialogue,"[8] followed the wanderings of the Goddess as she mourned the Kore, going to different locations within the walls of the Sanctuary which were, according to legend, the actual landmarks in the *Homeric Hymn*. At the disappearance of the Maiden, her name was called out and the initiates were startled by the crashing of a great cymbal.[9] It is contestable that the wanderings included a terrifying sojourn into the underworld. Carl Kerényi insists the Drama must have been not a stage-play, but a mystic dance.[10] Certainly the interior of the Telesterion was ill-suited to a play in any realistic sense, there being no stage and altogether too many columns for everyone to have a clear view of things.[11] Whatever the details, we know the subject and the culmination. Lactantius (d. 310 C.E.) says that Persephone "is sought with lighted torches through the night, and when she has been found the whole rite ends with expressions of joy and brandishing of torches."[12]

Less accessible are the Legomena. "Scholars agree that the legomena were not sermons, or long religious discourses, but short liturgical statements and explanations, and perhaps invocations. They were brief comments accompanying the dromena."[13] Any who repeated the words later faced execution. Only one such saying has survived and its context in the mysteries remains unclear.[14] Although Mylonas feels it had no place at all in the Eleusinia, but belonged to the cult of Cybele and Attis,[15] most scholars have included it in their attempts at reconstruction.

The Deiknymena was the completion, and most profound part, of the rite. A special priest called the Hierophant ("Displayer of the Hiera") would emerge from the Anaktoron (a small "holy of holies" within the Telesterion which only he could enter) and, bathed in dazzling torchlight, display the Hiera. Clement of Alexandria claimed the Hiera included the following: sesame cakes shaped as pyramids, balls, and navels; salt-balls; a snake; pomegranates; fig branches; fennel stalks; ivy leaves; poppies; "unutterable symbols" of the earth goddess Themis; marjoram; a lamp; a sword; and a model of the female genitals.[16] Clement's witness has been undermined by more recent scholarship, and there is little confidence in our ability to know what the *kistai* contained. It is reasonable to assume that the Hiera were objects large enough for those present to see.

One year or more after experiencing the Telete, the initiate was entitled to attain the final degree in the mysteries of Eleusis, called Epopteia, "the Beholding." It is commonly believed that the rite was held in the Telesterion after the Telete, once the general initiates had been evacuated. We have a few ancient sources—nearly all Christian—which would purport to betray this ultimate mystery. Of these, the one most likely to have historical value[17] is the quotation Hippolytus gives us from the writings of a now-unknown Naassene teacher:

> The Athenians, when they conduct the Eleusinian mysteries, reveal in silence to the *epoptai* the great, wonderful, most perfect initiation mystery, the *epoptikon*, an ear of grain. This ear of grain is for the Athenians the great initiatory light-bringer from that which is unformed, as when the hierophant himself... at night in Eleusis beneath a huge fire, celebrating the great and unspeakable mysteries, cries aloud, "The Lady Brimo has brought forth a holy son, Brimos."[18]

After a day of libations and offerings, the initiates departed the Sanctuary, utterly convinced that they had truly witnessed unspeakable, divine mysteries. Herein lies the historian's problem. Exactly how are we to account for the superlative impact these rites had upon most, if not all, of the participants? Mylonas clearly defines this enigma:

> Whatever the substance and meaning of the Mysteries was, the fact remains that the cult of Eleusis satisfied the most sincere yearnings and the deepest longings of the human heart. The initiates returned from their pilgrimages to Eleusis full of joy and happiness, with the fear of death diminished and the strengthened hope of a better life in the world of shadows: "Thrice happy are those of mortals, who having seen those rites depart for Hades; for to them alone is it granted to have true life there; to the rest all there is evil," Sophokles cries out exultantly. And to this Pindar with equal exultation answers: "Happy is he who, having seen these rites goes below the hollow earth; for he knows the end of life and

he knows its god-sent beginning." When we read these and other similar statements written by the great or nearly great of the ancient world, by the dramatists and the thinkers, when we picture the magnificent buildings and monuments constructed at Eleusis by great political figures like Peisistratos, Kimon, Perikles, Hadrian, Marcus Aurelius and others, we cannot help but believe that the Mysteries of Eleusis were not an empty, childish affair devised by shrewd priests to fool the peasant and the ignorant, but a philosophy of life that possessed substance and meaning and imparted a modicum of truth to the yearning human soul. That belief is strengthened when we read in Cicero that Athens has given nothing to the world more excellent than or divine than the Eleusinian Mysteries.[19]

We are at a loss to explain how any mere dance, any mere torchlight, any mere manipulation of objects pulled from a basket could produce such life-renewing effects. No matter what sort of grain the perfected initiates of the Epopteia degree saw in the silent spotlight, we cannot imagine how it was perceived as so spectacular, divine, and fulfilling. And yet it was. All scholars agree that something extraordinary, bordering on the otherworldly, happened in the Telesterion.

In the earlier part of the century, it was fashionable among scholars to assert that the spectacular content of the mysteries was derived from the performance of a *hieros gamos*, or sacred marriage. Accepting the lewd insinuations of the early Christian bishops, Jane Ellen Harrison, Paul Foucart, Mircea Eliade, E. O. James, and many others concluded that a cultic *orgia* took place between the Hierophant and the priestess of Demeter in the indirect presence of the initiates.[20] In Asterios we read the accusation that at the height of the Telete, the Hierophant and a priestess of Demeter descend into a basement chamber (*katabasion*) in the Telesterion. "Are not the torches then extinguished," he asks, "and the vast crowd believes that its salvation depends on what those two act in the darkness?"[21] Clement of Alexandria does not mention any particular sexual act, but certainly implies something of the sort when he laments that "Formerly night, which drew a veil over the pleasures of temperate men, was a time for silence. But now, when night is for those who are being initiated a temptation to licentiousness, talk abounds, and the torch-fires convict unbridled passions."[22]

Apparently accepting the insinuations of Clement and Asterios as veracious, Foucart paints a seamy picture of the Telete. The Hierophant and priestess descend together. The initiates begin the Eleusinian chant *hie kye* ("Rain! Conceive!") as the two officiants consummate their sexual union. Suddenly they emerge victoriously with the child Brimos . . . and all present are saved.[23] Certainly such an experience would be memorable for all concerned. However, if this was indeed the explosive secret of the mysteries, we are unable—even considering the different sexual attitudes of pagan Greece—to realistically explain the historical impact of these rites. Furthermore, we are probably making a mistake if we take the testimony of the uninitiated Asterios and Clement over the loftier witnesses of the archaeological data itself [24] as well as such prominent (and initiated) ancients as Aristotle, Cicero, Horace, and Plutarch. One cannot imagine such men standing in supreme awe at what would have resembled but a diluted and ornamentalized Bacchanalia.

Pointing out the ancient attestation that the Hierophant was celibate,[25] Jung concludes that only a spiritual or ceremonial, not physical, marriage could have occurred at Eleusis.[26] The sexual relationship of Persephone and Plouton was not acted out or celebrated in itself. In the Homeric Hymn, the mysteries are not instituted at the rape of Persephone, but at her return. The birth of Brimos that was reportedly stressed refers more likely to Demeter's "fiery adoption" of the queen's son Demophon than to an otherwise unknown child of Plouton and Persephone.[27]

Another theory to explain the regenerative powers of the mysteries in sexual terms has been put forth in various versions by such scholars as Albrecht Dieterich, Alfred Körte, and Otto Kern. These solutions are inspired by Clement of Alexandria's so-called "password":

I fasted;
I drank the kykeon;
I took from the chest;
I did the work, [or "I tasted"]
I placed in the basket,
and from the basket into the chest.[28]

Dieterich took this as a suggestion that the mystic chest contained a phallus with which the initiate touched himself.[29] But not even Clement claims a phallus to be part of the inventory of the Hiera. Nevertheless, the idea that some bizarre sexual rite took place in the handling of the sacred relics became a favorite explanation for the impact the mysteries possessed. Any number of variations of this theme have made themselves known:

> Körte maintained that not a phallus but the female pudenda, the *kteis* . . . was contained in the *kiste* [chest]. According to Körte by sliding the *kteis* over his body, the initiate believed that he was reborn, that he had become a child of Demeter. Kern . . . going a step further, maintained that the initiate actually came into a symbolic union with the Goddess by manipulating his own genital organ in the *kteis*. Picard projected a mystic union of the initiate with Demeter and Dionysos effected by the manipulation of a phallus and a *kteis* . . . Wilamowitz suggested that by merely seeing or touching the *kteis* the initiate was bound to the Goddess with a bond that blessed and sanctified him.[30]

All this conjecture is drawn from Clement's password and the vague suspicions of Christian writers like Tertullian and Asterios. Quite apart from the unlikelihood that such rites could honestly leave thousands awestruck year after year *is their impracticality*. Unless we postulate the awkward image of multiple sets of Hiera and multiple hierophants working at the same time in different corners of the Telesterion, there would not have been enough time in the Telete to allow each initiate his turn in handling the sacred objects. Even initiating around the clock for forty-eight hours running, only 576 five-minute initiations would be possible. Furthermore, outside of the scholarly elucidations of *ergasamenos*,[31] we have no claim at all that the mysteries at Eleusis were culminated in something the initiate did or acted with his own hands: "If there is any point upon which all witnesses agree, it is that the climax of the Eleusinian Mysteries was not a ritual, or anything which the mystes did or physically experienced, but a *vision*."[32] All of the evidence points to the simultaneous revelation of the Hiera to all the initiates by the Hierophant.[33] Certainly Clement's "password" is not on this basis alone to be forbidden a role in the mysteries, but it cannot represent the Telete proper.

It is unlikely that eroticism was completely absent from the Eleusinian mysteries, but it is impossible to conclude from evidence that literal or symbolic sex acts constituted the sacred revelation of the *epopteia*. Such explanations, and others just as unlikely,[34] were put forward by learned scholars who were well aware of the inconsistencies involved. Perhaps such uses of the evidence were justified by the knowledge that the greatest inconsistency of all would be that *nothing* spectacular happened at Eleusis to leave such deep marks in the psychic life of Mediterranean antiquity.

The notion that consciousness-altering drugs might have been employed in the mystery rites was not new when R. Gordon Wasson, Carl A. P. Ruck, and Albert Hofmann proposed in a 1978 study that the sacred *kykeon* with which the initiates ended their week-long fast contained a hallucinogenic compound. As early as 1964 Huston Smith had reached that very conclusion.[35] Carl Kerényi, in conjunction with Hofmann, was considering the possible narcotic effects of pennyroyal in connection with the mysteries.[36] But of the three ingredients of *kykeon* mentioned in the *Homeric Hymn*—water, barley, and pennyroyal leaves—it is barley which is the most likely source of a hallucinogenic drug.

Barley, wheat, rye, and other cereals may be visited by the parasitic fungus ergot (*Claviceps purpurea*). Ergot contains a number of alkaloids, several of which are psychoactive, including ergine (*d*-lysergic acid amide) and ergonovine. Ergine is the botanical source of one of the most powerful psychedelic compounds known, the modern synthetic LSD, and produces similar effects.[37] The theory of Wasson and his colleagues (the Wasson-Hofmann-Ruck model) is that the inhabitants of Eleusis had discovered the psychedelic properties of ergot and that the mystery rites enacted there were an outgrowth of powerful hallucinogenic experiences.

What is particularly striking about this purport as opposed to others is that it explicates the surviving evidence without contradicting it in any way. It explains the importance of the *kykeon*. It explains the enhanced feelings of empathy which gripped the initiates as they sought the lost Kore. It explains the amazement of the initiates as the holy relics were displayed in the brilliant firelight. Most of all, it is the best solution yet to the question of how the Epopteia, in which the Hierophant in silence held out an ear of grain, could have been the profound culmination of the mysteries which it was perceived to be. Indeed, some of our witnesses seem to demand recourse to some form of altered state of consciousness. Although the *mystai* understood from the mysteries that "death is for mortals no longer an evil, but a blessing,"[38] we have the important testimony of Aristotle:

> Initiates do not need to understand anything; rather, they undergo an experience and a disposition—become, that is, deserving.[39]

This interesting assertion should be compared with Plutarch's description of the psychological condition of the initiate, whom he compares to one who would like to become a philosopher:

> Just as persons who are being initiated into the mysteries throng together at the outset amid tumult and shouting, and jostle against one another, but when the holy rites are being performed and disclosed the people are immediately attentive in awe and silence, so too at the beginning of

philosophy.

[...H]e who has succeeded in getting inside, and has seen a great light, as though a shrine had been opened, adopts another bearing of silence and amazement, and "humble and orderly attends upon" reason as upon a god.[40]

In a similar and even more descriptive passage, Plutarch compares initiation to the experience of death and the liberation from the body:

(At the moment of death) the soul suffers an experience similar to those who celebrate great initiations . . . Wanderings astray in the beginning, tiresome walkings in circles, some frightening paths in darkness that lead nowhere; then immediately before the end all the terrible things, panic and shivering and sweat, and amazement. And then some wonderful light comes to meet you, pure regions and meadows are there to greet you, with sounds and dances and solemn, sacred words and holy views; and there the initiate, perfect by now, set free and loose from all bondage, walks about, crowned with a wreath, celebrating the festival together with the other sacred and pure people, and he looks down on the uninitiated, unpurified crowd in this world in mud and fog beneath his feet.[41]

As if to elucidate this idea, the philosopher Proclus describes that the officiants of the Eleusinia "cause" alterations in the psychological states of the *mystai*:

They cause the sympathy of the souls with the ritual [*dromena*] in a way that is incomprehensible to us, and divine, so that some of the initiated are stricken with panic, being filled with divine awe; others assimilate themselves to the holy symbols, leave their own identity, become at home with the gods, and experience divine possession.[42]

This passage is cited by Burkert who holds it "should be taken seriously as containing authentic tradition," since Proclus knew the daughter of a Hierophant on a personal basis.[43] If we do take it seriously, it becomes clear that initiates did—in fact were "caused" to—experience extreme and subjective states of consciousness the specific details of which correspond quite directly with the reported effects of lysergic acid hallucinogens. Most notable are Plutarch's descriptions, quoted above, of the initial agitated confusion, sensation of cold or trembling, and increase in perspiration. The physiological effects of LSD, "especially conspicuous in the first hour, before the psychological effects become obvious [are]: dilatation of the pupils; increase in deep tendon reflexes; increased heart rate, blood pressure, and body temperature; mild dizziness or nausea, chills, tingling, trembling; slow deep breathing; loss of appetite; and insomnia."[44] Along with these effects, an increase in both perspiration and blood glucose levels are noted by Julien, who reports that the physiological effects of LSD, "although noticeable, seldom interfere with the psychedelic experience and are seldom serious."[45] The effects in question for this study, those mentioned in Plutarch, have been observed with the use of the natural substance ergonovine.[46]

It is explicit from Aristotle, Proclus, and Plutarch that the mysteries were experienced, not explained. In fact, they were considered *arrheta*, unspeakable, not just because it was illegal to disclose what transpired in the sanctuary, but because the transcendent nature of the experience defied attempts to communicate it in language. By *some method*, the initiates must have been conditioned to "receive" this message with some degree of accuracy and personal satisfaction. What the initiates "learned" during the mysteries was accomplished by sight and without explicit verbal teaching. The Legomena were not theological discourses but short, cryptic statements. W. K. C. Guthrie correctly noted that we "can scarcely speak of anything so definite as doctrine in connexion with Eleusis."[47] It is natural to infer the use of altered states of consciousness from the fact that nevertheless the mysteries did communicate a rather complicated message with more or less precision. "The initiate was *shown* things," says Guthrie, "and convinced of his salvation by the evidence of his own eyes."[48] That some form of altered state was responsible was the suggestion of Walter Otto even before the drug hypothesis became an issue:

> the truth, disclosed to the mystai by images, signs, or words, must have been something absolutely new, astonishing, inaccessible to rational recognition. This is almost self-evident. And yet it has often been forgotten. . . . During the sacrosanct action the mystes is passive; he receives no teachings, but is *put into a state which is not subject to natural explanation* (emphasis added).[49]

One natural explanation, however, for an altered state of consciousness which would enhance human visual perceptions and add seemingly spiritual significance to them is the hallucinogenic properties of ergot. It is specifically the perception of visual stimuli that is most affected by these psychedelic compounds.[50] The subject's perceptions are magnified in contrast and intensity. Cross-sensory perceptions are also reported: the "texture" of a color, for instance, or the "sight" of a sound. Even this cross-modality perception is suggested by one of the ancient witnesses, Aristides the Rhetor, who writes, "Eleusis is a shrine common to the whole earth . . . it is both the most awesome and the most luminous. At what place in the world have more miraculous tidings been sung, and where have the dromena called forth greater emotion, where has there been greater rivalry between seeing and hearing?"[51]

Taken on their own merits, surely these psychological testimonies from ancient times sound fantastic. Yet either Aristotle, Plutarch, Proclus and Aristides were conspiring to deceive their contemporaries, or *the fantastic did happen*. According to Kerényi, we must accept this as self-evident if we are to imagine the mysteries "worked" and fulfilled their purpose:

> It was essentially a wordless initiation that led to a knowledge which it was neither necessary nor possible to clothe in words. We have to assume, in the history of the Eleusinian mysteries, a certain period during which the

ear of grain, under whatever circumstances it was shown, was transparently clear in meaning to the celebrants. We must take it as axiomatic that such a transparent meaning was there in the very fact of the mystery-festival being celebrated and experienced at all.[52]

A *mystes* whose perceptions had been reconditioned with ergine or ergonovine actually *would* feel such deep meanings had suddenly and inexplicably become transparent. Like the mysteries, must of what has been reported about the psychological effects of hallucinogenic drugs is difficult, and perhaps impossible, to imagine without benefit of experience. In both cases it is stated that the effects are so great that they preclude description. We have no choice but to work with the attempted accounts given us in scientific literature, such as the following:

> The psychic changes and the attendant abnormal states of consciousness induced by hallucinogens differ so utterly from ordinary experiences of the outer and inner world that *they cannot be described* in the usual language of the daily pattern of the outer and inner universe. The profound changes in conception of the universe towards either the diabolical sphere or celestial transfiguration may be explained by alterations in space and time perception—the two basic elements of human existence. The experience of corporeity and the spiritual being may likewise be deeply affected. *The partaker of an hallucinogen forsakes the familiar world and, yet in full consciousness, embraces a kind of quasi-dream world operating under different standards, strange dimensions and in a different time* (my emphasis).[53]

As shown above, all of the traits of the telete given by Plutarch and by Proclus are closely paralleled by the known common physiological and psychological effects of lysergic acid-based drugs. For these reasons the Wasson-Hofmann-Ruck model is remarkably strong, explaining as it does the subjective psychological state of the initiates and doing so with elements which can be traced directly to the origin of the cult. Furthermore, it is in thorough accord with the ancient testimonies regarding the sacred activities at Eleusis.[54] The drug hypothesis fits.

How future scholarship will deal with this interpretation of the facts has not yet become clear. Few new major studies of the mystery religions have appeared since 1978, when *The Road to Eleusis* was published. In *Ancient Mystery Cults* (1987), Walter Burkert does mention both Kerényi's and the Wasson group's drug theories, the latter of which he calls a "more sophisticated guess."[55] Burkert raises three very brief objections[56] to the Wasson-Hofmann-Ruck model, all of which we will examine:

Did ergot really infect the grains of the Rharian field?
Would Eleusis have been able to get enough of the drug for
all the initiates?
Is not ergot poisoning very unpleasant? If so, how could
it produce euphoria?

The question of whether ergot was extant in that place in Greece during the times in question is one which cannot be answered definitely. However, given the widespread persistence of the various types of ergot (*Figure 3*), it is unlikely that the grains and grasses of ancient Greece somehow escaped playing its host. Hofmann insists that we are not "pulling a long bow" in assuming that some of the Eleusinian barley was prey to the *Claviceps purpurea* with its hallucinogenic alkaloids.[57] Indeed, theories far more improbable than this one are regularly given serious consideration by historians, and rightly so. The complete absence of ergot, and not its presence, would be difficult to justify.

Burkert's skepticism that the Eleusinians could have consistently obtained "the quantities needed" for all of the initiates is similarly unjustified. It is true that ergine and ergonovine both are only 5–10% as potent as LSD. (See *Figures 1* and *2*.). However, LSD is extremely potent, producing its most notable effects in doses as miniscule as 100

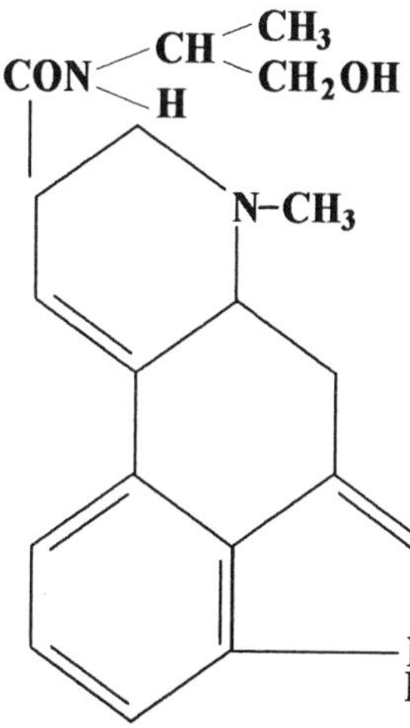

Figure 1. Ergonovine

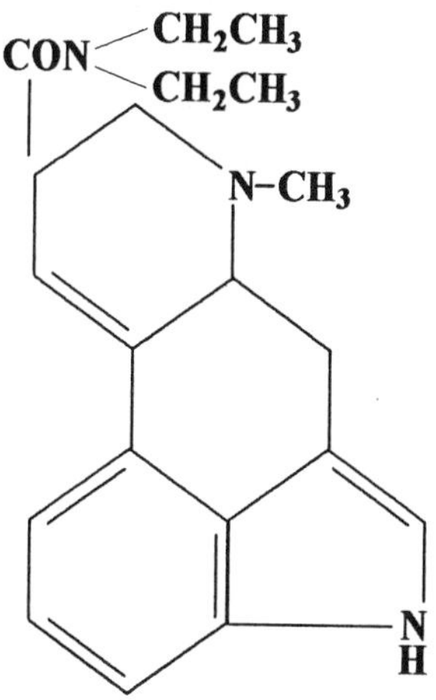

**Figure 2. Lysergic Acid
Diethylamide**

Ergonovine is an hallucinogenic alkaloid often found in ergot (*Claviceps purpurea*). It is water-soluble and thus may be easily isolated. It has 5–10% the potency of LSD, and taken in doses of 1 to 2 mg, produces nearly identical effects.

Lysergic acid diethylamide (LSD[25]), first synthesized in 1938 by Dr. Albert Hofmann, was once the most powerful psychedelic drug available, being active in remarkably small doses.

millionths of a gram (μg). Ergine and ergonovine produce the same effects in doses of 1 to 2 thousandths of a gram (mg). Several grams of the drug would be perfectly enough for one year's initiations.

Although to *ensure* the successful collection of the drug on an annual basis would require a not insignificant amount of grain, it is extremely unlikely that a religious center as famous and powerful as Eleusis would not be able to procure in a year's time the small amount of ergot alkaloids needed for the initiations. From the fifth century B.C.E., a decree was in effect that all of Greece should send a portion of its barley and wheat crops to Eleusis. These offerings were kept in a special silo at Eleusis wherein any ergot contamination would be able to spread rather quickly.[58] If anything, the problem was the same then as it was in later European history: not how to get *enough* ergot, but how to keep the pure grain from becoming infected.

The question of ergot poisoning (ergotism) is a more valid one. However, it is not the Wasson-Hofmann-Ruck theory that the initiates suffered this illness. Ergotism was a serious, often deadly, problem during the Middle Ages, when infected grains were used in bread-making.[59] Known as "St. Anthony's Fire," its symptoms included delirium, muscle spasms, hallucination, even gangrene. Today we know that ergotism is caused by specific ergot alkaloids such as ergotoxine and ergotamine. Dr. Hofmann's chapter in *The Road to Eleusis* is devoted specifically to the question of whether the Greeks could have isolated the valuable properties of ergot. Because the poisonous alkaloids are not water-soluble, Hofmann concludes that it would have been elementary to eliminate this problem:

> The separation of the hallucinogenic agents by simple water solution from the non-soluble ergotamine and ergotoxine alkaloids was well within the range of possibilities open to Early Man in Greece.[60]

This portion of Burkert's critique is thus not a problem. It was possible to receive the pharmacological benefits of ergot without its painful and destructive poisons,[61] as our medical industry in fact does

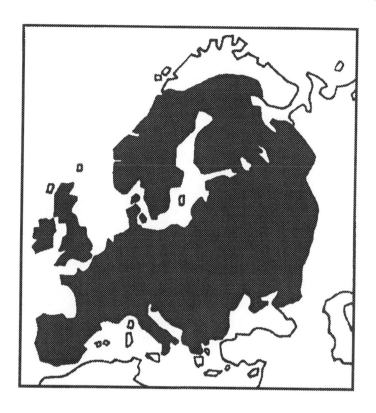

Figure 3. Map of Europe showing the extent
of ergot's natural range in modern times

today in commercial preparations of ergonovine.

Burkert's concerns have some validity, but they were some of the same concerns Wasson and his associates felt when they were developing their model. All of them are treated, I feel satisfactorily, in the original thesis.

There is, however, a final objection which is not scientific but philosophical: namely, whether drugs of this sort can in fact produce desirable religious states or if they instead are inherently destructive. After raising the questions just treated, Burkert continues: "What is perhaps more important is that the use of drugs, as our time has been doomed to see, does not create a true sense of community but rather leads to isolation."[62]

Whatever truth there is in this statement may stem more from our cultural biases than any actual reality.[63] It is, rather, a value judgement unbecoming one trained in either anthropology or psychology. It resembles the caveat once raised by the great orientalist R. C. Zaehner. Reacting strongly against the sentiments of Aldous Huxley, specifically that mescaline could induce a mystical state, Zaehner made the derisive comment that:

> It must therefore follow, if we accept the fatal "platitude," that not only can "mystical" experience be obtained artificially by the taking of drugs, it is also naturally present in the manic. It must then follow that the vision of God of the mystical saint is "one and the same" as the hallucination of the lunatic.[64]

This is a drastic overgeneralization. Even before the consideration of hallucinogenic drugs, the mystical state had already long been compared with that of the psychotic, and rightly so. The comparison is neither unreasonable nor irrelevant. Extreme religious experiences, like other types of experience, may be had by the psychotic and non-psychotic alike. "It follows," answers Huston Smith, "that religion is more than religious experiences."[65]

At the same time, professor Burkert acknowledges that the initiates must have been put into an altered state of consciousness verging on if not identical to the psychedelic:

> In psychological terms, there must have been an experience of the "other" in a change of consciousness, moving far beyond what could be found in everyday life. "I came out of the mystery hall feeling like a stranger to myself"—this is a rhetor's description of the experience at Eleusis.[66]

It is, then, a question of whether it is allowable for a drug to be the generative factor of the expanded state. While surely there is no drug which is by itself "religious vision encapsulated," it would be too reckless anthropologically speaking to say that drugs serve no important function in mankind's religious life. Drug researchers Grinspoon and Bakalar found that the religious experiences common to psychedelic sessions are produced ultimately *not* by the drug, but by the individual:

> The fact that a simple compound like nitrous oxide as well as the complex organic molecule of . . . LSD can produce a kind of psychedelic mystical experience suggests that the human organism has a rather general capacity to attain the state and can reach it by many different biological pathways.[67]

This same conclusion has been reached by Stanislav Grof, who has conducted decades of research on LSD and similar psychedelics, and may be the world's authority in the field:

> Most researchers studying the effects of psychedelics have come to the conclusion that these drugs can best be viewed as amplifiers or catalysts of mental processes. Instead of inducing drug-specific states, they seem to activate pre-existing matrices or potentials of the human mind.[68]

It is, then, by no means a sacrilege to think that the mysteries of Demeter and Kore might have utilized the naturally-occurring compounds which sporadically appeared on the heads of grain which were sacred to the goddesses. The question is not whether extreme altered states of consciousness are accessible without the use of drugs, but whether there was any realistic means to be certain hundreds and thousands of initiates could be inducted into such states *reliably and regularly* through the use of fasting, music, and dance alone. Perhaps the ancient authors all exaggerated the fantasticity or the universality of the rite, omitting to mention that a large proportion failed each year to see the "great light," or become "possessed" by the gods, or know the "rivalry between seeing and hearing." While I am prepared to go so far as to accept that it was possible for *some* (even many) of the initiates to achieve an expanded consciousness as a side-effect of the physical rigors of the week combined with autosuggestion based upon deeply-felt expectations, it does not seem plausible that a majority of Greek-speaking people of random classes and levels of education could like clockwork attain a natural, advanced trance state in which perceptions are changed after the order of psychedelic drugs.

The secret of what really happened at Eleusis remains one of the premier problems for historians of religion. That a trance state played an important role in the initiation is being suggested by more and more scholars. While there are various possible means of entering a mind-altering state of consciousness resembling that described in ancient sources, the use of a botanical stimulus is by far the most reliable. The model expressed by R. Gordon Wasson, Albert Hofmann and Carl Ruck, must therefore be taken seriously. Their theory is perhaps the first truly *realistic* explanation for the most-documented aspect of the sacred mysteries: their profound, beneficial, and lasting effects upon the millions of initiates who, at one time or another, stood enraptured on the steps of the torch-lit Telesterion.

Notes

1. Burkert, *Mystery Cults in the Ancient World*, 11.

2. Pausanias, *Description of Greece* 10.31.11.

3. Willoughby, *Pagan Regneration*, 46–47; Mylonas, *Eleusis and the Eleusinian Mysteries*, 224–226.

4. Mylonas, *Eleusis*, 316.

5. Otto, "The Meaning of the Eleusinian Mysteries," 14.

6. Aristophanes preserves an interesting example of such a procession song in his play *The Frogs* (324–459). Although he has adapted it to a comic setting, it probably retains something of the typical mood of the celebrants.

7. Euripides, *Ion* 1074.

8. Mylonas, *Eleusis*, 261.

9. Apollodoros, fr. 36.

10. Jung and Kerényi, *Essays on a Science of Mythology: The Myth of the Divine Child and the Mysteries of Eleusis*, 141.

11. Otto, "Meaning of the Eleusinian Mysteries," 26.

12. Lactantius, *Epitome of the Divine Institutes* 23.7.

13. Mylonas, *Eleusis*, 272.

14. Cf. Meyer, *The Ancient Mysteries*, 19; Jung and Kerényi, *Essays on a Science of Mythology*, 143.

15. Mylonas, *Eleusis*, 305–309.

16. Clement of Alexandria, *Exhortation to the Greeks* 2.22.

17. There has, however, been some controversy regarding the veracity of the tradition recorded in Hippolytus. George Mylonas in particular insists that nothing in Hippolytus' account can be attributed to the mysteries of Demeter (275–276, 305–310). "How can we maintain," asks Mylonas, "that the showing of 'cut wheat' was considered 'the great and marvelous mystery of perfect revelation' when we find that even the candidates of the telete had to bring with them cut wheat, and when cut wheat is freely exhibited on buildings and works of art?" (275–276) But Mylonas' reasoning is circular in this regard, for elsewhere he argues that Tertullian's statement (*Against Valentinians* 1) that the *epoptai* beheld silently a *phallos* cannot be true because such items are not found depicted in the Eleusinian edifices and are not

symbols of the goddesses in question (Mylonas 276). If the Epopteia *cannot* center around something symbolic of the goddesses, and the Epopteia cannot center around something *not* symbolic of the goddesses, we are in a tight spot. Furthermore, the mere depiction of grain around the sanctuary of Demeter, the "Grain Mother," is no surprise and would not at all suggest the Epopteia ritual Hippolytus describes—if anything, it would tend to throw one off the track. Surely it was not the spectacular nature of the Hiera, but the context of their revelation which caused such a deep effect on the *mystai*. Mylonas and others overlook that Hippolytus is not writing on his own, but is quoting a Gnostic who was in turn trying to argue that the divine mysteries were ultimately confluent with the *gnosis* of his own sect. Walter Burkert believes we are dealing with the account of a legitimate insider: "Presumably such a Gnostic, like other *homines religiosi* of late antiquity, had himself initiated in as many mysteries as possible; at the same time, conscious of the 'freedom of God's children,' the Gnostic felt himself above all traditional commandments and prohibitions" (Burkert, *Homo Necans*, 251).

18. Hippolytus, *Refutation of All Heresies* 5.8.39.

19. Mylonas, *Eleusis*, 284–285. And this is the same Cicero who ridiculed even the Delphic Oracle (*On Divination* 2.115–117).

20. E. O. James goes so far as to suggest in his *Sacrifice and Sacrament* that "From the general character of the ritual it is clear that the Mystery was connected with the seasonal drama in which a sacred marriage was a *prominent feature*" (242, emphasis mine). Harrison calls the sacred marriage "as integral a part of the mysteries of Eleusis as of the rites of Sabazios and Dionysos" (*Prolegomena*, 548). Eliade makes the *hieros gamos* the culminating act of the Epopteia: "We know that the torches were put out, a curtain raised, and the hierophant appeared with a box. He opened it and took out a ripe ear of grain. . . . Soon afterward the sacred marriage between the hierophant and the priestess of Demeter took place" (111). Many of Eliade's details are unsupported by the texts.

21. Asterios, *Enkomion to the Saintly Martyrs* 113B.

22. Clement of Alexandria, *Exhortation* 2.22.

23. Foucart, *Les Mystères d'Éleusis*, 496.

24. Excavations at Eleusis have proven conclusively that there was at no

time in the history of the Telesterion a *katabasion* into which anyone could descend (Mylonas 314). The only other option for performance of the act— if we discount it being done in the open, which we may—would be within the *anaktoron*, into which only the Hierophant was permitted.

25. Hippolytus, in that very passage so often cited as a witness for the sacred marriage hypothesis, in fact relates that the hierophant was chaste and used an anti-aphrodisiac drug, a hemlock potion, to keep himself sexually impotent (*Refutation* 5.8.39). We also have it from Lucian of Samosata that the priestesses of Demeter were "good girls" as opposed to courtesans (*Dialogues of the Courtesans* 7).

26. Jung and Kerényi, *Essays on a Science of Mythology*, 96.

27. Referring to the Naassene witness preserved by Hippolytus, Burkert proposes a very interesting parallel from the Isis mysteries, which we know were often compared in ancient times to the Eleusinia:

> These testimonies are not totally isolated: an earlier pagan witness— Mesomedes, a poet of the Hadrianic epoch—brings confirmation. In his "Hymn to Isis," he refers with cryptic allusions to the "marriage underground" and the "birth of plants"—which clearly recalls Persephone—and to "the desires of Aphrodite, the birth of the little child, the perfect, unspeakable fire, the Kuretes of Rhea, the reaping of Kronos, cities for the charioteer—all this is danced through the *anaktora* for Isis." Here we see the birth of the child and the great fire, the reaping of grain . . . and finally a reference to Triptolemus, the charioteer: clearly an Eleusinian scenario, which even provides a definite sequence rather than unconnected glimpses (Burkert, *Ancient Mystery Cults*, 94).

28. Clement of Alexandria, *Exhortation* 2.21.

29. Dieterich, *Eine Mithrasliturgie*, 123.

30. Mylonas, *Eleusis*, 296.

31. A popular emendation suggests that the word might originally have been *engeusamenos*, "I tasted." This would accord with certain evidence. In particular we have a large number of unique artifacts at Eleusis called *kernoi*. In Athenaios there is a reference to their use in the distribution of some edible

substances: "he who has carried them, that is he who has borne the *kernos* aloft, tastes these articles" (11.56). Elsewhere Athenaios relates the cups of the *kernoi* contained poppy-heads, barley and wheat, peas, okra-seeds and lentils (11.476f).

32. Otto, "The Meaning of the Eleusinian Mysteries," 23.

33. Guthrie, *The Greeks and their Gods*, 289.

34. For example, Loisy and Wehrli suggested the presence at Eleusis of something like a pagan Mass, wherein the initiate would partake of the substance or blessing of the goddess in the form of *kykeon* (Mylonas 260n). Scholars have reacted strongly against a quasi-eucharistic interpretation of the Eleusis cult (E. O. James 242; Mylonas 259–260). Nilsson offered a rather unspectacular interpretation, that the resurrection of Persephone was revealed to be nothing more than the opening of grain stores in springtime (51–52). This view is "extremely artificial" (Otto 17) and would have made the mysteries insufferably anticlimactic.

35. Smith, "Do Drugs Have Religious Import?," 518.

36. Kerényi suggested that the mint pennyroyal (*glekhon*) might have been used as a catalyst—in conjunction with the week of fasting and the walk to Eleusis—for altered states of consciousness (177–180). However, pennyroyal acts primarily as a stimulant, with marked toxicological effects in large doses. Pennyroyal itself lacks psychedelic potency (Wasson et al 46).

37. Grinspoon and Bakalar, *Psychedelic Drugs Reconsidered*, 10–11.

38. Inscription at Eleusis, quoted in Angus, *The Mystery-Religions*, 140.

39. Aristotle, frag. 15.

40. Plutarch, *Progress in Virtue* 10.

41. Plutarch, frag. 168 (Stobaeus 4.52.49).

42. Proclus, *Commentary on Plato's Republic.* 2.108.17–30.

43. Burkert, *Ancient Mystery Cults*, 114.

44. Grinspoon and Bakalar, *Psychedelics Reconsidered*, 11–12.

45. Julien, *A Primer of Drug Action*, 181–182.

46. Wasson et al., *The Road to Eleusis: Unveiling the Secret of the Mysteries*, 31.

47. Guthrie, *Greeks and their Gods*, 289.

48. Guthrie, *Greeks and their Gods*, 289.

49. Otto, "The Meaning of the Eleusinian Mysteries," 24.

50. Julien, *A Primer of Drug Action*, 182–183.

51. Aristides the Rhetor, *Orationes* 22.

52. Jung and Kerényi, *Essays on a Science of Mythology*, 152.

53. Schultes and Hofmann, *The Botany and Chemistry of Hallucinogens*, 20.

54. Wasson et al, *The Road to Eleusis*, 50.

55. Burkert, *Ancient Mystery Cults*, 108.

56. "Even if the Rharian plain at Eleusis might have been infected with this pest, as Wasson and his adherents surmise, one may wonder about the quantities needed for thousands of participants in order to provide happy visions for all; in addition, ergot poisoning is normally described as quite an unpleasant and not at all a euphoric state" (Burkert, *Ancient Mystery Cults*, 108).

57. Wasson et al, *The Road to Eleusis*, 32.

58. The text of the decree is in *Inscriptiones Graecae* I² 76.1–46. The actual site of the silos has been discovered at Eleusis and is described by Mylonas (125–127).

59. Schultes and Hofmann, *Botany and Chemistry*, 15–16.

60. Wasson et al, *The Road to Eleusis*, 33.

61. Regretfully, Burkert's brief comments reflect some mistaken impressions about the model described by Wasson, Hofmann, and Ruck. He is also incorrect in saying that ergot contains "traces of LSD" (*Mystery Cults* 108). This is impossible, as LSD does not occur in nature. LSD is a synthetic molecule which must be prepared in a laboratory.

62. Burkert, *Ancient Mystery Cults*, 109.

63. It is interesting that while there is an objection to the attribution of the Eleusinian mysteries to drug effects, no similar statement is brought against the Dionysos mysteries, famous for using every form of intoxication and excess it could discover.

64. Zaehner, *Mysticism: Sacred and Profane*, xii–xiii.

65. Smith, "Do Drugs Have Religious Import?," 529.

66. Burkert, *Ancient Mystery Cults*, 90, quoting Sopatros, *Rhet. Gr.* 8.114.

67. Grinspoon and Bakalar, *Psychedelic Drugs Reconsidered*, 36.

68. Grof, *Beyond the Brain: Birth, Death and Transcendence in Psychotherapy*, 29.

Author's note: An earlier edition of this paper was read at the annual meeting of the Ohio Academy of Religion, March 13, 1993, held at Wright State University. The author would like to express his gratitude to Dr. Jon Daniels and Dr. Kenneth Christiansen of The Defiance College, Dr. Adela Yarbro Collins of the University of Chicago, and Mr. George Vellios for valuable comments and insights throughout the course of this study.

Bibliography

Angus, S. *The Mystery-Religions: A Study in the Religious Background of Early Christianity*. New York: Dover, 1975 (orig. 1928).

Burkert, Walter. *Ancient Mystery Cults*. Cambridge: Harvard University Press, 1987.

————. *Greek Religion*. Cambridge: Harvard University Press, 1985.

————. *Homo Necans: the Anthropology of Ancient Greek Sacrificial Ritual and Myth*. Berkeley, CA: University of California, 1983.

Dieterich, Albrecht. *Eine Mithrasliturgie*. Third edition. Leipzig, 1923.

Dodds, E. R. *The Greeks and the Irrational*. Boston: Beacon, 1957.

Foucart, Paul François. *Les Mystères d'Éleusis*. Paris, 1914.

Grinspoon, Lester and James B. Bakalar. *Psychedelic Drugs Reconsidered*. New York: Basic Books, 1979.

Grof, Stanislav. *Beyond the Brain: Birth, Death and Transcendence in Psychotherapy*. Albany: State University of New York Press, 1985.

Guthrie, W. K. C. *The Greeks and their Gods*. Boston: Beacon, 1954.

Harrison, Jane Ellen. *Prolegomena to a Study of Greek Religion*. New York: Meridian, 1959.

James, E. O. *Sacrifice and Sacrament*. New York: Barnes & Noble, 1962.

Julien, Robert M. *A Primer of Drug Action*. Fifth edition. New York: W. H. Freeman, 1988.

Jung, C. G. and C. Kerényi. *Essays on a Science of Mythology: The Myth of the Divine Child and the Mysteries of Eleusis*. Princeton: Princeton University Press, 1969.

Kerényi, C. *Eleusis: Archetypal Image of Mother and Daughter*. New York: Pantheon, 1967.

Luck, Georg. *Arcana Mundi: Magic and the Occult in the Greek and Roman Worlds.* Baltimore: Johns Hopkins University Press, 1985.

Metzger, Bruce M. "A Classified Bibliography of the Graeco-Roman Mystery Religions 1924–1973 with a Supplement 1974–77," *Aufstieg und Niedergang der römischen Welt* 2.17.3, 1259–1423.

Meyer, Marvin W., ed. *The Ancient Mysteries: A Sourcebook.* San Francisco: Harper & Row, 1987.

Mylonas, George E. *Eleusis and the Eleusinian Mysteries.* Princeton: Princeton University Press, 1961.

Nilsson, Martin P. *Greek Folk Religion.* New York: Harper, 1961.

Otto, Walter F. "The Meaning of the Eleusinian Mysteries," in *The Mysteries: Papers from the Eranos Yearbooks,* Joseph Campbell, editor. Princeton: Princeton University Press, 1955.

Rice, David G. and John E. Stambaugh. *Sources for the Study of Greek Religion.* Chico, CA: Scholars Press, 1979.

Schultes, Richard Evans, and Albert Hofmann. *The Botany and Chemistry of Hallucinogens.* Springfield, IL: Charles C. Thomas, 1973.

Smith, Huston. "Do Drugs Have Religious Import?" *Journal of Philosophy* 61(1964): 517–530.

Wasson, R. Gordon, Albert Hofmann, and Carl A. P. Ruck. *The Road to Eleusis: Unveiling the Secret of the Mysteries.* New York: Harcourt Brace Jovanovich, 1978.

Willoughby, Harold R. *Pagan Regeneration: A Study of Mystery-Initiations in the Graeco-Roman World.* Chicago: University of Chicago Press, 1929.

Zaehner, R.C. *Mysticism Sacred and Profane.* Oxford: Clarendon, 1957.

Clement of Alexandria, Pausanias, Plutarch, and Asterios are cited from the Loeb Classical Library editions of these authors. *The Homeric Hymn to Demeter*, Lactantius, Hippolytus, and Aristotle are cited from Rice and Stambaugh's *Sources for the Study of Greek Religion*.

The Science and Art
of Animating Statues

DAVID FIDELER

For John Michell

ACCORDING TO the ancient Egyptian Hermetic writing entitled the *Asclepius* or *Perfect Discourse*, one of the magical arts of antiquity involved the animation of statues. Through this art, the statue became the home of a living spirit

> so that what is of heavenly nature, being drawn down into the images by means of heavenly use and practices, may be enabled to endure with joy the nature of mankind, and sojourn with it for long periods of time.[1]

Elsewhere, in the same writing, it is told how our ancient ancestors chanced upon the "art of making gods" out of some material substance:

> And to this invention they added a supernatural force whereby the images might have the power to work good or hurt, and combined it with the material substance; that is to say, being unable to make souls, they invoked the souls of spirits and implanted them in the statues by means of holy and sacred rites.[2]

The notion of statues being so carefully wrought that they come to life is an archetypal, universal notion. It appears, for instance, in the Greek myth of Pygmalion. He fell so in love with Aphrodite that he made, with great care and exquisite craftsmanship, a beautiful ivory image of her. The goddess, impressed by Pygmalion's devotion, entered into the image and brought it to life as Galatea, who bore him Paphus and Metharme. In ancient Egypt, not only were the bas reliefs of the temples designed to become the receptacles of living spirits, but the temple itself was conceived of as the very incarnation of the god. As E. A. E. Reymond notes in his book on *The Mythical Origin of the Egyptian Temple*,

> The temple was regarded as a living entity. We are already familiar with the ideas of the temple and its reliefs being animated, but it appears that there was more than mere animation. Reasons are cited for suggesting that the temple was conceived as the material embodiment of the *God-of-the-Temple* who attained concrete form in the temple, and who was the Son of the Earth.

In antiquity, the practice of animating temples, bas reliefs, and statues was conceived of as both an art and a science. In its scientific aspect, the art of animating statues drew upon the ancient canon of proportion, itself based on those ubiquitous geometrical ratios which underlie the forms of nature and the unfolding patterns of life. In the *Laws* 656D, Plato refers to the canon of music and proportion which maintained the integrity of Egyptian art for no less than ten thousand years. As Plato writes,

> If you inspect their paintings and reliefs on the spot, you will find that the work of ten thousand years ago—I mean the expression not loosely but in all precision—is neither better nor worse than that of today; both exhibit an identical artistry.

The ultimate origins of the canon remains mysterious; evidence of its use is very early. Plato concluded that it "must have been the doing of a god, or a godlike man—as, in fact, the local tradition is that the melodies which have been preserved for so many years were the work of Isis."

The existence of such a canon is confirmed by the research of archaeologists and universally accepted by all Egyptologists. There were two Egyptian canons: the earliest divided the height of a human being into 19 squares; the later canon was based on a division of 22 squares. These canons provided a framework for Egyptian artists when rendering the human form and the forms of the gods. No one can deny the existence of the canon, for in some instances the gridwork is still visible on surviving temple walls. Interestingly, the 19-square Egyptian canon was taken over by the early Greek artists and sculptors, as has been shown by the studies of archaeologist Eleanor Guralnick.[3]

Despite the acceptance of the use of the canonical grid in Egyptian art, few Egyptologists have any awareness of the types of geometrical ratios and proportional schemes that were widely employed in Egyptian art. One such geometrical proportion is the so-called phi ratio or Golden Section. In this article, I will show how this proportion was incorporated into the design of a bas relief that is also based on the canon of 19 squares. This bas relief depicts Amenophis III (1391–1353 B.C.E.) facing a goddess, and is plate 4 in Erik Iversen's *Canon and Proportions in Egyptian Art*. While Iversen's work is an excellent study of the canonical grid system, he fails to discuss the use of the dynamic and canonical ratios in Egyptian art.[4]

The "Divine Proportion"

The so-called Divine Proportion, Golden Section, or phi ratio is one of the most ubiquitous ratios found in living forms. It controls the spacing of seeds on a sunflower, the distribution of leaves on plants, various forms of natural spirals, and the ratios of the human form. It is generally associated with the principle of gnomic growth. Mathematically speaking, it is defined as $(\sqrt{5}+1)/2 = 1.618034...$ It is the controlling ratio of the pentagon and is also associated with the double square, whose diagonal is $\sqrt{5}$. Earlier in this century it was entitled the phi ratio or ϕ, named after Phidias, the Greek sculptor who is famous for the colossal Athena in the Parthenon and the colossal Zeus at

Olympia, one of the seven wonders of the ancient world.

The simplest way to generate the phi ratio is shown in *Figure 1*. This technique produces a Golden Rectangle, which can be infinitely continued into a series of "whirling squares." These squares are linked with one another in continuous geometrical proportion (in Greek, *analogia*) which embodies the ratio φ.

The ancient Greeks referred to φ as "the extreme and mean division of a line" (Euclid 6.30), which is the unique property of this proportion. In other words, the smaller division is to the larger division as the larger division is to the whole: .618 is to 1 as 1 is to 1.618.

In *Figure 2* we see how φ is related to the geometry of the pentagon. Here, if length AB = 1, then BC = φ.

A useful method for dividing any line segment at the φ division is illustrated in *Figure 3*.

Figure 4 shows a well known property of φ in relation to the proportions of the human body: while the height of the body is divided in half by the genitals, the position of the navel indicates the φ division.

The φ ratio possesses many unique and magical properties. For example:

$$\phi + 1 = \phi^2 \text{ or } 1.618 + 1 = 1.618^2 \text{ or } 1.618 \times 1.618 = 2.618$$
$$\phi \times (\phi - 1) = 1 \text{ or } 1.618 \times (1.618 - 1) = 1 \text{ or } 1.618 \times .618 = 1$$
$$\phi^2 \times (\phi - 1)2 = 1$$
$$\phi^2 + (\phi - 1)2 = 3$$

In the Renaissance, Luca Pacioli wrote a book about the Golden Section entitled *The Divine Proportion*, a work illustrated by Leonardo da Vinci. According to Pacioli, the phi ratio is "divine" for five reasons:

1) Like God, it is unique; 2) As the Holy Trinity is one substance in three persons, so the Section is one proportion in three terms; 3) As God cannot be defined in words, the Section cannot be described by any number or rational quality because it is irrational and, hence, occult and secret; 4) Like God, it is always similar to itself; 5) As celestial virtue or

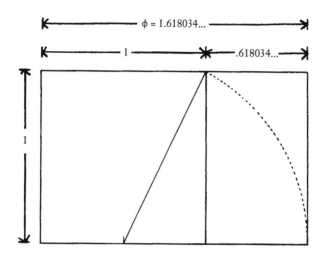

Figure 1.

The construction of a Golden Rectangle from a square brings out the proportion of ϕ, 1.618034...

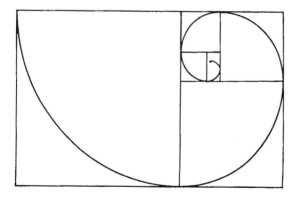

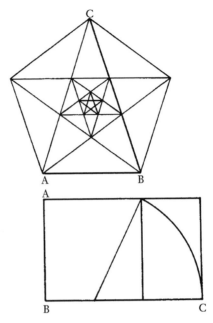

Figure 2. Phi as the Controlling Ratio of the Pentagon

If length AB = 1, then BC = ϕ = 1.618034

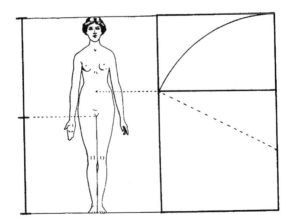

Figure 3. Phi and the Location of the Navel

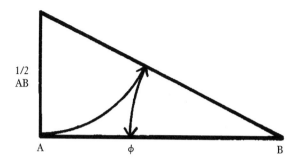

Figure 4. Technique for Cutting Any Line at the Phi Division

To cut any line AB at the phi division, erect a perpendicular that is 1/2 AB at the end of the line, and connect to the opposite end. Arcing the compass as shown will divide the line at the phi division, so that the smaller part is to the larger part as the larger part is to the whole.

quintessence has made possible the creation of the four elements out of which the whole of nature was made, so the Divine Proportion makes possible the construction of the dodecahedron, the fifth and most complex Platonic solid and the epitome of quintessence.

Analysis of the Bas Relief

As I studied the bas relief in Iversen's book, it became obvious that there was more more going on in the piece than the square grid would account for. For example, there seems to be a mysterious symmetry present between the goddess and the pharaoh as gaze meets gaze. Additionally, the hair of the goddess which falls down her front is obviously one unit wide. Why, then, didn't the artist make the hair of the goddess and the similarly positioned headdress of Amenophis perfectly align with the grid? It certainly would have simplified the composition.

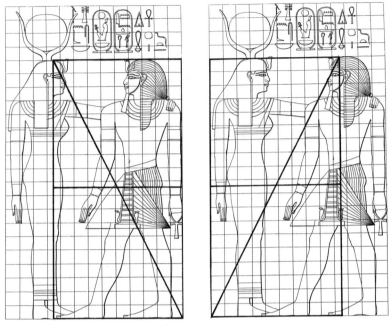

Figure 5.   **Figure 6.**

If we superimpose a double square on both the goddess and
Amenophis as shown in *Figure 5* and *6*, we can begin to see the
geometrical reciprocity between the two figures. The diagonal of the
double square is √5, the root of φ, and the eyes of the two figures are
clearly positioned at the apex of the resulting triangles.

In *Figure 7*, we see how the φ ratio determines the placement of the
navel on the pharaoh.

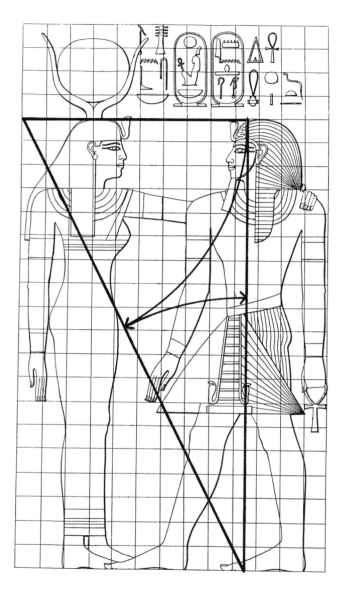

Figure 7.

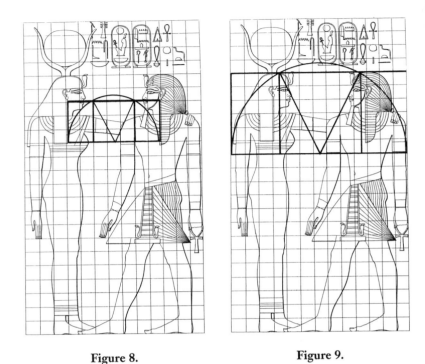

Figure 8.   **Figure 9.**

Figure 8 illustrates the underlying ratio which determines the placement of the goddess' hair and the pharaoh's headdress. They are positioned by reference to a "double sided" Golden Rectangle which has the proportion of 1:√5.

Figure 9 shows a larger √5 rectangle based on the double squares of *Figures 5* and *6*.

In *Figure 10* the two previous geometries are combined, with the armbands highlighted. The phi ratio controls the placement of every arm band in the composition!

Figures 11 and *12* show the precise harmonic division of a square based on the phi ratio. The phi ratio determines the placement of the arm bands. In *Figure 12* this square is centered on the ankh which is being carried by the pharaoh. The ankh is the Egyptian hieroglyph which denotes the unfolding principle of life.

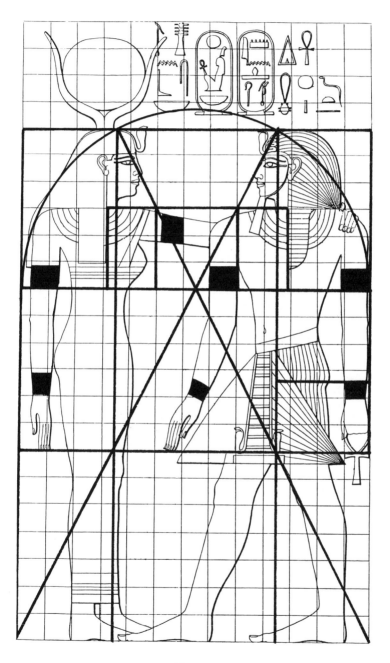

Figure 10.

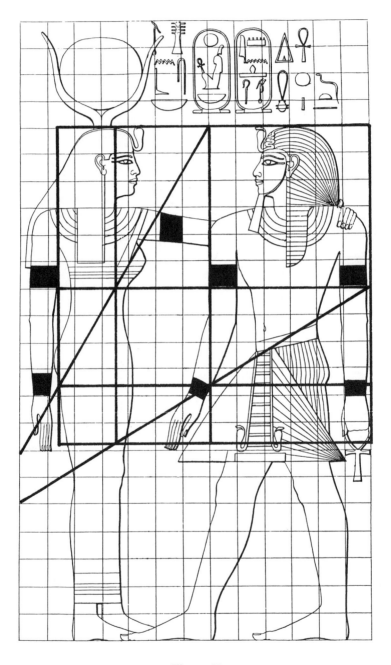

Figure 11.

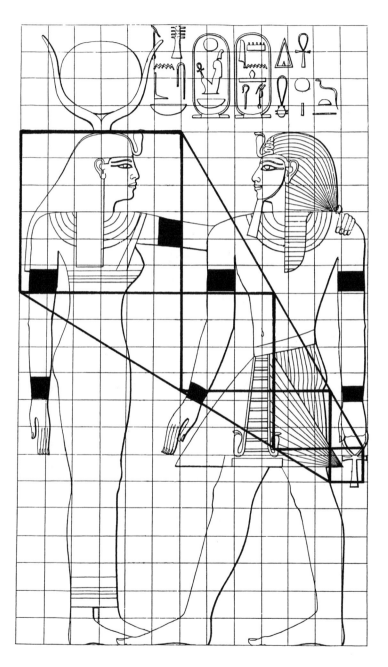

Figure 12.

The Meaning of the Composition

This particular bas relief, controlled by the geometrical forming principle of φ, is not a unique occurrence; it is a specific instance of a widespread practice and tradition which has rarely been studied by professional Egyptologists. In very ancient times, the scribes, artists, priests, and temple architects were trained about the nature of geometrical forming principles, which they applied to their work. Considering the fact that such training is not readily available, it is no wonder that the old tradition is in most respects unknown to contemporary archaeologists.

The bas relief we have examined, dating back some 3,300 years, is clearly structured on the accepted canon of 19 squares. However, the 19-square grid is not a true canon of *proportion*, but a canonical rule of thumb that was used in Egyptian art. True *proportion* involves the use of *ratio*, and one of the most dynamic ratios is the Golden Section, reflected in the process of unfolding life. Students of geometry draw a distinction between the principles of static and dynamic symmetry.[5] The square grid is useful but static; the phi grid is dynamic and brings the piece to life.

In this composition, a window opens onto the true nature of the ancient proportional canon and its employment in the science of animating statues. The square grid represents the body or raw *materia* of the composition; the phi ratio is the animating principle which brings it to life. In the same way that the universe is a harmonic union of spirit and matter, so too did the Egyptians reflect this understanding in their temple art. As we can see in *Figure 12*, the phi geometry seems to emanate from the ankh, the symbol of life; this is reinforced by the emanating lines on the pharaoh's ritual apron. From this we conclude that the Egyptians consciously understood the relationship between the phi ratio and the patterns of unfolding life.

Ancient art, at its highest, embodied scientific realizations and reflected a far more inclusive world-view than most individuals can imagine in the contemporary world. There is also a magical dimension to the old view which transcends reductionistic description. The entire culture of ancient Egypt, for example, was structured around the temple and the invocation of the gods. The pharaoh fulfilled a symbolic role within the framework of Egyptian cultural alchemy; he was seen as the personification of the Ideal Man, humanity made in the image of God. In the words of the Hermetic tractate,

> the man who, in virtue of the Mind that is in him, through which he is akin to the gods, has attached himself to them by pious devotion, becomes like the gods . . .
>
> It is for reasons such as these, Asclepius, man is a mighty wonder— an animal worthy of our worship and our respect. Man takes on the attributes of a god, as though he himself were a god . . .[6]

In our bas relief, a god gazes into the eye of a mortal; the mortal meets the god. The god welcomes the mortal with a gesture of acceptance. The pharaoh has become a god and is mortal no more. God and mortal are thus reciprocally entwined, mirror images of one another, mirror images of one life. This reciprocity between the divine and the human worlds—the interpenetration of spirit and matter—is why the Greeks depicted the gods in human form. As Heraclitus wrote, "The immortal becomes mortal, the mortal immortal, each living in the other's death and dying in the other's life."

True art is always rooted in a sacred vision of life which affirms the divine role of humanity as the living image of God. It is only through the phenomenon of humanity that consciousness or Mind, the mysterious Light of Nature, becomes cognizant of its existence and meaning. Thus, in the traditional view, humanity is seen as the central pivot of an alchemical drama which is occurring on a universal scale. Through creativity, harmony, and art, matter is transformed into spirit. Man thereby affirms his essential nature as a creature of light and life, and as the ultimate mediator between all perceivable opposites.

Notes

1. *Asclepius* 38

2. *Asclepius* 37.

3. See, for example, her article "Proportions of Korai," *American Journal of Archaeology* 85 (1981), 3, 269–80.

4. Erik Iversen, *Canon and Proportions in Egyptian Art*. Second edition, fully revised in collaboration with Yoshiaki Shibata (Warminster: Aris and Phillips, 1975).

5. For examples of dynamic symmetry see Jay Hambridge, *The Elements of Dynamic Symmetry* (New York: Dover, 1967); Matila Ghyk, *The Geometry of Art and Life* (New York: Dover, 1977); Jay Hambridge, *Dynamic Symmetry: The Greek Vase* (New Haven: Yale University Press, 1920). For an excellent introduction to geometrical forming principles, which contains a remarkable analysis of the phi ratio as the basis of an Egyptian Osiris temple, see Robert Lawlor, *Sacred Geometry: Philosophy and Practice* (London: Thames & Hudson, 1982). For more on phi, see H. E. Huntley, *The Divine Proportion: A Study in Mathematical Beauty* (New York: Dover, 1970).

6. *Asclepius* 5–6

"Matrix of Creation"

Drawing with compass and straight-edge.

DAVID FIDELER

A Meditation on the Third Gregorian Mode (Lydian)

On a capital from the abbey church at Cluny, now in the Cluny Musee Ochier.

The Alchemical Harp of Mechtild of Hackeborn

THERESE SCHROEDER-SHEKER

> When a world-view is based explicitly on a metaphysical system which takes into account the transcendental dimension and which, furthermore, shows itself in concrete realizations, we are then in the presence of Tradition. When the spirit no longer breathes in the works, even if the activities exist, then it is no longer tradition but custom.
>
> —Jean During[1]

THE HISTORY of the medieval European harp includes every enigma possible, because it remained a fiercely guarded oral tradition[2] until the middle of the sixteenth century. As such, by the time oral tradition had become written custom, its true wealth had become obscured and splintered, waiting to be remembered. Subtle traditions which involved a lifetime commitment to an interior practice became lost and forgotten when placed alongside the dazzling products of the *scriptoria* and printing press. The pure and objective notation of music itself became the primary documentation of the end product of an essentially interior journey.

Musicians have long been thrilled to have, study, and learn these steps when we digest a written repertoire. Yet this repertoire, when carried by a real artist, ceases being score, comes to life again, and links again with Tradition. This brief article is an excerpt from a larger study; it explores a little-known monastic history in which an exterior historical harp tradition became a completely interior practice through the rhythm of prayer. I am referring to this interior practice as the *alchemical harp* of religious communities and individuals in the Middle

Ages. This is also an effort to explore precious moments in the history of sung prayer, personal acts of piety, modes of transformation and individuation, and inspired symbols. I specifically probe the intentionality of a medieval female contemplative named Mechtild of Hackeborn.[3] She came to a deeper understanding of the love of the crucified and risen Christ through the teaching process inherent in the plucked-string tradition. This multi-dimensional Mechtild provides us with an exemplary model of a Christian musical-alchemical initiation. In Mechtild, contemplation, prayer, and music merge and wed, bringing to birth a profoundly integrated human being who harmonizes and strengthens her entire community, although she retains a rather anonymous personal identity in the ideal of monastic humility. Mechtild is an initiate of peace and reconciliation. With one hand she is metaphorically linked to distant brothers Pythagoras and Plato in her own profoundly musical initiation, and with the other she explicitly opens herself to Christ's love and the depths of the Christian mysteries. Her entire narration serves as a paradigm of nuptial mysticism, where harmonized body, soul, and spirit become liturgy, and she becomes Christ's harp.

The Medieval Harp

Fragments of harp history are currently woven together by scouring written chronicles, diaries, histories, tax accounts, mythologies, monastic records and constitutions, architectural records, and the full spectrum of religious and secular literature. There are numerous historical documents associating harps and psalteries with monastic communities from the tenth to the fourteenth centuries in Ireland, Wales, Germany, Italy, England, Switzerland, Spain, and possibly France. In gathering many examples, I have come to believe that the continental and romanesque harps, in substance and symbol, remained a living tradition for many members of religious communities, although this can only be adequately explored as an aspect of contemplative musicology, not Canon Law.[4] These episodes accumulate powerfully, though they have been previously dismissed as exceptions to the rule by historians who record systematic patristic denunciations of the use of instruments within liturgy. When studied together, however, these previously unrelated though exceptional narratives reveal an entirely new genre of literature. This genre creates a matrix and structure in which we can understand more fully a medieval experience of symbol, icon, psyche, spirit, and harp, thus offering us much worthy contemplative material.

One must differentiate between the Irish harp of the Western Isles and the continental European harps. The massive, calendric wire-strung Irish harp is associated with the Nature religions and the phases of the moon; therefore, it was shunned by the ecclesiastics. The harp of Celtic tradition is preserved in many myths and royal accounts, and has long been associated with entry into the supernatural world, the elemental world of nature spirits and forces now hidden from our physical eyes. The one who would finally carry Irish tradition studied years to master the three roads: the sleep song, the tear song, the laughter song.[5] The epic cycles recount how the Irish harper (like Orpheus) could call up nature-forces to aid a king in battle, put soldiers to sleep, soften women's hearts, and make mirth abound.[6] The heavy truncated wire-strung harp with its strong, bell-like clarity has a regal stature, wields power and authority, has a startlingly unique voice, and stirs the memory. Its fascination with triplicate-riddles demands things from us, asks us to pay attention, forces us to ask questions of ourselves and our meanings, and is penetrating, like lightning or the gaze of an eagle. Its royalty teaches and leads.

How completely different from its continental European cousin! The Irish missionary monks preferred small eight-stringed harps (*ocht-Trdach*)[7] suspended from their girdles, and brought these harps with them as they founded the monasteries of Europe, stringing them with gut, silk, or horsehair. In central Europe they gradually metamor-phosed, by district and county, into the triangular romanesque harps seen so prolifically in psalter iconography. By the eleventh and twelfth centuries, the romanesques received a small softened shoulder and heightened pillar, and became the elegant, slender, light-weight gothic harp strung with eight to twenty-four gut strings, full of melting warmth and generosity. Both romanesque and gothic harps were held and/or contemplated by religious musicians, who composed new Offices on them, or heard them being played by angels in mystical visions. These narratives are found in specific moments of Benedictine, Cistercian, Franciscan, and Carmelite spirituality. What could this have meant then, and what could it mean to contemplative musicians today?

As will be explained in the development of this essay, the medieval monastic harp tradition seems to revolve solely around the processes of spiritual and emotional harmonization *and* the lessons of love: sacrifice, purification, surrender, and transformation. For these and other reasons, it is appropriate to refer to these collective episodes as an alchemical harp tradition, rather than a concrete musical performance practice. One writer described alchemy with sacramental and mystical overtones by portraying it as a triadic process involving the transmutation of the physical body by the soul within it, the exaltation and transfiguration of the soul by the spirit, and the illumination and deification of the spirit by contact with the Divine.[8] In this sense, the alchemical harp was an inner musical reality that permeated meanings, thoughts, words, symbols, and was the ensouled substance of allegorical, hermeneutic, and exegetic literature of the day. The alchemical harp tradition provided immediate meaning for some medieval religious contemplatives and mystics. This body of meaning (without any trace of elitism or heresy) flourished outside but alongside canonic sources, scriptures, doctrines, and theologies, and revolved around the transformation of the interior life, not musical finger-tip virtuosity. This alchemical harp served (and still serves) as a well-spring: it is situated in the heart of daily activity and is available for all singing the *opus Dei*. It is the revered harp of prayer, praise, heroic struggle, and love lyric. It seeks to serve, comfort, and soothe. It teaches indirectly through tenderness, and enters one's life quietly like moisture, or the quiet beauty of a swan's ascent into the air. It is this harp tradition that elects Mechtild as a rare and stellar guardian from whom we can learn so much today.

Mechtild of Hackeborn and the
Christian Alchemical Initiation

Mechtild of Hackeborn (1241–1298/99) came from high nobility and entered the convent of Rodarsdorf in northwestern Germany at the age of seven in the year 1248.[9] When she was fifteen, the nuns moved to Helfta near Eisleben where the Saxon monastery flourished. Theirs was a center of religious culture and scholarship where spiritual revelations were preserved and honored, nurturing the entire community. Under the direction of her sister, the Abbess Gertrude (not to be confused with Gertrude the Great), books of poetry, prayer, and spiritual exercises were written, collected, and transcribed by nuns in the scriptorium. Scholarship and spiritual activity were equally valued at Helfta. The momentum of intellectual discernment and discipline born in the study of the seven liberal arts was never set in opposition to the profound current of religious devotion so characteristic of Helfta spirituality.

No doubt this harmony supported the possibilities of both serenity and integrity within community. Active devotion to the Eucharist was cultivated, as was a devotion to the Passion and humanity of Christ, the wounds of Christ, and the cult of His Sacred Heart. Simultaneously, the Helfta women studied, among others, Augustine, Bernard of Clairvaux, Gregory the Great, and Hugh of St. Victor.[10] These nuns observed Cistercian spirituality in general and repeatedly found voice in the luminous expressions of personal love, spiritual friendship, nuptial mysticism, and mystic espousal.

Mechtild as chant-mistress or *cantrix* trained the choir[11] and earned the tender sobriquet "God's nightingale" from her sisters. Her singing was renowned and inextricably linked with a lyric and transparent spirituality. It was something about the totality of her ability to enter prayer when she sang and when she heard music that brought about these special visionary states. Under the direction of the Abbess Gertrude, two-hundred and thirty of Mechtild's visions were compiled under the title: *Liber Spiritualis Gratiae* (The Book of Special

Grace) and later translated into Middle English.[12] These visions disclose a Mechtild whose special graces are both clairvoyant and clairaudient, and an interior life wherein the sheaths of music, love, and prayer are seamlessly integrated, and interpenetrate each other flawlessly. The scribe assures us that there were many more visions, but they couldn't write them all down. The visions explored in this article will reflect stages of transformation rather than chronological events.

Mechtild's Visions

> Clay is molded into vessels, and because of the space where nothing exists we are able to use them as vessels. Doors and windows are cut out in the walls of a house, and because they are empty spaces, we are able to use them. . . . Be vacant, and you will remain full.
> —Lao Tzu[13]

In a vision immediately following her mystic betrothal, Christ tells Mechtild that he "worships himself in her when she worships him."[14] He finds himself in her! He tells her to "rest her weary head on his heart,"[15] which is elsewhere described as a "five-petalled rose."[16] When she gives away all her desires in the practice of inner-emptiness, the monastic vow of poverty becomes a potent spiritual expression of vast freedom. In this condition, she has made room to become the receptacle of tender longing, which strikes her like a lightning-bolt. During the Secret[17] of the Mass, she is transported to another level where she meets Christ intimately. He wants to fill her with every sweetness; he wants to know her requests. Mechtild replies three times that her only longing concerns the knowledge and perfection of his will. This can be seen in a particularly Christian context, not as the reply of a bashful maiden so much as it is the inversion, reflection, and transformation of the third request in the time-honored *Pater Noster*: "give us this day our daily bread."[18]

As she draws near to her Beloved, she is startled by a blinding new kind of union. From his divine heart emerges a harp,[19] and a numinous voice informs her that "the harp is our Lord Jesu" and the many strings are all "chosen souls, sounding together in his love." Mechtild continues like a bride, describing how he gives her his singing voice, surrounds her in his song and the most refined movements of his fingertips as the strings begin to sound. She calls him the "high chanter of all chanters" and he becomes a minstrel for her. She says that he "smote the harp" and all the quivering angels, no longer able to contain their gladness, intoned "delectable sound" with him singing: "Regem, Regum, Dominum."[20]

Here, the languages of love, alchemy, poetry, psychology, and mysticism collide and engender a highly individual and shimmering series of symbols, which she receives in full power. The contents of her inner life ignore the canon of rules that historically legislated against the use of instruments within liturgy.[21] Those confines mean nothing to her! She makes her own history, stands literally in her own tradition, weaving her spirituality from every thread of beauty and harmony in her life. For her, Christ is the tactile and fragrant celebrant of a threshold liturgy which she hears, receives, and then shares with her community. She enters the mysteries of Christ's love as a faithful equal, a polar opposite, living from the leaven of the perfectly tuned strings sounding in his perfectly formed hands. His sung holy words become Eucharist, thanksgiving, suspended and offered in melody, Mechtild's most highly developed sensibility. Again, like the exchange of true lovers, he gives her his gift in the one modality that she can return eight times daily in Divine Office. This picture of the audible, tactile, fragrant *troubadour*-Christ, singing and playing his harp for her, is an *icon*, not a metaphor.

There is yet another vision[22] which concerns the inspired nature of these medieval plucked-stringed instruments:

> It seemed to her sight that Love stood at the right side of God and from the heart of God showed out an instrument of melody and of merry sound. This instrument reached forth to the heart of this maiden. This

instrument was a psaltery to her sight which had ten strings, and of that is written in the Psalms of the Psalter "My God, I shall sing to thee in a psaltery with ten strings" (Ps. 32.2). By the nine strings were betokened the nine orders of angels in which are ordained all the persons of the saints. The tenth string betokened our Lord himself, who is the King of angels and the sanctifier of all the saints.

A feminine form, a "maiden," a being of pure love stands next to "God" who seems to be an equally benevolent figure. Mechtild's tenderness often engenders deeply relational pictures: the alchemical marriage of two standing together mutually fructifying each other. The alchemical marriage creates, from pure resonance, the birth of another stringed instrument: the psaltery. As the two face each other, they co-create from the matrix of their reflected luminosity a ten-stringed psaltery, which she calls an instrument of "merry melody." Each string "betokens" one of the nine orders of celestial beings or angels who "ordain" the saints. The tenth string "betokens" the Lord himself, the "king of the angels." She touches each one of the strings, but not the tenth! Her tenderness overflows in generosity and joy. She wants all the souls of heaven and earth to become "partners" of this divine grace. Her marriage mysticism is completely relational.

The Theological Mysticism of the Harp

Why has revelation chosen harp and psaltery as an archetype of the mystic call, or "spiritual election" as Mechtild calls it? What do these strings-held-over-the-heart signify in the contemplative life? Why is the "Lover of all lovers," Christ, the harper and minstrel divine? His actual corporeality is shown as a harp, and it is here on earth, not in a heavenly cloud. Mechtild's body-of-Christ has incarnated, and like a beacon of light, suffuses her entire consciousness with heavenly music. But how? Why?

Strings stretching must do so between two equal polar opposites. This is the alchemical wedding of one's soul to one's spirit, or in another interpretation, head and heart. Vertical strings anchor themselves firmly in the body or soundboard of the harp, and stretch high into the harmonic curve. Vertical strings maintain and image the earth-sky axis. Suffering and sacrifice, the intimate and essential aspects of the Eucharist and the self-purification so necessary for the mystical or alchemical betrothal, are even physically present in these inspired instruments. The very strings for the harps and psalteries come from the animal kingdom, where goats and sheep (Lamb of God) are destined for sacrifice. The wood from the fallen willow, hornbeam, spruce, or cherry tree is offered up from the plant kingdom. Choirs of plant, animal, human, and celestial kingdoms join together to offer praise. Jesus Christ stretching on the wood of the cross becomes at once the new sounding board for lament (of our suffering humanity) and the Eucharistic string for celebration (for our transformation).

The body of the harp, any harp, is a huge empty womb or sepulcher. The non-mechanized medieval harp is played on the left shoulder, where Jesus carried the cross, and is therefore always held over the heart and the genitals, the two most vulnerable aspects of our humanity.[23] The risen Christ *becomes* a harp when he appears as the divine groom, the husband of our nightingale, who sings in his hand. He longs to be played. Mechtild (the Soul or the Bride) has spent years fine-tuning herself to reflect heavenly harmonies. She also lived her vow of poverty as the interior practice of inner-emptiness, an alchemical sepulcher, in order to make room in herself for the reception of revelation. Mechtild, like Christ, creates pure tone from her finely tuned body, from her throat, the larynx: the metamorphosis of the motherly womb. The singing minstrel Christ walks the feminine way and joins all women, by giving birth when he sings the Logos. Mechtild becomes the harp, and in her obedience, the very harp played by the "high chanter of all chanters." The boundaries dissolve and Christ worships himself when she worships him.

I believe this is Mechtild's way to her resurrection body. When she creates during long years a completely purified body of images, memories, feelings, desires, and hopes, it is woven from the borderline material substance of song, of hymnody, of Christ's song. Like the secret intimacies in marriage, which are hidden from the casual glance, the interior work of harmonizing (of fine-tuning pitch and proportion) supersedes mere external musical technique. It demands conscious spiritual activity. While she weaves her Christian resurrection body (or the rainbow body of Buddhism), she is also becoming more and more complete, more whole, in her physical body. One final story makes this fact eminently clear.

Harmonious Presence-of-Being Despite Adversity

In a strange twist of fate, Mechtild experienced a political intrigue which resulted in the punishment of monastic silence. An interdict imposed on the convent forbade the singing of chant and the celebration of the Mass. The well-known tradition of loving friendship at Helfta (compassion, tenderness, consolation), seems to have been sorely tested, initially causing the women serious grief. As would be expected, the momentum of their years of fine-tuning did not fail, but contributed strength and great serenity at a time most needed. The women weathered this attack with a victorious blessing from their troubadour Christ, who once again healed with the sound of his voice.

On the feast of the Assumption, Christ appeared[24] covered with roses of gold and silver, along with his mother, Mary, who "held the chalice." Together they con-celebrated Mass, with John the Baptist reading the Epistle, and Christ is described as one who "sang high Mass." John the Beloved served for Mary as she stood at the right side of the altar clothed in vestments as bright as the sun. It is this John who reads the Gospel. Descriptions are given detailing Christ and Mary's voices, singing this Mass. They sing together! He sings the *Gloria* in a "full, high voice"; she sings the *Sanctus*! They are arrayed in shimmering, precious stones, and give golden wedding rings to the many Helfta brides, who receive him despite the interdict! This is a vivid Christian monastic imagination of the alchemical wedding. The nuns married Christ inwardly in a most intimate Eucharist of heavenly sound and color. They remained subtle and steadfast in their experience, despite external turbulence. The trademark at Helfta had always reflected the harmonious balance between scholarship and devotion, head and heart. This agreement had fortified the unitive experience, where individually and collectively the nuns sought and found balance and serenity in angelic sound that had become incarnated in their interior practice. Luminous and proportionate, they kept their sense of pitch, their feeling for truth and harmony, and received graces instead of psychic wounds and legal deprivations.

Conclusion

Mechtild's Christian alchemical initiation resulted in a series of authentic stages, heard and seen inwardly, creating a new kind of certainty that manifested itself as a body-wisdom. It sang or resonated on all three levels of body, soul, and spirit. It was so inward that it did and could bypass or dissolve the barriers of the dense body, and could ring, instead, all around her like a protective sheath. The unique detail here is that it seems to have been infectious at Helfta, spreading inwardly to benefit, heal, comfort, and nurture other nuns. This relational boundless love seems to be the ultimate harvest of marriage mysticism. A young and foolish soul may want to hide the light of a handsome lamp in the isolation of her own house, lest someone covet it. Mechtild, on the other hand, was so at home with her purified singing sheath that her life became the hymn of the wise virgin. Her loving heart had generated a physical body that had become a "chapel spun of sound. Every door and window gleams and motion crowns." [25]

I must admit that sometimes I wonder if Mechtild actually had a harp, or if someone in her close proximity had one. The depth, frequency, and detail of these plucked-stringed visions would suggest great personal intimacy with actual physical harps. We do know that Welsh Cistercian abbots maintained resident harpists, and that the harps may have been used in the monastic infirmary at St. Augustine's in Canterbury. We do know that both troubadours Bernard de Ventadorn and Bertran de Born retired to the Cistercian abbey of

Dalon. The harp was a substantial force and a symbolic presence in monasticism. Regardless of literal proof, Mechtild certainly lived the harp tradition so completely that physical harp was experienced as the exterior reminder of the interior practice, the alchemical harp. When a contemplative musician goes so far as to abandon even the physical tool or prop, she or he freely lives harp as the interior path of fine-tuning. This is the alchemical harp of medieval monasticism: a timeless and resonating icon singing only of an anointed love.

Notes

1. Jean During, "Poetry and the Visual Arts," *World of Music* 24 (1982), n. 1.

2. Select bibliographical sources: Edward Bunting, *The Ancient Music of Ireland* (Dublin: Waltons, 1969); Robert Bruce Armstrong, *The Irish and Highland Harps* (New York: Praeger, 1969); Roslyn Rensch, *The Harp* (London: Duckworth, 1969); Joan Rimmer, *The Irish Harp, Clairseach na hEireann* (Cork: Mercier Press, 1977); Grainne Yeats, *The Belfast Harpers Festival 1792* (Dublin: Gael Linn, 1980); Donal O'Sullivan, *Carolan: The Life, Times and Music of an Irish Harper* (Lincolnshire: Celtic Music, 1983); Christopher Page, *Voices and Instruments of the Middle Ages* (Berkeley: University of California Press, 1986); Ann Heymann, *Secrets of the Gaelic Harp* (Minneapolis: Clairseach Publications, 1988); Roslyn Rensch, *Harps and Harpists* (Bloomington: Indiana University Press, 1989).

3. Mechtild of Hackeborn was a nun at the convent of Helfta and a friend of both Gertrude the Great and Mechtild of Magdeburg (with whom she is frequently confused). During a serious illness, she confided her visions to two companions, who, for the next eight years recorded them without her knowledge. On learning of this activity, she was greatly distressed, but Christ reassured her that it was his will that the experiences be made known.

4. See a forthcoming survey by the author entitled *The Alchemical Harp of Christian Monasticism*, St. Dunstan's Press.

5. See Bunting, 18–36. Another rendering: soothing, affecting, and exhilarating.

6. Classic texts of the Mythological, Ulster, and Ossianic cycles are readily available in many translations. See Jeffrey Gantz, *Early Irish Myths and Sagas* (New York: Penguin Books, 1981); Kenneth Hurlstone Jackson, *A Celtic Miscellany* (Baltimore: Penguin Books, 1975); Charles Squire, *Celtic Myth and Legend* (Van Nuys: Newcastle Publishing, 1975); David H. Greene, *An Anthology of Irish Literature* (New York: Modern Library, 1954).

7. See Bunting, 42. Also, Aloys Fleischmann, "References to Chant in Early Irish MSS," in *Essays and Studies Presented to Professor Tadgh Ua Donnchadha* (Cork: Cork University Press, 1947).

8. See page 26 in the Arthur Edward Waite introductory essay on the four treatises by Thomas Vaughan (Eugenius Philalethes) in the George Redway, London, 1888 edition. He also continues saying "contemplation and quiet" are the keys to this "modification," to this "New Birth."

9. Her dates are variously disputed, one source says 1244–1310, another says 1241?–1298/99. I have worked from the Theresa A. Halligan microfiche edition, *The Booke of Gostlye Grace of Mechtild of Hackeborn*, Studies and Texts 46 (Toronto: Pontifical Institute of Medieval Studies, 1979). Further references to this text will be cited: BOGG.

10. See Caroline Walker Bynum, *Jesus as Mother: Studies in the Spirituality of the High Middle Ages* (Berkeley: University of California Press, 1982), 176.

11. For a thoughtful discussion of this office, see Alejandro Enrique Planchart, *The Repertory of Tropes at Winchester* (Princeton: Princeton University Press, 1977), 14–16.

12. Two fifteenth-century MSS are extant: Oxford, Bodleian Library MS Bodley 220B and London, British Library MS Egerton 2006E.

13. *Tao Te Ching* 11 and 22, trans. Ch'u Ta-Kao (London: 1953), 23 and 34.

14. BOGG, part 3, vision 8, 430–1.

15. BOGG, prologue, 34; also part 2, vision 29, 382–3.

16. BOGG, part 3, vision 1, 412.

17. *Secret*: the name given to the prayer said by the celebrant after the offering of the bread and wine. BOGG, part 2, vision 2, 333–4. Her question is a paragraph long. It is here paraphrased.

18. See also "Concerning the Our Father," in the *Simone Weil Reader*, ed. George Panichas (New York: McKay, 1977).

19. BOGG, part 2, vision 2, 328–34.

20. These details from BOGG, part 2, vision 2, 328–34.

21. See James McKinnon, "Music in Early Christian Literature," in *Cambridge Readings in the Literature of Music* (New York: Cambridge University Press, 1987).

22. BOGG, part 2, vision 35, 392–3. See also Pseudo-Dionysius, *The Mystical Theology and the Celestial Hierarchies* (North Godalming, Surrey: Shrine of Wisdom, 1949); also Adam Bittleston, *Our Spiritual Companions: From Angels and Archangels to Cherubim and Seraphim* (Edinburgh: Floris Books, 1980).

23. The orchestral pedal harp is today played on the right shoulder.

24. BOGG, part 1, vision 61, 251–5. The text reads: "It seemed to her that He appeared to all the congregation." She also sees her sisters in procession.

25. This is a line from an unpublished art song composed by the author. It is a sequence in praise of Mechtild but has not yet been recorded at the time of this publication.

The Fish Bride

JANE THIGPEN

ONCE LONG AGO, an old King fell in love with a beautiful young girl and brought her back to live as his wife in a tiny kingdom of crags and cliffs that stretched between a desert wilderness and a great salt sea. As the years went by, the Queen produced no heirs. The rumour grew that her barrenness had brought the entire land under a curse, for the earth withered with drought and dust clung to the mountains in a haze. Finally, the King's advisors argued that he should consider the future of his people and choose another bride.

He refused because he loved his wife dearly, but felt such guilt over this decision that the sight of her came to fill him with sorrow and pain. He took to hunting and spent his days among the conies and sheep on the mountainsides. Most of the Court rode with him, so the Queen watched over an empty house.

Late one afternoon as the hunters rode homewards, they found the road blocked by an enormous cart piled high with hay. The King shouted crossly that the driver should make way, but the cart kept plodding forwards. As he shouted again, it went yet slower. At his third cry, the cart stopped dead. The press of men and horses surged forward and pushed it off the road into a deep ditch where it overturned and splintered, scattering hay in all directions.

An old, old woman crawled out of the wreckage and limped forward until she stood just below the King. She spat the straw from her mouth and hissed,

> For this your wife shall bear a son:
> A heartless beast, despised and slain,
> then left to rot as carrion.

The crowd shouted in outrage and several nobles closed in with raised fists, but the King motioned them back. He pulled the crone up onto the road and set her on his horse, then walked down into the ditch, braced his back against the far side of the cart, and pushed. Slowly one, then another of his men followed suit. Finally the vehicle stood again upon the highway. He helped the woman into the driver's seat and handed her his signet ring:

"Take this to the palace and my seneschal shall repay you for your load at thrice its market value."

As the cart rolled up the road, a sudden gust of wind blew back the sacking from the woman's head. A flash of gold shone in the afternoon sun, then wagon and driver both vanished. A white dove circled overhead, singing,

> When twice one wife he woos and wins
> your child will gain both life and heart
> and turn his curse to blessedness.

Nine months later, the Queen gave birth to a son. He was a healthy child except for one thing—he never showed the least affection for anyone or anything. At the age of three, he watched in silence while his puppy lost its tail beneath a wagon wheel. When his mother died in childbirth on his eighth birthday, her son asked his nurse why everyone was making such a fuss—surely his father could find a replacement easily enough. Several years later, a fire gutted the palace nursery. The boy listened to the screams of those within and never shed a tear. By his twelfth birthday, he was so hated that his father placed him under protective custody.

At last, the Prince came of age and the King set about finding the prescribed cure for his condition. Marital inquiries went forth to every eligible maiden in the land, from the richest merchant's daughter to the lowliest chambermaid. It soon became clear that no woman would have the Prince as a husband, for it was generally agreed that he was not quite human.

Late one night after a day of hopeless matrimonial interviews, the King fell into an exhausted sleep and received a strange answer to his problem. He dreamed that he stood again upon the highway as he had 18 years ago. This time the crone rode to meet him upon a milk-white stallion with a golden bridle and saddle.

She handed him a golden ring and said, "Tomorrow at noon your son will notice beauty for the first time in his life. Have him throw this ring as far as he can in the direction of his gaze, then wait. His bride will carry the ring back to him."

The King awoke in the deep of the night and found the ring glittering in the moonlight upon his pillowcase.

Father and son rode out at dawn. A strong wind had cleared the air and the mountain peaks flushed purple then dusky rose in the sunlight. Dew shone on the grass and the sky glittered like mother-of-pearl. The Prince rode in silence and kept his eyes fixed upon the gravel and dusty rocks along the roadside. As the path wound beside a cliff, the boy's horse stumbled and threw its rider. The Prince landed with his head slightly over the cliff-edge and stared out to sea at water which shimmered every imaginable color of blue and green.

"What a remarkable place," he said. "How lovely!"

His father glanced up at the sky and sighed. The sun poised precisely in mid-heaven.

Well, that was that, then. The sea did not seem a logical place for a bride, but the King followed his instructions precisely, handed his son the ring, and told him to throw it out as far from shore as he could. Then they tethered their horses to a tree, climbed down the winding path that led to the beach, and waited.

They had sat all day long in the blistering sun when something dark appeared against the horizon. An enormous grouper swam towards the shore, wearing a bridal wreath and veil. A school of tuna accompanied it, pulling a barge piled high with driftwood. Six sharks, with a net of seaweed in their teeth, brought up the rear. As the tuna touched land, they turned into a team of white mares harnessed by golden ropes to a wagon loaded with trunks and boxes of the finest leather. The sharks became black stallions which pulled an enormous clear fish bowl brimming with salt water and mounted on golden wheels. The grouper rolled its eyes at the Prince, spat the ring at his feet, and flopped into its bowl.

The wedding party ambled down the beach to the harbor and then went straight to the cathedral. By the time the procession emerged again from the building, the entire town had assembled at the church steps. Everyone applauded the King's wit and agreed that the couple was astoundingly well-matched, at least in blood and temperament. Then they pelted the newlyweds with seaweed and fish-heads all the way back to the palace.

The palace cooks threw together a lavish feast and the Court had a great time, dancing and drinking far into the night. The bride and groom themselves seemed strangely apathetic. The Prince eyed the monster lolling beside him and slipped his supper under the table to the dogs. The grouper eyed the repast of diced worms and minnows that floated overhead and shrank against the bottom of her bowl. At last the time for retiring arrived. The Court escorted the couple to their chambers and tucked them into bed as best as they could, allowing for the fish-bowl. Then they tiptoed out and left the young man wondering what in the world he was supposed to do with a fish in his bed.

At the stroke of midnight, the rays of the moon struck the bowl and its water began to shake violently. Sounds of furious splashing echoed round the room. When darkness fell again, all grew still. The Prince lit a candle and peered at his roommate. A crinkled fish skin floated on one side of the bowl while in the other swam a young girl, naked except for her wreath and veil and a cloud of long brown hair. A knock came at the door and the Prince rose, bemused, to open it. A line of women waited outside, clad in white and gold and bearing armfulls of silk and lace, and trays of jeweled brushes, combs, and jars of creams and powders.

The glass bowl was soon surrounded by a flurry of activity. As the Prince watched in amazement, another knock sounded at the door.

Again, he rose to answer it and found six black footmen outside, clad in red and gold. Each balanced a lacquered tray upon his head, loaded with golden bowls, plates and goblets. Each cradled a stringed instrument inlaid with rare and costly woods. Two viols bore scenes of harvest time: peasants pounded great vats of grapes beneath their dancing feet as wagons heavy with corn wound through fields dotted with sheaves of wheat. The great bass viol depicted a hunt, complete with falcons, lords and ladies, horses and dogs. Stag and boars crashed through the brush, while partridges winged overhead. Two violins bore orchards of pears and apples across their backs. And last, a harp, twined with veins of gold and silver and clearest crystal, bore scenes of craftsmen hard at work with anvil and forge, hammer and tongs.

One of the women snapped her fingers. The great canopied bed became a musicians' gallery. A long table, draped in white damask, appeared in the middle of the room. Two thrones, heavy with carving and heaped with cushions, sat at either end. The golden bowls, plates and goblets floated down and arranged themselves upon the tablecloth while the men climbed into the gallery, tuned their instruments, and began to play. As the bass viol struck a chord, sides of venison and breasts of pheasant appeared on the platters. The viols joined in and red wine shimmered within the goblets. Fruit tumbled into the bowls, accompanied by a run of violins, and golden knives and forks and crystal candelabra chimed into place with a sweeping arpeggio from the harp.

The Prince felt a gentle touch upon this shoulder and looked up. His wife stood beside him, dressed in yards of lace and ropes of pearls.

The night passed swiftly. Just before down, the attendants bowed to the couple and left. As the first rays of the sun entered the palace, the sound of horse hooves echoed down the corridor. The Princess vanished and a monstrous fish swam again within its bowl. No trace remained of the night's festivities except for a small note pinned to a pillow-case which read, "Keep this a secret, please."

For one year, the Prince lived a double life. During the day, he took his grouper on outings in her bowl. During the night, he wined, dined, and explored other activities which made the Princess blush and order her servants out of the room. As a result, one morning two tiny groupers appeared wriggling beside their mother. The Royal veterinarian examined the babies and declared them male.

The Prince's feat disturbed his people greatly. Everyone had assumed that this marriage was a mere formality and would be dissolved as soon as a proper bride appeared. But now it seemed that their nation was saddled with a dynasty of fish. A delegation of nobles forced the King to decree a divorce and disinherit the offspring.

When he was told the news, the Prince declared that he would have his fish or no one.

"But why?" people asked. "What can she do other than swim, bubble, and grow? Surely any replacement could easily outpace those accomplishments."

No, it could not.

The young man listed his wife's beauty, grace, and poise. When he mentioned her excellence as a dancer, the room exploded into laughter.

"Look at the finny ballerina!" someone said, and a group of boys linked arms around the bowl and spun it in a circle.

As water sprayed across the room and swam upon the floor, the Prince blurted out, "No, truly it all makes perfect sense. You see, my wife's not really a fish, she's a lady—" and then he gasped, remembering her request. But it was too late.

The grouper moved jerkily within her bowl, swam upside down for a few minutes, then floated to the surface. A sign appeared upon her body,

> If you would see me live again,
> eat all of me from head to tail
> then throw my wishbone down the Well of Life.

The Prince called for a huge cauldron and had the fish boiled right in front of him. He rolled up his sleeves, caught up knife and fork, and set to work. It took him several days to gulp her down, but at last the skeleton lay clean and bare upon the table. A wishbone poked up at the very base of the tail. The Prince pried out the bone and went to bed.

When a valet entered the royal bed chamber the next morning, he found no sign of the Prince but noticed an exceedingly ugly little dog sleeping in the bed with its snout wedged between the pillows and its paws draped over the coverlet. He caught up a broom and gave the animal a smack. It awoke with a yip, rooted briefly in the bedclothes, then ran out the door with a bone in its mouth.

Several other smacks of the broom propelled the creature through the halls, out the front door, and high into the air. It landed on its tail just outside the palace gate. A rain of stones, tin cans, and rotten fruit sent it squealing through the town, through the north gate, and out into the countryside. Eventually, the beast outran its persecutor. The run had whet its appetite, but it soon discovered that drought had baked the earth hard and nothing grew. All the other animals had either gone far north or had ended up in soup pots long ago. Late that evening, the dog crept back to town and searched through the garbage at the dump. It survived in this fashion for a week before it was discovered by a pack of mongrels. Thereafter it hid under the docks and ate fish heads. When a tribe of cats slashed its nose open, the dog padded out into the countryside again. It loped all day long, always heading north. As night fell, it found itself climbing a narrow pathway that inched up the back of a mountain. At the crest of the ridge, the road suddenly ended in a blaze of torches and shouting men. Several feet away huddled an old woman, crouching beneath a pile of bloody sacking. A white horse kicked and reared nearby, dragging against the reins which bound it to a tree.

As stone after stone whizzed over its head, the dog grew more and more frightened. It barked and ran in circles, snapping and biting. In the confusion, the woman slipped over to the horse, cut its reins free, and escaped. At that moment, the stones abruptly changed course and hit the dog thick and fast.

When the morning dawned, a hunter discovered the animal lying under a pile of rocks, stiff as a board. He picked the corpse up by its tail and threw it off the road. Later that day, a group of villagers found the body and argued over its proper disposal. No one wanted to go to the bother of burying it and a fire was out of the question because of the drought. So finally, one woman said, "How about that old dry well in Grishom's field?"

This field was widely considered a Fairy dancing ground. Grass grew lush and green there although the rest of the kingdom had long since dried to dust. The climate of the place was curiously regular. Roses and violets bloomed there untouched by frost or heat. More-over, music and lights visited the property at odd hours of the night when any decent human lay in bed. All in all it was quite uncanny and avoided by most sensible folk. Still, the well did make a splendid dump, so the group bribed a young boy and sent him racing off, dragging the dog behind him.

After the child got rid of the carcass, he noticed a strange object lying at his feet. It looked just like a wishbone, so he picked it up, snapped it in half as he made a wish, then dropped it into the well on top of the dog.

The Prince awoke in darkness, swimming hard. A flood of cold water drove him upwards, out into the sunlight, then gently dropped him onto a grassy meadow. His Princess lay beside him, still and pale as a block of alabaster. Her body twisted sharply at the waist and her head bent so far backward that bones pressed against the skin of her throat. As he reached out to touch her, she vanished. A grouper lay at his side, mouth open and eyes glazed.

A strange cry burst forth from the young man. His mind suddenly swam with a host of images: a puppy leaping from his arms then running out into the street, his father staring blindly at a casket, men pulling a body from a smoke-stained room, an elegant woman fading from his arms as dawn broke through shadows and candlelight. Tears began to trickle down his cheeks, falling faster and faster until the fish lay slick and wet in a pool of water. A slight twitching began at its tail then spread upwards until the entire body shook and trembled.

Finally, it exploded in a brilliant flash of light. The Princess stood whole and well above him, holding out her hands and smiling.

They walked a day and a night without ceasing and reached the royal city at dawn. It was market day and the streets were already full of people. Vendors hawked hot rolls and cups of water. Behind curtains of red and blue, puppeteers readied their creatures of paper and string. Children chased scrawny dogs and half-starved cats while their parents waited in long lines for the family's weekly ration of grain, withered vegetables, and tiny sack of water. As the Prince and Princess passed the stands of food, a gasp arose from the people. Bags of grain burst their seams and wheat streamed onto the ground until tall mounds hid the tables from view. Vegetables swelled, then split and trebled until plump piles of green, red, white and yellow rolled about the Princess' feet. Water began to well from her footprints and soon a broad stream ran through the center of town. As the couple reached the palace doors, the sky rippled with lightning and a strong wind brought down the first drops of rain.

On that day the Court vanished without a trace and fish suddenly appeared within the city stream with curiously human expressions upon their faces. The King lived the rest of his life happy with his son, daughter-in-law and grandsons (who were normal little boys with a zest for all sorts of water sports). After the King's death, the Prince and Princess ruled well and long and were greatly beloved by their people, particularly the poor and homeless, who never left their presence empty-handed.

Editor's Introduction

The principle of *harmonia*—the mediation between extremes through the application of *logos* or proportion—is the preeminent, central concern of Pythagorean cosmology and philosophy. According to Philolaus (b. *c.* 470 B.C.E.), the earliest Pythagorean whose fragments have survived, "Nature in the universe was harmonized from Limited and Unlimited elements, both the totality of the *kosmos* and all the things in it." Moreover, "*Harmonia* comes to be in all respects out of contraries; for *harmonia* is the unity of multiplicity, and the agreement of things that disagree." The nature of *harmonia*, the "fitting together" of extremes, was studied by the Pythagoreans on the monochord. The importance of these harmonic studies is indicated by a story which has come down to us from antiquity: as Pythagoras lay dying on his deathbed, his final exhortation to his students was that they should continue their investigations on the monochord.

We believe that Siemen Terpstra is the leading expert on the monochord alive today. He has produced a vast corpus of highly illustrated technical and philosophical work, spanning hundreds of pages, which documents the natural genesis, morphology, and structure of tuning systems, including the regions of microtonality. His work on the mathematical nature of *harmonia* not only illuminates the work of the ancient Greek philosophers, it also extends the Pythagorean science and philosophy of whole systems into the present day. In this article, he describes how to build a monochord, its fundamental principles, and beginning exercises and investigations for the student of harmonic science.

—DAVID FIDELER

An Introduction to the Monochord

Siemen Terpstra

THE MONOCHORD is essentially a tool for measuring musical intervals. In its simplest form it consists of one string stretched between two bridges on a plank or suitable sound-box. A movable bridge is then placed under the string and calibrated. The various positions of the movable bridge define fret placements, demonstrating the numerical foundations of consonant and dissonant musical intervals. (See *Figure 1.*) Thus the theoretical approach is to calibrate interval size by changing the string length alone, always keeping other parameters (for example, string tension) constant. As the name implies, only one string is necessary to do the experiments; but, since ancient times, several strings were used, all tuned in exact unison, each with a movable bridge, so that various intervals can be compared to each other. The monochord described by the ancient theorists Aristoxenus and Ptolemy had eight strings, so that a whole scale could be erected; hence they called it an *octachord.*

The monochord principle is acoustically sound, although certain limitations are present which we will describe later; indeed, no more accurate tool for investigating musical tuning was invented until after the research of Helmholtz in the latter half of the nineteenth century. It is still a worthwhile instrument for the investigation of ratios and intonation.

The monochord had various names in ancient cultures. In classical Greece it was also called the *kanon* or "law." The Middle Eastern multi-stringed zither called a *canon* is a direct evolution from the monochord. The Chinese *k'in* or "philosopher's lute" is essentially a multi-stringed monochord. The Japanese *koto* is also directly a monochord with movable bridges. The Hindu *vina* is another evolution from it; indeed, all fretted instruments are descendants of the primordial stretched string. In Europe, the *hurdy-gurdy* and the *clavichord* (hence all keyboard instruments) developed from it. The medieval Europeans used the instrument as an aid to proper vocal intonation and as a measuring tool in the design of bells and organ pipes.

The origin of the monochord is obscure. The Greeks attributed its invention to Pythagoras; however, like most Greek musical technologies, it was probably imported from Babylonia or Egypt. The mathematics associated with monochord work reached a very high level of evolution in the earliest known literate civilization, the city-states of Sumer. In fact, some historians of science contend that the division of the monochord string is possibly one of the earliest scientific-empirical experiments ever to be carried out with mathematical rigor. The mathematics associated with the monochord include the multiplication table, the concept of least common multiples, and the concept of prime and composite numbers. This level of arithmetical proficiency is of an unknown but certainly very early origin.[1] The origins of the instrument will probably always remain a mystery. In view of the simplicity of the associated mathematics, it is entirely possible that the monochord predated the advent of urban civilization.

The monochord is a valuable practical device, but the ancients prized it even more as a source of scientific-philosophical speculation. It was the source of much ancient number-lore and cosmological thinking. Its theoretical significance is thus even more important than its practical influence, although the two aspects can never be separated completely. Throughout the whole of history, right up to the eighteenth century, the monochord was associated with cosmic concerns. For example, it was often seen as a symbolic device showing the mystical unity between man (the microcosm) and the universe (the macrocosm). The stretched string stood for the universe, with the various pitches representing the planets in the solar system (*musica mundana*), the Muses, and the parts of the human body. The string was often pictured being tuned by the hand of a god. Music, mathematics, and astronomy were inexorably linked in the monochord. The uni-

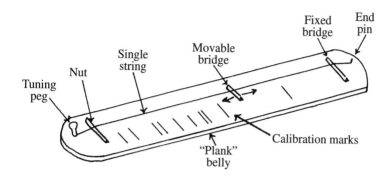

Above: A simple, one-stringed monochord with a plank belly.
Below: A more complex polychord with a sounding box.

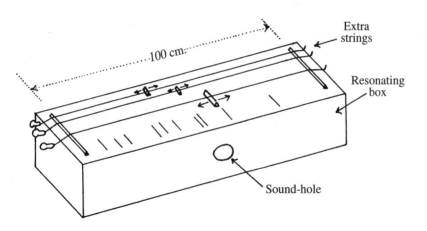

Figure 1. The Construction of the Monochord

verse was thought to obey musical laws; therefore, the study of the monochord yielded information considered relevant to the other sciences, the humanities, and religion.

The monochord was the primary source for the ancient science of HARMONICS, which had applications in tuning theory, arithmetic, geometry, and astronomy. Out of this mathematical matrix we also see the evolution of sacred architecture and sacred geometry, as well as the other high arts. The sacred songs and chants of the *rishis* in India and the Homeric bards in the West were invented in a musical context. The early philosophers, such as Empedocles, sang their poems to the accompaniment of stringed instruments. Much of the content of early philosophical speculation concerned issues that stem from monochord work; for example, the meaning of harmony, the relations between the One and the Multiplicity, the powers and properties of numbers, the deeper meanings of justice and reciprocity, and the cosmogenesis of patterns of order in nature.

We also see monochord principles underlying the prevalent configuration of ancient cosmogonies. This pattern is similar in the cosmology of the Egyptians, Babylonians, Greeks, and Celts. First there is the silence of pre-manifestation (the Egyptian *Nun*). Secondly, there arises the first vibratory event (the Egyptian *Atum*), which is an undifferentiated unity—the open string of the monochord before the movable bridge is applied. Then the One becomes Two through the act of division, creating the possibility of "the other" and setting the stage for the evolution of a world order. In the monochord context, the division of the open string by two (accomplished by putting the movable bridge in the exact middle) creates the interval of the octave, which is the natural boundary for all scale formation. It is the matrix out of which the musical intervals emerge. Next, the Two becomes the Multiplicity (for example, the *Ogdoad* of Egyptian divinities) by the separating out of reciprocal pairs, to generate life. Hence the diversity of manifestation is related to the whole, just as the scale elements are related to the open string which generated them.

The Orphic religious movement in Greece, and contemporary

religious movements in Egypt and Persia, saw the sanctification of Harmonics as a pathway to yogic liberation. Orpheus represented the power of the cosmic musician whose lyre was the universe. He was associated with Dionysus who represented the power of the Multiplicity inherent in the One, and Apollo, who represented the power of the One inherent in the Multiplicity. The Orphics deified Number in a manner reminiscent of the ancient Babylonians, for whom the first 60 numbers were gods.

The most visible manifestation of this Orphic spirit was the school of Pythagorean philosophy, which sought to integrate scientific inquiry into the nature of Number and a mystical awareness of the musicality of universal law. Naturally, the monochord was the chief vehicle for their researches. Other branches of mathematics which do not seem to have a direct bearing on monochord work, such as geometry, and even gematria, were also integrated into the science. When the school was dispersed throughout Greece in the fifth century B.C.E., the "fallout" resulted in major developments in mathematics and the sciences. Many of the greatest ancient scientists were directly or indirectly influenced by Pythagorean lore.

The monochord has had such a major influence on the spiritual, intellectual, and cultural history of mankind that it is a shame so little is known of it today. This lack of awareness has resulted in the removal of tuning theory from the center stage of spiritual, cultural, and scientific pursuits to become an esoteric discipline of interest only to musicologists. Also, it has created major misunderstandings of the "mind-set" of ancient culture, and the mathematical-musical origins of our common spiritual heritage. Ancient cultures, before the invention of the printing press and the proliferation of books, were far more sonically oriented than visually focussed, and their elaborate aural traditions of storytelling required great feats of memory. Music was used as an aid to memorization, and musical concerns were of far greater import in antiquity than they are today for our modern, visually oriented and linear culture.

In order to better understand the sources of ancient cosmology, and to make the monochord accessible today, I offer this introduction to monochord technique. The mathematics involved in basic monochord work is very simple; and yet, at the same time it is very profound, because it forces us to confront philosophical issues which were of great concern in the ancient world. It is the gateway to a type of thinking now largely forgotten, but very fruitful for understanding the ancient approach to verifiable truth.

It is not difficult to build a monochord. (See *Figure 1*). It is also possible to adapt another instrument, say a guitar, to be used as a monochord. The ideal monochord, though, has a longer string length than the guitar (which is about 65 cm), say from 90 to 120 cm. The long string length minimizes inaccuracy and facilitates the calibration of micro-intervals which are essential to the study of harmony. The string material itself creates a slight imprecision which we can ignore; but the main source of inaccuracy is the movable bridge, which must deflect the string a little bit, altering the string tension. Remember that the monochord idea is based on the principle that the string length is the only variable factor, and that the string tension must remain constant. The use of a long string length minimizes this deflection. Even though there is a slight deviation from the true norms, it is still accurate to a surprising degree—easily enough to demonstrate all of the important micro-intervals, such as the *diesis* and the *comma*. In fact, the comma (ratio 81:80), which is a very small interval of about a quarter of a semitone, can easily be divided into several parts, so that all of the practical concerns of tuning theory can be demonstrated.

I use an active string length of 100 cm, which is about 40 inches. I find that this decimal system is most convenient for calibration, since I can then use a calculator to do the arithmetic in short order.

The ancients saw the scale as a falling pattern starting at the octave point (called by the Greeks the *mese* or middle) and proceeding to the open string (called the *proslambanomenos*). Every note in the scale, regardless of scale type, had a name according to its position within the tetrachord system; but we will the ignore the technicalities of the

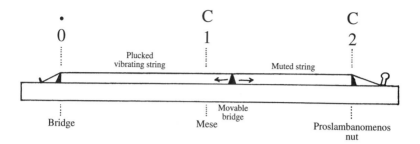

Figure 2. Monochord Division 1–2

Greek names. It is more convenient and relevant for us to use modern-style pitch names, although they must be slightly modified to reflect micro-tonal inflections. Hence, I have arbitrarily designated the open string as pitch C. The octave point is thus also pitch C. The octave point is found by putting the movable bridge in the exact middle of the string length. (See *Figure 2.*) Note that the string length is the active string length from the bridge to the nut, using standard guitar terminology. We have now divided the string by two. Since scale patterns repeat at the octave, only one octave is necessary to erect a scale. The classical Greek system and terminology used two octaves, one above and one below the Mese.

The octave is called the miracle of music, since it creates a microcosm of cyclic identity within the macrocosm of the pitch continuum. There is an infinity of pitches from the lowest note we can hear to the highest; but this infinity repeats at the octave. Therefore, the octave is the matrix number, the "womb" out of which the other scale elements are born. The number two is the first even number. The Pythagoreans called it female, the hearth of harmony, Hestia, the *Dyad*. All even numbers are female because they contain an element of 2 in their divisors.

The open string is One, androgynous, the source, Zeus, Apollo, the immovable *Monad*. All numbers are divisible by one and maintain their identity when multiplied by one: $n \times 1 = n$. The One, when divided into

Two, maintains its 'C'ness, hence the concept of cyclical identity. Powers of 2 define octaves; for example, $4=2^2$ or two octaves, $8=2^3$ or three octaves. In order to find the frequency of a pitch an octave above another one, multiply it by 2/1; to find a pitch an octave below, multiply by 1/2. Thus the division by 2 can be expressed as the number series 1:2, as shown in *Figure 2*. The numbers One and Two are so closely related and so fundamental to harmonic theory that they were not considered numbers at all by the Pythagoreans; rather, they were seen as the principles of number. The first real number (which creates new tonal material) is Three.

The ancient approach to monochord division is to divide the string into an arithmetic number of equal sized units. This technique is called the ARITHMETIC PROPORTION.[1] The technique called the GEOMETRIC PROPORTION is more advanced and does not concern us now. We always measure this arithmetic series from the bridge to the nut. In the division just given, the Mese sits at position 1, the open string is position 2.

The string can be divided into any number of arithmetic components, yielding various scales; but a little reflection leads to the conclusion that the open string must be divided into an even number of components so that there is a position for the Mese. Therefore, let us now divide the string into 4 components, so that the Mese sits at position 2. (See *Figure 3*.) We have now produced the scale sequence 2:3:4 or, in pitches C:F:C. Note that 1:2::2:4, so that the C for our open string and octave point are preserved in this new sequence. In all various further divisions of the Arithmetic Proportion, we get a sequence of numbers "ruled by a double." Our former division was ruled by the double 1–2, the next one by the double 2–4. We can investigate the divisions of the Arithmetic Proportion in a systematic manner by examining each series in order. Thus, the next sequence is 3:4:5:6 or C:G:E♭:C. (*Figure 4*.) After that we get the sequence 4:5:6:7:8 or C:A♭:F:D♯:C. (*Figure 5*.) The creation of these series can easily be continued.

We will pause here, however, because we have generated enough

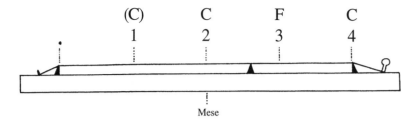

Figure 3. Monochord Division 2–4

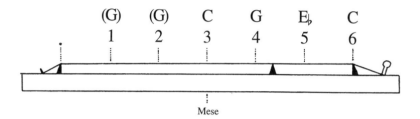

Figure 4. Monochord Division 3–6

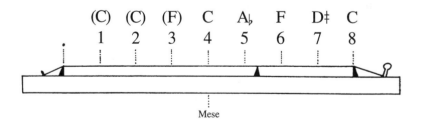

Figure 4. Monochord Division 4–8

material to clarify various monochord concepts and principles. First, a practical note. Rather than mark the monochord belly directly, it is better to use a paper or cardboard template on which to mark our divisions, a different template for each division we use. In antiquity, this calibration template was known as the canon. In a group of sequences like 1–2, 2–4, and 4–8 it is tempting to put them all on one template distinguished by layers. In that case, put 3–6, 6–12, and 12–24 together on another template. Various divisions have "family relations" to each other.

In expressing the division as a sequence ruled by a double, we are eliminating the cumbersome use of proportional fractions through the use of a least common multiple, chosen as our string length. But it is important to be aware of the inherent ratios in the series. Let's look more closely at our series 2:3:4 or C:F:C. The musical interval from C at the Mese down to F is a fifth in pitch. In order to find the frequency of the pitch F in relation to the Mese C, just take the frequency number of our C and multiply it by 2/3. In other words, the ratio 2/3 represents a fifth down in pitch. Looking at F from the other side, it is a musical fourth in pitch up from the C of the open string. A musical fourth up in pitch is frequency ratio 4/3. Do you see how easy it is to derive musical ratios from our arithmetic series? Let's try it with the more complicated series 4:5:6:7:8 or C:A♭:F:D♯:C. The ratio of the musical fifth from C down to F is 4/6 which equals 2/3. Similarly, the musical just major third down in pitch from C to A♭ is ratio 4/5. Ratios which represent musical intervals down in pitch have the denominator larger than the numerator; the opposite situation applies for musical intervals up in pitch. This convention in the expression of musical ratios makes the arithmetic straightforward.

All of the ratios which are inherent in a given monochord series can be expressed by using an INTERVAL TRIANGLE as shown in *Figure 6*. Note that the shape of this interval triangle is identical to that of the Pythagorean *Tetraktys*. This is one of the many meanings for this pattern. We shall find that the Tetraktys and many other Pythagorean symbols and concepts have multiple meanings that ultimately can be

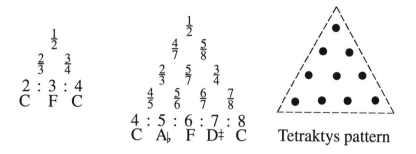

$$\frac{1}{2}$$
$$\frac{2}{3} \quad \frac{3}{4}$$
$$2 : 3 : 4$$
$$\text{C} \quad \text{F} \quad \text{C}$$

$$\frac{1}{2}$$
$$\frac{4}{7} \quad \frac{5}{8}$$
$$\frac{2}{3} \quad \frac{5}{7} \quad \frac{3}{4}$$
$$\frac{4}{5} \quad \frac{5}{6} \quad \frac{6}{7} \quad \frac{7}{8}$$
$$4 : 5 : 6 : 7 : 8$$
$$\text{C} \quad \text{A}\flat \quad \text{F} \quad \text{D}\sharp \quad \text{C}$$

Tetraktys pattern

Figure 6. Examples of Interval Triangles

derived from monochord work.

Next we will clarify the monochord PRINCIPLE OF HARMONIC IDENTITY. Every harmonic structure can be expressed in smallest integers; but it can also be expressed in larger numbers without a change of structural identity. The pattern C:F:C is expressed in smallest integers as the series 2:3:4; but it can also be expressed as 4:6:8 with no change of meaning. It is often useful to increase the "numerosity" of a sequence. The meaning of the numbers used depends on the context of the particular series. As a general rule, a sequence will always be expressed in the smallest numerical terms appropriate to bring out a particular harmonic meaning.

When we increase the numerosity of the series from 2:3:4 to 4:6:8, more potential harmonic elements can be interpolated, as illustrated in our series 4:5:6:7:8. This situation illustrates the PRINCIPLE OF HARMONIC EXPANSION. As the numerosity increases, more elements can be "caught in the net," so that the scale or the field of harmonic relations becomes more complex. We can increase the numerosity as much as we want, so that the series 4–8 could become 8–16, and so on. The number series is infinite. Thus the number 2 and the octave is associated with the concept of the APEIRON or the INFINITE, the tendency to complexity. This tendency to complexity exists without even adding new elements. For example, the series 4:6:8 is harmonically identical to 2:3:4, but potentially contains the more harmonically complex series 4:5:6:7:8.

Note in series 2:3:4 that the prime number 3 adds a new structural element to the scale (the pitch F). When we doubled the series 2:3:4 to form 4:6:8 nothing new was added. But when we interpolated the prime numbers 5 and 7 to the series, new harmonic elements were added to the scale. This illustrates one of the fundamental truths about numbers in the harmonic context. PRIME NUMBERS are the power numbers that generate new harmonic material. Any number is either prime or composite. Composite numbers can be uniquely expressed as a product of primes. Thus in the series 4:6:8 the number 6 is an F because 6=3x2. Composite numbers are formed as a result of "marriages," by multiplication between prime numbers. This arithmetical fact has important practical and symbolical consequences for the science of Harmonics. Odd numbers, and especially prime numbers, are associated with the concept of PERAS or LIMIT, since they define the elements of the scale.

As the numerosity of our number sequences grows incorporating new elements through the principle of Harmonic Expansion, interval complexity results, for the sequence of prime numbers is potentially infinite. There must be some practical rubric for checking the expansion of the sequences. Therefore, the ancient tuners conceived of the PRINCIPLE OF HARMONIC LIMIT. Certain types of numbers are allowed into the sequences, others are forbidden. You may have noticed in our sequence 4:5:6:7:8 that the number 7 presents a pitch which is foreign to our normal system of harmony, the pitch D♯ (semisharp). Most historical and practical tunings that were in use in China, India, Babylonia, and Greece used numbers that were derived from the prime numbers 1, 2, 3, and 5 alone.[2] Higher prime numbers like 7, or 11, or 13 were not allowed. This move reduced the potential complexity of relations to more manageable levels. To use modern terms for this concept, the sequence 4:5:6:7:8 would be called 7-Limit because there is a factor of 7 in the inherent ratios. We could convert this sequence to a 5-Limit harmony by making it 4:5:6:8. We could further reduce this sequence to a 3-Limit harmony in the sequence 4:6:8. 3-Limit harmonies are a sub-set of 5-Limit harmonies, which are a sub-set of 7-Limit harmonies, and so on. In the history of musical tuning, 5-Limit harmonies are the norm; 3-Limit harmonies as an important subset of 5-Limit harmonies; and 7-Limit harmonies are an esoteric extension of the usual norms.

This use of the concept of LIMIT is another example of the Pythagorean concept of PERAS, which is naturally associated with odd, and especially prime numbers. The concepts of Peras and Apeiron are central and multi-faceted in tuning theory and Pythagorean philosophy.

We are now ready to present a more complex but very important practical ancient Greek-Hindu scale—the double 24–48. We can derive it from the 5-Limit double 4:5:6:8 by multiplying each element by 6 to give us 24:30:36:48; then we add various other elements to create the 5-Limit diatonic scale 24:27:30:32:36:40:45:48—in pitches C:\B♭:A♭:G:F:E♭:D♭:C. Note that every one of these numbers is made of factors of the prime numbers 2, 3, and 5 only. We could convert this sequence into a 3-Limit scale by leaving out all numbers that have factors of 5, resulting in 24:27:32:36:48 or C:\B♭:G:F:C, which is a subset of the other scale. Note that we could also derive this 5-Limit scale from double 3–6, becoming 6–12, then 12–24, then 24–48. We now have a practical scale which has been used for music-making since very early times and is still used as a North Indian raga scale.

We have one more monochord principle to clarify, the PRINCIPLE OF RECIPROCITY. This one may be a bit more difficult to comprehend than the others, but it is indispensible to tuning theory. We have been dividing the monochord string, but it is theoretically possible to multiply it. Now this can't be done in actual practice, since we can't make the string longer than it is, but we can do it theoretically since division and multiplication are reciprocal operations. Looking at it another way, we can consider our number sequences as rising in pitch rather than falling in pitch. To illustrate this principle, let's go back to our simple sequence 2:3:4. On the monochord, this sequence gives a

falling scale which is an aspect of the SUBHARMONIC SERIES SPEC-
TRUM—the pitches C:F:C. We could also consider the sequence as
components of the HARMONIC SERIES SPECTRUM with C defined as
the second harmonic. Then the sequence 2:3:4 becomes the rising
scale C:G:C.

The reason for this inverse relation is that the Harmonic Series is
asymmetrical; hence it has a "flip-over" or "mirror" pattern in the
Sub-harmonic Series. There are always two ways of seeing an interval
pattern: up or down. For example, if we build a chord by piling up the
intervals of a major third, then a minor third, we get C–E–G. If we now
pile the intervals in a downward direction we get C–A♭–F. Now look
at our 5-Limit series ruled by the double 4–8, that is 4:5:6:8. On the
monochord, it yields the Minor Triad associated with the Sub-
harmonic Series C:A♭:F:C. The reciprocal (rising) sequence yields the
Major Triad associated with the Harmonic Series C:E:G:C. In other
words, if C is defined as the fourth and eighth harmonic in the
Harmonic Series, then E is the fifth harmonic, and G is the sixth
harmonic. You can verify this by examining the harmonics of a string
tuned to C.

Every number sequence of the Arithmetic Proportion can also be
defined as a rising sequence which is the reciprocal of the falling
(monochord) sequence. The rising sequence is associated with the one
other tuning procedure (besides the monochord) which has been
prevalent since ancient times. It is called the HARMONIC PROPOR-
TION. In this technique, various strings of different pitches are tuned
to each other by the comparison of harmonics between the strings.
Through this method we can yield simple or complex ratios just as we
can using the monochord. These two tuning methods can also be used
to cross-check each other. We will not explore this topic here, since
it is beyond the scope of this article, but it is helpful to be aware that
these two ancient tuning methods have this reciprocal relation to each
other.

Ultimately, the reciprocal nature of our sequences can be derived
from a basic and fundamental principle of physics: frequency (string

harmonics) is inversely proportional to wavelength (monochord string length).

Generally, when a sequence is presented, both the falling and the rising pattern are given, for the sake of comprehensiveness. One reason for this is that when the falling pattern is musically useful or significant, the rising pattern is almost always so. For example, the monochord series 24–48 yields a significant just intonation Phrygian Minor scale. However, if we define C as the 24th harmonic in the rising sequence, we get the famous Ionian Major scale C:D:E:F:G:A:B:C—a useful scale indeed!

Do not worry that only a minor chord or scale is demonstrable on the monochord. The monochord sequence 10:12:15:20 yields the major chord C:A:F:C. Its reciprocal in Harmonic Series components gives C:E♭:G:C. In fact, any type of chord or scale can be calibrated on the monochord, if you know the right number in which to divide the string. The many possible sequences yield a wealth of just intonation tunings which have been at the heart of monophonic music culture throughout the ancient world.[3]

Although most monochord sequences are asymmetrical, there are a minority of patterns which are SYMMETRICAL; in other words, they make the same scale in both an upward and a downward direction. Such patterns have heightened theoretical and even metaphysical meaning in ancient culture. The numbers associated with these sequences appear repeatedly in the cosmology, calendars, and mythology of Babylonia, Egypt, and Greece. Significantly enough, the simplest such sequence is the 3-Limit series 6:8:9:12, which is both C:G:F:C and C:F:G:C. It was called the MUSICAL PROPORTION and was, according to Iamblichus, brought home to Greece from Babylonia by Pythagoras. Now this pattern defines the tetrachords of ancient music theory. The musical fourth, fifth, and octave were also the only acknowledged consonances. We still define them as the only perfect consonances, the major third and sixth being the medial consonances, and the minor third and sixth being the imperfect consonances. Interestingly enough, the perfect consonances are the 3-Limit root ratios 3/2, and 4/3; whereas the other consonances are the 5-Limit root ratios 5/4, 5/3, 6/5, and 8/5. In ancient theory, the perfect consonances are immutable—the axis of the scale; on the other hand, the imperfect consonances are amenable to various "mutations" of size as scale elements.

The double 6–12 is often expressed in the form of a proportion as 6:8::9:12. This presentation highlights the symmetrical nature of this series, and informs us that symmetrical series have added prominence. As an example of another symmetrical series of great musical and cosmological significance, try the 5-Limit double 60–120, which yields as a rising and a falling scale 60:72:75:80:90:96:100:120 or, in pitches C:A♭:A♭:G:F:E:E♭:C. This sequence puts into smallest numerical terms both the perfect and the imperfect consonances. *Figure* 7 shows a number of symmetrical monochord sequences which are ruled by doubles having important cosmological significance as well as great musical import. It appears that, in the ancient cultures of Greece, Egypt, Babylonia, India, and China, the ubiquitous cosmological numbers are also the most significant musical numbers.

Figure 8 shows a sampling of some of the most interesting of the non-symmetrical monochord sequences. Although the significance of these divisions can be derived purely from musical considerations, again we have convergence with ubiquitous cosmological numbers. Many of these numbers were associated with the calendar and the measurement of time cycles in general. This is understandable, since the measurement of time is at the heart of all procedures in Harmonics, whether it be the relatively fast cycles of the vibrating string, or the relatively slow cycles of planetary movement. Over time, the seven visible planets were coupled with the seven notes of most scales.

It would be helpful here to remind ourselves of the ancient meaning for the term harmony. In its etymology, *harmos* means "joint," and *harmozein* means to join or connect together unlike elements. These elements or roots are the simple prime numbers which create "offspring" by "marriages" with themselves and each other, through the use of least common multiples. In the mainstream of tuning history

Some examples of prominent symmetrical divisions taken from the 3-Limit sequences:

6–12   6 : 8 : 9 : 12
      C   F   G   C—rising in pitch, harmonic series components
      C   G   F   C—falling in pitch, monochord sequence

72–144   72 : 81 : 96 : 108 : 128 : 144
      C   D   F   G   \B♭   C
      C   \B♭   G   F   D   C

432–864   432 : 486 : 512 : 576 : 648 : 729 : 768 : 864
      C   D   \E♭   F   G   /A   \B♭   C
      C   \B♭   /A   G   F   \E♭   D   C

Examples of symmetrical 5-Limit sequences:

60–120   60 : 72 : 75 : 80 : 90 : 96 : 100 : 120
      C   E♭   E   F   G   A♭   A   C
      C   A   A♭   G   F   E   E♭   C

360–720   360 : 348 : 400 : 405 : 432 : 450 : 480 : 540 : 576 : 600 : 640 : 648 : 675 : 720
      C   E♭   \D   D   \E♭   E   F   G   A♭   A   \B♭   B♭   B   C
      C   B   B♭   \B♭   A   A♭   G   F   E   E♭   D   \D   D♭   C

Figure 7. Some Symmetrical Monochord Divisions in the 3-Limit (Pythagorean) and 5-Limit (Just Intonation) Families

In the monochord divisions indicated above, the rising scale (tone numbers or Harmonic Series) and falling scale (monochord divisions or Sub-harmonic Series) are perfectly symmetrical and produce the same tuning.

these are the prime numbers 1, 2, 3, and 5. If the number 1 is understood as omnipresent, then the numbers 2, 3, and 5 are the trinity of three greatest gods present in many cultures. Looking at the Babylonian-Sumerian gods, the greatest are Anu-An (60/60), Ea-Enki (40/60), and Bel-Enlil (50/60); by number association they couple with the efficacy of the numbers 2, 3, and 5 respectively. As a musical harmony they form the 4:5:6 triad.[4]

Beyond the four elements, which I believe were represented by the numbers 1 (fire), 2 (earth), 3 (air), and 5 (water), the Pythagoreans also recognized a fifth element, the Aether, which would have embodied the power of the prime number 7. Philolaus called it "motherless."[5] Note that these five prime numbers are all of the primes between one and ten. For the Pythagoreans, the first ten numbers were special—the archetypes of harmonic order. We can also define them as the ratios 1/1, 2/1, 3/2, 4/3, 5/4, and so on. This is another meaning for the symbol of the Tetraktys, which, according to the Pythagorean Oath, was "the spring of all our wisdom, the perennial fount and root of Nature." This statement is literally true when refering to the sources of 7-Limit Harmony, which was extensively explored bv the Pythagorean Archytas.[6] It is interesting that if we want to express all of the Tetraktys ratios as a monochord sequence in smallest terms, we must use the double 2520–5040. This number is the number of "citizens" in Plato's "city" of Magnesia (*Laws* 73). Many of the allegories in Plato use significant monochord numbers and refer to the monochord in oblique ways.

It is useful to explore one more meaning for that potent symbol— the Tetraktys. This one comes from a practical context. We have been generating various scales which have been expressed as number sequences ruled by a double. We could also generate the same scales through the Harmonic Proportion. It would be a useful tool to be able to designate the harmony itself, independent of the method of generating it, or the particular sequence with which it is expressed. The Pythagoreans did this by the use of a simple matrix of tuning opera-

12–24   12 : 15 : 16 : 18 : 20 : 24
           C   E   F   G   A   C
           C   A♭   G   F   E♭   C

24–48   24 : 27 : 30 : 32 : 36 : 40 : 45 : 48
           C   D   E   F   G   A   B   C
           C   \B♭   A♭   G   F   E♭   D♭   C

30–60   30 : 32 : 36 : 40 : 45 : 48 : 54 : 60
           C   D♭   E♭   F   G   A♭   B♭   C
           C   B   A   G   F   E   \D   C

36–72   30 : 40 : 45 : 48 : 54 : 60 : 64 : 72
           C   \D   E   F   G   A   \B♭   C
           C   B♭   A♭   G   F   E♭   D   C

72–144   72 : 80 : 81 : 90 : 96 :108:120:128:135:144
           C   \D   D   E   F   G   A   \B♭   B   C
           C   B♭   \B♭   A♭   G   F   E♭   D   D♭   C

90–180   90 : 96 :108:120:128:135:144:160:162:180
           C   D♭   E♭   F   \G♭   G   A♭   \B♭   B♭   C
           C   B   A   G   F♯   F   E   D   \D   C

120–240   120:135:144:150:160:180:192:200:216:225:240
           C   D   E♭   E   F   G   A♭   A   B♭   B   C
           C   \B♭   A   A♭   G   F   E   E♭   \D   D♭   C

180–360   180:192:200:216:225:240:270:288:300:320:360
           C   D♭   \D   E♭   E   F   G   A♭   A   \B♭   C
           C   B♭   \B♭   /A   A♭   G   F   E   E♭   D♭   C

Figure 8. Some Non-symmetrical Versions of 5-Limit Harmonies

tions, called the "pebble arithmetic." It was so named because in its most abstract form it appears simply as an array of pebbles in triangular patterns. This is the shape of the Tetraktys! This "notation" is a practical device which helps the tuner know what particular harmony he or she has produced. It is also an indispensible morphological model of the structure of harmony, eliminating redundancies in the expression of scale elements, and "mapping" the regions of the harmony matrix in an unambiguous way. Each type of musical scale has a unique and defining "pebble" pattern.

The axes of the harmonic matrix model are shown in *Figure 9*. Octaves denote cyclical identity; hence they are marked as identity of position. Tuning in musical fifths or fourths (i.e., 3-Limit ratios) are marked by "pebbles" in a horizontal line. For example, the sequence 6:8:9:12 can be marked as three horizontal "dots" which stand for the line of fifths F:C:G. When tunings are expanded to include 5-Limit ratios, this simple line is transformed into a triangular matrix. The major triad becomes the simple up-pointing triangle; the minor triad becomes the down-pointing triangle. The "pebble patterns" for the other scales we have looked at are also shown in *Figure 10* and *Figure 11*. Any 3-Limit or 5-Limit harmony can be defined by this triangular-hexagonal grid.

We cannot conclude an introductory paper on monochord technique without adding something about the Geometrical Proportion, although any advanced work in this field is beyond the scope of this article. In order to explain the rationale behind this technique, we must examine the Pythagorean concept of the MEANS. Again, this concept is multi-leveled in its meanings, and most of its aspects will not concern us here. We will focus on its origins from and application to the monochord.

According to Pythagorean tradition as expressed in the fragments of Archytas, there are three Means between any given number pair: the ARITHMETIC MEAN, the HARMONIC MEAN, and the GEOMETRIC MEAN. Note, first of all, that we have a conceptual convergence with the three tuning techniques associated with the monochord. Here is

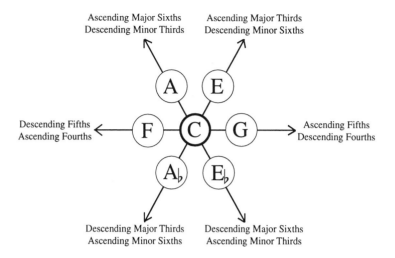

Figure 9. The Interval Axes of the Harmony Matrix Model

The central tonic C is the starting point of the matrix and represents unison (1/1). Identity of position indicates ascending octaves (2/1) and descending octaves (1/2).

another of the many examples in which Pythagorean concepts form a satisfying and integrated whole. The universe is a KOSMOS in which the practical and the metaphysical aspects are inexorably intertwined.[7]

Let us look at the Arithmetic and Harmonic Means first. Rather than relating the somewhat complicated methods of generation given in Archytas,[8] here is a simplified method which also shows the close relation of this "numbers game" to our familiar monochord procedures. In order to find these two Means within the octave 1/2, simply double the numbers to 2/4 and interpolate the number 3. Now the Arithmetic Mean of the 1/2 is the fifth 2/3, and the Harmonic Mean is the fourth 3/4. Again, to find the means between the fifth 2/3, double

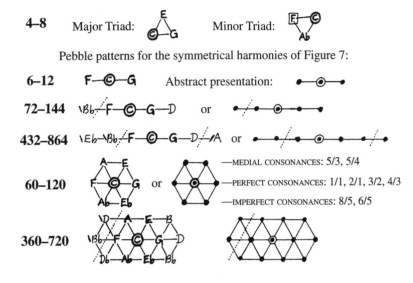

Figure 10. Examples of the Matrix Grid ("Pebble Arithmetic")
Showing the Symmetrical Harmonies of Figure 7.

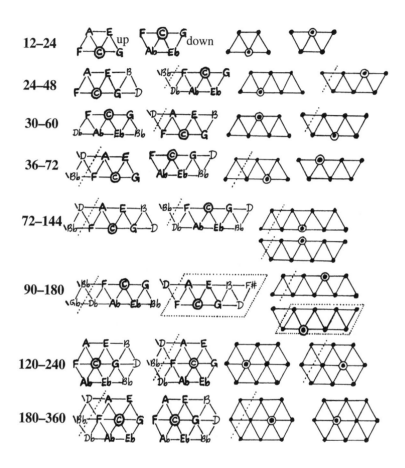

Figure 11. Pebble Patterns for the Non-symmetrical
5-Limit Harmonies of Figure 8.

the numbers to 4/6, and interpolate the number 5. The Arithmetic Mean is 4/5, and the Harmonic Mean is 5/6. Similarly, the Arithmetic and Harmonic Means of the fourth 3/4 are 6/7 and 7/8. The Arithmetic and Harmonic Means of the just major third 4/5 are 8/9 and 9/10.

The simplicity of this procedure belies its important metaphysical significance. The Greeks, as well as the Chinese, Babylonians, and Egyptians, saw life as a dynamically balanced "middle path" between opposites. Hence it is natural for the Pythagoreans to value an orderly and finite numerical mean between two "opposites" or extremes. The means are the "offspring" of the "parents," and share in their absolute powers. In this procedure we see complete integration with monochord thinking. Note the essential similarity between this procedure and our Arithmetic Proportion. In fact, the whole operation could be viewed as an example of the principle of Harmonic Expansion. The series 1:2 becomes the series 2:3:4 in complete agreement with the 1/2 becoming the 2/3 and 3/4. We could consider these two Means as another expression of the Arithmetic Proportion.

However, the theory of the Means offers more. We saw that the octave generated the root 3-Limit ratios 2/3 and 3/4. The next strongest musical interval, the fifth, generated the root 5-Limit ratios 4/5, and 5/6. Then the musical fourth generated the 7-Limit root ratios 6/7 and 7/8. Hence we have here a systematic way of "birthing" the whole conceptual framework of 3-, 5-, and 7-Limit harmonies. Note that the major third 4/5 generated the two sizes of whole-tone of just intonation—the 8/9 and 9/10. The difference in size between these whole-steps is the Syntonic Comma (ratio 80/81). In ancient tuning tradition, as preserved in the Vedic text called the *Natyashastra*, the comma (Shruti) is the smallest building block out of which all harmonies are aggregated. We are again reminded here of the Tetraktys ratio series which concludes its "primal harmonic archetypes" with the ratios 8/9 and 9/10. Therefore, in the context of Harmonics, the Means can be said to generate the whole "cosmos."

We have yet to examine the Geometric Mean. The technique is simple enough. To find the Geometric Mean between any two numbers (as a ratio), multiply the two numbers together and find the square root. For example, the G.M. of the octave 1/2 is the √2. It is the exact harmonic midpoint between the extremes—it cuts the octave exactly into a harmonic half to form the equal-tempered tritone associated with 12-tone equal temperament. This number represents the first of a new class of numbers which are called irrational or incommensurable numbers. The square root of two cannot be expressed as a discrete ratio fraction; rather, it forms one of those never-ending decimal fractions which we only approximate on our calculators—1.4142136... Consequently—and this is important for monochord technique—we can never accurately express it as a member of an Arithmetic Proportion number series. We can approximate it with various levels of accuracy, for example as 7/5, 10/7, 45/32, and so on, but these expressions are only substitutes for the "real thing." How is it possible then to find the fret position on the monochord for the √2?

The answer is surprisingly simple, and shown in *Figure 12*. We use a geometrical method rather than an arithmetical method. First, we define the string length as 2 units; in other words, we use the simplest division, number series 1:2. Now at position 1 (the Mese), we draw a semi-circle with diameter equal to the string-length. Next, at the Mese, we draw a perpendicular to cut the semi-circle. Finally, with center at the bridge, we draw another arc from the top of the perpendicular to cut the string at the desired position. The proof of this construction hinges on the fact that the diagonal of a square whose length and width are 1 is equal to √2. This operation is the simplest procedure of the Geometric Proportion on the monochord.

According to tradition, it was the Pythagoreans who first systematically investigated incommensurable ratios. If we assume that they applied these investigations to the monochord, then they must have explored the implications of what we call "tempered" tunings. For these ratios are heard as controlled "mistunings" or temperings of the harmonic series norms that control the Arithmetic Proportion and just intonation. The study of these systems of harmony is considered as esoteric, even today, and raises many questions about the nature of a continuum, the degree of acceptable error in harmonic norms, the nature of justice, and other issues that have metaphysical import.

In conclusion, let us re-examine the ancient concept of KOSMOS. The term generally signifies "world-order" or "the ordered-world," but its etymology includes the meaning of "ornament," hence "the world ornamented with order." As a philosophy of whole systems, what better metaphor could one use than the structural implications of harmony? For in the realm of musical harmony we see the architectonic wholeness of unity within multiplicity. All numbers, as "masks" of the Monad, are aspects of the One in a differentiated image of wholeness. Even dissonance is not in essence different, only a more complex set of relations to the One. The notion of the ubiquity of opposites stems from the fundamental experience of reciprocity— reciprocity in pitch direction, and the reciprocity of the monochord sequence with its harmonic series mirror.

One of the most satisfying and most potent images for the notion of reciprocity within wholeness is the Lambdoma Table of ratios.[9] It is also potentially one of the oldest, since it can be conceived simply as a re-interpretation of the MULTIPLICATION TABLE. (See *Figure 11*.) The Multiplication Table becomes the world of musical ratios as soon as we introduce the concept of an "over" number and an "under" number. The horizontal line defines the ratios which make up the Harmonic Series. The vertical line defines the monochord divisions and/or the Sub-harmonic Series. The diagonal line is the boundary zone between the two "realms." All the elements of the Harmonic Series and its mirror can be systematically explored through this simple but comprehensive model.

It is interesting that the experience of musical phenomena in nature can always be referenced to the Harmonic Series, whether it be on a

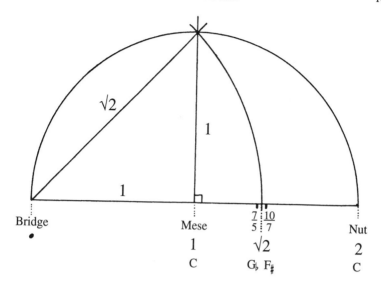

Figure 12. The Placement of the √2 Interval on the Monochord

stringed instrument, wind instrument, or brass. The Sub-harmonic Series does not exist in nature, apart from electronic or other artificial production. Hence it seems strange to us now that the ancients would give predominance to the monochord patterns over Harmonic Series components. We moderns would always give the Harmonic Series priority. Nevertheless, for the ancients, the monochord comes first. It is natural for us to associate the Harmonic Series with the realm of actual, vibratory phenomena. By implication then, the Sub-harmonic Series can be associated with the unseen inner world that underlies the vibrating outer experience. This inner world is experienced through the monochord as a mirror image of the world of harmonics. As above, so below. In giving priority to the monochord patterns (all the time recognizing the equality of the two in reciprocity), the ancients expressed the conviction that the inner harmony is more significant than the phenomenal experience. Music, as a meaningful gesture-language, must comprehend and emerge from silence, returning to it when its cycle is complete. Only when profound silence is encountered, only then can we experience or create the profound states of consciousness transformation that the best music induces in us.

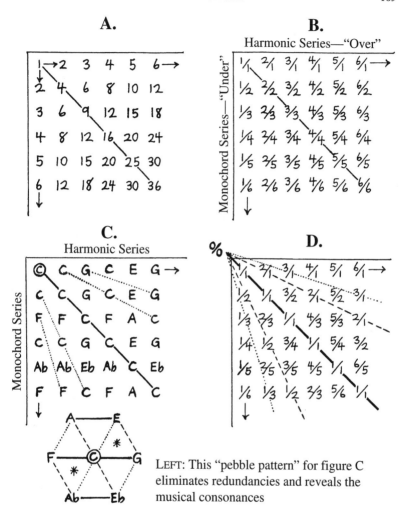

LEFT: This "pebble pattern" for figure C eliminates redundancies and reveals the musical consonances

Figure 13. The Multiplication Table as the Probable Source of the Lambdoma Table of Ratios.

A) The beginning fragment of the multiplication table; B) The table re-interpreted as an array of ratios; C) The ratios shown as an array of pitches; D) Shown as an array of ratios in smallest terms. Note the "identity rays" which converge beyond 1/1 at 0/0, symbolic of silence.

Notes

1. For alternative accounts of the Arithmetic Proportion on the monochord, see Harry Partch, *Genesis of a Music* (New York: Da Capo Press, 1974), 174–76. See also Ernest G. McClain, *The Pythagorean Plato* (York Beach: Nicolas-Hays, 1978), 169–75. Complexities in both of these accounts, and many years of work with monochords, encouraged me to reformulate the procedures so that the basic concepts are more comprehensible to the novice.

2. These numbers, which have the general form $2^a x 3^b x 5^c$ were called *regular numbers* by O. Neugebauer in *The Exact Sciences in Antiquity* (New York: Dover, 1969), 33. They are also sometimes called *Babylonian numbers* because of their association with Babylonian sexagesimal (base 60) arithmetic and cosmology.

3. For a systematic layout of the materials of the Arithmetical Proportion, see my Monochord Numbers Reference Material.

4. Also, note the importance of the 3x4x5 right-angled triangle, which is associated with the "Pythagorean Theorem" (which was already in use in Babylonia a full millenium before Pythagoras). $3x4x5=2^2x3x5$. Here we have another expression of the traditional sacred roots.

5. Kenneth Sylvan Guthrie, *The Pythagorean Sourcebook and Library* (Grand Rapids: Phanes Press, 1987), 175.

6. Archytas' tunings, as given by Ptolemy in his *Harmonics*, contain prominent 7-Limit ratios.

7. This integration of the practical and the metaphysical also covers important aspects of Greek music theory. For example, the traditional categorization of tetrachord tunings into the three Genera or "levels of resolution" called diatonic, chromatic, and enharmonic, can be intricately linked to the notion of 3-Limit, 5-Limit, and 7-Limit harmonies. For an in-depth study, see my paper *Musical Metaphors in Pythagorean Philosophy*.

8. See the fragments of Archytas in *The Pythagorean Sourcebook and Library*, 185.

9. The Lambdoma Table was rediscovered in 1868–76 by Albert von Thimus and formed the basis for the Harmonics investigations of Hans Kayser. Its very simplicity indicates that it is possibly very old.

A Note on Ptolemy's Polychord
and the Contemporary Relevance
of Harmonic Science

DAVID FIDELER

[While] philosophers initiated in the mysteries of music . . . expounded
some things in their writings, they reserved the more esoteric secrets for
their discussions with one another. The reason lay in the enthusiastic
affection of the men of those times for all that is finest. But now, when
indifference to music (to put it politely) is so widespread, we cannot
expect people with only a mild interest in the subject to tolerate being
faced with a book in which not everything is explicitly spelled out.

—Aristides Quintilianus, *On Music*

The numbers to do with music are sacred and of perfect efficacy.

—Aristides Quintilianus, *On Music*

All things began in order, so shall they end, and so shall they begin again;
according to the ordainer of order and the mystical mathematics of the
city of heaven.

—Sir Thomas Browne

Introduction

THE MONOCHORD is a one-stringed musical instrument with a
movable bridge used, from antiquity up until the present day, to study
the principles of harmony and tuning theory. The ancient Greek
philosopher Pythagoras discovered that the intervals of the musical
scale originate from naturally occurring whole number ratios, which
are easily demonstrated on the monochord. This led him to conclude

that musical harmony originates from the pure principle of Number-in-itself.

The Pythagoreans believed that the laws of music and the laws of the cosmos have something in common with one another: both are shaped by the underlying archetype of Number, which spontaneously gives order, proportion (*logos*), symmetry, harmony, limit, and form, to all phenomena. The Greek word *harmonia* means, literally, "to fit together," and the ancient mathematical science of harmonics clearly shows how all the parts of the musical scale fit together to form a greater, interconnected whole. Conversely, the musical scale may be seen as a harmonically differentiated image of natural wholeness. According to the Pythagoreans, it is the perfect image of harmony, sharing, reciprocity, and unity in multiplicity.

From this perspective, the language of music and tuning theory was applied, by analogy, to describe the harmony of the universe, the harmony of the soul, as well as harmony in the civic sphere. The ancient Pythagorean definition of *justice*—whether in the soul or society—revolved around the idea of *proportion*, and is described as that state in which "every part of the whole receives its proper due." The project of Plato's *Republic* is to define the principle of justice, whether in the state or the soul, and Plato suggests therein that the guardians of the ideal state should be required to study the Pythagorean sciences of arithmetic (number in itself), geometry (number in space), harmonics (number in time), and cosmology (number in space and time). Today in a world characterized by narrow self-interest, ecological imbalance, and a lack of concern for the whole, the philosophical perspective offered by the science of harmonics once again becomes self-evident.

As the Pythagoreans realized, one of the best ways to truly understand the nature of *harmonia* is by investigating the principles of harmony on the monochord. While it is possible to have an intellectual appreciation of Pythagorean concepts without recourse to the monochord, the actual, firsthand experience of the harmonic realities leads to deeper levels of understanding and true knowledge. *Harmonia*, like other universal principles, is not merely a mental abstraction based on observation of the physical world, but an *a priori* factor which underlies and conditions phenomenal reality. It is a transcendental organizational principle which, like light, gravity, and other universal phenomena, exerts its influence in every corner of the cosmos. The perfect consonances of music such as the octave (2:1), perfect fifth (3:2), and perfect fourth (4:3) are not invented but discovered and are the underlying basis of all musical expression. Different cultures have different musical syntaxes, but the same perfect intervals are found everywhere. We are led from these considerations to conclude, along with the ancient Pythagoreans, that *harmonia* is truly universal. If we are to extend the conclusion, it then follows that these perfect consonances would be reflected in the music of other civilizations, on other worlds. The music of an extraterrestrial civilization might well have a syntax unlike anything we are used to, but the underlying harmonic intervals would, of necessity, be the same. In this sense, the reality of *harmonia mundi* becomes obvious, and music is thereby revealed as a universal language, which people have always imagined it to be.

The Revival of Harmonics: Its Cultural, Cosmological, and Therapeutic Dimensions

From ancient Greece through the Renaissance, Harmonics was a widely-studied discipline that elevated the mind of the student to experience firsthand the root principles of music and universal harmony. Every major Greek mathematician and scientist, judging by Andrew Barker's anthology of *Ancient Greek Musical Writings*, seems to have written on the topic. With the so-called Enlightenment, however, a linear, reductionistic, economically-driven, and materialistic view of the universe arose which, for most people, eclipsed the perennial vision of a multi-dimensional, hierarchical cosmos, in which the various levels of being are linked together by universal harmony and sympathy. All of a sudden, we were left stranded in Flatland.

The contemporary revival of interest in Harmonics is a phenomenon with important cultural, therapeutic, artistic, and cosmological implications. In antiquity, for example, the healing and psycho-therapeutic power of music was widely perceived. More recently, the great psychologist C. G. Jung observed a fascinating phenomenon at work in his patients involving the spontaneous appearance of compensatory archetypal material. In short, Jung observed that the dreams of individuals experiencing psychic distress or disequilibrium spontaneously produce mandala symbolism and other numinous representations of psychic wholeness. Jung discovered that this symbolism, often of a geometrical nature, functions as a psychic "compass" or "view finder" to help orient, equilibrate, and restore balance to the distressed system.

From this standpoint, despite its purely scientific and philosophical value, the spontaneous, renewed interest we see in Harmonics today is not unexpected and should also be seen within the wider perspective of an emerging "cultural therapy." Materialism "works," and it works well within its own particular context. However, the path of materialism can only lead to physical comfort and never to true happiness of the soul or spirit. The exclusively linear, mechanistic, and materialistic view must therefore be seen for what it is: an example of diseased cosmological thinking and cultural pathology which can only lead to alienation and a distorted view of reality. Thus, it is only appropriate that the study of Harmonics should reassert itself at this point in time. Heraclitus wrote that "In opposition there is true friendship" and Philolaus maintained that "*Harmonia* is the unity of multiplicity, and the agreement of things that disagree." Out of disequilibrium shall arise images of wholeness; out of opposition, friendship; from discord, there shall arise *harmonia*.

The relative health of a culture may be judged not only by the quality of its bread, but also by the quality of its music. By these two yardsticks, the current state of our cultural distress cannot be overestimated. In terms of the former, we Americans have let our taste evaporate to the point where we accept, as a culture, baked loaves of styrofoam paste exuded by machines. In terms of music, our culture presents it as a commodity rather than a path of spiritual development. Most musicians learn technique, or how to play a particular piece, and don't even know what a perfect fifth *really* is in an ultimate sense; this fact alone bespeaks the need for a return of the monochord to our schools and academies. Let us therefore seek quality and knowledge in every domain, and seek that which is good and lasting over the quick and easy fix. Moreover, let us see the return of Harmonics for what it is, in at least one of its guises: a true example of "music therapy," which can help to heal our cultural fragmentation and the harm that has been done by our inadequate cosmological and educational models. Let us restore the pursuit of music to its rightful place in our lives and society, and let us recall those lines of Congreve on the magical and therapeutic power of harmony, the magical music of Orpheus:

> Music hath charms to soothe the savage breast,
> To soften rocks, or bend a knotted oak,
> By magic numbers and persuasive sound.

Ptolemy's Polychord Revived

In Ptolemy's remarkable work *On Harmonics* (translated in Barker, *Ancient Greek Musical Writings II*), the second century C.E. astronomer, mathematician, geographer, philosoper and cosmologist of Alexandria, describes the construction of the monochord or the single-stringed *kanôn* in book 1.8. Later, in book 1.11, he describes the use of an eight-stringed polychord or *kanôn*. Finally in book 3.1, supposing "that someone's enthusiasm should make him want to fill out on the *kanôn* the double-octave *systêma*, to achieve a complete repertoire of complexity," he describes the construction of a fifteen-stringed polychord or *kanôn*, which might be described as "the mother of all monochords." The virtue of the fifteen-stringed polychord, shown in *Figure 1*, is that it allows the researcher to set up two different scales side-by-side for purposes of comparison, or lay out the entire Greek Greater Perfect System which spans two octaves.

In *Figure 1*, the *kanôn* is divided to produce the regular diatonic scale

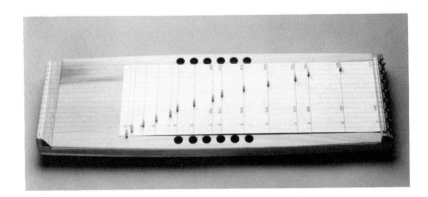

Figure 1. Ptolemy's Fifteen-stringed Monochord or Polychord

This polychord with fifteen strings is described by Ptolemy in his treatise *On Harmonics*, book 3, chapter 1. It allows the researcher to set up a double-octave system, the Greek Greater Perfect System, two different tuning systems side-by-side, and so forth.

In the photograph above is shown the regular diatonic scale described in Plato's *Timaeus*, spanning two octaves. In order to set up this scale on the polychord, the length of the *kanôn* needs to be divided into 972 parts. In the table below, both string divisions and the tone-numbers are expressed in the lowest possible whole-number terms:

String divisions (Length)	Tone numbers (Vibration)	Tones (in key of C)	Intervals between tones
486	768	C	
			leimma (256:243)
512	729	B	
			whole-tone (9:8)
576	648	A	
			whole-tone (9:8)
648	576	G	
			whole-tone (9:8)
729	512	F	
			leimma (256:243)
768	486	E	
			whole-tone (9:8)
864	432	D	
			whole-tone (9:8)
972	384	C	

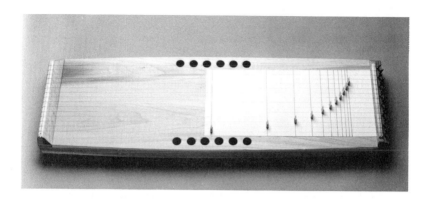

Figure 2. The Harmonic Overtone Series on the Polychord

Above: The naturally occurring harmonic nodal points are indicated on the polychord: (1) whole string; (2) one-half string; (3) one-third string; (4) one-quarter string; and so on. By gently touching the string at the nodal point and plucking it, the overtone can be emphasized and made to ring out.

Below: If a polychord is not readily available, the overtone series can be demonstrated on a piano. Play the progression here as a sustained chord, starting with the fundamental tone (1) and adding the overtones in sequence. The notes are (1) C; (2) C; (3) G; (4) C; (5) E; (6) G; (7) B flat; (8) C; (9) D; (10) E. When a single string is plucked, all these overtones are produced. See how well you can hear them by just striking the fundamental tone and carefully listening to the sound decay. The octave, fifth, and fourth are perfect consonances.

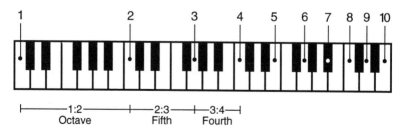

described in Plato's *Timaeus*, shown here spanning two octaves, which is the ancient Three-Limit version of our major scale in Pythagorean tuning.

In *Figure 2*, the naturally occuring harmonic nodal points are indicated on the polychord.

Calibration of the *Kanôn:* A Digital Approach

Following the suggestion of Siemen Terpstra in his "Introduction to the Monochord," the active string length of this polychord is exactly 100 centimeters (or 1000 millimeters), which allows for easy calibration of the removable tuning templates. The polychord itself is built to fit in a standard carrying case made for electronic keyboards.

Using a spreadsheet program, this writer has developed a simple calculator entitled "Monochord Tuner" which automatically computes the division of the 100 millimeter *kanôn* based on whole-number divisions of the string length, the way that monochord divisions were expressed by the Greek philosophers and mathematicians. In addition, the Monochord Tuner computes the decimal ratios between adjacent tones and string divisions, and other factors.

Shown in *Figure 3* is the division of the *kanôn* in the smallest possible whole-number terms required to produced the Major Pythagorean scale of Figure 1. In order to produce the Major Pythagorean scale on the monochord, the string needs to be divided into 972 parts. This value is entered into cell A2. This results in 972 string units, each 1.03 cm in length, reported in cell A3. The whole-number divisions of the string are then entered beneath in column A, and the spreadsheet computes the rest:

> Column B: Division of the 1000 millimeter tuning template from the end
> Column C: Division of the 1000 millimeter tuning template from the center
> Column D: The ratio of the produced tone, shown to three decimal places
> Column E: The ratio of adjacent tones to one another
> Column F: The ratio of adjacent string division to one another
> Column G: The notes are not computed, but manually entered

Note that the values in columns of E and F are reciprocals of one

	A	B	C	D	E	F	G
1	Pythagorean 972-486						
2	972.00	- MONOCHORD DIVISIONS					
3	1.03	- LENGTH UNIT					
4							
5	DIVISIONS	MILLIMETERS	FROM CENTER	TONE RATIO	TONE INCREMENT	STRING INCREMENT	NOTE
6							
7	972.00	1000.00000	500.00000	1000.00000			C
8	864.00	888.88889	388.88889	1125.00000	1.125000	0.88889	D
9	768.00	790.12346	290.12346	1265.62500	1.125000	0.88889	E
10	729.00	750.00000	250.00000	1333.33333	1.053498	0.94922	F
11	648.00	666.66667	166.66667	1500.00000	1.125000	0.88889	G
12	576.00	592.59259	92.59259	1687.50000	1.125000	0.88889	A
13	512.00	526.74897	26.74897	1898.43750	1.125000	0.88889	B
14	486.00	500.00000	0.00000	2000.00000	1.053498	0.94922	C

Figure 3. The Calibration of the Major Pythagorean Scale on a 1000 mm String Depicted on the Monochord Tuner

	A	B	C	D	E	F	G
1	6:8::9:12 "Musical Proportion"						
2	12.00	- MONOCHORD DIVISIONS					
3	83.33	- LENGTH UNIT					
4							
5	DIVISIONS	MILLIMETERS	FROM CENTER	TONE RATIO	TONE INCREMENT	STRING INCREMENT	NOTE
6							
7	12.00	1000.00000	500.00000	1000.00000			C
8	9.00	750.00000	250.00000	1333.33333	1.333333	0.75000	F
9	8.00	666.66667	166.66667	1500.00000	1.125000	0.88889	G
10	6.00	500.00000	0.00000	2000.00000	1.333333	0.75000	C
11							
12							
13	12.00	1000.00000	500.00000	1000.00000			C
14	9.00	750.00000	250.00000	1333.33333	1.333333	0.75000	F
15	8.48528	707.10678	207.10678	1414.21356	1.060660	0.94281	F#
16	8.00	666.66667	166.66667	1500.00000	1.060660	0.94281	G
17	6.00	500.00000	0.00000	2000.00000	1.333333	0.75000	C

Figure 4. Calibration of the 6:8::9:12 Musical Proportion

another. In others words, if these two ratios are multiplied together they will equal 1 or Unity, the root principle of *harmonia*.

In *Figure 4*, the ratios of the 6:8::9:12 "Musical Proportion" attributed to Pythagoras are shown in the Monochord Tuner. In the upper part of the figure, 9 is the Arithmetic Mean between the extremes and 8 is the Harmonic Mean, and the ratio between them defines the whole tone in Pythagorean tuning.

In the lower version of the Musical Proportion, the Geometric Mean between the two extremes has been inserted, which is the *axis of harmonic symmetry* of the octave and corresponds with F♯ in twelve-tone equal temperament. These three Means of the octave, Arithmetic, Geometric, and Harmonic, can be illustrated on a circular graph as in *Figure 5*, where they are shown as whole numbers; in *Figure 6*, where they are shown as fractions or whole-number ratios; and as in *Figure 7*, where they are shown as decimal ratios. These diagrams are adapted from Siemen Terpstra's work, *Means and Music: The Generation of the Consonant Ratios Through the Application of Means*. Finally, *Figure 8* shows the ratios of the Pythagorean whole-tone, which is the difference between the Arithmetic and Harmonic Means, the perfect fifth and the perfect fourth.

The axis of harmonic symmetry divides the octave into two perfectly equal parts and is the most perfect mean between its extremes, if we accept the view of Plato who states in *Timaeus* 31B–32A that "of all bonds the best is that which makes itself and the terms it connects a unity in the fullest sense; and it is of the nature of a continued geometrical proportion to effect this most perfectly." As I have shown in chapter four of my recently published book *Jesus Christ, Sun of God: Ancient Cosmology and Early Christian Symbolism*, the decimal ratios of the Arithmetic, Harmonic, and Geometric Means of the octave define the numerical values of the ancient divinities who were seen as personificiations of the Logos (literally, *ratio*), the cosmic power of *harmonia*: THE GOD HERMES ('Ο ΘΕΟΣ ἙΡΜΗΣ=707); APOLLO ('ΑΠΟΛΛΩΝ=1061); THE GOD APOLLO ('Ο ΘΕΟΣ 'ΑΠΟΛΛΩΝ=1415), and JESUS ('ΙΗΣΟΥΣ=888). These gematria values are rounded off expressions of the string ratios of the Geometric Mean (.707); the half-tone in Pythagorean tuning (1.061); the tone ratio of the Geometric Mean (1.415); and the string ratio of the Pythagorean whole-tone (.888) respectively. According to ancient sources cited in my study, the names of the gods were first revealed by Orpheus, the musician-theologian whom tradition records as the founder of the Greek mysteries. According to Iamblichus, it was from the Orphic writers that the Pythagoreans received the doctrine "that the essence of the gods is defined by Number."

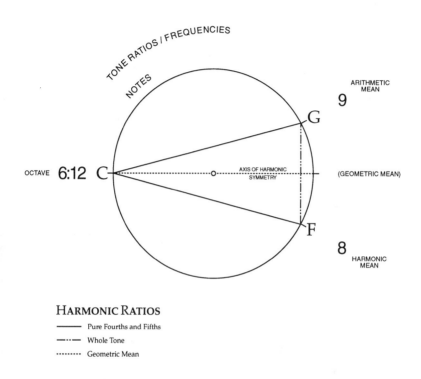

Figure 5. The Musical Proportion on the Circular Graph

The logarithmic representation of the octave on a circular graph or "tone mandala" allows one to visually discern any harmonic symmetries. Here the 6:8::9:12 Musical Proportion is shown with the corresponding intervals. The *axis of harmonic symmetry* is the Geometric Mean between the two extremes of the octave; it is also the Geometric Mean between the Arithmetic and Harmonic Means.

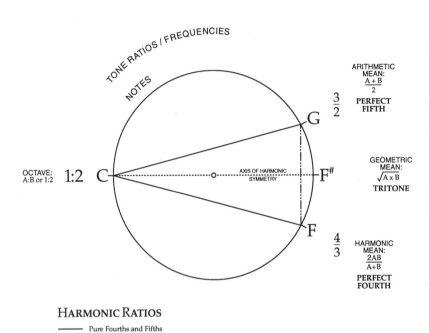

Figure 6. The Arithmetic, Geometric, and Harmonic Means

Shown here are the formulas for arriving at the values of the Arithmetic, Geometric, and Harmonic Means. They are given here as whole-number ratios in the smallest possible terms.

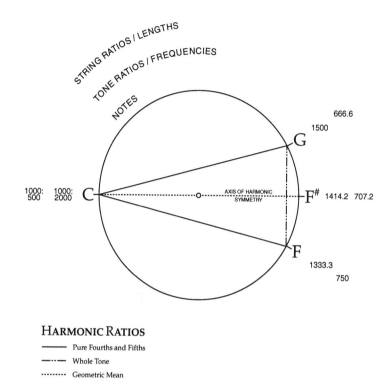

Figure 7. The Ratios of Harmony Expressed in Decimal Form

Shown above are the tone and string ratios of the Means expressed in decimal form if Unison is taken to be 1000. Each pair of ratios is a set of reciprocals.

The tonal frequency of the Geometric Mean, at the precise, harmonic center of the octave is a fraction off from 1415, the numerical value of the ancient Greek title THE GOD APOLLO, the Hellenistic god of musical harmony. The string ratio which gives rise to this value is 707, the number of THE GOD HERMES, who invented the lyre and gave it to Apollo as a token of their harmonic friendship. Hermes and Apollo are "brothers" of one another in Greek myth, mirroring their unique harmonic relationship: 1.414 x .707 = 1.

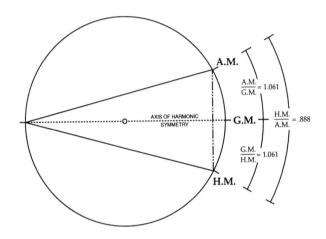

HARMONIC RATIOS

——— Pure Fourths and Fifths
—··— Whole Tone
········ Geometric Mean

Figure 8. The Ratios of the Tone

The Pythagorean whole-tone, the ratio between the Arithmetic and Harmonic Means, encompasses the canonical numbers 1061 and 888. The ratio 1061, the number of APOLLO, links the Means together in one continuous geometric proportion. 888, the number of JESUS, the string ratio of the whole-tone. Clement of Alexandria portrayed emerging Christianity in musical terms as the "New Song," a new manifestation of the preexisting Logos: "Behold the might of the New Song!" he wrote. It has "composed the universe into melodious order, and tuned the discord of the element to harmonious arrangement, so that the whole *kosmos* might become *harmonia*."

A Concluding Notion: The "Pebble Arithmetic Challenge"

Returning to our discussion of the Monochord Tuner, it must be possible to create a more comprehensive program that would automatically fill in all the Pythagorean (Three-Limit) or Just Intonation (Five-Limit) values between any two octave extremes, calculate the corresponding tone numbers in lowest possible terms, and plot out the "pebble arithmetic" patterns of the Harmonic Series and Sub-harmonic Series on the network grid of the matrix model, which could then be output on a high resolution imaging device. Should enthusiasm for research into harmonics lead some reader to undertake this type of project and "achieve a complete repertoire of complexity," we'd certainly like to hear from you.

For futher reading:

• *The Pythagorean Sourcebook and Library.* Compiled and translated by K. S. Guthrie. Phanes Press, 1987.

• "An Introduction to the Monochord" by Siemen Terpstra. Copies of his other papers and monographs may be obtained directly from the author, who may be contacted through Phanes Press.

• *The Manual of Harmonics of Nicomachus the Pythagorean.* Translation and commentary by Flora Levin. Phanes Press, 1993.

• *Ancient Greek Musical Writings II: Harmonic and Acoustic Theory.* Translation, introductions, and notes by Andrew Barker. Cambridge: Cambridge University Press, 1989. (581 pages of primary texts.)

• *The Pythagorean Plato: Prelude to the Song Itself* by Ernest McClain. York Beach: Nicolas Hays, 1978. (An interpretation of Plato's "ideal cities" as tuning systems.)

• *Tone: A Study in Musical Acoustics* by Siegmund Levarie and Ernst Levy. Kent: Kent State University Press, 1980. (Contains a valuable chapter on the monochord, along with exercises.)

• *Jesus Christ, Sun of God: Ancient Cosmology and Early Christian Symbolism* by David Fideler. Wheaton: Quest Books, 1993. (Chapters 4 and 10 deal with the science of harmony and the harmonic basis of some ancient cosmological symbolism.)

Mysticism and Spiritual Harmonics in Eighteenth-Century England

ARTHUR VERSLUIS

For Joscelyn Godwin

ALTHOUGH CONTEMPORARY SCHOLARSHIP has brought to light many aspects of musical and harmonic symbolism in Asian religions, and suggested something of its affiliations with sacred words, or *mantra*, comparatively little has been written about these subjects in the Western religious traditions. A happy exception, of course, are the works of Joscelyn Godwin, whose extensive and wide-ranging research has revealed much about Western esoteric traditions of musical and linguistic mysticism.[1] What follows is a brief introduction to a very rare text from the late seventeenth century in England, an essay and an illustration whose significance ought not go unnoticed, for they reveal a little-known aspect of Western musical esotericism, and demonstrate that practical harmonic mysticism along the lines of that found in Sufism, in Shaivite Hinduism, and in Tibetan Buddhism can also be found in, of all things, relatively recent Protestant Christianity in England.

This essay, "A New Theory of Musick"—and the accompanying illustration—are found in *Theosophical Transactions*, the journal of the Philadelphians, a mystical community based mostly in London, England during the late seventeenth and early eighteenth centuries. The Philadelphians held that they were not a sect, and in fact, since they followed in the tradition of Jacob Boehme (1575–1624)—the great German mystic—they opposed on principle the formation of sects or denominations, because they thought that sectarianism created a kind of "astral shell" preventing one from authentic spiritual awakening. The Philadelphians (their name connoting a community of love) developed around Jane Leade, a visionary mystic in her own right whose many works document her spiritual experiences and her conviction that divine mercy extends to all beings, so that eventually all must be saved and restored to divine unity.

Theosophical Transactions, which was published during 1697, was largely the product of the brilliant Dr. Francis Lee, a specialist in Hebrew and the Kabbalah, a man who willingly resigned his academic career in order to live in the small spiritual community surrounding Jane Leade. Lee and a few friends published the journal in order to give Philadelphian spirituality a public vehicle, and although it won them few adherents—"orthodox" ruffians on more than one occasion violently tried to break up the prayer meetings of the Philadelphians, and the group was rather frequently publicly vilified by sanctimonious clergy—it is very useful as a means for understanding the spirituality of this remarkable English movement, whose closest analogue is probably Sufism.

Like the Sufis in Islam, these adherents of the school of Jacob Boehme tended—whether in Germany, the Netherlands, England, or Pennsylvania—to practice both silent meditation and singing with dancing as rhythmic, harmonic manifestations of (and as a path to) the spiritual truths realized through contemplation. I have documented elsewhere the precise nature of the Boehmeans' meditative practices, especially in the school of Dr. John Pordage, to which Jane Leade and her group belong.[2] Pordage, who died in 1681, practiced a silent meditation that left his body inert for extremely long periods of time, and also was known, along with his wife and colleagues, to practice a variety of English folk dancing adapted—perhaps along the lines of Sufi adaptations of indigenous dance—to their particular spiritual discipline.

There are several elements of "A New Theory of Musick" and of the accompanying illustration to which I think it important to draw attention. One feels compelled to note that this essay fits precisely into the long Western tradition that runs through Pythagoras, Orphism, Platonism, and Judeo-Christian mysticism or esotericism, and that emphasizes the harmonic nature of the cosmos. We should emphasize the term "Judeo-Christian" here, for this essay and illustration rather subtly incorporate aspects of kabbalistic mysticism, revealed in the mysticism of the word in the essay and, of course, in the geometric diagram of the six-pointed "Seal of Solomon" with its numerical, alphabetical, and musical significances.

"A New Theory of Musick" also demonstrates provocative parallels with Islamic, Hindu, Greek, and Buddhist doctrines of harmonics, *mantra*, and geometrical or mathematical correspondences. It would be particularly interesting to compare the harmonic mysticism evidenced here with that of Shaivite mysticism, and to investigate further the implications of the author's recognition that a given note is connected by an "Umbilical Ray of Communication" to its center, or "Ground Note," and that indeed the "Original Note" is "the *Central* Point or Unity, branching out it self every way, in the form of a *Sphear* or *Globe*, wherein each Ray, as it proceeds from the Centre, still opens its self by Division into Multiplicity; as the Rays of Light do according to their distance from the *Sun*: . . . [so as to] constitute a Sphere of Light." This is a profound and concise expression of the fundamental relationship between unity and multiplicity—said by some to be the essential problem of philosophy—and it does have spiritual implications, especially as regards the metaphysics of light and sound. Undoubtedly one could find correlate expositions in Buddhism or Islamic mysticism of the relation between unity and multiplicity, but I have space here only to suggest such avenues of possible enquiry.

Regardless, it is important to recognize that this essay stands on its own as one among many examples of the hidden Western esoteric tradition. Particularly significant is its implicit embrace of the Neoplatonic Christian tradition rooted in the work of Dionysius the Areopagite, which recognizes that "the True outward Harmony of Nature" is "an Image or Manifestation of the *Angelical*, and *Divine* Harmony." This recognition is further extended to a mysticism of the

Word, or Logos, seen as a variation of celestial music. The deep interconnectedness of geometry, music, number, language, and symbolism is perhaps best exemplified in the accompanying illustration, which incorporates so many elements of Judeo-Christian sacred symbolism—from the 144 (12x12) radiating numbers, to the superimposed triangles of the Seal of Solomon, to the mystical relationship of the six hexagonal points to the seventh, their center—that we cannot begin to explicate it all. Suffice it to say that this is a preëminent example of the Western esoteric tradition, one that should be read as a document of spiritual and cosmological implications. With that I leave it to the reader to draw his or her own conclusions about the meanings inherent in these works from seventeenth-century English Boehmean Christianity.

A New Theory of Musick[3]

AS ALL ARTS AND SCIENCES have in these times arrived to a more than ordinary height; so has *Musick* in Particular by some extraordinary Genius's in this last Age been brought to such Perfection, that it may be esteemed one of the Wonders of it. Their Compositions have been most judicious and accurate, full of Air, sprightly, and nervous withal: (for there is an emptiness and thinness of Air, answerable to that of *Sence* in an Oration) but the great Excellency and Beauty has been in their near Approach to, and Imitation of *Nature*. In which the Performances of Mr. *Purcell*[4] have been so happy, as may justly give him the Preference of all others, even of those Countries where this Art has been most encouraged. Indeed *Nature* her self is the best Mistress, though *Art* has almost in every thing intruded it self, usurping her Seat and keeping her out; and by a set of Rules and Caveats, it fetters and confines the Mind, and baffles the Genius, keeping it down in the common and beaten Track: which if left to its Native Liberty, and free to hearken to the Direction of Nature her self, might be lead by her, to view her in her Simplicity, and learn her Secrets, and bring her forth in her Varieties and Wonders; in which she is endless, as being bottom'd and founded on that Infinity which gave her Being; and has shadow'd out Himself in her. What is here offer'd, will we hope sufficiently approve it self, when throughly examin'd, to be grounded in Nature; and though, as a New thing, it may appear to some strange, or difficult at first; yet they are desired to forbear any hard censure, till what is here but Proposed and a rude Draught of it only offer'd, shall come to be deduced more largely, both in Theory and Practice.

It is then suppos'd, that Musick is an outward Representation of the Harmony of the Divine Powers and Properties in the Nature of God: who exists and manifests himself in infinite variety and multiplicity, all in perfect Concord and Unity. The *Unity* as Fundamental, comprizing and containing all in it self. And thus the One Ground Note, or Bass contains in it self all the whole *Scale* above it; not only the *Artificial Scale*, but all as high as we can imagine; and its Tone is an Aggregate of them all; as the roaring of the Sea is made up of the noise of each particular Wave contain'd in it. Out of the Bass then all the other Notes proceed, as a Birth from it; and together make up its adequate proportion and Image. Let us suppose the Bass or ground to be G. and consider briefly the process of the first Octave from it. First the note A is divided from it; and set up by it self. This being the first recess from the simple Unity is at greatest disproportion to it; and whereas in the Ground Note, A is founded in unity with the rest, therein also contain'd; now it is founded out of it likewise: so that A being twice taken, when the others are but once, causes that disagreement; which is to be made up, as the other Notes come forth and joyn with it, to make up the full proportion of the Ground Note, that they may agree and unite with it perfectly. As yet A (as containing also its own Concords) stands as an opposite party; this being in reality the product or Birth of a new Ground or Key. Then B comes forth in Agreement with the Ground, and Discord to A, but in far less proportion; bearing something more of affinity to it as another single Note come forth. The next, C, is of the family of A; and has a less proportion of Contrariety to the first Note than that. In D there is a fuller Concord with the Ground, being its 5th. still less at variance with A; to which it is but a fourth. Thus way being made by advance of the opposite Parties to each other, they come in the next Note to an Agreement, where E, who is of the Family of A, is received as into that of G, in the imperfect Concord of a 6th. In the next Note, F, the breach is widened again in the Discord of a 7th. (the first breach downwards, or recess from the Unity in G above:) but mightily qualified by its Relation of a 3d. to D, (5th. to the Ground) and of a 5th. to B, (third to it). Lastly comes forth the Great Concord of the 8th.; or G again, i.e. in its Octave: where it is truly but half of the first (apparent in that it recurrs in the exact half of the String in any Instrument). Now should we go on forwards to gain the other half of proportion, yet lacking, to the Ground Note; we should be deceiv'd in our expectation, forasmuch as all possible Octaves about this superior G, are but adequate to it (unless we could determine and take them all in). But there's a shorter way, and that is by Returning and taking the same Notes over again, the Octave backwards: which compleats the proportion. Sound spreads as from a point every way; and the Proportions are to be reckon'd here as well backwards as forwards; the Reflexion of the Sound being equally necessary to the full Harmony.

We proceed then backwards from G in the Octave. F is the first recess or division; but not so much as A from G, being rather the recess of the greater from the lesser, whose Proportion it carries in it, and with it: so that in the descent, what was lost before, is now by degrees all gathered up, (every Note containing all above, as before) so here we find F in a considerable degree Harmoniz'd, by the relations already mention'd. But E much more being a lesser third to G in the Octave; and C becomes a 5th. or perfect Concord. D also being 5th. to G below, is near related, and shews a 4th. capable of being made a Concord. B is made another Concord, or 6th. as it was before a third. And last of all, A the first great Discord, by its relations to G above, through its 3d. and 5th. to G above; is near allied to its Ground Note, and brought into Concord with it.

And thus we see the *first* great Discord *Harmonized* with all the other arising from it. That which went out *First*, must come in *Last*: the Great *Breach* or *Division* cannot be made up and restored to *Unity*, till by a Progress forwards and backwards through the whole Circle of alienation it has begun, it has work'd off the contrariety of Disproportion; and by degrees gather up the Proportion it lost, it returns again into its own Original. The Circle is here *compleat*, and the *End* has found its *Beginning*, the *Multiplicity* received into *Identity* and *Unity*. There is a Birth of a *new* Octave, or Series of Harmony, existing in its outflown and manifested Essence, and also in its Original: not only in its Original, as *Archetype*, containing the first Seeds and Grounds of it; but in its *new Essence* admitted into, and made one with it.

Here we see the Natural Motion, and the End of the Seven Notes of Musick: contributing their proper Qualities, Powers, and Proportions in joint operation; tending and driving on towards a state of Rest and Union, in *Concentration* of all their Powers, as the End and Consummation of their Labour: which is obtained in the full Musical Close. Similitudes of this may be offered in the Seven *Planets* working in like manner in their variety of Motion and Influence. The *six Working Days* of the Week ending in the Sabbath, recurring in an Octave. The 6000 Years of the World in Labour and Misery ending, as is supposed, in the 7000th Year, as its *Sabbatical Jubilee*. And lastly, as the Archetype and Ground of all, the Seven Working *Spirits of God* manifesting themselves through the whole Creation, operating in their peculiar Powers, and bringing all things through a state of Action and Motion, into Stillness and Rest, Joy and Triumph; their End, Perfection, and Crown.

Hence as there was no Discord any where in *Nature* arising from the distinction and variation of the Unity, till *Lucifer* would divide, by extending himself beyond all Proportion: so there is naturally no Discord at all in *Musick*; properly so call'd. And confrequent of this, it may be affirm'd that *all* the Seven notes of Musick, duly conducted and wrought out, may be founded together; even the whole Octave, in full Consort, with a new and surprizing Harmony; and if the whole Octave, then of consequence All possible Octaves: which would make it yet more wonderful and delightful.

It is further Observable, that every Note is diversified as to its Property and difference of Sound; by the Relation it bears to its Bass or Key note; according to the Distance it has sprung out from it.

Now this different Relation (as suppose a 4th or 8th) directs or determines the Mind to regard this Distance or Proportion it bears to its Bass or Center; to which, though it goes forth, it still keeps fast tied (as an Infant to its Mother) by an *Umbilical* Ray of Communication; which consists of most minute Division, often beyond what can be exprest to the outward Ear, but perceptible by the Intellect, judging of the different appulses of Sound. Where upon this Ray of Division the Mind is naturally carried back, and runs to the Centre; and makes as

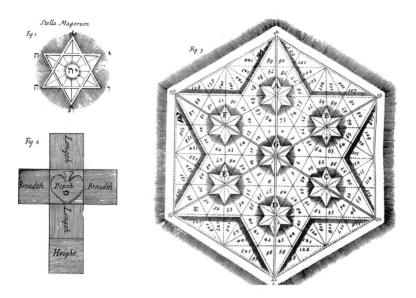

it were an Instantaneous Comparison of the distance of the Sound from it, and the Proportion to it. So that still the Respect is to be observ'd to the Original or Ground Note: which in the Plan of Natures Harmony stands as the *Central* Point or Unity, branching out it self every way, in the form of a *Sphear* or *Globe*, wherein each Ray, as it proceeds from the Centre, still opens it self by Division into Multiplicity: as the Rays of Light do according to their distance from the *Sun*: and as These constitute a Sphere of Light, so do the others proceed on till they come to be so minute and close rang'd, as to form a *Circumference* of continued Harmony. Wherein the Modus or way of Procession by Skipping from Note to Note, is chang'd into a new sort of Musick, that takes in every Interval of Sound, and moves after the same manner, as when on a *Lute* or *Viol*, we don't Skip upon the String from Fret to Fret; but sliding down with the Finger take in all between the Frets in a continued movement. Which is easily Imitated by the Voice, as for Instance, sliding thus continuously and quick from the 5th. above to the Key Note. Which way if follow'd as Nature it self will direct us, in proper Passages or expressions of Passion, would add

many Elegant Graces in mixture without common Musick, and give
it a peculiar sweetness, Solemnity, and Majesty. Thus is the True
outward Harmony of Nature, an Image or Manifestation of the
Angelical, and *Divine* Harmony. The Bass or Centre stands continually
sounding; and sounding All Harmony in Unity; also working and
shooting forth it self into Variety, and Multiplicity; and in the
Circumference uniting again, in a Sphere of continued Unities. And
every one of these, as also all intermediate Ones, is as a Centre it self;
opening, and proceeding in a Sphere of its own. So that as proceeding
forwards they increase their Circle, so each one, at whatever distance,
has also its motion back again, and return to its Originals: and Ecchoes
to it that Proportion which it bears of it. So that the Reflex Act of the
whole Circumference, and of all contain'd within it, is but the
Returning of the Outflown Image into its own Centre and Original;
or the True *Eccho* of the first Unity: which as it gave out, so it must
receive again, and contain all in it self.

Thus will the Theory of *Musick*, duly applied and Spiritualiz'd lead
us on to glorious Contemplations, and give us a Key of the great
Mysteries of *Nature*. It will furnish us with sublime Idea's of the Beauty
and Harmony of *God*, and of his Works in the Creation: in the
Contemplation and Joy whereof all the Angelick Hosts, as they first
began, so still continue their Songs of Triumph and Praise: the
Morning Stars singing together, and all the *Sons of God* shouting for Joy.
And it will be a great excitement of Emulation in us to joyn with them,
both in Heart and Voice: and raise especially in the Sons of this Art,
a generous Indignation to see it debased and prostituted to the vanity
of common Amours; to the Luxury, and too often, even the Obscenity
of the Age: Rising now for her Vindication, both in themselves and
others; and for the Employ and devotement of that Divine Talent to
the Praise and Glory of him that gave it; and takes himself delight in
it. In which we are most Emulous to concur. . .

The Ground on which we proceed, is a New Discovery arising from
this Theory; Which is This:

That the Natural Pronunciation, or the Tone, Accent, and Emphasis, which we use in speaking our Words; and that variety of it that

appears in the Expression of our Passions; is nothing else but Musick; it is True and Natural Harmony; and may be prick'd down and perform'd in Comfort; running in minute and swift Division. Which Division coming near to the Modus or continued flux of Sound in Speaking, it will be discerned and demonstrated to the Ear, that it agrees exactly with it; and that this Division is only taking the Stamina, or more Substantial and Fundamental Notes, of the Harmony in Continuity; which upon these, as their Ground, runs out into yet more minute Division; even till they exceed the reach of the Ear, and become united (as to all perception): after the same manner as it happens to the Eye in the Continuity of the Circle, when a lighted Match or Coal of Fire is swung swiftly about; or after that which a very Ingenious and Sublime Author has hinted to us, of the Termination and Passage of Quick Motion into Rest. And here the Transition from the manner of expressing the Notes in Division, into that of expressing them in Continuity will be plain and obvious: And 'tis observable, that Mr. *Purcell*'s great Excellency lay in this, that in his Compositions, by listening to Nature, he falls frequently upon those Radical Notes, which support, and may be branched out into this Natural Harmony. Some instances whereof may hereafter be produced; with the Natural Divisions annexed to them. In the mean time the whole is submitted to the Ingenious, in hopes of favourable Acceptance, and of their free Concurrence, either for Discovery of any Mistake, which shall be freely acknowledged, or for the further Improvement of this Art.

Notes

1. See Joscelyn Godwin, "The Golden Chain of Orpheus: A Survey of Musical Esotericism in the West," *Temenos* 4 (1984) 7–25 and *Temenos* 5 (1984), 211–39; *Music, Mysticism, and Magic: A Sourcebook* (London: Routledge & Kegan Paul, 1986); *Harmonies of Heaven and Earth* (London: Thames & Hudson, 1987); *The Mystery of the Seven Vowels in Theory and Practice* (Grand Rapids: Phanes Press, 1991); *The Harmony of the Spheres: A Sourcebook of the Pythagorean Tradition in Music* (Rochester: Inner Traditions, 1993).

2. See Arthur Versluis, *Theosophia: Hidden Dimensions of Christianity* (Hudson: Lindisfarne Press, 1994) for the first extensive introduction to Christian theosophy in English.

3. I must here express my indebtedness to the Bibliotheca Philosophica Hermetica of Amsterdam for access to this rare work. The essay is anonymous, is probably the work of Dr. Francis Lee, and is found in *Theosophical Transactions* 1 (March, 1697), 60–65. Original punctuation and spelling has been scrupulously retained.

4. The English composer, Henry Purcell (1659–1695).

Mentalism and the Cosmological Fallacy

JOSCELYN GODWIN

IN THE LAST issue of ALEXANDRIA I offered a cautionary tale to cosmologists, in an analysis of how one man's cosmology came into being. Through a combination of study, intuition, and psychic experience, Saint-Yves d'Alveydre became convinced that he had rediscovered the ancient key to all religions, arts, and sciences, as well as the proof of a primordial, "cosmic" inscription of the names of Jesus and Maria. My analysis of Saint-Yves' "Archeometric" system carried the discreet suggestion that other, more familiar cosmologies might perhaps have no better pedigree than his.

Cosmology is an essential part of the Western esoteric tradition—sometimes the most important part. Its function is to provide a framework that "saves the appearances" of both outward and inward reality. While there are radical differences between the cosmologies of the various schools—Pythagoreanism, Kabbalah, Sufism, Gnosticism, Christian theosophy, etc.—they all start from the assumption that there is an objective world or plane that they call material, physical, or gross, comprising stars and planets; fire, air, water, and earth; and living bodies made from these elements. But scarcely any religion, and certainly no esoteric doctrine, stops at this point, because the appearances requiring to "saved" are not exhausted by those of the sense-world. The cosmological systems mentioned above, as well as the personal ones of Boehme, Swedenborg, Saint-Yves, and the rest, all give due place to the immaterial or spiritual world to which the soul, not the bodily senses, is the witness. These appearances, too, demand to be integrated into an acceptable world view, with the result that traditional cosmologies have both a material and a spiritual department. The best known example is the medieval cosmology, in which the spheres of earth and the other elements reside within the ethereal spheres of the planets, and these within a further series of immaterial spheres assigned to the angelic hierarchies, the whole enclosed within the infinity of God. Such a system answered the medieval need for situating "all things visible and invisible" in a logical and integrated creation.

Having once developed such an integral cosmology, the esoteric traditions differ even within themselves over how to evaluate its visible or material component. In their quest for the perfection of the human being, there are those who accept and welcome it, and those who reject it in favor of a purely immaterial existence. In the Hermetic tradition, for example, there is a contrast between the Trismegistian treatises of the *Corpus Hermeticum*, and the art or science of alchemy. The treatises lean strongly to the anti-material side, their supreme image being that of the bodiless soul ascending through the starry spheres to the immaterial world of the Elect. In alchemy, on the other hand, the goal is the consecration of matter by raising it to its noblest form, gold. (Alchemists who work only on the soul or spiritual levels evidently lean towards the Trismegistian side of Hermeticism.)

Christianity also has room for contradictory attitudes to the material world, each finding ample support in the Scriptures. The anti-materialists can turn to the sayings of Jesus that contrast this world with the Kingdom of Heaven, then to the Apocalypse to learn of the eventual fate of heavens and earth alike, after which all things shall be made anew in a celestial and immaterial state. Those who have warmer feelings towards Nature can point to the Johannine doctrine of the Word made Flesh, and to the consecration of matter through the Incarnation. Esoteric traditions such as that of the Grail envisage the salvation and sanctification of the entire natural world without requiring it to be translated to Heaven. The archetypal images of the two tendencies are the New Jerusalem and the Earthly Paradise.

Such distinctions, important as they are, lose their force in the light of a further philosophical position, which holds that the material world does not exist as an objective, independent cosmos, but that all is of the nature of mind. The student of philosophy will know this mainly as the "idealism" of Bishop Berkeley. Academic philosophers periodically re-examine it, but it has never become a popular world view because of the conceptual challenge it presents to the habits of a lifetime. One does not expect the majority of people to change their ways, any more than one expects them to join the ranks of esoteric cosmologists. But the latter, at least, might be willing to follow up some of the consequences of mentalism as a practical philosophy.

After two hundred years of philosophical argument, the general consensus regarding the physical cosmos remains unchanged. This is that, while the cosmologies of ancient and non-European peoples are the understandable but mistaken constructs of their minds and cultural expectations, the same cannot be said of the universe as modern science has discovered and defined it. The politest response to anyone who questions the latter is an invitation to repeat the relevant experiments, from Galileo's rumbling cannonballs to the particle accelerators of today, in order to follow in the steps by which Western scientists have attained their unrivalled knowledge of the nature of the universe.

Scientists with more philosophical depth know this to be shaky ground. It is a mistaken prejudice to think that it confirms the materialist hypothesis of a world "out there" waiting to be discovered, any better than the mentalist one of a world projected from "in here." Given that our only possible experience is of our own mental states, then those can include going to the moon, accelerating subatomic particles, or simply living lives in which number, measure, and weight condition much of our existence. There is no evidence whatever that the "things" of our experience are anything but thoughts; and the suspicion arises that these, too, may be strongly subject to personal and cultural conditioning.

The chief stumbling-block to the practical acceptance of this "strong anthropic principle" (according to which the human mind constructs its own cosmos) is the commonality of our experience, as much in the everyday world as in the laboratory. We are conditioned to think of ideas and the mental world as personal, private, and relatively unreal, but of the physical world as shared, common, and real. Mentalism replaces this distinction by another one. Some of our ideas, it says, are personal, private, and real to us alone. These include our dreams, thoughts, emotions, and much of our everyday experience. Other of our ideas are held in common with other people and animals. These include the environment and physical bodies, including our own anatomy. But they are none the less ideas. Stones are no less hard, injuries no less painful, when one knows them to be hard and painful ideas. The regular courses of the heavenly bodies are no less regular when one recognizes them as mathematical ideas made visible, as any Pythagorean should know. Nor is the supposed confirmation of the Big Bang theory other than the coincidence of one idea (the interpretation of signals) with another (the imagination of an event in the past). It is comparable to Galileo's observations through his primitive telescope, which coincided with the heliocentric theory and hence clarified—we cannot say confirmed—a new spatial image of the cosmos that is now recognized as adequate, but far from definitive. Each case is but a portrait of the human mind at a certain stage of its history.

Perhaps the hardest step demanded by mentalism concerns the human body, and of accepting that it, too, is of a kindred stuff with the human mind. In the dream state one creates a body out of mind-stuff, and lives quite convincingly in it. But others cannot see or dissect the dream-body. If it were sufficient for us to live the dream-life alone, with whatever modes of experience it affords, it would not be necessary to have an anatomical body. However, it seems to be the destiny of humans, as of animals and plants, to garner the experiences that only communal living can provide. For this it is necessary for one's individuality to have an extension that impinges on the consciousness of others, and in turn supplies our own consciousness with new experiences both pleasant and disagreeable. It is this temporary extension of consciousness that we call our body.

The bodily senses are like amplifiers that bring these experiences to our consciousness, some people's more efficiently than others'. If we should be deprived of sight or hearing, our existence would lose a certain dimension but lack nothing in reality or intensity. If we lose all five senses, as in sleep, mystical rapture, or meditational trance, we may continue to live through our inner senses, but without the fertilizing input from the environing world that defines the normal human state. In dreamless sleep we have no experience at all, but our bodily extensions continue to be present to the waking worlds of others, like disconnected radios no longer broadcasting or receiving messages.

In speaking of the body, I mentioned that it "seems to be the destiny of humans" to have certain experiences. This begs the question that troubles scientific cosmologists: that of the intention, if any, behind the cosmos, and the source of the commonality of ideas. They are afraid that if they admit these, they will have to "include God in their hypotheses," as Laplace declined to do when questioned by Napoleon. Since even distinguished scientists are usually familiar only with exoteric religion, they understandably hesitate to take on the baggage that accompanies the God of Church and Bible. In present company, however, one can safely assume that the universe is suffused with intelligence, without anthropomorphizing the latter. The common elements of our experience come from our participation in this world-idea, to which we each contribute our own nuances whether we be angels, humans, or insects.

This relieves us from a common objection to mentalism, namely that it is solipsistic and hence alienating; that it shuts us up in a bubble, spinning our own world-experience without any certainty that other beings are real in their own right. This is very far from the truth. It is the materialistic world view that alienates us from each other as fortuitous centers of conscious matter, whereas mentalism links us, through our common participation in the universal idea, to every being in the cosmos. Though every creature emanates a unique version of the world-idea, it bears a close resemblance to those of its fellows. It challenges the imagination, but brings a strange sense of sympathy, to recall that every person or animal we meet is projecting its own universe, which includes its own body, and ours.

The second consideration of mentalism, which is more important to esotericists, concerns the immaterial department of cosmology. Esoteric cosmologists may well agree that the World Mind (or God) emanates the cosmos, but they will add that this is not restricted to the universe of the astronomers and physicists: that it may include tier upon tier of states, and of beings native to them. Typical images of the integral cosmos are the linear one (e.g., Jacob's Ladder, the Great Chain of Being, or the Kabbalistic Tree), and the spherical one (with matter either compressed at the center or relegated to the circumference). Thanks to the writings of Henry Corbin and his admirers, most students of esotericism are now familiar with the concept of these worlds as a "mundus imaginalis": an imaginal world which lacks a physical substratum but which is no less real than the world we call material.

Knowledge of this imaginal world usually comes through visionary or mystical experience. Traditional Kabbalah, for example, develops Moses' vision of Yahweh's Throne, and Ezekiel's vision of his Chariot, supplemented by the insights of post-biblical mystics. Mohammed's nocturnal ascent through the heavenly spheres is the essential precedent for the mystical flights of Sufism. The Platonic cosmology and eschatology as given in the "Myth of Er" (*Republic* 10) is presented as coming from the "near-death experience" of the Pamphylian soldier. The image of crystalline spheres enclosing the earth in the Ptolemaic cosmology, which is also that of Hermeticism, may not be mystically based, but is an awe-inspiring achievement of the imaginative faculty working at the highest degree of abstraction from observed reality, which reveals nothing of the sort to the outer eye. Such non-mystical penetration of the imaginal world is sometimes achieved by poets, painters, and musicians, though the borderline between some of their experiences and those of the mystics is undefinable.

The imaginal world stands under the same warrant of certainty as the physical one, namely that if one wishes to prove the received theories about it, one must follow the experimental path of the greatest authorities. On the one hand, a single-minded dedication to theoretical and experimental physics is required; on the other, a lifetime of mystic practice, meditation, or yoga. Since this is far beyond most of us, we lesser mortals are supposed to take both cosmologies on trust. However, we may notice that the esoteric schools that teach the exploration of the imaginal world under one name or another have each their own view of it, or as one might say their own inner cosmology. Within each school, its objective nature is taken for granted, and its scenery and *dramatis personae* are consistent. The Egyptian and Tibetan "Books of the Dead," the visionary recitals of Ibn Sina and Suhrawardi, the Sephiroth and Paths of the Kabbalah, and the *Divine Comedy* of Dante are among the best known guides. Evidently this world or plane appears quite differently to different peoples. The pagan wanderer through the spheres does not find them populated by the cast of Dante's epic; the Sufi will not find Mohammed in Hell, nor the Kabbalist become the Bride of Christ.

Consequently, whereas the religious mystic takes his experiences as the objective revelation of the spiritual world, the philosopher knows that cultural and religious conditioning are active even there. The cosmological fallacy is to posit a single, objective reality, whether this is perceived by the outer or inner senses. When this illusion is sacrificed, it becomes laughable to pretend that our little minds could ever have grasped the master-idea of the Universal Mind that is thinking us. It is particularly arrogant to believe, as Saint-Yves d'Alveydre did, that one's own conclusions about the structure and system of the universe invalidate those of everyone else.

No one has been more guilty of this kind of arrogance than the scientists who believe only in an objective, material universe. When the Big Bang theory was "proved," in April 1992, the London *Times* explained it on its front page with a diagram bearing a remarkable resemblance to certain Renaissance engravings of the world-system. Now at last, each seems to say, we can picture the cosmos as it really is, in time as well as space. What vanity! In a sense, the Renaissance cosmos was "truer" than the one of medieval flat-earthers, because its spherical globe corresponded to the new findings of voyagers and astronomers. Likewise, the cosmos of background radiation and condensing galaxies is "truer" than the crystallized universe of Newton, because it answers to the discoveries of today's instruments. But to a medieval mystic like St. Hildegard of Bingen or Dante, a cosmology that included the circles of Paradise saved the appearances much better than one that stopped with the material worlds. And to the Persian theosophers, the superior reality of Hurqalya (the imaginal world) made all haggling about the shape or history of Terra irrelevant.

Some modern cosmologists, however, have gone far beyond the common, objective world view. To a philosophical mind like Stephen Hawking's, the notion that science is describing "things as they really are" (or "were") is naïveté itself. Hawking is willing to entertain the hair-raising theory of the "Sum over Histories" proposed by Feynman, which involves the idea that the universe has not just one history, but all possible ones. This is very close to the mentalist view, namely that the history and nature of the universe are constituted by the perceptions and ideas of every conscious being that has ever, or ever will, exist—including the World Mind.

One consequence of mentalism as a practical philosophy is that the material world is no longer devalued in favor of a spiritual one. The mentalist's attitude to matter is not the contemptuous one of the Platonic, Gnostic, or Christian ascetic, but is nearer that of the pantheist or nature-mystic who sees the Universal Mind present in everything. Far from being separate from Nature, we are co-creators of it and thus nothing if not responsible. The fictitious barrier between spiritual and material life begins to dissolve as we realize that we are all modifying the universal idea after our own fashion, and in so doing are affecting the destinies of other beings as well as our own.

Human consciousness may be our own standard for experience, but it is not the universal model. As the universal idea is infinite, so there can be infinitely different types of conscious participation in it, not necessarily limited by the categories of human logic or even by the "laws" of mathematics. Being human seems especially to entail two crucial dichotomies: of mind from matter, and of self from other. But why should we suppose that other centers of consciousness labor under the same assumptions? It seems especially unlikely in the light of those rare occasions, which in retrospect seem the most significant of a lifetime, when this separation dissolves in the encounter with a reality that is indescribable in visual, verbal, or logical terms. But then one is no longer dealing with cosmology.

The pluralistic view of mentalism provides the key to accepting, and respecting, every cosmological view (including one's own) as the self-portrait of a person, an epoch, or a civilization. Cosmological discovery appears to be an endless game, in which progress is made on one front only at the expense of ignoring another. It seems doubtful that an endpoint of absolute truth will ever be reached, whether by science or by esotericism, for the simple reason that absolute truth, as hinted above, does not take a cosmological form. Mentalism turns the attention away from these shifting sands and focuses it on the sole certainty of our existence: our own consciousness. Its lesson is above all to observe, and perhaps one day to know, oneself.

A R S   M E M O R I Æ.

The Art of Memory

This illustration from the works of Robert Fludd illustrates the "third eye" or *oculus imaginationis* which, through its visionary faculty, sees into the *mundus imaginalis*—the intermediate, Imaginal world between the purely spiritual and physical levels of existence.

Printing, Memory, and the Loss of the Celestial

ARTHUR VERSLUIS

IS MODERN HUMANITY irrevocably caught in history? To judge by many modern authors, the answer is yes. To most of us, life is apparently like a train, moving along rails. Some expect an apocalypse, or a millennium; others still anticipate constant evolutionary progress toward some as yet only barely glimpsed future state. And of course there are the many modern writers whose fiction or poetry betrays a chaotic world full of cruelty and mayhem. All of these views, however disparate, have one thing in common: all are caught in history, trapped in the linear. How did we become trapped in history? This entrapment, I think, began with modern printing and in a forgetting of the celestial dimensions of life—and freedom from it lies in the art of memory and Imagination.

It is strange to compare modern cosmology with ancient and more traditional cosmologies. For all of these ancient cosmologies—including European, Greco-Roman and Judeo-Christian—are based in an ahistorical vision of life, a vertical perspective that might be termed emanationism, and that holds that this world emanates from a celestial, imaginal realm (to use Henry Corbin's term), which in turn emanated from what Plato called the realm of Ideas or Forms. These archetypal Forms are refracted through the intermediate, subtle realms, and in turn are embodied in the material world we see around us. Modernity appears to be fundamentally a forgetting of this vertical, ahistorical dimension of life, and an immersion in the Lethean river of historical dreaming.

The difficulty we have in grasping this traditional, vertical relationship with a divine realm bespeaks our distance from it. How did we come to lose sight of the vertical, and become a prisoner of a merely horizontal, dialectical view of the world? Clearly the question is immense in scope, and one can only suggest directions to pursue both in tracing the loss of the vertical dimension, and in attempting to recover it. But the best place to begin is with the European Renaissance, and the most revolutionary change in our history: the shift from the oral and written tradition to the printed word. For if as Plato wrote long ago, a written tradition is inferior to an oral, the printed word is still another step down from the manuscript.

Prior to the Renaissance and the advent of the printed word, there were two modes for transmitting literature: the laborious preparation and copying of handmade manuscripts; or oral transmission, which required memorization. Both of these entail considerable personal investment in the work—in fact, both entail an assimilation of the work into oneself. By copying a manuscript, and adding one's own decorations and elaborations, by memorizing an oral tradition, the scribe or scop would make that work part of himself, and contribute to it as well, subtly altering it to suit himself. Every recitation, every copy of a manuscript in this way became a variation on a theme, much like a musical composition, a harmony.

But with the advent of the printing press, literature was no longer assimilated in the same way. The pattern of individual assimilation and subtle variation that held the traditional culture together was effaced. The art of memory, both individual and cultural, was lost. Instead of making literature—the storehouse of our inner mythic and spiritual pattern—into a part of us, as had been the case in the oral and manuscript tradition, the printing press severed those ties. We were free to appropriate or ignore culture as we willed. Literature—the inner reflection of the celestial realms—became external to us.

If the traditional, rooted, oral tradition is conceived of as a planetary system orbiting a spiritual sun, then memorization is the gravity holding it together. The oral tradition, through which the individual bathes in and is warmed by the light of the sun, is the individual entryway into the celestial realm of the Imagination. In the traditional, vertical vision of the world, memorizing literature is the opening through which the celestial light shines from above—not from some "lower" "unconscious," as some psychologists would have it. Through hearing the familiar myths, one is surrounded by a mythical realm and through it we perceive the archetypal images that the myths mediate to us. We walk for a timeless moment among gods. We circle the sun, and all is in order again.

By making literature external, by making it a commodity, the printing press effaced this point of contact with the higher realm. No reader of books assimilates literature in the same way that one who copies or memorizes must assimilate it. Reading rides on the surface of the mind. Without that deeper assimilation of oral and manuscript traditions, literature becomes unrooted, and its revelation of the vertical dimension disappears. The ensuing chaos of a world without Memory's gravity we see in much modern fiction and poetry. Indeed, this prompted Yeats to begin his "The Second Coming":

> Turning and turning in the widening gyre
> The falcon cannot hear the falconer;
> Things fall apart; the center cannot hold;
> Mere anarchy is loosed upon the world.

The widening gyre begins with the printed word. The printing press signalled repeatability and homogeneity: literature became a commodity.

Plato in the "Myth of Er," which concludes the *Republic*, suggests that the soul—before it descends to the earthly sphere—drinks of the river Lethe, the river of forgetfulness. Therefore, the purpose of true education is to teach the soul to remember its origins, its place in the higher realm. This premise, that the incarnate soul is asleep, or forgetful, and that its purpose is to awaken and remember its origins, is reflected in Gnostic and Manichaean teachings. Henry Corbin, the late French Islamic scholar, drew attention to the similarity of the

Gnostic *Hymn of the Pearl*—a song of remembering— to the innumer-able Sufi recitals, and in particular to those of Avicenna (Ibn Sina). All these show spirituality as the soul remembering its origins.

With this higher definition of memory in mind we can approach the shift from the memory-based oral cultures to the modern, print-based culture. The shift to the printed word meant that the scholar could simply look up his references in a book; encyclopedias were born. The poet began to give readings rather than recitals. The heart of Euro-pean culture was becoming external, bound in the form of a book, rather than instilled internally through memory. This shift is embod-ied in a drama of the Renaissance, a conflict that neatly telescopes the nature of the time. For during the Renaissance and the appearance of the printed word, a new art arose, one that vigorously championed the suddenly declining vertical, symbolic realm: the art of memory.

The art of memory is, to the modern mind, a curious and almost forgotten discipline. As Frances Yates points out in her book on the subject, the art of memory was extant long before the Renaissance—its mythical founder was said to be the poet Simonides, who recited a lyric poem at a banquet, dedicating the poem to the gods Castor and Pollux, and to the host. The host suggested that since he received half the dedication, the gods would provide the other half of the payment. Later in the evening, the poet was called to the door to meet two unknown visitors. When he left, the hall collapsed, killing the guests in so horrible a manner that they couldn't be identified. The gods had rendered their payment by saving him. The poet Simonides was able to name the guests by remembering their places in order. This situation suggested to him the art of memory, and Cicero in turn drew on this story in his writing on classical rhetoric, illustrating the practical matter of remembering speeches by forming a mental picture of a given building or street, and associating images with words.

But while the Renaissance art of memory drew on its classical origins, and in particular upon the system of Metrodorus of Scepsis, its intent was quite different; for while the classical art was focused upon the practical ends of rhetoric, the Renaissance art took on a cosmological and religious aspect. Since the advent of the printed word had begun to obliterate the traditional vertical relation to the divine, it is not surprising that the art of memory appeared at just this time—for the art of memory as practiced in the Renaissance became a vehicle to reëstablish the symbolic, vertical dimension of existence. And its disappearance signalled the modern tyranny of the linear dialectic.

The Renaissance art of memory was based in the traditional Hermetic concept of the correspondence between man's soul and the universe. In this vision of the world, the individual soul bears the imprint of the divine realm. Microcosm: macrocosm. The new art of memory was based upon the idea that the individual could realize within himself the divine realm—it was a means to that end. Hence the great memory wheels of Ramon Lull, or Giordano Bruno, the memory theaters of Giulio Camillo, all organized according to images—in the form of planetary influences and Greek mythical figures—all phenomena, mineral, vegetable, animal, human, or cosmic. Intuitively recognizing the imminent loss of the vertical, emanatory vision, thinkers like Bruno sought to reinstill the gravity that the oral tradition had provided. Indeed, many, like Bruno, identified the art of memory with Egypt, because Egypt implies a return to the original, ancient vision, and Egypt also suggests the heart of the Renaissance memory systems: images.

For it is no accident that the most ancient languages, like Egyptian hieroglyphs, are based in images or representations of what is being conveyed. In Platonic terms, they invoke the vertical essence of things, their Forms or celestial origins. Because modern languages are by nature devoid of images, medieval Christian monks and Islamic calligraphers spent days, weeks, months, and years inscribing myriad images within each letter in a manuscript page, thereby injecting the vertical world of images into the horizontal written lines. Hence a single letter in an illuminated manuscript can reflect worlds. Illuminated manuscripts were a means of continuing the primal form of imaginal language. When the art of illuminated manuscripts was lost, due to the printing press and its repeatable homogeneity, the correlation between words and images, tenuously maintained through medieval illuminated manuscripts, became even more hidden.

The art of memory was an attempt to infuse the realm of images into the horizontal world of the printed page, and to give the practitioner an opportunity to ascend to the celestial realms. Like Egyptian hieroglyphs, memory wheels were associative and visionary in nature, relying on groupings of ideas around a striking image. This image was itself a reflection of the higher, symbolic realm. As Hermes Trismegistus has it, "As above, so below." By memorizing these images of a "huge dark man with burning eyes, dressed in white," or of "a man bearing a key," the practitioner sought to unite himself with that which they represented.

The struggle between the proponents of the art of memory and the rationalist Aristotelians continued throughout the Renaissance, their irreconcilable antagonism deriving from the former's insistence upon the supra-logical, imaginal, associative use of memory as a means to human perfection, while the Aristotelians steadfastly maintained that the art of memory, if at all useful, was suitable only as a means for more efficient use of rational, linear faculties. Because universities were dominated by Aristotelians, the reception was unfriendly of those who, like Ramon Lull, Giordano Bruno, and Robert Fludd, sought to reintroduce the vertical realm of images into the culture.

Probably the greatest disseminator of the art of memory was Giordano Bruno who, in the late sixteenth century, was driven from one university after another, across Europe and back again, until he was betrayed to the Inquisition and finally burned to death for heresy. Bruno, a somewhat quixotic figure, sought to reëstablish with unparalleled vigor the art of memory based in Ramon Lull's work. But even then, when he spoke with King Henry III of France, Sir Philip Sidney and Queen Elizabeth I, King Rudolph II in Prague, and Pope Pius V, his cause was lost: both he and his art were consigned to ashes and dust.

But that was not the end of the art: it simply changed form, being carried on by the poets. One sees the transition most clearly in Bruno's eruption into the Elizabethan circle of poets, which included Sidney, Sir Walter Raleigh, George Chapman, Edmund Spenser—and, rumors persist, Shakespeare himself. It was as if Bruno was passing the torch, for his visit to London had a profound influence. After it, references to his imagery abound in Elizabethan drama too: some of Ben Jonson's plays bear striking resemblances to Bruno's play *The Torch-Bearer*, and Bruno is referred to numerous times in Marlowe's *Faustus*. John Donne's debt to Bruno has been catalogued more than once as well.

The same fire to know, to pierce through to the celestial, impelled Nerval's journey to Egypt, and his use of strange, numinous alchemical imagery; it appears too in Coleridge's work. In fact, Coleridge once sought copies of all Bruno's writings, locating many in Copenhagen, and explicitly drew upon Bruno for many essays, including one in which he quotes long passages from *De Immenso*. Goethe, Novalis, Hölderlin and William Blake all also reveal in their works, if not always the direct influence of, then certainly aims similar to those of the Hermetic philosopher and poet Bruno. All sought to manifest archetypal poetic imagery in their works, which seen in this light, resemble individual efforts to incarnate in poetry symbolism that had been systematized in the art of memory.

But poetry is nearly as esoteric as the art of memory itself, and could not restore cultural gravity either, try as a Novalis or a Hölderlin might. The mere fact that memory and images had to be condensed into a system implies its exclusionary nature: few could grasp and assimilate memory wheels even then, and looking back upon them now, one is baffled: to memorize hundreds of images, from Juno in the clouds to Hercules cleaning the Augean stables, and then to relate those images to one's daily life seems a feat utterly beyond us, unapproachable, superhuman. The symbolic realm, in such concentration, is alien to us.

The consequences of this loss are visible in every sphere of modern life. Consider the disarray in the world of art. Modern, abstract art has no sun; it is profane abstraction, breaking an image down into elemental forms of color and pattern, as if to confess that the artist cannot reunify the world through art. One sees this disarray in the world of poetry, too: poetry about difficulties with the mailman, or about the noise the dishwasher makes can isolate discrete things or events, but gives them no meaning. By contrast, abstraction in its higher sense means investing an image with mythopoetic power, as the greatest works of art have always done—and some still do today.

The modern world seems trapped under the tyranny of the linear dialectic: mythological, vertical history has been supplanted by or dragged down to the horizontal level. Myths are destroyed by trivialization and literalization, and perhaps the clearest evidence of our loss we can see in how the word "myth" has become synonymous with "lie," as in "the myth of scarcity," or "myths about pregnancy." For myths reveal timeless truth, and speak to us of who we really are; myths allow us to walk among gods. To abandon myth means to abandon meaning itself.

Diagnosing this loss itself gives hope. But we should not transpose this hope itself onto the horizontal plane, and expect the "spiritual evolution of humanity" to solve our problems. To place our hope in history alone is to take the path of a Teilhard de Chardin, and to substitute the illusion of an inevitable historical transformation for personal responsibility. If the art of memory tells us anything, it bespeaks the need for individual effort. Here, after all, is our hope: in realizing individually and then perhaps even culturally the supra-historical, mythological dimension of life. This path we see in all art that we truly feel in our hearts.

If Yeats was right, if the gyre is out of control, our historical future may look bleak—but only from an historical perspective. There is an ironic truth in the modern cliché assertions that "it's all Greek to me," and "that's nothing but a myth." Both imply our distance from the vertical realm of mythology in which the gods are living principles. But modern pessimism is valid only in the world under the tyranny of the linear dialectic, the sleep that produces monsters like toxic waste, nuclear weapons, and cancer. And a Bruno would tell us that we need not stay asleep.

In a wonderful poem, Bruno tells us that if we can but move toward the symbolic, the vistas that will open around us will surpass our greatest hopes, our most cherished aspirations, as we spread our wings, one light and one dark, rising beyond the most infinite spheres. To the side of a planet facing away from the sun, all is dark; yet when the planet turns, it is suffused with light that was always there. If the printed word marks our loss, perhaps it also can lead to renewed life. This is the message of countless authors and artists whose work continues to call us to a celestial ascent, to become what we always are. There is, perhaps, a meaning there—if we only remember.

LA
MONARCHIE
DV TERNAIRE EN
VNION, CONTRE
LA
MONOMACHIE
DV BINAIRE EN
CONFVSION:

PAR GERARD DORN,
Docteur Physicien.

M. D. LXXVII.

The Monarchy of the Ternary in Union Versus the Monomachia of the Dyad in Confusion by Gerhard Dorn

TRANSLATED BY DANIEL WILLENS

Introduction

LITTLE IS KNOWN with any certainty about Gerhard Dorn, a Belgian follower of Paracelsus who flourished towards the end of the sixteenth century.[1] The fact that his works published during the late 1570s were printed in Basle suggests that he was living in Switzerland at that time, presumably connected with the university and studying under Adam von Bodenstein, Paracelsus' "closest disciple."[2] In the 1680s his books were appearing in Frankfurt, implying a change of residence. He evidently knew Michael Toxites, one of the editors of Paracelsus' works.[3]

Dorn describes himself as an "intermediary and translator-physician in the Germanic language" to Prince Francis de Valois, the brother of the ill-starred King Henry III. It is not entirely clear what duties Dorn performed as an "intermediary," although they do not seem to have been so numerous as to prevent him from leaving a wealth of alchemical writings behind. In addition to his works which appeared in the *Theatrum Chemicum* of 1602–1661, he also produced a *Dictionarium Paracelsi* (Frankfurt, 1583); *Chymisticum artificium naturae, theoricum et Practicum . . . liber plane philosophicus* (1568); *Artificii chymistici physici, metaphysici, secunda pars et tertia . . . accessit etiam tertiade parti, de praeparationibus metallicis in utroque lapidis philosophorum opere maiore minoreque* (1569); *Congeries paracelsicae chemicae de transmutationibus metallorum. ex omnibus quae de his ab ipso scripta reperire licuit hactenus Accessit genealogia Mineralium atque metallorum omnium* (Frankfurt, 1581). Dorn also edited and illustrated a collection of classical, medieval and Islamic alchemical works entitled *Trevisanus: De chymico miraculo, quod lapidem philosophiae appellant* (Basle, 1600).[4]

His most important literary activity, however, was probably his editing and translation of the works of Paracelsus into Latin for Peter Perna, an important publisher in Basle.[5] It is believed that his "translations" may have contained much embellishment of his own.[6] The *Aurora thesaurusque philosophorum*, for example, attributed to Paracelsus, first appeared bound with Dorn's *Monarchia*, leading A. E. Waite to suspect its provenance, and some modern scholars are of the opinion that *De Occulta Philosophia*, first published in Huser's edition of Paracelsus' *Opera, Buecher und Schrifften* (Basle, 1589–90), may have been entirely the work of Dorn.[7]

The present work, as noted above, first appeared in Latin, bound with Paracelsus' *Aurora*, in 1577. An edition in the French language was published the same year for the benefit of Dorn's patron. It is not clear in which tongue the book was originally composed.

The *Monarchia* is an attempt to distill all the knowledge of the arts and sciences into a series of geometrical figures, not unlike John Dee's *Monas hieroglyphica*, which was published in Antwerp in 1564. Dorn was clearly influenced by Dee, whose *monas* glyph appeared on the frontispiece of his *Chymisticum artificium*.

Although Dorn heaps scorn on those who would "rank themselves with pagans,"[8] he draws very freely from non-Christian sources: Pythagorean, Platonic, and kabbalistic references abound. The very premise of the work, that the genesis and nature of the cosmos is susceptible to numerical and geometrical exegesis, is of course quintessentially Pythagorean, as is the tacit identification of odd and even numbers as being "male" and "female," and hence having generative and potentially destabilizing functions.

Dorn describes in cryptic terms the generation of the Platonic solids. For example, "One says to Three, / Receive Four: / And henceforth / Let us live in peace" refers to the tetrahedral pyramid, the simplest three dimensional object, which consists of four equilateral triangles arranged to form a single solid object with four faces and six edges. In the Platonic cosmology, this solid, elemental "fire," forms one of the basic building blocks of all matter.

The two "enigmas" which Dorn advances bear a superficial resemblance to the kabbalistic *otz chaim*, or "Tree of Life." The letters which he uses on these figures are not defined in the text, and it is possible that he may have been assuming a familiarity on the part of the reader with Raymond Lull's *Ars Demonstrativa* and *Ars Brevis*, in which letters of the Latin alphabet are used to signify open categories which stand in fixed, logical relationship, a concept which Lull himself may have derived from the sephirotic speculations of the Spanish kabbalists of his own era.[9]

Another kabbalistic allusion might be found in "One says to Ten, / Live in Six: / Don't hazard Five . . ." On the "Tree of Life," there is a "Pillar of Equilibrium" running from the first and highest sephirah, Kether, the Crown, to the tenth sephirah, Malkuth, the Kingdom. In Christian Kabbalah, the sixth sephirah, Tipheret, Beauty, which is located in the exact center of this column, is identified with Christ, suggesting that Six is the soteriological mediator which elevates the base matter of Ten towards the wellspring of the primal Monad. The fifth sephirah, Gevurah, Strength or Power, lies on the "Pillar of Severity" and has no connecting channel to the tenth sephirah.

Conspicuously absent are overt references to Christian dogma. Despite the prominence of the Ternary, it is identified only with alchemical Mercury, Sulphur and Salt, and never with the Christian Trinity. Also missing are the hieroglyphic images of green lions, androgynes, ouroborean serpents, etc., so beloved of students of alchemy. This is due to the Paracelsian approach to the art, which tended to express itself much more "scientifically," in the modern sense. Another noteworthy absence is the lack of color transformation symbolism, so important to modern followers of "Fulcanelli" and R. A. Schwaller de Lubicz. This is certainly due to the work's theoretical orientation towards cosmogenesis through number and geometry as opposed to any attempt to provide a handbook for practical laboratory work.

The structure of the work reflects the number symbolism of its text. It falls into three basic sections: an "arguement" in verse, a dedicatory epistle in prose, and then the exposition in verse. The "arguement" is itself divided into three stanzas, and the main body of exposition moves through three phases: the generation of a series of figures which recapitulate the evolution from the monad into the "confusion of the multitude," an "enigma" and commentary which set out the "anatomy which is the friend of Life," and, finally, an "enigma" and commentary which expose the "basis of errors" in all the arts and sciences. The verse sections rhyme: ABAB for the "arguement" and the first section of the exposition, but changing to AABB for the "enigmas." Given the emphasis on the disruptive nature of the dyad, this translation attempts to retain the original lineation so as to permit the reading of alternate lines; much of the text remains comprehensible when read in this fashion. Similarly, the original punctuation and use of the ampersand has been closely followed. No attempt has been made to retain the original rhyme-scheme or meter.

This translation is based on the facsimile of the 1577 edition published by Gutenberg Reprint, Jugain, Alençon, France, 1981.

—DANIEL WILLENS

The Monarchy of the Ternary in Union, Versus the Monomachia[10] of the Dyad in Confusion:

By Gerhard Dorn, Doctor Physician

1577

Arguement:

Great is the grace that God communicates
to His children who love and fear Him:
Following the true & only unique imprint,
are vigilant, benign & learn
To understand Him in His extreme goodness
(without disguising His majesty in anything)
To be the center & supreme wisdom
where every knowledge of man is stopped.

Whatever leaves the center, so divine,
   is intoxicated by the cursed beverage
that falsehood brews and serves for wine
   to whomever follows it, & holds its edict.
Off the path, lost in vagrant error,
   Like the drunk, brutal and bestial,
Knowing neither God nor self, self-ensnared
   In the labyrinth of misfortune he has prepared.

Christians, why do you rank yourself with Pagans?
  Ethnic people, & full of rage:
All enemies of God, of Christians,
  Among whom there is nary a sage.
How then can you learn
  That which they themselves never knew?
Is it well to render one's self in Hell
  Amongst them, who died in darkness?

II

To the most illustrious, most high & most powerful Prince, Francis of Valois, Son of France & only brother of the king, Duke of Anjou, Bourges, Alençon, Touraine, &c.

Most illustrious & most magnanimous Prince, since it pleases Your Highness to employ me in your service as intermediary and translator-physician in the Germanic language, to translate the medical works of the late Dr. Theophrastus Paracelsus, a man of great erudition, I have started with his *Aurora, Treasure of the Philosophers, & Anatomy of the Living Body*, to which I would like to add my *Monarchy of the Ternary in Unity*, by which I approve the foundations of the said Paracelsus, my preceptor in medicine & philosophy, against which it is impossible to resist, as learned as the common man thinks himself to be. And so that Your Highness does not think that these are things of little value, as certain Academicians, our enemies, might presume; I offer to defend them by pen & press, against all who would wish to oppose them, by writings equally public, that in that place everyone can judge what is right. This science[11] is so high & worthy, that no other can be compared to it. But seeing that the work is very great, I could not achieve it so soon, & so that Your Highness, who employs me daily at your service, (to whom I myself and my labors are dedicated), can see it, it seemed very reasonable to me to send a small commencement of the said work. I supplicate Your Highness to deign to receive it in pleasure: for it is the true aim of all medicine, the most ancient that has ever been practiced, & that by very few wise & holy persons. This having been long hidden, as though buried, until the present, God wished it to be resuscitated by the said late Theophrastus Paracelsus. As for the rest, most illustrious Prince, I pray God that He wishes to keep Your Highness in His holy protection & health. Given at Basle this 1st day of September, 1577,

Of Your Highness,

The humble servant,

Gerhard Dorn

BRIEF DISCOURSE

ON THE MONARCHY OF THE TER-

nary in Unity, versus the Single Combat

of the Dyad confused in the multitude.

MONAD

Always self-resembling,
God reposes in a point.[12]

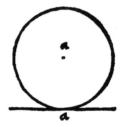

DYAD

The Devil is variable,
And has no repose.[13]

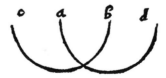

TERNARY

The semblance of God,
  Being peaceful in man,
Was troubled in that place
  By the hurtful serpent.

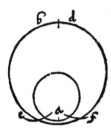

The apple of knowledge[14]
  Disrupted the Monarchy,
Wounded conscience,
  By its Single Combat.[15]

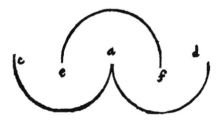

The great mercy
    Of God the Creator,
Of man re-strings itself,
    Like a true zealot.[16]

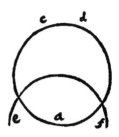

The most worthy Ternary,
    The lost Ternary,
By Holy medicine
    Restored in its virtue.

Enigma, in which is contained all the goal, secret, basis
& perfection of all knowledge.

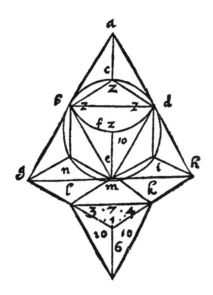

One says to Ten,
   Live in Six:
Don't hazard Five,
   Put yourself on guard:
The apple of knowledge
   Provides ignorance
To the soul, to the body: in sum,
   Every abundance of evil.

Every ailment thus,
  Comes from the bitter apple:
Whatever other origin,
  Has but vice for its source,
As much for the body, as the soul
  Caused corruption:
That little morsel of the First
  Lady placed us into the subjection
Of the cursed Dyad.[17]
  But the most holy Unity,
By means of the Ternary,
  Sets us free.
It is the fountain of Life,
  Which can give us health,
When the Dyad, from envy,
  Plants ailments:
What do we seek in Four,
  The child of Two, & the fruit,
Other than to revel
  In all that destroys us.
May Two the beast
  Prepare no evil for you,
Stealing cure
  From your house.
Conceived before long,
  Ten was deceived.
One replies to him,
  For heretic,
Return to Three,
  The King of Kings.
Tell him that Four
  Does not wish to destroy,
Thus re-invest it,
  Re-instate it in Six:

Of Three, face him
  To shine his face,[18]
Triple and unique,
  So magnificent.
That was done
  By a beautiful stroke.[19]
One says to Three,
  Receive Four:
And henceforth
  Let us live in peace.

Whoever will understand these verses,
  He will win his trial,[20]
Where the basis of the work is,
  Which discovers Medicine:
Separate the true from the false,
  And favor virtue over every vice.
That which anatomy perfects,
  Leading the cause to its effect.
And that which falsifies everything
  Never verifies anything.
Here is the end of the Anatomy,
  Which is the friend of our life.

Enigma, which contains all the falsity of arts & science,
with the basis of errors.

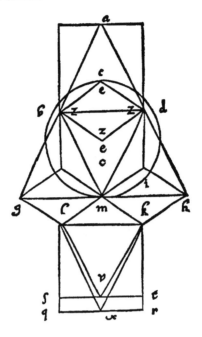

By finesse, Two
    Addresses itself to Five:
Says as a bluff,
    To be foolish
To believe in One
    More than the generality.[21]
It is necessary to try
    Without taking fright,
And to know everything
    In order to have everything,
And to best be able
    To see the world.

To revenge himself,
  Five did eat
The dearly sold
  Forbidden bread.
Thus Ten died,
  As it appeared.
This Two does not cease
  To oppose the body,
Torment & kill it.
  The fallen soul
Is become of this Two
  A hideous monster.[22]
He who will resolve this enigma
  Will extract the powder
From the confused multitude:
  Shall follow the simple, flee the ruse
Of the Squared Duality,
  Prepared of vice and misfortune.
In which there is but despair
  Of amendment, as one can see.
Here is the end of the Anatomy
  Which is the enemy of Life.

Notes

1. Charles Nicholl, *The Chemical Theatre* (London: Routledge & Kegan Paul, 1980), 5.

2. Mark Haeffner, *The Dictionary of Alchemy: From Maria Prophetissa to Isaac Newton* (London: Aquarian Press, 1991), 104.

3. *Ibid.*

4. *Ibid.*

5. *Ibid.*

6. Allen G. Debus, *The English Paracelsians* (New York: Franklin Watts, Inc., 1966), 44.

7. Arthur Edward Waite, *The Hermetic and Alchemical Writings of Paracelsus*, I (Berkeley: Shambhala, 1976), 48.

8. Perhaps an overreaction to a contemplated political alliance between France and Ottoman Turkey.

9. Lull's system is too complex to cover here, but the interested reader is refered to *The Selected Works of Raymon Lull*, translated and edited by Anthony Bonner (Princeton: Princeton University Press, 1985) and Dame Frances A. Yates' *Lull & Bruno: Collected Essays* (London: Routledge & Kegan Paul, 1982).

10. Dorn seems to have coined this word from the Greek *mono*= "one, single" and *machia*= "combat, struggle," hence, "single combat." The "single combat" of the dyad is in opposition to the "single rule" of the ternary.

11. Fr. *science*="knowledge."

12. Compare this image with the Hermetic/Platonic aphorism which Rabelais (*circa* 1492–1553) gives in his *Cinquiesme Livre*: "cette sphere intellectuelle de laquelle en tous lieux est le centre et n'a en lieu aucun circonference, que nous appelons Dieu": "that intellectual sphere which has its center everywhere and its circumference nowhere, which we call God." This image also appears in Cusanus and the Scholastics.

13. There is a pun here in French on the double meaning of "point": in addition to its geometrical meaning, "point" is also a negative meaning "none at all."

14. "*Science*." The identification of the "fruit of the tree of knowledge" with an apple suggests a connection with the myth of Eris, or Discordia, who

creates dissension amongst the gods by engraving a golden apple "To the most beautiful."

15. *Monomachia.*

16. The punctuation and syntax of this passage are problematical. Without the first comma, it could be paraphrased "The mercy of God, who created man, restrings itself." With the comma, it might be paraphrased "God the creator's mercy restrings itself out of man," in the sense that man is the material out of which the strings are made! The expression translated as "restring" is also of note: *se recorder* is a reflexive verb based on the noun *corde*, which can mean the "string" of a musical instrument, a rope, or, more relevant in this context, a chord in the geometrical sense: a line segment connecting the ends of an arc on a circle. Why God's mercy doubling a chord upon itself makes it a zealot probably has more to do with rhyme than metaphysics.

17. Irreconcilable differences in French and English grammar make it necessary to deviate from the practise of translating line-by-line at this point. For the benefit of those who might wish to hunt for hidden meanings by reading alternate lines, etc., the original versification reads: "Ce morcellet de la Dame / Premiere, en subiection / Nous mit du maudit Binaire."

18. "Face," not "visage." The allusion is to gem cutting. *Face* can also mean "face" in the English sense, perhaps in this case a reference to the Macroprosopus of kabbalistic lore. The gemological imagery also suggests the Platonic solids.

19. Or "treatment." Dorn is implying a set of concrete operations on a material.

20. *Proces* means "trial" in the legal sense, although in the period that Dorn was writing, it might also have retained the connotation of "process" in the English sense of the word.

21. This translation accurately portrays the enigmatic nature of the original. Given that the work is dedicated to a member of the royal family, it is difficult not to suspect that this passage has political overtones.

22. Or, perhaps, "is shown to be hideous."

Imago Magia, Virgin Mother of Eternity: Imagination and Phantasy in the Philosophy of Jacob Boehme

Hugh Urban

FOR MOST contemporary Westerners, the term "imagination" is equated with "fantasy," "day-dream," illusion, and even madness or drug-induced hallucination. It is generally considered to be an "unreal" product of the subjective human mind, in opposition to the "real" world of materialism and scientific fact. Today, at best, imagination might be identified with artistic inspiration or poetic fancy; at worst, it is relegated to the domain of psychosis, schizophrenia, and the uncontrolled fantasies of the unconscious. In any event, it no longer has any significant place in the cold, intellectual universe of modern science and technology.

It is indeed ironic that just a few centuries ago, the concept of the Imagination held a much higher and more profound position in the Western tradition. Some of the most influential medieval and Renaissance thinkers[1] even considered the Imagination to be divine cosmogonic power—the creative power of God himself. In fact, such great Christian mystical philosophers as Jacob Boehme (1575–1624) conceived a vast metaphysical system centering around the concept of the "Imagination." Amidst the growing triumphs of science, physics, rationalism and empiricism, Boehme envisioned a universe in which Imagination occupied a more important place than matter, more important even than reason itself. For Boehme, Imagination is not merely the subjective faculty of dreamy illusion; it is in fact a cosmogonic power, the creative energy of God which conceives and manifests the universe. And, simultaneously, this Imagination is a divine power lying within the human heart, the Image of God in man, bearing the power to re-create man in imitation of this Divine model.

As such, Boehme carefully distinguishes this higher Imagination from the lower, human faculty of *phantasia*. The latter is only the deceptive illusion of the human mind or ego, and in fact a dangerous delusion which entices the soul away from God toward its own selfish desires. What most contemporary Westerners now call "imagination" is not Imagination in the true sense, but only the day-dream world of fantasy and reverie—what Paracelsus had called the "cornerstone of lunacy,"[2] or what Boehme called "the dark realm of fantasy, which is constituted by the fallen angels."[3] Fantasy is but the deluded realm of our own ignorance, veiled from the divine.[4]

In contrast to this deluding and destructive power of *phantasia*, *Imaginatio* is the will of God himself. *Imaginatio* (or sometimes *Einbildung*) is none other than the divine cosmogonic power which "imagines" the created universe in its ideal form; it is the Divine *Magia*, the magical creativity, which weaves the fabric of the cosmos, spinning the web of time and space out of the ineffable, Absolute Reality: "For the beginning of all being is nothing else than an imagination of the *Ungrund*, whereby it introduces itself through its own desire in an imagination and sets itself into images."[5] Franz von Baader, a later student of Boehme, suggests that the concept of *Imago Magia* is in fact closely related to the Indian doctrine of *Maya*;[6] it is the creative power of God, the power of the divine illusion, which at once veils and reveals, conceals and discloses the divinity hidden within the realm of forms and multiplicity. It is the power of transformation—of a divine *alchemy*.

In himself, in his own pure and perfect essence, God is utterly imageless and unimaginable; he is an infinite Will, having no distinction, no opposition, and therefore no conceivable determinations—a "groundless Abyss," the *Ungrund* or *Ewige Nicht:* "Within the groundlessness [the 'Non-Being'] there is nothing but eternal tranquility, an eternal rest without beginning. . . . It has no origin, but conceives itself within itself."[7] However, this Ineffable Abyss eternally desires to manifest itself, to objectify and view itself outside itself; the Godhead seeks to know itself: "If everything were only One that One could not become manifest to itself."[8]

Therefore, in its desire to know itself, this Will eternally begets its own image in the "Mirror" of its own self-consciousness, the mirror of its Wisdom (Sophia, *Weisheit*): "Divine Wisdom is the mirror wherein God eternally sees Himself, He being that mirror Himself."[9] This Mirror of Wisdom is the beginning of all manifestation, and therefore also the essence of the Divine Imagination.[10] However, in Boehme's complicated and often convoluted descriptions, this Divine Wisdom appears in three different forms, in three stages of the emanation of the universe, corresponding to the three basic levels of the cosmic hierarchy.[11] Often, these three forms are referred to as: 1) Eternal Imagination or the Infinite Mother in the divine realm; 2) the Virgin Sophia in the intermediary or celestial realm; and 3) Eternal Nature in the material realm.[12] But in all cases she is intimately associated with the power of Imagination. For none can grasp the ineffable Absolute Reality save its own Magical Imagination: "It can be represented by no conceivable, creaturely image … but rather only by the divine Imagination, as the first, inner ground of *Magia*."[13]

In her first and most profound aspect, Wisdom is the "empty" Mirror of God's self-consciousness, which precedes all determination whatever, before even the Holy Trinity Itself. Within this Mirror, the Will of the Abyss casts its own Image, to reflect upon and know itself;[14] the Will "imagines" within itself, begetting its own mirrored likeness: "The Will creates in its Imagination spirit only and becomes pregnant with the eternal knowing of the *Ungrund*."[15] Within the womb of the Virgin Sophia, the *Ungrund* projects Itself as a "seed" and so begets the second person of the Holy Trinity, the Son or Logos. Within Wisdom, the "empty mirror of consciousness," eternal subject conceives its own object, which is the *Image* and Word of God.[16] In begetting the Son, the Will of the Abyss becomes the Father of the Trinity; the Son, conceived in the womb of Wisdom, subsequently returns the love, knowledge, and reflected Image of the Father; and the bond of union between Father and Son is the Holy Spirit, as the harmony and bliss which flows between them. Thus does the Godhead know and love Itself in Itself—and in the eternal ground this knowing is Divine Wisdom and Imagination herself. Within her mirroring womb, the Divine Abyss reveals itself in its threefold spirit: as the radiating Will (the Father), as the reflected Image of the "Love, center or heart" (the Son), and as the unifying "power issuing from the Will and Love" (the Spirit).[17]

While God knows Himself *in* Himself (*ad intra*) in the Trinity, this knowledge is still in a sense incomplete and "abstract"; God does not yet know himself *outside of* himself, that is, as other than himself (*ad extra*). He is like a pure Mind, which knows its thought, but which does not yet know its own visible form; he still requires a *body*, which would reveal his exterior as well as his interior image. Thus, God must manifest himself in a mode external to the Trinity—and this is the second aspect of Boehme's Divine Wisdom. In this form, Wisdom is not only the Mirror of the *Ungrund*, but now becomes the reflected image of the Trinity as a whole, the "full" Mirror which manifests the form of God outside of Him.[18] As Alexandre Koyre explains, the Holy Trinity requires a "fourth"—not of course a fourth person of the Trinity, but a person outside the Trinity, which reflects its Image a*d extra*: "to realize itself," the Triad must have a "real object, a 'fourth term,' which it could oppose to itself in order to know itself."[19]

This "fourth" term is Wisdom in her role as the external reflection of the Trinity, the "radiance" which shines from the Divine Mirror. For Boehme, she now becomes the "*body*" of God himself, the outer form which surrounds the inner Unity of the Trinity as its "temple," "house," or "matrix." She is God's Imagination or Magical "Body," with which he "clothes" himself. As the "outflown Word of the Divine Power," Wisdom is the passive "subject and resemblance of the infinite Unity" wherein "the Holy Ghost forms and models" all things.[20]

It is through this Body of Wisdom that God will create and *imagine* the universe itself. Herein the Spirit conceives the image of the universe in its ideal form, "imagining" the plan of creation within his own mind, in its perfect state. The Body of Wisdom is, then, the corpus of divine images or Platonic Ideas, the imaginal archetypes which precede the creation of the material cosmos: "She is the Divine Chaos, wherein all things lie, a Divine Imagination, in which the Ideas of Angels and Souls have been since Eternity."[21] As Koyre writes,

> In the Mirror of Divine Wisdom, the Divine Will . . . "traces" the "plan" . . . of its creative action; the Divine Imagination incarnates its thought in forms and figures. . . . The Great Artist has conceived His work; He reflects . . . and knows Himself in it.[22]

In this sense, the Body of Wisdom constitutes an entire plane of existence, the intermediary plane of Idea-Images which lies between God and the world, between pure spirit and matter. Everything that God creates in the physical cosmos has an archetypal *form* in this Celestial or Imaginal world of the Divine Sophia, as an "image of the eternal image."[23] It constitutes the divine Paradise or primordial state of Pure Creation, in its spiritual and Edenic condition. According to Henry Corbin, this Intermediary Plane is the *mundus archetypus imaginalis*, the Imaginal realm, a dimension which lies betwixt heaven and earth, but which also participates in both. It is the realm of *transformation* and transition, transmuting spirits into bodies and bodies into spirit.[24]

Thus, the entire hierarchy of the cosmos, from its height to its base, is constructed of Divine Imagination and Magical Wisdom; all that is other than the Absolute Reality Itself is but the Imaginal creation of the One Will, and all existence descends in progressively less real, more Imaginary levels of being. At the bottom of the cosmic hierarchy, God's Imagination solidifies or crystallizes into concrete form—the visible structure of the physical world. This material realm, the realm of our own mortal existence, represents the third aspect of the Virgin Wisdom. The Imaginal or Ideal realm now becomes realized in physical, tangible form. In a sense, the Imaginal plane represents the "subtle" or "Celestial Body" of God, which is yet immaterial, while our ordinary world represents the "physical body" of God, now become visible and sensible. This material world is the Virgin Wisdom as Eternal Nature, the realization of Divine Imagination in the natural cosmos. In Eternal Nature, God completes his creative process in its "final objectivation," in which "He sees Himself mirrored as He really is." As Howard Brinton writes, "This is Wisdom in her third capacity. The second mirror of Wisdom showed God his possibilities, the third showed Him His actualities."[25] As embodied Wisdom, Nature now carries out the plan of creation which had existed ideally in the Imaginal Realm; it executes the commands of the Son and Spirit, that is, the creative Word of God, according to the Idea-Images of Divine Wisdom. Following the pattern of the Word, "Nature is like a carpenter, who builds a House which the mind figured . . . before in itself."[26]

Eternal Nature acts through seven fundamental "principles" or qualities, seven different aspects of the Divine Will embodied in the cosmos. These seven constitute an ascending scale in Nature, rising from matter to spirit, and inversely reflecting the descent of the creative emanation from God. Beginning in the dark ternary of contraction, expansion and motion, Nature evolves out of a chaotic, dynamic "wheel of anguish"; as Nature evolves into the fourth principle or "flash," however, this dark ternary is transformed into a higher, light ternary, composed of the spiritual principles of divine Love, Speech, and the Kingdom of Heaven.[27] Now, this final, seventh Principle is again associated with the Virgin Wisdom and the Divine Imagination: for the seventh is the summation and consummation of the other six Principles, and so represents the totality of Eternal Nature as embodied Wisdom or Incarnate Imagination: "The Seventh Principle is the corporeal comprehension of the other qualities. It is *Essential Wisdom* or *the* Body of God."[28]

Thereby, the Creative Process which manifests the Absolute to Itself is now complete; in the material world, the *Ungrund* knows and loves itself fully, in all its infinite possibilities and forms. For Boehme, the Imaginal power of Wisdom is both the beginning and the end of this process of divine self-consciousness. She is both the "Mother" or Source and the "Daughter" of the Trinity, both the creatrice of the universe and the created result. As the Mother, she is the receptive and empty Mirror which receives the light of the Divine Will and gives birth to all this Imaginal existence. However, as the Daughter, she is herself the radiance, the "utterance" and finally the material crystallization of God, that is, the expression of the Trinity which manifests its glory. She is like the eye of God whereby he sees, but also like the eye of his reflection in a mirror, whereby he sees himself seeing—"the eternal beginning and end by which the spirit sees what is in eternity and what it might reveal therein."[29]

However, if the Imagination is a creative power of divine revelation, it also bears the possibility of being misused, of being turned toward the powers of evil, darkness, and concealment. Indeed, Boehme attributes the fall of the rebel Angel Lucifer himself to a perversion of imagination. Originally an angel, Lucifer was intended to "put his imagination into the light of God," to "receive the Divine substantiality in his Imagination," and to aid the Divine Imagination in the process of creation;[30] but he tried to supplant it with his own selfish, proud will and imagination. He desired to be God himself and to replace the divine image with his own vain idol. Instead of aiding God's imagination in creation, he desired to "bring into form his own thoughts," to imagine "his own effects and figurations."[31] Thus, turned away from God, he became an enemy of God, and his imagination was perverted into the delusion of *phantasia*. This is the dark and hellish world, the world of the ego's own self-deception—"the realm of illusion"[32]—which vainly pursues its own desires in opposition to the Will of the Divine Imagination.

In the vast metaphysical system of Jacob Boehme, everything that occurs in the Divinity and in the macrocosm has a parallel reflection in the human realm, in the microcosmic spirit of man. The human being himself is a mirror of the created universe, and each part of his body is an "image and analogue of the world."[33] More profoundly, however, man is also the mirror-image of God himself, God's representative on earth, who cognizes, comprehends, and "translates" the signatures or symbols in the Book of Creation.[34] In either case, man contains within himself the power of Magical Wisdom and Imagination, which is manifest in both the Divinity and the created world. In fact, the very origin of humanity lies in the Virgin Sophia herself. Within the Divine Imagination, man has eternally existed, not in his manifest form, but rather as an Idea and Image of God, as the reflection of the Word in the Mirror of Wisdom. "Like a shadow stood the image" of man in the Divine Mind, "wherein God knew all things from eternity, in the mirror of His Wisdom."[35] From this ideal state, Adam was manifestly created by the Son, the Word of God, in conjunction with Sophia, the Divine Mirror of Wisdom. He proceeded from the "eternal *Magia*" of the Virgin, as a "perfect symbol of God" and a true union of the Word and Wisdom:

> God created him in His likeness.... In the Ground of the soul ... moved the ... Word of God, together with the Eternal *Idea*, which was known from eternity in the Divine Wisdom, as a ... Form of the Divine Imagination.[36]

In his primordial nature, Adam was a perfect union of the two fundamental aspects of the Divinity—a wedding of the masculine Word and the feminine Sophia: "Adam was man and wife in one individuality, a pure virginal power."[37] Thus, Boehme calls Adam an "androgyne" or "masculine virgin" (*mannliche Jungfrau*), neither male nor female, but rather one whole and perfect being without duality. In fact, before the fall, man carried his feminine counterpart within himself, as an intimate part of his nature; the Virgin Sophia herself originally dwelt within him, and was even in a sense "incarnate" in his form. She was his eternal "consort" or "bride," and yet really his own true Self—his celestial ego. As the image of the Archetypal or Imaginal world as a whole, the Virgin Sophia contains within herself the eternal Image and essence of Man:

> Adam was an androgyne . . . in his celestial body . . . he possessed the
> plenitude of magic power . . . of the eternal feminine . . . or Divine
> Wisdom . . . she was incarnate in Adam as his celestial companion.[38]

Indeed, in his primordial condition, with his immaterial, magical body, Adam did not need to procreate by physical sexual means; to beget offspring, he need only use his imagination or magical power, and unite with his celestial companion Sophia. Thereby, he united in magic union with his own eternal image or ideal self in the Imaginal realm. As Koyre summarizes,

> To procreate . . . he had to *imagine in her*, realize her within himself and
> . . . unite with her. The Eternal Virgin . . . is none other than the Image
> (*Vorbild*) of Adam in God . . . Wisdom is the ideal image of the world
> which contains the images of all beings. . . . By uniting with Wisdom
> . . . Adam united with his own ideal self.[39]

Thus, in its original and true function, the Imagination was for Man the perfect means of self-realization and self-integration.

Again, however, the Imagination is always a power which can be misused, misdirected, and perverted into egotism and sin. Like Lucifer before him, Adam turned his Imagination and desire away from God and the Divine Images, to imagine within his own mind, to desire his own image in place of God's. However, in Boehme's complex interpretation of Genesis, this fall of man away from God happens in several successive stages; and in each stage, the fall of man is associated with a misuse of his imagination. First, before the creation of Eve, man descended from his celestial and eternal state to his terrestrial and temporal existence. For Boehme this is represented by Adam's sleep, signifying ignorance and forgetfulness of his true nature. Man was in fact deluded by the power of *Magic*, and so descended into the dream-world of earthly life. Now "a victim of *Magic*" and the sleep of ignorance, he was "conquered by the terrestrial realm."[40] At the same time, man also lost his eternal companion and counterpart, his virgin bride Sophia; he fell to the earth, while she ascended into the upper heavens. Adam "fell asleep in the angelic world and awoke to the external world," however, "the celestial Virgin went into the celestial ether."[41]

Separated from his Heavenly Companion and own true Self, Adam became divided within and externalized to himself. When he awoke, he found that his immortal spiritual corpus had become a mortal and corruptible shell—"his celestial body became flesh and blood."[42] Moreover, he found that his original unity and androgyny was destroyed; he was no longer one simple being, but was severed into male and female—that is to say, the woman Eve had been extracted from his rib. His counterpart and bride was no longer within himself and above him, but rather outside of himself and beneath him. Nevertheless, Adam still desired to unite with his bride through his imagination. Just as he had "imagined" into and desired the Virgin Sophia in his primordial state, so too did Adam "imagine" into and desire Eve in their terrestrial state. But now their imagination was no longer turned upward toward the divine, but instead downward toward the earth, toward their own bestial, selfish lust:

> When Adam awoke from his sleep, he saw Eve by his side. He *imagined* into her (fell in love with her). . . . Eve likewise put her imagination into Adam, and each ignited the desire of the other. . . Has not the eternal image become an animal?[43]

Thus, instead of uniting man with his celestial archetype, the imagination was perverted into uniting man with the earth and flesh.

Of course, the Fall of Man, in the traditional sense of the term, had not yet occurred at this point. The true Fall came about only after man had descended to the terrestrial plane, and after Eve had been separated from Adam. Only then could the devil have tempted them with his dark power of imagination or *phantasia*, and deceived them into disobeying the Divine Will. Lucifer implanted his own corrupt imagination into the human soul, and sowed the seed of evil and pride:

"The Devil introduced his poisonous imagination into the human quality. Therefrom resulted the ardent desire to live in self-will."[44] And, simultaneously, Lucifer himself crept into, transformed and "poisoned the serpent" with his "imagination." Through his evil power of phantasy, the Devil was able to weave a web of cunning and lies, and so deceive the woman Eve, by "making illusions as his own god."[45]

The sin of Adam and Eve, in the traditional Christian account, is that of disobedience, pride and desiring to be like God; however, in Boehme's interpretation, it is also a sin of "imagination," that is, of "changing their imagination."[46] By eating the fruit of knowledge, Adam and Eve turned their imagination and desire away from God, toward themselves and their own "self-knowledge." They desired their own images in place of God's; and they desired the illusory images of earth to the eternal Images of Heaven: "he lusted after vanity and brought his imagination into the earth."[47] Thus, by "imagining" or desiring themselves and the earth, Adam and Eve *became* selfish and earthly. They ceased to know or seek God, but instead came to "seek after their imaginary self, that they may exalt themselves."[48] They ceased to know the celestial realm of Imagination, but instead knew only the illusory, "imaginary" terrestrial realm, which is "only like a smoke or a fog."[49] By corrupting his power of imagination into a selfish *phantasia*, man simultaneously corrupted his soul as the image of God, and thence became an image of his own self and his own dark dreams: "he imagined therein, and was imprisoned in his imagination—powerless and weak...he fell victim to magic, and his glory was lost."[50]

However, if the image and imagination of man have been distorted by the Fall, they have not yet been completely destroyed. And if man has separated himself from the Divine Word and the Virgin Sophia, he has still not entirely lost the mercy and compassion of God, or the presence of the divinity within. First of all, immediately after the fall, God spoke his Word into Eve, implanting within her the seed of the future Savior. Thus, the same woman who was divided from the original unity of man, the same woman who caused him to fall, became a manifestation of the Divine Wisdom, Sophia herself;[51] she became a reflection of the Divine Virgin Imagination, which bore the seed of the coming Messiah. Second, throughout the later history of mankind, as recorded in the Old Testament, God revealed images, signs, and prophecies of the future redemption. In all the rituals, symbols, and visions of the Old Covenant, "the Divine Imagination saw through" and prefigured the future Incarnation of the Son:[52] "The Word of promise was within the Covenant . . . God conceived of a symbol . . . by means of the Imagination."[53]

Ultimately, however, both the Divine Word and Imagination have been newly revealed and manifest through the incarnation of Jesus Christ. What existed symbolically, through the figures of Imagination in the Old Testament, has now become flesh, through the physical manifestation of the Divine Imagination in the world of men. For Boehme, the incarnation itself is a product of God's Imagination and Wisdom, which in fact closely mirrors the eternal begetting of the Son in the Trinity. For the Divine Wisdom herself has descended and become manifest in the person of the Virgin Mary, the Mother of God. "The soul of Mary took hold of the Celestial Virgin," which clothed her with "a pure garment of the holy element."[54] Thus, Boehme writes,

> The immaculate Virgin in whom God was born is before God and an Eternal Virgin. She was . . . before heaven and earth were created; this Virgin was incorporated in Mary, and made her a new being.[55]

As in the eternal begetting of the Trinity, the Heavenly Father "imagined" into the womb of the Virgin, and so conceived the image of the Son in physical form: "As God bears his Son . . . Mary bore Jesus . . . This comes about through Imagination, by which the Will acquires substance by uniting with the objective Idea."[56] Just as the Holy Spirit imagines in the Mirror of the Eternal Virgin Sophia, so does he again imagine in the womb of the Virgin Mary, to beget the Word.

The incarnate Christ is none other than the "Second Adam," the new primordial Man, though in his true state of perfection as the

Image of God. Like Adam, he is an "androgyne," a union of the male and female principles, and a "masculine Virgin"; and he too is intimately associated with the Virgin Wisdom, the Divine Imagination. In the person of Christ, the Eternal Word and the Heavenly Sophia come together once more, in the original state of unity lost by Adam. Thus, the Heavenly Wisdom and Imagination is not only manifest in Mary, but also, through her, in the Son: in this Second Adam, or *männliche Jungfrau*, the "Divine Wisdom is newly incarnate."[57]

Christ reveals to mankind the perfect way to salvation. Through his own life, teachings, suffering, and death, he shows the way of denying the sinful human self, of passing through death, and of re-ascending to Heaven. To follow Christ the human soul must, first of all, turn its Imagination away from the false illusions of the world and the self, and back towards God. By "Imagining" and desiring God, the soul actually partakes of and "eats" God. For Boehme, this is the meaning of true faith:

> Faith is a partaking of the substance of God . . . an introducing of the substance of God into one's soul by means of Imagination . . . thereby the soul becomes clothed in the substance of God.[58]

Ultimately, like Christ, the soul must be made completely free of its own false and "imaginary" selfhood, of the "vanity (selfishness) which the devil introduced into the flesh by his imagination."[59] It is this imaginary or phantastic self which must be crucified in the human soul, and completely purged along with all its selfish dreams and fancies: "We must continually die in Christ and kill the man of sin within us, so that the New Man may live."[60]

This long and difficult process of self-abandonment in imitation of Christ is accomplished through many different spiritual disciplines— asceticism, the practice of virtue, the sacraments, etc.—however, perhaps the most significant and powerful for Boehme is the mystery of prayer. In order truly to pray, the soul must crucify and sacrifice all its own false imaginings and egotistic phantasies, it must renounce its own selfish image, and call upon the image of God, Christ. It must be silent to all of its mind's babbling words, and call upon the One Word, the name of Jesus. "Thus all images (opinions and conceits) die in him, and the soul's life falleth into the only living Word."[61] Symbolically, the Word is the essence and "Spirit" of all the "letters," that is, of the external images and forms of the material world. In prayer, the soul must die to all the "letters" and outward images of the world, and live only to the One Word and name of Jesus:

> There is no way . . . to bring us to union, that we may become One again . . . than to destroy all the images . . . of letters in us . . . not desiring to know . . . save only what God willeth to know in us . . . we immerse . . . the soul's desire merely . . . into the great holy Name of Jehovah or Jesus (the living Word).[62]

Thus, in order truly to pray, to crucify his old ego, and to cleanse himself of all false "imaginings," man must become pure, empty, and receptive to the Spirit of God—he must become a "Virgin." He must regain his original nature as a manifestation of the divine Virgin Wisdom herself, and so reascend to the celestial plane where he and Divine Wisdom were originally united. For it is ultimately only the Virgin Mother and Divine Imagination that can give brith to the Word and Image of God. If man is to conceive this Word and Image within his own heart in prayer, he must be one with this Virgin Wisdom. Man must join himself with his celestial bride, uniting so intimately as to become one being, one androgynic Virgin:

> the inner soul from the eternal Word is married to Sophia . . . she is again transformed into the image which God created in Adam.[63]

> We ought to exist in the same . . . substantiality in eternity wherein exists the Virgin of God, and we must clothe ourselves with the Virgin, for Christ has clothed Himself with her.[64]

When he has perfectly sacrificed his own selfish ego, and perfectly wedded himself to the Virgin Sophia, man is then ready to receive the Word and Son of God within his own heart in prayer. When he has become "Virgin" in his own soul, free of all selfish fantasies, Man can be made the receptacle and bride of the Holy Spirit; and he may, ultimately, become the Virgin "Mother" of Christ the Word himself. That is to say, he may give birth to, and himself be reborn in, the original Image of God in Man: "Out of the same virginity from which Christ was born must we all be born."[65] This is accomplished through the transforming power of Imagination. Man directs all his "will together with the Imagination, into the heart of the Father, into the Word of love"; and God in turn "Imagines" into the human soul, giving birth to His Divine Image (*Vorbild*) in the receptive womb of the heart. "In our Imagination we are impregnated of His Word," for "as the Virgin Mary bore Jesus, the soul unites with the Virgin, Heavenly Wisdom and a Son is born."[66] As Koyre notes,

> The soul ... "imagines into Christ" ... it "reconstructs" itself in the image of Christ. A plastic, magical power, *imaginatio* "casts" man in the form it imagines. It transforms him into this image . . . and this transformation is the incarnation of Christ in man, who becomes . . . the image, incarnation, and expression of God.[67]

In short, the Imagination has the power to transform the one who imagines into that which he imagines.[68] It is the power of *alchemy*, which can transmute matter into spirit, the lead of man into the pure gold of divinity.[69] If the Imagination was directed toward the earth and the ego, making man selfish and mortal, it can also be re-directed toward Christ, making man selfless and immortal. True Imagination is the power to re-integrate the divided nature of man, to re-cast him in his primordial Image, and to return him to his own celestial origin, in perfect union with the Divine Wisdom and *Magia*. If the soul can crucify and bury all of its false imaginings and selfish fantasies, it may be at last reborn and resurrected from the dead, with Christ, in the true image of God:

> All that God is and all that is in Him, will then appear within *me* (in Man) as . . . an image of the divine world. All powers and virtues of His Eternal Wisdom will be manifest in *me* as His true Image. I shall be the manifestation of the spiritual world and an instrument for the Spirit of God wherein he plays with Himself.[70]

Ultimately, the power of Imagination makes it possible for man to realize his own final end and goal—both in the universe and beyond it. On the one hand, man becomes the instrument of the Divine Imagination in the created world, the mirror of the Eternal Magia in the temporal realm. By conforming to the Divine Will, he regains his original title as the Lord of creation, and becomes in fact a "channel" through which the Divine Magia works in creation. It is in this way that Man brings love, art, religion, wisdom, freedom, and truth into the finite world. United with God, man then "creates as God creates, through the power of Will and Imagination":

> Love is the creative Imagination, which . . . manifests the good. "Imagination makes substance." By living in the Kingdom inwardly, I create it outwardly. I become a channel through which divine light streams into the . . . world.[71]

But finally, on the other hand, the Imagination has the power to take Man beyond all Images, all forms and all imaginations whatever, to the absolute ineffability of the *Ungrund*. It has the potential to realize that particle of the Ultimate which lies within the human heart, to return man to the Absolute Will from which he has sprung. If man can free himself of all illusions of individuality and separateness, he may at last return to the Unity of the Form-less, Image-less Reality. Then, indeed, "he is bound to no form."[72] As Boehme writes,

> Man is then to himself nothing, for he is dead . . . to all things . . . God

is in and through all, and yet . . . nothing can comprehend Him. . . . this will be the state of a person . . . if he entirely surrenders himself to God. Then will his will drop back into the unfathomable Will of God, wherefrom it came in the beginning.[73]

As a whole, from beginning to end, from creation to salvation, the Imagination plays a crucial role in the cosmology of Jacob Boehme. Indeed, its true importance is far greater than we could possibly describe in so short an article; we have here only given a brief sketch of a truly intricate metaphysical doctrine of the Divine Imagination. Nevertheless, even from these few remarks, we can see that the Imagination has a much more profound and powerful significance than is ordinarily acknowledged in modern Western civilization. Far from merely a false and deluding "fantasy," the Divine Imagination is both a cosmological and a soteriological reality; it is the power of transformation, which reveals the Absolute Reality within the illusion of creation, and returns humanity from the illusion of the ego to the reality of God. For Imagination can penetrate into and grasp truths which elude ordinary human reason or perception. As the power of transformation and transition between levels of existence, Imagination partakes of both reality and illusion, Being and nothingness. For Boehme, it is even "superior to discursive reason, for it can grasp the One and the Many simultaneously," while reason can only "isolate and break up" the unity of life.[74]

Thus, without an understanding of these more profound dimensions of the Imagination, modern science and cosmology are missing an essential aspect of the universe and of humanity itself.[75] Unless we comprehend the significance of the Imagination, humanity is doomed to chase after the deceptive illusions of the material world and the finite human ego—without realizing the Divine Image within.

Notes

1. Such as Ficino, Paracelsus, Bruno; cf. Frances Yates, *Giordano Bruno and the Hermetic Tradition* (Chicago: University of Chicago Press, 1964), 103–04, 191–92.

2. Cf. *Schriften, Theophrasts von Hohenheim*. Ausgewahlt und Herausgeben von Hans Kaiser (Leipzig, 1924), 458.

3. *Von der Gnaden-Wahl*, 4.46. Unless otherwise noted, all references to Boehme's works are from the *Samlichte Schriften*, edited by Will-Erich Peuckert and August Faust (Stuttgart: Frommans-Verlag, 1955–61); translations from the *Samlichte Schriften* will be my own.

As Boheme clarifies this distinction, "just as there is a great difference between a false and wicked soul (which imagines in a bestial manner . . . and desires bestial things) and a pious divine soul, wherein the Spirit of God is manifest; so too, the magical imaginations . . . in the astral spirit are different. For a beast dreams according to *fantasy*, and so too does a bestial man" (*Mysterium Magnum*, 67.5).

4. "The Imagination as a creative magical potency which, giving birth to the sensible world, produces the Spirit in forms and colors; the world as *Magia divina*, 'imagined' by the Godhead, that is the ancient doctrine . . . this *Imaginatio* must not be confused with *fantasy* . . . fantasy, unlike Imagination, is an exercise of thought without foundation in nature" (Henry Corbin, *Creative Imagination in the Sufism of Ibn 'Arabi* [Princeton: Princeton University Press, 1969], 179). In order to avoid confusion between these two ideas, Corbin uses the term "Imaginal" to designate the divine power of Imagination.

5. *Von Christi Testamenti*, 1.5. Cf. Howard Brinton, *The Mystic Will* (New York, Macmillan, 1930), 113.

6. *Speculativ Dogmatik. Samlichte Werke*. Anton Lutterbeck, ed. (Scientia Verlag Aalen, 1963), 9, 181. As Lutterbeck summarizes the various meanings and associations of the Imagination, "The concept of *Imaginatio* or *Magia* of J. Boehme corresponds to Sophia among the Hebrews, to the *Idea* of the Greeks, and to *Maya* according to the Indians" 16, 257).

7. *Von der Menschwerdung Jesu Christi*, 21.1.

8. *Mysterium Magnum*, 4.22.

9. *Erste Schutzschrift gegen Balthasar Tilken*, 141.

10. "Magic is the Mother of Eternity, of the being of all beings. . . . It is . . . nothing but a will, and this will is the great mystery of all wonders and secrets, but brings itself by the Imagination . . . into being. It is the original state of Nature. Its desire makes an Imagination" (*Kurtze Erklarung sechs Mystischer Puncte*, 5.1–4).

11. Boehme himself is not always clear in his discussion of these three aspects of Wisdom; we are relying here on the interpretation of Howard Brinton, who has disentangled some of Boehme's confusing descriptions. (*The Mystic Will*, 185ff.)

12. Adam McLean, *The Alchemical Mandala* (Grand Rapids: Phanes Press, 1989), 110.

13. Boehme, quoted in von Baader, *Speculativ Dogmatik*, 81.

14. "Eternal Wisdom . . . resembles an eternal eye without essence. It is the unground, and yet sees all . . . as a mirror which embraces all that appears before it" (*Von sechs theosophischen Puncten*, 1.11).

15. *Nine Texts*, 4.3, in Brinton, *The Mystic Will*, 178.

16. Brinton, *The Mystic Will*, 187.

17. *Mysterium Magnum*, 1.2.

18. "Then the mirror of the eye, which is the Wisdom of the Father and the Son, becomes manifest; Wisdom stands before the Spirit of God, who manifests the Unground within it. . . . Wisdom is that which . . . the Father utters out of the center of the Heart by the Holy Spirit, and it stands in divine forms and images . . . as a Virgin . . . all is together an eternal *Magia* . . . and manifests itself endlessly in the eye of Virgin Wisdom" (*Von sechs theosophischen Puncten*, 1.16–7).

19. *La Philosophie de Jacob Boehme* (Paris: Librairie Philosophique J. Vrin, 1929), 335.

20. Boehme, *The "Key" of Jacob Boehme* (Grand Rapids: Phanes Press, 1991), 23.

21. *The "Key" of Jacob Boehme*, 23.

22. Koyre, *La Philosophie de Jacob Boehme*, 263.

23. *Psychologia Vera*, 1.74.

24. On the Imaginal Realm, see Corbin, *Creative Imagination in the Sufism of Ibn'Arabi* .

25. Brinton, *The Mystic Will*, 188–9. Cf. *Beschreibung Der drey Principien Gottliches Wesens*, 22.77. In the words of Kathleen Raine, "The imagination opens . . . into heavens and hells of the mind, beyond which lies boundless mystery . . . nature itself, for the imagination, becomes a living image, incarnation and language of spiritual realities" (*The Inner Journey of the Poet* [London, 1982], 23).

26. Boehme, *The "Key" of Jacob Boehme*, 26.

27. *Cf.* Basarab Nicolescu, *Science, Meaning and Evolution: The Cosmology of Jacob Boehme* (New York: Parabola Books, 1991), 27ff.

28. *Von der Gnaden-Wahl*, 4.10.

29. *Von der Menschwerdung Jesu Christi* 1.11.

30. "As a son in the house helps his father to . . . manage his work . . . so too, in the great house of God . . . Lucifer was to help . . . imagine all the forms and ideas in the *Salitter* of God" (*Aurora*, 15.88).

31. "Adam was drawn into the earth by the Devil's strong will and *Imagination*. . . . The Devil can move mountains, so powerful is his Imagination. The Devil was created from the Great Magia of God and was a Prince of this throne, but he entered into the strong power of fire" (*Von der Menschwerdung Jesu Christi*, 1.5.7).

32. *Theosophischen Fragen*, 10.1. "When Lucifer exalted himself . . . the spirit went forth . . . from Lucifer's angels . . . as a fiery dragon and imaged . . . all sorts of fiery and poisonous images, like to cruel and evil beasts" (*Aurora*, 15.91).

33. Koyre, *La Philosophie de Jacob Boehme*, 99.

34. Cf. *De Signatura Rerum Naturum*.

35. *Bedenken uber Stiefels Buchlein*, 2.143.1.

36. Boehme, *The "Key" of Jacob Boehme*, 43.

37. *Vom dreyfachen Leben des Menschen*, 2.24.

38. *La Philosophie de Jacob Boehme*, 230.

39. *The Way to Christ*, 230.

40. *Von der Menschwerdung Jesu Christi*, 1.5.

41. *Mysterium Magnum*, 19.4.

42. *Beschreibung der drey Principien des Gottlichen Wesens*, 13.2.

43. *Viertzig Fragen von der Seelen*, 36.6.

44. *Mysterium Magnum*, 27.37.

45. *Mysterium Magnum*, 20.16.

46. "That in which the imagination of the spirit enters becomes expressed in corporeal form by . . . the spiritual desire. Therefore God commanded Adam . . . not to eat with his imagination from the tree of self-knowledge . . . so that he should not sink into suffering and death" (*Baptism*, 1.22; in Hartmann, *Personal Christianity*).

47. *Beschreibung der drey Principien*, 13.36.

48. *The Way to Christ*, 157. Cf. Hartmann, *Personal Christianity*, 188.

49. *Mysterium Magnum*, 3.10.

50. *Von der Menschwerdung Jesu Christi*, 1.5.6.

51. *Von der Gnaden-Wahl*, 7.33.

52. *Erste Schutzschrift gegen Balthasar Tilken*, 1.289. The Imagination is also the means through which the Old Testament prophets—and all true mystics, such as Boehme himself—received their visionary inspiration. "A true vision is seen . . . by the soul's modellising, when it co-imagines . . . a figure in its Imagination. Then the image . . . appears in the human understanding . . . .True visions occur when man's will rests in God: then God's Will is manifest in man's will, and the soul sees with God's eyes from its most inward ground . . . in the Word of God . . . then the soul sees what the Most High has prefigured and what shall come to pass . . . thus are the magic visions of all the prophets" (*Mysterium Magnum*, 67.6).

53. *Von der Menschwerdung Jesu Christi*, 1.7.12.

54. *Beschreibung der drey Principien*, 27.44.

55. *Beschreibung der drey Principien*, 27.38.

56. Brinton, *The Mystic Will*, 201. Cf. *Aurora*, 7.42.

57. Koyre, *La Philosophie de Jacob Boehme*, 232.

58. *Von der Menschwerdung Jesu Christi*, 2.8.1. In the words of Paracelsus, "*Imaginatio* is confirmed and rendered perfect by the belief that it really takes place . . . faith must confirm Imagination."

59. Hartmann, *Personal Christianity*, 168.

60. *Bedenken uber Stiefels Buchlein*, 1.63.

61. *Mysterium Magnum*, 36.42–3. At the same time, in prayer, man must "imagine" that he stands in the presence of God, and also that the Magical

Presence of God is within him: "he must firmly imagine to himself that this very . . . instant he standeth before the face of the Holy Trinity, and that God is really present within and without him" (*The Way to Christ*, 18).

62. *Mysterium Magnum*, 36.43–8.

63. *Mysterium Magnum*, 52.13.

64. *Von der Menschwerdung Jesu Christi*, 1.8.12.

65. *Von der Menschwerdung Jesu Christi*, 1.11, 1.10.2. "When we with our imagination enter into God, and wholly give ourselves up to Him, we enter into God's flesh . . . and live in God. For the Word is become man" (*The Confessions of Jacob Boehme*, trans. W. S. Palmer [New York: Harper & Brothers, 1954], 140).

66. *The Confessions of Jacob Boehme*, 143; Brinton, *The Mystic Will*, 200.

67. Koyre, *La Philosophie de Jacob Boehme*, 481–2.

68. "To whatever the mind inclines itself, in that is it figured in the eternal fiat" (quoted in Brinton, *The Mystic Will*, 112).

69. "The divine Mercury changes the wrathful Mercury into its property and Christ is born, and a new man appears as hidden gold out of the earth. Hereby . . . the adept shall seek [the philosopher's stone]; not otherwise than as he has sought in himself the . . . pure gold . . . for man and the earth . . . lie shut up . . . in death and need the same restitution" (*De Signatura Rerum*, 8.52–3).

Corbin has also discussed this theme in the Sufi tradition of alchemy: "this organ of the heart (with the spiritual energy of the *Imaginatrix*) effects a transmutation of the sensory, so that it is perceived . . . on the plane of the *mundus imaginalis* . . . wherein 'what is corporeal becomes spirit and what is spiritual assumes a body' ('our method is that of alchemy,' said Najm Kobra)" (*The Man of Light in Iranian Sufism* [Boston: Shambhala, 1978], 106).

70. *De Signatura Rerum*, 12.12. Thus, as man gained an earthly, mortal body through a misuse of his Imagination, so may he regain his immortal celestial body through a proper use of his Imagination: "How happened it that Adam . . . lost his perfection and became earthly? . . . through imagination . . . he introduced his desire into the outer earthly realm. . . . So it goes also with the new birth. Through imagination and earnest desire we are again impregnated with the deity and receive a new body" (*Informatorium*, 2.7.8).

71. Brinton, *The Mystic Will*, 221–22.

72. *De Signatura Rerum*, 15.24.

73. *Mysterium Magnum*, 56.

74. Koyre, *La Philosophie de Jacob Boehme*, 86. As Paracelsus said, "*Magic* is a great occult wisdom, as Reason is a great open folly."

75. In the words of Franz von Baader, "Theology and Physics have lost their . . . vitality as philosophies of Nature, because neither of them any longer understands the significance . . . of the Imagination, nor do they comprehend the concept of Magic, which is fundamental in the relationship between Man and God, as well as between Man and Nature" (*Vorlesung uber der Lehre Jacob Bohmes*, 15).

Select Bibliography

Baader, Franz Von. *Speculativ Dogmatik. Samlichte Werke*. Book IX. Edited by Anton Lutterbeck. Scientia Verlag Aalen, 1963.

Boehme, Jacob. Unless otherwise noted, all references to Boehme's works are from the *Samlichte Schriften*, edited by Will-Erich Peuckert and August Faust (Stuttgart: Frommans-Verlag, 1955-61). The following works are cited in this essay:

    v. 1. *Morgenrothe im Aufgang (The Aurora)*

    v. 2. *Beschreibung der drey Principien Gottliches Wesen*

    v. 3. *Vom dreyfachen Leben des Menschen. Viertzig Fragen von der Seelen.*

    v. 4. *Von Menschwerdung Jesu Christi. Von sechs Theosophiscen Puncten. Kurtze Erklarung sechs mystischer Puncte.*

    v. 5. *Schutzschriften wieder Balthasar Tilken. Bedenken uber Stiefels Buchlein*

    v. 6. *De Signatura Rerum. Von der Gnaden-Wahl.*

    v. 7–8. *Mysterium Magnum.*

————*The Confessions of Jacob Boehme*. Translated by W. S. Palmer. New York: Harper & Brothers, 1954.

————. *Six Theosophic Points*. Translated by J. R. Earle. Ann Arbor: University of Michigan Press, 1958.

————. *The Way to Christ*. Translated by Peter Erb. New York: Paulist Press, 1986.

Brinton, Howard. *The Mystic Will*. New York: Macmillan, 1930.

Corbin, Henry. *Creative Imagination in the Sufism of Ibn'Arabi*. Princeton: Princeton University Press, 1969.

———. *The Man of Light in Iranian Sufism*. Boston: Shambhala, 1978.

Hartmann, Franz, ed. *Personal Christianity, A Science*. New York: Macoy, 1919.

Koyre, Alexandre. *La Philosophie de Jacob Boehme*. Paris: Librairie Philosophique J.Vrin, 1929.

McLean, Adam. *The Alchemical Mandala*. Grand Rapids: Phanes Press, 1989.

Nicolescu, Basarab. *Science, Meaning and Evolution: The Cosmology of Jacob Boehme*. New York: Parabola Books, 1991.

Paracelsus. *Schriften. Theophrasts von Hohenheim. Ausgewahlt und Herausgeben von Hans Kaiser*. Leipzig, 1924.

Raine, Kathleen. *The Inner Journey of the Poet*. London, 1982.

Yates, Frances. *Giordano Bruno and the Hermetic Tradition*. Chicago: University of Chicago Press, 1964.

The Castle of Heroes:
W. B. Yeats' Celtic Mystical Order

PETER CAWLEY

> While the men of action could mobilize active resistance or political parties, the occultists, by virtue of their peculiar temperament, could manufacture nations out of dreams.
>
> —James Webb[1]

EVERY ACCOUNT of the Hermetic Order of the Golden Dawn includes a roll-call of its more notable initiates and every roll-call gives a prominent position to the poet and dramatist, W. B. Yeats. Yeats was the one order initiate to receive universal recognition for his contributions in disciplines apparently unrelated to those of the Order of the Golden Dawn. Standard reference works remember him as the leader of the Irish Literary Revival, as a Nobel laureate (1923), and as a Senator in the first Senate of the Irish Free State (1922–28).

Many volumes of literary criticism have explored the artistic aspirations of Yeats as poet and dramatist. His political career, from member of the Irish Republican Brotherhood (parent organization of the Irish Republican Army) through Senator to Elder Statesman, has also been documented. Yeats' occult life, however, remains, for the most part, unexamined, discounted, or devalued by researchers.

Both the standard reference works and the historical accounts of modern magic fail to give due regard to Yeats' magical accomplishments. One Golden Dawn historian suggested, rather facetiously, that Yeats' ability to make a good income as a poet and dramatist must have had a magical cause.[2] But Yeats was very serious about his magic. In 1892 he wrote "I decided deliberately . . . to make [magic], next to my poetry, the most important pursuit of my life."[3]

It is unfortunate that the most significant magical project that Yeats ever attempted, a project with the potential for changing the course of British and Irish history in the twentieth century, was never completed. Forgotten or ignored today, hidden away among the footnotes and parentheses of literary criticism, is the story of Yeats' plan to found a Celtic mystical order, a Castle of Heroes, modelled on the Order of the Golden Dawn.

The Castle of Heroes project synthesized three basic spiritual dynamics that energized Yeats' inner world throughout his working life. Yeats visualized his Celtic mystical order as a magical fraternity that would combine artistic idealism with ceremonial magic in the service of Irish nationalism.

Yeats scholar Kathleen Raine explained the type of difficulties academic critics meet while trying to appraise the occult elements in Yeats' work:

> The kind of knowledge to which members of that Order (the Golden Dawn) aspired cannot of its nature be understood in academic terms. The merely academic study of magical symbolism may be likened to the analysis of musical scores by a student who does not know that the documents he meticulously annotates are merely indications for the evocation of music from instruments of whose very existence he is ignorant. Magic . . . is an art. [4]

Part of Yeats' genius was to communicate the hidden through words, and it is possible to excavate at least the foundations of the Castle of Heroes from his writings and from isolated clues uncovered by various critics.

Yeats' relationship with Maude Gonne, romantic and ideal love of his life, was the catalyst which activated his triad of personal spiritual motivators, art, Irish nationalism, and the occult. Like Yeats, Maude's background was Anglo-Irish of the Protestant ascendency class. Her appearance was striking, but not photogenic. Yeats considered her to be the most beautiful woman of the age. She shared his passionate Irish nationalism on an intensely activist level, and she was keenly interested in the occult. Maude, in later life, was to entitle her autobiography *A Servant of the Queen*, and this title echoed the key-note of her life. The Queen served was not the Britannic Majesty of Maude's childhood, but the Triune Goddess personified as Banda–Folta–Eire, and representing the spirit of Ireland.

Unfortunately for Yeats, Maude did not reciprocate his romantic feelings and their relationship was to remain largely Platonic: as she wrote to a friend, it was "a perfect friendship though nothing else."[5] Yeats never concurred with this opinion. First he found his political involvement increasingly stimulated by the opportunities it provided for frequent meetings with Maude. He anticipated that mutual work in magic and occultism would cause a spiritual closeness to grow between them. Maude and magic became inseparably intertwined during a significant portion of Yeats' career.

Golden Dawn membership was a consistent thread through thirty productive years of Yeats' life. He was initiated at the Isis-Urania Temple on March 7, 1890, the year after he met Maude. For a short time he was chief of the temple. After the break-up of the Golden Dawn, he continued work in the Stella Matutina faction, even though this meant re-taking all the grades. In 1916 he was accepted as Adeptus Exemptus, the highest degree attainable while still living in the body. The date of his resignation from the order is not known, but evidence in his letters suggests he was a member until 1922 or 1923.

Just a year after his own initiation in 1891, he persuaded Maude Gonne to join the order so she could train for a "secret spiritual propaganda" campaign to be launched in the interests of Irish nationalism. The "spiritual propaganda" did not materialize, but Yeats continued to be profoundly affected by the Golden Dawn rituals. He wrote in his *Autobiography*: "After I had been moved by ritual, I formed plans for deeds of all kinds. I wished to return to Ireland to find there some public work."[6] Earlier vague ideas for the regeneration of Irish literature began to crystallize into a plan for an Irish mystical order using specifically Celtic symbols; a mystical brotherhood that would combine artistic ideal with ritual magic in the service of Irish nation-alism. The concept was approved by Maude, who also saw in it the seed of a secret organization, similar to Freemasonry, with the capability of using Masonic political methods against the Masons to counter-balance their influence amongst the Unionists in Ireland. [7]

Elements of the plans for the Celtic mystery school begin to appear in Yeats' writing almost at once. The theme of the mystery school is particularly noticeable in three short stories written between 1893 and 1897. In the story "Out of the Rose,"[8] a medieval provenance for the Irish order, every bit as antique as that of the Golden Dawn's, is related. It tells of a Knight of St. John in Palestine "to whom the truth of truths was revealed by God Himself." He had seen a great Rose of Fire and a voice out of the Rose had told him "to avoid the corruption inherent in life" by "dying in the service of the Rose." On hearing this, a group of Knights of St. John believed that "the very Voice of God" had spoken to them through the knight; in response they formed an oathbound secret order and went into the world seeking "good causes and to die in doing battle for them." The last knight of the secret order died an obscure death in Ireland. Critic George Mills Harper suggests "Out of the Rose" had its origin in a vision. It is probable that, in the light of other work connected with his Celtic mystical order, Yeats was conducting during this period, the "vision" was in fact a guided meditation or pathworking.

"A half-prophecy of a very veiled kind"[9] was Yeats' own description of the short story "The Adoration of the Magi." A dying woman

> told . . . the secret names of the immortals of many lands, and of the colours, and odours, and weapons, and the instruments of music and instruments of handicraft they held dearest; but most about the immortals of Ireland and of their love for the cauldron, and the whet-stone, and the sword, and the spear.[10]

This passage was deleted from the final published version of the story. Perhaps it revealed too much material that Yeats preferred to remain private. Here, in a fictionalized format is described the reception of tables of correspondences for god-forms and the elemental weapons of the new Order: all secret ritual material that Yeats and his Golden Dawn companions were busily acquiring by less terminal methods during the period in which the story was written.

"Rosa Alchemica," a description of a fictional contemporary mystical order, the Order of the Alchemical Rose, indicates the direction of Yeats' thoughts for his own mystery school. The fictional Order was founded by six students of Celtic descent who had each solved a key mystery of alchemy. They defined alchemy as the "distillation of the contents of the Soul until (one) is ready to put off the mortal and put on the immortal." Alchemical Rose neophytes were taught "the independent reality .. of thoughts, . . . the doctrine from which all true doctrines arose." The curriculum continued with the making of forms in which soulless divinities and demons could manifest. "In this way all great events were accomplished."[11]

"Out of the Rose" was first published in a collection of stories entitled *The Secret Rose*. "The Adoration of the Magi" and "Rosa Alchemica" were originally intended for inclusion in *The Secret Rose* collection but were published separately with another "Michael Robartes" story. The 1897 edition of *The Secret Rose* was issued in a beautifully elaborate binding, fraught with occult significance, designed by Golden Dawn initiate Althea Gyles. The spine decoration was a pattern of peacock feathers and leaves. The front cover showed male and female faces kissing in a stylized rose tree, a Kabbalistic Tree of Life, rooted in the skeleton of an armoured knight (perhaps the skeleton of the Knight of St. John?). Three roses at the top of the Tree represented the Supernal Sephiroth, Kether, Chockmah and Binah. The branches of the Tree intertwined like a symmetrical serpent. At the center of the Tree, and of the design, representing the four elements, was a four-petalled rose joined to a cross. This ornately decorated binding for *The Secret Rose* closely resembled the cover of the Alchemical Rose Order's textbook described in the story "Rosa Alchemica."[12]

The temple of the fictional Order of the Alchemical Rose was located in a circular building at the end of a pier protruding into the Atlantic off the west coast of Ireland. The intended home of the Celtic mystical order was even more striking and evocative in its placement. In his *Autobiography* Yeats described his discovery of the location he selected for the headquarters of the Celtic mystical order:

> On a visit (in the Spring of 1895) to Dr. Hyde (later to become the first president of the Irish Free State) I had seen the Castle Rock . . . in Lough Key. There is this small island entirely covered by what was a still habitable but empty castle . . . All around were the wooded and hilly shores, a place of great beauty. I . . . had long been dreaming of making it an Irish Eleusis or Samothrace.[13]

It is tempting to speculate that Yeats may have sensed in the Castle Rock a real-world manifestation of his dream Castle of Heroes. The castellated island is an apt image of the mystic's "Interior Castle," imposing the qualities of discipline, strength and purpose onto a lake island very similar to the poet's romantically escapist "Lake Isle of Innisfree."

For Yeats the need to create a mystical order was an "obsession more constant than anything but my love itself." Part of this "obsession" was a projection of his artistic values. The proposed rites were to be a "mystical system of evocation and meditation to reunite the perception of the spirit, of the divine, with natural beauty." William Blake's influence is reflected in Yeats' belief "that instead of thinking of Judea as holy, we should think our own land holy, and most holy where most beautiful." The "beautiful" places were the sites for establishing communication with invisible beings. "I meant to initiate young men and women in this worship, which would unite the radical truth of Christianity to those of a more ancient world, and use the Castle Rock for their occasional retirement from the world."[14]

Developing a coherent mythos of background material to convey the teachings of the order and from which the rituals of the Castle of

Heroes could be derived, was a monumental undertaking. Yeats drew heavily upon his connections within the Golden Dawn for assistance. MacGregor Mathers, the head of the order, his wife Moina, and several other members were keenly interested in the Celtic Revival and were very willing to assist in Yeats' Celtic mystery school project. Magical skills learned in the Golden Dawn were applied to the task. MacGregor Mathers had previously taught Yeats the techniques of using symbols to induce visions from a "deeper source than the conscious or unconscious memory." Yeats wanted to check and double-check the ensuing visions and he saw in the work a way to come closer to Maude Gonne. "My own seership was, I thought, inadequate . . . I would therefore use her [Maude Gonne's] clairvoyance to produce forms that would arise from both minds."[15]

The work went well. Inner contacts were established and the ensuing material was prolific:

> We obtained in vision long lists of symbols. Various trees corresponded to the cardinal points, and the old gods and heroes took their places gradually in a symbolic fabric that had for its centre the four talismans of the Tuatha de Danaan, the sword, the stone, the spear and the cauldron, which related themselves in my mind with the suits of the Tarot.[16]

Further research linked the stone, the cauldron, the sword and the spear with the elements of earth, water, air and fire, with the god forms of Dagda, Danu, Brigid, and Lugh, and with the mystic cities of Falias, Murias, Findras, and Gorias.[17]

Yeats' uncle, George Pollexfen, also a Golden Dawn member, checked their results and made his own contributions. The concentration became so intense that some of the thought-forms began to assume a semblance of physical reality. When the poet A.E. (George Russell) came to visit, he inquired about the white jester he had seen in the corridors. Yeats responded that the jester was the form he associated with the god Aengus, the god of love. Aengus was not to be the only manifestation.

In the winter of 1897–98 Yeats broadened his magical research with a small group of London-based Golden Dawn members who were especially interested in Celtic mythology. The group included E. A. Hunter, Dorothea Hunter, Mary Briggs, Annie Horniman and William Sharp. Sharp, a Scottish Nationalist, was later invited to Paris to work on the actual rituals with Yeats and the Matherses. Yeats also corresponded with "Fiona Macleod" and sought "her" opinion. It was in deference to "her" Scottish sensibilities that the mystery school was designated as Celtic rather than Irish. Yeats was not aware that "Fiona Macleod" was the pen-name William Sharp attached to the poetry, plays and essays produced by his *anima*-figure that had begun manifesting after Sharp's own Golden Dawn initiation.[18] "Fiona Macleod" was responsible for a separate published output in "her" own distinctive literary style by way of automatic writing. To assure a feminine hand-writing, "she" dictated correspondence for Yeats, and others, via William Sharp to his spouse, Elizabeth.[19]

In addition to identifying symbols, the Golden Dawn sub-group were presented with the names of various gods and heroes from Celtic mythology. The intuitively received ritual signs and words associated with these personages were then carefully noted. Yeats also conducted loosely structured pathworkings based on Irish saga material. The group-visions were recorded and cross-checked. A recurring Guardian in these pathworkings was Connla the Druid (as distinct from Connla, son of Cuchulain).

On these occasions Yeats, using the initials of his Golden Dawn magical name *Daemon Est Deus Invertus*, would simultaneously lead and participate in the group's inner vision using a technique comparable to mutual hypnosis. These journeys commenced with Yeats performing a Celtic ceremony of invocation. The group was led into the mountains to an ancient well beside a mountain-ash tree. The ripe red rowan berries fell into the water like "drops of blood." (The hazelnut, symbol of wisdom, is the fruit tradition more usually associated with this well.) Connla the Druid appeared as a luminous figure and D.E.D.I. questioned him. The responses would take the form of reflective visions in the pool, or sometimes further journeys were made using the well as a doorway. Connla was saluted with an X sign on departure. When the group was conducted back to a place and state of consciousness from which they could safely return to reality, D.E.D.I. disappeared from the vision.[20]

It seems that Connla, like Aengus before him, began to take on something of an independent existence. Moina MacGregor Mathers reported seeing Connla in Paris even though she was not cognizant with the details of the workings in London. Moina and MacGregor during this period were assisting the project by annotating Celtic mythological data with zodiacal and planetary sigils and the appropriate colors from the Golden Dawn color scales. The following year, Yeats and Sharp joined the Matherses and Maude Gonne in Paris to begin work on the rituals. Despite an incompatibility between the personalities of MacGregor Mathers and Sharp, some progress was made.

The 140 pages of notes for the Celtic order rituals that still exist have been described as "incoherent and incomplete." But some material survived and something can be inferred from the remains. It is known that the order candidates were to pass through a series of six initiations: the Opening Ritual, and the Initiations of the Stone, of the Cauldron, of the Sword, of the Spear, and of the Spirit. The four symbols represented the four elements and the ceremonies were intended to parallel Golden Dawn rituals. The fifth and final initiation, that of the spirit, exhorted:

Active Spirit of the Divine Life, awake to consciousness,
Informing Genius, awake in this man.
Life that has descended, awake in him.
Light that has descended, illuminate him.
Joy that has descended, shine in him.
Be the sap of his bones and the life of his blood.
Rejoice, rejoice, a new staff is in the hands of the Eternal,
A new sword is in the hands of the Eternal.[21]

It was intended to use the legendary Cuchulain hero cycle as the background mythos for the order.

In his *Autobiography* Yeats noted: "I wished my writings, and those of the school I hoped to found to have a secret symbolical relation to these mysteries [the Celtic Mystery School]."[22] Assuming that he indeed acted on this wish, it may be possible to reconstruct a skeletal outline of Yeats' intentions for the major order rituals from his writings, especially from the five plays in his Cuchulain cycle, written after the plans for the mystical order were abandoned.

In a later work, *A Vision*, Yeats explicated in detail his theory of cosmic cycles and gyres. Ingeniously incorporating background from *A Vision* with information contained in the poem, "The Phases of the Moon," and from other sources, Reg Skene, in *The Cuchulain Plays of W. B. Yeats*, analyzes the ritual elements in the plays and locates each play on Yeats' solar wheel/lunar cycle calendar, which relates the twenty-eight moon phases to the solstices and equinoxes. In the resulting "marrying of the Sun and the Moon" may be discerned the remains of a basic outline of Yeats' scheme for the Celtic mystical order rituals.

The play cycle enacts the spiritual adventures of Cuchulain as the story of the progression of the human soul; each play contains abundant material for a ritual. The cycle commences at the autumnal equinox and at the first phase of the moon with the play *At The Hawk's Well*. The theme is the Dawn of Consciousness, a variation of the Garden of Eden story. The second play in the cycle, *The Green Helmet* is placed on the eighth moon phase and the winter solstice with a theme relating to the Cup of Temptation. Here Cuchulain, through noble self-sacrifice, finds his place as Champion of Ireland. The central play of the cycle, *On Baile's Strand*, falls on the twelfth moon phase ("the phase of the hero") and the Celtic festival of Imbolc. The nature goddess is worshiped and her sun-god consort, Cuchulain's son, meets the sacrificial death at the hands of his unwitting father. The fifteenth moon phase (the full moon) and the vernal equinox celebrates the resurrection of the solar-hero with *The Only Jealousy of*

Emer. The last play, *The Death of Cuchulain*, starts at the summer solstice and the twenty-second moon phase. As the solar power diminishes and the moon travels through its last six phases, Cuchulain meets his six antagonists and receives his six mortal wounds, thus completing the ritual cycle. The death of Cuchulain ritually represents birth into the spiritual world.

There are skeleton notes for at least two drafts of the Castle of Heroes rituals. The original draft required the candidate to make various gestures or choices during the four rituals of the elements; the way the candidate responded was "symbolical and very important . . . the undirected impulse . . . should be recorded."[23] The results of these actions decided the color and decorations on the candidate's order staff. The depth of the shade of the staff's violet coloring depended on the depth the candidate's hands were thrust into a basin of water; "the complete and forceful immersion of both hands shows that the purification and initiation are real in spirit."[24] The staff was adorned with a beast's head according to the candidate's choice of a planet, with an emblem representing the adept to whom the candidate presented an eagle feather, and with a zodiacal sign assigned according to which of twelve lamps was lighted. "Fiona Macleod" objected to evaluating the candidate's choices in this fashion. Consequently, the rituals were reconstructed; and while the partial rewrite may have satisfied "her" sense of occult correctness, the feeling of cohesiveness and unity is much less than that of the original.

While Yeats' impulse to create these rituals was derived from his Golden Dawn membership and obeyed the Flying Roll injunction to "prepare a ritual," very little of the material in the Castle of Heroes was directly derived from Golden Dawn material. The allusions and mythos are stringently Irish. There are only two direct "borrowings" from the London order. One is an oath sworn with a hand placed on a Rose of the World. The other is a fragment of a ritual entitled "The Opening of the Gates" that echoes the "Lesser Banishing Ritual." The Candidate stands in the East and calls on the gods associated with the four Treasures of Ireland: "Before me Brigid, upon my left hand

Dagda, upon my right hand Lugh, behind me Danu." Fire, water, the flowering bough, and the stone are then invoked. The fragmented note ends suddenly with the words: "Lift your hands above your head and say . . ."[25]

After such extended effort, what considerations could be strong enough to cause Yeats to abandon this promising and powerful project before the Celtic mystery school could be established? The idea had been incubating, in some form or other, since his initiation into the Golden Dawn and had been defined, refined, and sharpened for almost thirteen years.

Its abandonment was slow and protracted and the events that led to the abandonment were personally painful.

As early as 1898 the seeds of an internal struggle for dominance between Yeats' values as an artist and as an adept began to surface in the drafts of an uncompleted novel, *The Speckled Bird*. The novel was largely autobiographical. At one point the MacGregor Mathers-based figure significantly tells the Yeatsian character, "I have come to recognize that you are not a magician, but some kind of an artist."[26] In the course of the narrative, London occultists are depicted as dull, eccentric, petty, jealous, and willing to compromise idealistic goals with hastily conceived and occasionally shoddy means.

All these negative qualities were assumed and personified by the principal members of the Golden Dawn who participated in the "Great Schism" of 1900. The quarrel which split the Golden Dawn into rival factions also brought about a permanent estrangement between Yeats and the Matherses. MacGregor Mathers' autocratic attitude in the governance of the order and his misplaced trust in Aleister Crowley (whom Yeats had refused to admit to the Second Order on the grounds that "a mystical fraternity is not a moral reformatory") placed too great a strain on his relationship with Yeats. The antics of Crowley, acting as Mathers' London agent, drove the final wedge between Yeats, who was at this time Chief of the Isis-Urania Temple, and Mathers. All contact with Mathers, including collaboration on the Celtic mystical order, was terminated.

Meanwhile, Maude Gonne had begun to develop her own reservations about the Golden Dawn, mainly on account of what she perceived as Masonic influence on the order. Some order rituals were being worked at the Mark Masons' Hall in London. Any Masonic connection, however tenuous, made her uncomfortable. Maude was disturbed by Macgregor Mathers' use of Masonic emblems. When she tested Golden Dawn passwords on Claude Lane, a Freemason, both were horrified by the results: he, because an outsider and a woman possessed the words for some of the higher degrees of Masonry, and she because Mathers seemed to be linking the Golden Dawn with Masonry.[27] Maude shared the view of many Irish nationalists that Freemasonry in Ireland was an institution for the promotion of Unionism and British Imperialism, and that it had secretly sponsored the Orange Order as a front-organization to channel Protestant working-class bigotry and violence in support of those ends. But however painful for Yeats, and however damaging to his plans her withdrawal from the Golden Dawn may have been, worse was to follow.

In 1903 Maude Gonne married John McBride. It is ironic that McBride was to become in reality the type of hero that Yeats and Maude Gonne had dreamed of creating in their Castle of Heroes. Thirteen years later, John McBride was to be one of the signatories of the Declaration of the Irish Republic, was to be executed by the British for his part in the 1916 Easter Rising, was to be eulogized by Yeats in the poem "Easter 1916" as

A drunken, vainglorious lout . . .
Transformed utterly:
A terrible beauty is born.

But in 1903 McBride was instrumental in shaking the foundations of Yeats' spiritual well-being. The McBride marriage was to prove an unhappy failure for all concerned. However, its early break-up and the ensuing separation were to bring no comfort to Yeats; as an unrepentently independent Maude Gonne McBride was to say: "If a woman has something worthwhile doing in this world . . . marriage is a deplorable step."

For Yeats, Maude's marriage was a stunning emotional blow. It led him to undertake an extensive reassessment of both his own personal qualities and of his life's work. As a consequence, any remaining hopes for saving the Celtic mystical order were finally abandoned. The underlying impulse for the order was now transformed and redirected into the creation of an "Irish ritual theatre like that of Aeschylus and Sophocles." Much of the material originally intended for the order was utilized in the Cuchulain Cycle of plays. For example, Connla and his well played an important role in *At The Hawk's Well.*

The Cuchulain Mythos was to deeply affect Irish nationalism during the first decades of the twentieth century. The spiritual charge behind the original impulse for a Castle of Heroes, even after its dilution into theatrical format, energized the participants in the 1916 Easter Rising and changed the subsequent course of Irish history. Yeats deeply regretted that he was not informed of the Rising in advance. (He had resigned from the Irish Republican Brotherhood in 1900 because of its violent policies.) Yet his contribution to the cause is tacitly acknowledged; the memorial to the insurrectionists in the Dublin Post Office, site of the main battle, is a statue of Cuchulain. James Webb, the rationalist historian, wrote sixty years after the events:

> If there existed any "national spirit" in Ireland at the time of the Rising it was to a large extent formed by the mystical elements gathered by Yeats . . . around the concept of "Ireland."[28]

One might speculate as to what the state of the "national spirit" of Ireland would have been if the Celtic mystical order had been at work during the ten years leading up to the 1916 Easter Rising. Yeats expressed his views on the importance of creating, maintaining, and protecting the "magical personality" of occult organizations in his 1901 pamphlet *Is the Order of R.R. & A.C. to Remain a Magical Order?*

He would certainly have endeavored to follow his own advice and ensured that his own magical order developed into a strong and disciplined "Actual Being, an organic life holding within itself the highest life of its members" and that it grew into a "Talisman" acting on the souls of those who were attached to it; and all this with the magical intention of creating a strong "ripple effect" that would extend well beyond the anticipated elite order membership.[29]

Would the rituals of the Castle of Heroes have been magically potent enough to energize a "national spirit" capable of liberating and unifying four provinces into a united Ireland that included Cuchulain's Ulster, instead of a Free State comprising only twenty-six of the thirty-two counties of the island? If so, could the greater result have been attained with less violence? Would the history of the last seventy-five years have been any happier as a consequence?

The concept of the Castle of Heroes may, however, have sent out other strange, but perhaps, significant ripples into the world of magic. John Michell cites Yeats critic John Parisious as ascribing the revival of the Mysteries at Glastonbury in the 1920s to the influence of W.B. Yeats' Celtic mystery school. The ambiance generated by the Glastonbury Festivals in its turn influenced many contemporary personalities. One of those attracted to Glastonbury by the Festivals and whose subsequent work was profoundly affected by that location, was Violet Firth, better known by her pen-name, Dion Fortune. Another ripple from the Castle workings which touched her Society of the Inner Light was Connla the Druid, who re-appeared in 1936–38, in his role of guide in the writings of C. R. F. Seymour.[30]

A century after the first Celtic Revival a resurgence of interest in the Matter of Britain and its Celtic roots is again attracting a wide interest. Yeats' spiritual dynamics are still activated in the 1990s, modified only slightly by the perceptions of a new age. The impulse Yeats expressed through Irish nationalism is today found in a wider search for collective and personal freedom. True artistic values are now being articulated in a growing desire for an wholistic integrity in all aspects of life. More people are interested in the occult than at any other time in history. As the modern seeker labors to build the Interior Castle, the writings of researchers like John and Caitlin Matthews offer an abundance of material for a modern Celtic mystery school; a plenitude of symbols for a modern revival are available in mass-market artifacts such as the *Arthurian Tarot* and the *Celtic Tarot* decks. Would the shades of Yeats object to a modern revival of his Celtic mystery order, suitably updated? Probably not. Maude Gonne McBride records that in his old age, during their final conversation together just prior to leaving Ireland for the last time before his death, Yeats said to her:

> Maude, we should have gone on with our
> Castle of the Heroes, we might still do it.[31]

Notes

1. James Webb, *The Occult Underground*, 321.

2. Ithell Colquhoun, *Sword of Wisdom: MacGregor Mathers and the Golden Dawn*, 174.

3. Richard Ellman, *Yeats: The Man and the Masks*, 95.

4. Kathleen Raine, "Yeats, the Tarot and the Golden Dawn," 177.

5. William H. O'Donnell, ed., *The Speckled Bird by William Butler Yeats*, 265.

6. William Butler Yeats, *Memoirs*, 123.

7. Richard Ellman, *Yeats: The Man and the Masks*, 125.

8. William Butler Yeats, *Mythologies*, 157–164.

9. Richard Ellman, *Yeats*, 122.

10. Richard Ellman, *Yeats*, 122.

11. William Butler Yeats, *Mythologies*, 283–4.

12. William Butler Yeats, *Mythologies*, 283

13. William Butler Yeats, *Memoirs*, 123.

14. William Butler Yeats, *Memoirs*, 124.

15. William Butler Yeats, *Memoirs*, 124.

16. William Butler Yeats, *Memoirs*, 125.

17. Virginia Moore, *The Unicorn: William Butler Yeats' Search for Reality*, 72.

18. Virginia Moore, *The Unicorn*, 76.

19. Ithell Colquhoun, *Sword of Wisdom*, 167.

20. Richard Ellman, *Yeats*, 127.

21. Virginia Moore, *The Unicorn*, 80.

22. Virginia Moore, *The Unicorn*, 82.

23. Virginia Moore, *The Unicorn*, 74.

24. Virginia Moore, *The Unicorn*, 74.

25. Virginia Moore, *The Unicorn*, 79.

26. William H. O'Donnell, ed., *The Speckled Bird by William Butler Yeats*, 92.

27. Maude Gonne, *A Servant of the Queen: Reminiscences* 259.

28. James Webb, *The Occult Underground*, 325.

29. William Butler Yeats, "Is the Order of R.R. and A.C. to Remain a Magical Order?", in Harper, *Yeats's Golden Dawn*, 267.

30. John Michell, *New Light on the Ancient Mystery of Glastonbury*, 34.

31. See "Meditations for Temple Novices" and "Children of the Great Mother" in Seymour, *The Forgotten Mage: The Magical Lectures of Colonel C. R. F. Seymour*.

32. Ithell Colquhoun, *Sword of Wisdom*, 159.

Bibliography

Ithell Colquhoun. *Sword of Wisdom: MacGregor Mathers and the Golden Dawn*. New York: G. P. Putnam's Sons, 1975.

Richard Ellman. *Yeats: The Man and the Masks*. London: Macmillan, 1949.

Maude Gonne. *A Servant of the Queen: Reminiscences*. London: Victor Gollancz, 1974.

George Mills Harper. *Yeats's Golden Dawn*. New York: Harper and Row, 1974.

———. *Yeats and the Occult*. Toronto: Macmillan of Canada, 1975.

John Michell. *New Light on the Ancient Mystery of Glastonbury*. Glastonbury: Gothic Image, 1990.

Virginia Moore. *The Unicorn: William Butler Yeats' Search for Reality*. New York: Macmillan, 1954.

William O'Donnell, ed. *The Speckled Bird by William Butler Yeats*. Toronto:

McClelland and Stewart, 1976.

Kathleen Raine. "Yeats, the Tarot, and the Golden Dawn" in *Yeats the Initiate: Essays on Certain Themes in the Works of W. B. Yeats.* Mountrath: Dolmen, 1986.

C. R. F. Seymour. *The Forgotten Mage: The Magical Lectures of Colonel C. R. F. Seymour.* Edited by Dolores Ashcroft-Nowicki. Wellingborough: Aquarian, 1986.

Reg Skene. *The Cuchulain Plays of W. B. Yeats.* New York: Columbia University Press, 1974.

James Webb. *The Occult Underground.* LaSalle: Open Court, 1974.

William Butler Yeats. *Memoirs.* Edited by Dennis Donaghue. New York: Macmillan, 1972.

———. *Mythologies,* London: Macmillan, 1959.

The Availability of the One:
An Interpretive Essay

MICHAEL HORNUM

MODERN SCHOLARSHIP has traditionally divided ancient Platonism into several major phases: the Old Academy, the Skeptical Academy, Middle Platonism, and Neoplatonism. While these distinctions roughly follow a chronological development from the fourth century B.C.E. to the sixth century C.E., there are also doctrinal differences between the "schools." Doctrinal variance is particularly important in the relationship to Middle and Neoplatonism, which overlap chronologically and represent, after Plotinus, divergent sets of solutions to the many issues raised by Platonic metaphysics.

One of the major differences between Middle Platonism and Neoplatonism is the manner in which they view the Ultimate Principle and its relation to the hierarchy of reality derived from it. The present essay shall discuss this distinction, and attempt to work out the logical implications of the Plotinian Neoplatonic revision of the Middle Platonic position. The essay does not strive to merely replicate the ancient doctrines of a long dead system, but to extend the development of "pagan" Neoplatonic ideas which had been arrested by the "triumph" of Christianity.

The Middle Platonists regard the Ultimate Principle as a *Mind* (νοῦς). This holds true for both those philosophers who see the Supreme Principle as identical with the immediate creator of the physical cosmos, the Demiurge of the *Timaeus* (Plutarch), and those who make the Ultimate not creator but both beyond and the source of the Demiurge (Alcinous, Numenius). All of these Platonists also place the archetypes of sense-perceptory objects—variously called the *True*

Being (τὸ ὄν), the *Forms* (αἱ ἰδέαι) or the *Intelligibles* (τὰ νοητά) in that mind which is identical with God.

It is possible that already in the thought of the Platonic Successor Xenocrates (late fourth century B.C.E.) the archetypes had been placed within the mind of the Demiurge, called the Monad.[1] Certainly this position is better represented by Plutarch (late first century–early second century C.E.), who identifies the One/Good of the *Parmenides* and the *Republic* with the cosmic creator, and places the Forms in that mind which is God. The Forms taken as a whole are therefore identified with the Demiurge, and the order and excellence of the cosmos therefore are seen to rely upon the paradigm of God himself.[2] A similar first century C.E. account has been identified in Seneca's *Epistulae* 65 and in the writings of the Jewish philosopher Philo of Alexandria, heavily indebted to Platonism and Stoicism.[3]

By the second century C.E. some Platonists had rejected the identification of the Supreme Principle with the creator of the cosmos. Such a rejection has been traced to a concern to absolve the One from any contact with Matter, the principle of disorder in the cosmos.[4] This concern is already manifest in Philo, who attempts to make the active, creative divine mind a derivative aspect of God, intermediate between the Supreme and Matter, since "it was not lawful for the happy and blessed One to touch limitless chaotic matter."[5] One can also point out that the creative aspect of the Divine is one which only exists in the context of the creative process itself, is interdependent with it, and therefore logically evokes an ontologically prior pre-creative aspect or principle as substratum for both creator and creation. In any case, the second century Numenius and Alcinous clearly distinguish the Demiurge from the non-cosmological First Principle, making them two distinct Gods.[6]

In order to avoid the danger of an instrumentalist interpretation of the Forms as constituted by the divine mind purely for the purpose of serving as the model for creation—a notion which would abrogate the eternal, unchanging reality of the Forms—Alcinous and Numenius make the Ultimate a mind eternally thinking its own unchanging self, both intellectual and the Intelligible. Thus, they alter the position of Plutarch by making the Divine Mind/Being entirely self-contemplative and not involved in the making of the physical cosmos. The Demiurge, instead, is said to look to the Intelligible beyond as the model for its creative activity.[7]

Plotinus presents a marked contrast with all of the Middle Platonists. He places the Ultimate Principle beyond both Nous and Noeton/Being. The One does not think others nor itself. The idea that the One thinks others is specifically rejected in several passages, on the grounds that, for example, thinking things not as perfect as itself would lessen its perfection, introducing into it some measure of the multiplicity and/or changeability of those things.[8] The idea that the One is self-conscious is unambiguously rejected by Plotinus in tracts which range from the early through the middle to some of the very latest portions of his writing period.[9]

The only instance in which self-consciousness is explicitly predicated of the One is in the early tract *Enneads* 5.4 (chapter 2, lines 17–18). Here the One is apparently identified with the Intelligible and is said to have a thinking of itself (κατανόησις αὐτοῦ) which is itself and to exist by an immediate self-awareness (συναίσθησις). This is a passage for which the influence of Numenius' idea of a passive and an active Intellect has been invoked.[10] While one might be tempted to explain away the text as Plotinian experimentation with certain Numenian ideas that were later rejected, intimations of a type of self-consciousness for the One have been detected by scholars in *Enneads* 5.7 and 6.8.[11]

In *Enneads* 6.8.16, for example, the One is said to "look at himself" with a self-looking identical with his being (lines 20–21), and to possess a "wakefulness" (ἐγρήγορσις) and a "superintellection" (ὑπερνόησις) as his activity which is identical with his essence (lines 33–34). It has even been suggested that the predication of "wakefulness" and "superintellection" to the One directly parallels the "self-awareness" and "thinking of itself" attributed to the One in *Enneads* 5.4.2, and argued that this parallel proves that Plotinus had continued to regard the One as self-conscious.[12] In *Enneads* 6.18.21–22, the One is said to possess, on the evidence of the nature of the Nous derived from it, "something like Intellect which is not Intellect." Finally, in *Enneads* 6.7.39.1–4 the One is attributed a simple attention (ἐπιβολή) on itself, an attention which is itself.

In analyzing this issue, it should first be emphasized that Plotinus is very clear that he is using concepts that are "strictly inapplicable" to the One throughout the entire tract *Enneads* 6.8.[13] It must then be pointed out that if there is indeed a parallel in terminology between *Enneads* 5.4.2 and 6.8.16, a persuasive case can be made that the parallel actually shows a major change in Plotinus' perspective on the One's consciousness. First, the intellection implied in *katanoêsis* is explicitly rejected by the word *hypernoêsis*, a faculty beyond intellection. Second, the identification of the One's activity, which is identical with itself, as "wakefulness" is a sharp rebuke to the notion of self-awareness. For if the One is all wakefulness through and through, what need could it possibly have for self-consciousness?

Regardless of whether there exists some parallel between *Enneads* 5.4.2 and 6.8.16, it may be asserted that some measure of consciousness is still predicated of the One in the sense that "wakefulness" is a form of awareness. However, given the discussion of free-will which comprises the context of the passage it is clear that the main sense of "wakefulness" here is not as a form of awareness. Indeed, if this is what was intended the consciousness of the One would be that of the barest level of awareness, the simple state of being awake. Instead, the main sense can be traced to the root-meaning of ἐγείρω—to awaken, to rouse up. The One's activity is its own self-rousing, its own self-determination. Plotinus is attempting to demonstrate that the One is absolutely free, completely self-determined.

The other passages pointed to as evidence of a self-consciousness of the One are similarly problematic. The "looking at himself" in 6.8.16.20–21 does not necessarily convey the impression of self-awareness. The verb βλέπειν does not elicit the reflectivity of the self-conscious "I," but merely the notion of self-inclination, not being directed outside itself, which is exactly how Plotinus characterizes the One's activity in the succeeding lines (24–27). As for the One's simple attention on itself in 6.7.39.1–4, it must be noted that the primary meaning of ἐπιβολή is "to throw or cast upon," with the secondary, metaphorical meaning of intuitive consciousness or immediate attention. Perhaps this word was intentionally chosen by Plotinus in order to convey something quite different than self-consciousness, a contact which is something like the self-union beyond thought evoked in *Enneads* 6.9.6.48–50.

The statement in 6.8.18.21–22 that there is "something like Intellect in the One" is in a context in which Plotinus is not emphasizing consciousness but the freedom of the One's causative power, that the One is not subject to chance. If Intellect acts as it wills and is not a slave to chance, so much greater must be the freedom of the One. That "something like Intellect" is not self-awareness, but, like "wakefulness" in *Enneads* 6.8.16, is the absolute freedom of the completely infinite One which is approximated in a limited way in the free-will of the Nous.

In general, what seems apparent in each of the passages under question is that Plotinus is struggling to refine the Numenian ideas expressed in *Enneads* 5.4.2. Even there, his concern for the unfortunately divisive consciousness imagery is evident in the qualification of the One's activity as identical with its very essence, a characterization maintained in several of the later contexts as well. But even this is not enough, as a careful examination of the above texts has shown. Plotinus has ultimately rejected the applicability of self-consciousness to the One.

A similar situation exists in the case of mystical union terminology. It has been suggested that there is a parallel between the description of the union of the soul or nous with the One and that of the One's relationship with itself, and that this also conveys the idea of the One's self-awareness.[14] *Epibolê, prosbolê, synêsis* used of the *unio mystica* do parallel the *epibolê* of *Enneads* 6.7.39.1–4. However, even if it can be interpreted to represent the language of some sort of immediate consciousness,[15] it is clear that they also all bear a non-conscious root meaning of touch or contact (a "thrusting or casting upon or towards," a "coming together with") which definitely conveys the impression that Plotinus is trying to push the reader towards something more basic, more unitative than consciousness. An impression confirmed in passages like *Enneads* 6.7.16.11–23 which speaks of the pre-intellective vision of the Nous, identified with the power by which the Nous experiences the One through *epibolê* in 6.7.35.20–34, and then rejects it as a "vision" altogether, or *Enneads* 6.9.11.5–6 where it is said of the union of the soul with the One that "the seer himself was one with the seen (for it was not really seen, but united to him)." It is also in accord with the many passages which describe the union as a presence, touch or possession rather than a knowing, thinking, or consciousness.[16]

Bussanich believes that the soul's "vision" of the One is largely synonymous with its "contact" or "union" with the One.[17] He may well be correct. However, this is not because consciousness persists in the union in the form of the One's self-vision, but because the "vision" is really something more than consciousness, a "different kind of seeing" which is more like touch. "Vision" is really only an approximation of the experience from a noetic perspective. Any interchangeability of "seeing" with "touching" is designed to indicate that we are dealing with an experience which does not really involve consciousness, but which only appears to be like it when we speak from the noetic level.

The One should therefore be properly regarded as beyond any self-consciousness. For self-awareness is both divisive to the One's absolute simplicity and unity, and limiting to its absolute infinity. It is divisive because it requires at least a subject and an act of awareness, and undoubtedly also an object as well. It is limiting because before or at the same instant that one can pronounce "I," one must encompass oneself, and in order to encompass oneself one must be a distinct thing, i.e. have boundaries. The infinite, on the other hand, has no boundaries to reach, upon the attaining of which the "I" can be thought. But then the truly Infinite does not need self-awareness or any consciousness at all, but has something much better: it *is* itself in a unified and infinite way, if by "itself" we do not mean some distinct thing but no distinct thing at all, having no separation in itself and no limits.

What are the implications of the Plotinian revision of the Middle Platonic Supreme Principle? One consequence is that when the One is placed outside of distinct being, its transcendence is of a kind quite different from that of the typical Middle Platonic Supreme Principle. The Middle Platonic God sits at the summit of a hierarchical universe, distantly removed from the lower levels by many intermediate strata of being and entirely unrelated to the material substratum of the lowest. Instead, the One is fully omnipresent,[18] and not merely by being immanent in the All, like the incorporeal Forms or soul are in relation to embodied things, but as the All. In other words, the One can become all things, even Matter, because the Middle Platonic concern about infecting the Supreme Principle with the imperfections of the world is alleviated when the the One is seen to have no distinct nature to be altered or changed.

In the usual Plotinian idea of Nous coming from the One, Soul from the Nous, Nature from Soul, etc., it might seem as if the One is still part of a hierarchy. However, while Plotinus does maintain an internal hierarchy within that which is derived from the One, with the Nous, Soul, Nature, Matter in a descending order of power and perfection, one must always bear in mind that the entire emanational sequence is, less spatially construed, a progressive transformation of the One. Plotinus treats it like a single life laid out at length with each part following one after the other.[19] Alternately, one can use the analogy of a single substance taking on many succeeding forms. In either case, while there is some internal hierarchy with one thing coming before another, each thing stands in an equal relation to the one substance or life which becomes it. Hence, there is equal continuity permitted between God and all levels of creation from Nous to Hyle.

Removing God from the summit of a hierarchy of Being and thereby establishing this intimate continuity dramatically alters the relationship between God and the All in another way. The view that God is both true Being and Mind, is both intelligible and intellectual, creates a special relationship between Man and God. Man, alone of all creation, both resembles God in being intellectual and can have access to God as the Intelligible through his own intellect. However, if the One is beyond both Intellect and the Intelligible, man does not stand in some special relationship to God. Instead, all creatures have access to the One in a way appropriate to their own natures.

Plotinus says as much in one late treatise: "All in me (the physical cosmos) seek after the Good and each attain it in accordance with their own particular power (to attain); for the whole of heaven hangs from it, and the entirety of my soul, and the gods in my parts, and all animals and plants and whatever there is in me (if there is anything) which seems to be without life. And some things seem to have a share only of being, others of life, others more fully of life in that they have sense-perception, others at the next stage have reason, and others full life."[20] Because all things are continuous with the One/Good, each can attain it. Because they are each distinctly different in nature and powers, each must attain the One in accordance with its own peculiar nature.

This is because as the One is beyond distinct being, each reaches the One by transcending its own distinct nature which the One has become. But this can only be accomplished once each has fully experienced that nature. One cannot go beyond what one has not yet achieved. This path cannot be the same for every type of creature because each possesses a different distinct nature to transcend.

All souls consist of one aspect which always looks towards the Nous, and one which tends to the body. For humans, the distinct nature of our souls is such that through the rational power, a power of that aspect of the soul tending the body,[21] we may, when we use it, become aware of the aspect of the soul always fixing its gaze upon the intelligible and thereby begin our ascent towards full experience of the nature available to us in the Nous. Animals and plants, however, possess body-tending souls in which the rational power is not active. Consequently, their distinct soul natures are such that the part of the soul always looking towards the Nous is not available to them.[22] Therefore, full experience of that distinctness of the being available to each, involves "higher" soul and Nous for humans but not for animals or plants. The distinctness of being which they must fully experience in order to be able to reach the One beyond is one involving the body and body-tending aspect of the soul with those powers active in it, sense-perception and growth in animals, growth in plants.

In this way intellect is not dispensed with as a path to God, but it is not the only way for all. It is only the way appropriate for Man, as a creature whose distinct nature has available physical, psychic, and intelligible realms. We must go through the Nous, not because the Nous is somehow closer to the One (for how could the One indeed be limited in such a way that it is less omnipresent to Nature than to Nous), but because in order to reach beyond the distinctness of Being, we must first fully experience Nous, as an aspect of that distinctness of being available to us. Creatures with nous not available to them need not live noetically to experience what lies beyond.

In the end, one can see that Plotinus' reworking of Middle Platonic approaches to the problem of the relationship between the Ultimate Principle and all else constitutes a major paradigm shift. The implications of this shift are extremely significant with regard to both the problem of Divine transcendence and immanence, and that of the availability of the One for its derivatives. In our world, where hierarchical conceptualizations of all kinds—from social class/caste structures to the phylogenetic order attributed to nature's life forms—are slowly beginning to break down,[23] it is time to re-evaluate the special relationship of man to God which remains a dominant feature of Western religion. The Judaeo-Christian theological mainstream still reflects a largely Middle Platonic framework to the extent that God is treated not as beyond Being and Mind but as a different kind of conscious Being, distinctly different from a Cosmos created from nothing, to whom humankind alone can relate by virtue of our unique gift of *imago Dei*, a mind analogous to that of God and thus capable of receiving his revelation. By contrast, the conclusions drawn here from Plotinian metaphysics allow us to envision all creatures and even the physical world as just as much transformations of the One as are we; we can also see them as able, in accordance with their own peculiar natures and abilities, to attain union with the One. The same conclusions, however, in no way attempt to demean humans or the special powers which we possess.

Notes

1. J. Dillon, *The Middle Platonists* (Ithaca: Cornell University Press, 1977), 29; and J. P. Kenney, *Mystical Monotheism, A Study in Ancient Platonic Theology* (Hanover & London: Brown University Press, 1991), 26–27.

2. Kenney 1991, 46.

3. For Seneca: Kenney 1991, 30–31; for Philo: Dillon 1977, 155–178; Kenney 1991, 32.

4. Dillon 1977, 46.

5. Philo, *The Special Laws* 1.328.

6. Dillon 1977, 46.

7. Dillon 1977, 280–283; Kenney 1991, 62–70, 76–79.

8. Plotinus, *Enneads* 6.7.39.20–24; 6.8.16.26–27.

9. *Enneads* 5.3.10.48–54, 5.3.12.47–50, 5.3.13.22–24; 5.6.5.1-5; 6.7.35.44–45, 6.7.37–41; 6.9.6.43–50.

10. J. M. Rist, *Plotinus: The Road to Reality* (Cambridge: Cambridge University Press, 1967), 44; Kenney 1991, 105–109.

11. J. Bussanich, *The One and Its Relation to Intellect in Plotinus* (Leiden: E.J. Brill, 1988), 218; J. N. Deck, *Nature, Contemplation, and the One: A Study in the Philosophy of Plotinus* (Burdett, NY: Larson Publications, 1991), 32–33; Kenney 1991, 108, 110.

12. Bussanich 1988, 218.

13. *Enneads* 6.8.13

14. Bussanich 1988, 95, 214–215.

15. Bussanich 1988, 115–116.

16. *Enneads* 5.3.10.43–44; 5.3.14.8–20; 6.7.35.19–20; 6.9.4.1–4.

17. Bussanich 1988, 146–148, as opposed to Rist 1967, 221, where it is argued that "vision" of the One is subordinate to "contact" or "union" with

the One.

18. A. H. Armstrong, *An Introduction to Ancient Philosophy* (Totowa, NJ: Littlefield, Adams & Co., 1981), 182.

19. *Enneads* 5.2.2.27–30.

20. *Enneads* 3.2.3.32–39. The passage in question could be interpreted differently, with the attainment of each being only as far as each is able, and the result being that some achieve only a "share in being, some in life, etc." However, I believe that this interpretation is faulty for two reasons. First, in the early part of the passage there is no strong contrast established between the seeking by all and a differential attainment by each, but rather, because of the placement of the mevn and dev next to the verbs, there is a weak contrast between the activities of seeking and attaining, which leads to my translation as seek "and" attain. Second, if the subsequent section really assigns to differential attainment a causality for the various shares which all things possess, we are left with the logically incoherent situation in which the various entities within the cosmos are seeking the Good before they yet have the traits which distinguish them (being only=rocks, life=plants, sense-perception=animals, etc.), the powers which make them what they are. Therefore, how can they be said to seek at all when they do yet exist as themselves, and thus do not yet exist. It is better to interpret the second portion of the passage as not related to the first causally, but in the explanatory manner of my translation and interpretation.

21. *Enneads* 4.3.18.2–3.

22. *Enneads* 1.1.11.10–12.

23. The idea that "all men are created equal" has at least given ideological pressure to change social and economic inequalities, even if there still exist in actuality many ranked societies, including our own. In the realm of biology and physical anthropology, the evolutionary "tree" gradation of species has begun to yield to the non-hierarchical "bush" model, as in K. L. Feder and M. A. Park, *Human Antiquity* (Mountain View, CA: Mayfield Publishing Company, 1989), 368.

The Magic of Romance:
The Cultivation of Eros
from Sappho to the Troubadours

Christopher Bamford

> To appreciate present conditions
> collate them with those of antiquity.
>
> To humiliate love,
> remember nothing.
> —Basil Bunting

Introduction

THIS PAPER (a fragment of a fragment of a larger history of Romanticism) seeks to conjure a mood, a new way of thinking about ourselves that connects us to a fundamental human experience, perhaps in a way we are unused to. By looking at something that is closer to us than usual, I hope to unsettle some habitual perceptions and provide an opening of perspectives onto our lives and work.

The theme is twofold: love and the evolution of consciousness.

The evolution of consciousness is central to the Romantic worldview, as Hegel and Schelling well knew. Usually, it is considered rather in the abstract—either in terms of the evolution of the great cultural epochs or, when looking at more recent history, in terms of philosophy and science: the evolution or history of ideas. This makes us forget that, if there is such an evolution, it is the whole human being that evolves—not only human thinking, but human feeling and willing as well, and even (may we say it?), the body itself, as Michel Foucault pointed out. I came to consider this controversial idea from the perspective of love—or relationship—when studying and thinking about psychotherapy. For central to psychotherapy or "the talking cure" is the therapeutic relationship—the "transference" or mutual space of healing speech where truth speaks in the play of difference between therapist and client—which all schools of psychotherapy (Freudian and Jungian) agree is (in Lacan's phrase) "the place of the unconscious," the place where I (or individuation) truly comes about, where transformation and real learning occur. In other words, this therapeutic relationship is gnostic: it confers knowledge that saves. It is redemptive, redeeming not just by new "information," but by a "new birth." A maieutic process unfolding between two individuals "midwifes" a higher reality. Indeed, it is as if the ancient spiritual relation between teacher and pupil was metamorphosing into a lay relation between human beings encountering each other as if for the first time and potentially as equals.

Of course, this possibility has always been present, but with significant changes still naturally incomplete. Ellenberger, the historian of the unconscious, for instance, shows the long pre-history of the phenomenon of rapport from the magical healing of shamanic and temple trance, through animal magnetism and hypnotism, to the contemporary understanding of the transference relation as a new kind of interpersonal clairvoyance, a heightened and exalted empathic cognition, in which human beings are enabled to experience each other's pain and joy in compassion and detachment.

Another insight into this same history of a quite different order is provided by Rudolf Steiner when he speaks of the Mysteries of Eleusis—of Demeter, and of her daughter Persephone (in his lecture cycle *Wonders of the World, Ordeals of the Soul, Revelations of the Spirit*). According to Steiner, Persephone names the ancient powers of clairvoyance that played out of the cosmos into human souls, while Demeter, her mother, invokes still more ancient powers of clairvoyance: the memory of a time when humanity and the cosmos were completely integrated and interpenetrated. At the time of the Mysteries of Eleusis, these ancient clairvoyances were disappearing. Demeter was distant, and Persephone was sinking deeper and deeper into the unconscious, carried off by Hades into the underworld. It was at this moment, according to Steiner, that Eros first arose, to take the place of Persephone in human consciousness and mediate the ancient clairvoyance. Standing in for Demeter and Persephone, Eros expands human awareness beyond the senses. In Steiner's view, nothing disappears; it is only transformed. Today, too, Eros is in the process of metamorphosis. Some new faculty is arising.

This is to say that the experience of being in relationship—of being as it were outside oneself in some liminal place or state in-between—is universal. Indeed, the idea of human "being" as being-in-relation—and the world as beings-in-relation—embryonically penetrates all aspects of the thought of our century. For our age could be called the Hermeneutic Age, after Hermes, like Eros, a mediator, interpreter, go-between, message and messenger. Whether in the field of physics or textual criticism the whole certainty of an independent outside observer and an objective world has been called into question in favor of a relational, interactive, less ego-bound view of the world.

This fundamental experience rests upon what Jung called "kinship libido," the desire for connection that is, as he said, "the core of the transference phenomenon" which "it is impossible to argue away, because relationship to the self is at once relationship to our fellow man, and no one can be related to the latter until he is related to himself." This "kinship libido" or affinity is the "mysterious sub-stance" that creates community. To be human is to be with, for, and toward others. There are no monologues. Otherness is always present. Even the creator, as creator, had an Other, as Genesis and the opening of St. John's Gospel affirm: "God said . . ." In this sense, to be human, as to be divine, is to be in relation. It is to experience encounter, the meeting with something—someone—other. Immediately we deliteralize and dematerialize this phenomenon, we realize that the real place of being human, where we meet one another, is not where we are but somewhere in-between, neither here nor there, some other no-place, where the other meets us. They are there, too. The nature of this no-place, this utopia, is suggested by James Hillman's insight that relationship is soul-making: where relations are, that no-place is soul.

In this paper, then, I want to look at the reality of relationship as this may be found in the cultural imagination of the West. It seems to me that, if the evolution of consciousness is a reality, then we ought to be able to see it in something as central to human life as love.

The Gap

> Whoever flees pain
> will love no more.
> To love is always
> to feel the opening
> to hold the wound
> always open.
>   (Novalis)

Sappho (b. 612 B.C.E.) was the first to celebrate Eros, the power or god of love, from a human, existential, phenomenological perspective. This is why we may call her the first Romantic, for Romanticism means not only to write in a Romance language, that is, in the vernacular, but also to stick close to experience. In her fragmentary verses, Sappho depicts in actual, lived detail the paradoxical experience or painful gift of the state of love, calling it "sweetbitter" (*glukuprikon*):

> Eros once again limb-loosener whirls me
> sweetbitter, impossible to fight off, creature
>   stealing up
>   (tr. Anne Carson)

In Sappho's language the description of the experience is precise. The event, the moment of love, is closely observed, caught forever.

Eros blows us away, knocks us down. In the instant of desire, love dismembers us. We fall apart, split open, as if by a great wind:

> Like a mountain whirlwind
> punishing oak trees
> love shattered my heart.
> (tr. Barnstone)

Swept away by love, ungrounded, we lose control. We are burned up: "You burn me." A being or creature, foreign to our will, to our everyday I, seems to flow in upon us, overwhelming our sense of who we are, transporting us into another time and place. Love indeed is this, as Sappho knew: a kind of rape, a Dionysian inflowing into the soul, forcing it open. Plato, in his *Cratylus*, confirms this when he derives *eros* from the Greek *eron*, to flow in from without. "The stream is not inherent," he writes, "but is an influence introduced through the eyes, and from flowing in was called Eros (influx) in the old time." Not only through the eyes, through the ears also:

> Some say cavalry and others claim
> infantry or a fleet of long oars
> is the supreme sight on the black earth.
>   I say it is

> the one you love. And easily proved.
> Did not Helen, who was queen of mortal
> beauty, choose as first among mankind
>   the very source

> of Trojan honor? Haunted by love
> she forgot her kinsmen, her own dear child,
> and wandered off into a remote country.
>   Weak and fitful

woman bending before any man!
So, Anaktoria, although you are
far, do not forget your loving friends.
        And I for one

would rather listen to your soft step
and see your radiant face—than watch
all the dazzling chariots and armored
        hoplites of Lydia.
                (tr. Barnstone)

Such love is more than a seduction; it is closer to magic: something like an enchantment or possession. We no longer know who we are. Something, someone else—a god—suddenly awakes, speaks, and sees in us. We seem to be born anew. For a moment everything is unknown, startling, transfigured. Caught between pleasure and pain, submission and resistance—two states in a single experience—we become many-minded, multiplicitous, clairvoyant. "Sweet wound," Sappho calls it, "bitter honey."

No wonder those who fall in love lose their bearings, suffer dizzying disorientation. Love plunges us (according to Sappho) into an impossible ambivalence. The comfortable, because habitual, boundaries—the fixed distinctions of body and mind, self and other—break down, become confused and mingled. Love seems to undo whatever binds soul to body and gives meaning to our lives. The sadness of love comes from this dying, this aspect of love that initiates us into death. Marsilio Ficino, in the Renaissance, thinking of Sappho's words, which he attributes to Plato and the ancient theologian, Orpheus, acknowledges this: "Love is called by Plato bitter, and not unjustly, because death is inseparable from love. And Orpheus also called love "glukuprikon," that is, sweetbitter, because it is a voluntary death. As death it is bitter, but being voluntary it is sweet."

"Even in Hades I am with you," writes Sappho. This is because death (and rebirth) deliteralize the soul, free it from the body, making it an organ of cognition, conjunction, and, even, a kind of union. With the experience of Hades, the modern experience of the soul begins. In a sense, "Hades' realm" refers to a new perspective that is wholly psychological, where the considerations of human life—the emotions, organic needs, the social connections of humanistic psychology—no longer apply. In Hades's realm (to paraphrase Hillman) psyche alone exists: all other standpoints are dissolved. Therefore the lover says: Even in Hades I am with you. Another poem makes this powerfully clear:

He seems to me equal to gods that man
who opposite you
sits and listens close
to your sweet speaking

and lovely laughing—oh it
puts the heart in my chest on wings
for when I look at you, a moment, then no speaking
is left in me

no: tongue breaks, and thin
fire is racing under skin
and in eyes no sight and drumming
fills ears

and cold sweat holds me and shaking
grips me all, greener than grass
I am and dead—or almost
I seem to me.

(tr. Anne Carson)

Catching us up in an interworld between this world and and that, Sappho's Eros burns away our fixed notions of who we are. Eros puts us into a liminal state, neither this nor that. Our reason and our heart go into oscillation. "Desire keeps pulling the lover to act and not to act," wrote Sophocles. And Sappho:

> I do not know what to do.
> I say yes—and then no.
> (tr. Anne Carson)

Eros thus opens a gap, a split, a hole in our lives. Eros is this gap, this space of desire, held between boundaries. It moves across it like lightning.

This is not necessarily pleasant. Mostly, it is difficult and painful. The first sensation is one of loss. "A hole is being gnawed in my vitals," Sappho reports. She speaks of being "pierced right through to the bone," worn away, sucked out, as in some shamanic rite of passage. Love here is an initiation, a transformation, beginning with dismemberment.

Aphrodite: The Flame

Remember that Aphrodite, Love's golden goddess, was born of the castration of Ouranos, the heavenly father. Recall how Saturn hacked off his father's genitals; how these hurtled earthwards and plunged into the ocean at great speed; and how, finally, out of the churning, white maternal foam caused by the heavenly genitals' explosive fall, bright-shining Aphrodite arose, gloriously whole, bearing in her being the wound of inexorable and painful memory.

Aphrodite's task—this is what love must do—is to redeem the titan Saturn's tragic act of violent, primal scission. Her throne is dappled, complex, shifting, as befits her painful origin; her nature is complex, ambivalent, unpredictable. According to the myth, however, she knows the cost of wholeness and moves laughing through the forms of otherness, making whole what pleases her, "present when wholeness emerges from the halves and when the resolved opposites become the indissoluble goldenness of life" (Kerenyi).

The mention of halves reminds us of Aristophanes' image of original human beings as spherical and sliced in half: "Sliced in two like a flatfish, each of us is perpetually hunting for the matching himself." Here, too, we may remember Plato's description of "true learning": "It is not something that can be put into words like other kinds of learning; only after a long partnership in a common life devoted to this very thing does truth flash into the soul, like a flame kindled by a leaping spark."

Knowing Eros

Eros in Greek means (according to another derivation) want, lack, desire for what we do not have. In a sense, it speaks of absence at the very heart of being. This lack is fundamental: at the same time an absence of and an openness to being itself. Not lack of this or that, the absence of something nameable, but the lack of being itself, something unnameable, unknowable, out of which being can come into existence. If being lacked nothing, there would be nothing, no images, nothing to say, nothing to know. It is because of eros—lack, desire, love—that the world is and becomes more and more itself as we know it. The more we love, the more we are, the more we speak and make. In love, we pursue what flees, living towards the future, giving to airy nothings a habitation and a name—"I begin with words of air / Yet they are good to hear," writes Sappho. The lover is forever naming the unnameable, a glance or glimpse of something always poised between appearance and disappearance, actuality and potentiality. Love places us at the very edge, on the cut between male and female, between I and Thou— between and before the two. Here we are not yet one, nor yet still wholly two. Not in this world, not in that. Eros is and appears on this delicate threshold or horizon, the instant between reach and grasp, when the inaccessible becomes suddenly accessible. Love, indeed, as we said before is a boundary condition. It is a drawn sword placed between lovers when they lie down together in the forest. It is that electric opening in our lives across which something then can leap: a spark, an insight, an image: a metaphor, a transference (for transference is the precise Latin translation of the Greek metaphor). When we love, we know: we love to know. For as Aristotle says, "All men by their nature reach out (desire) to know." Knowing and desiring are two sides of a single movement, and all knowledge, like all love, is metaphor or transference. "To give names to nameless things by transference from things kindred or similar in appearances," is how Aristotle defines metaphor. And metaphor, as Anne Carson says, is a species of symbol. "Each one of us is but the symbolon of a human being . . . and each pursues a never ending search for the symbolon of himself." Between two pairs of eyes, between glances "more melting than sleep or death," love comes to be in a gaze of seeing, a visionary state. Sappho wrote:

> Now in my
> heart I
> see clearly
>
> a beautiful
> face
> shining,
>
> etched
> by love.
>   (tr. Barnstone)

Imagination: An Eye Filled with its Vision

Love has also very much to do with seeing, as Plotinus noted. Not the seeing of the eyes, but the seeing of the heart, as Sappho knew. This heart is not the conical organ, not my heart in my body, but heart as a psychic organ and state of knowing. The Greek word *enthymesis* speaks of the power of this heart—as the act of meditating, conceiving, imagining, projecting, ardently desiring: intending. This heart is creative: it is the True Imagination, the mirror and projection of real presences. Plotinus puts it this way: Eros, whether a god, a spirit, or a state of mind, begins in the soul's affinity to beauty, which is its true nature and is divine. The soul therefore by its nature tends towards this perfection of itself, which is beauty, and from this innate intentionality of the soul Eros, the power to behold Beauty is born:

> Love, thus, is ever intent upon that other loveliness, and exists to be the medium between desire and the object of desire. It is the eye of the desirer; by its power what loves is enabled to see the loved thing. But it is first; before it becomes the vehicle of vision, it is itself filled with the sight; it is first, therefore, and not even of the same order—for desire attains to vision only through the efficacy of Love, while Love, in its own act, harvests the spectacle of beauty playing immediately above it.

Eros, for Plotinus, twinned with Imagination, is a quite special kind of contemplative healing seeing in which Beauty and love meet in the eye, the same eye of which Meister Eckhart says, the eye with which I see God and the eye with which God sees me are one. The real aim of love for Plotinus is contemplation, the perfection of the soul. He even derives *eros* from *orathis*, this seeing. Rightly so, for without eyes—without seeing—Love cannot be:

> In the absence of eyes
> all Aphrodite is vacant, gone.
> (Aeschylus, *Agammemnon*; tr. Anne Carson)

And Plotinus:

> There is a strenuous act of contemplation in the Soul; there is an emanation towards it from the object contemplated; and Eros is born, the Love which is an eye filled with its vision, a seeing that bears its image with it.

Psyche is and is not Eros

O Goddess! hear these tuneless numbers, wrung
      By sweet enforcement and remembrance dear,

And pardon that thy secrets should be sung
        Even into thine own soft-conched ear:
Surely I dreamt today, or did I see
        The winged Psyche with awakened eyes?
I wandered in a forest thoughtlessly,
        And, on a sudden, fainting with surprise,
Saw two fair creatures, couched side by side
        In deepest grass, beneath the whispering roof
Of leaves and trembled blossoms . . .
They lay calm-breathing on the bedded grass;
        Their arms embraced, and their pinions too;
Their lips touched not, but had not bade adieu,
        As if disjoined by soft-handed slumber . . .
        The winged boy I knew;
But who wast thou, O happy, happy dove?
        His Psyche true!
          —John Keats

It was James Hillman who placed the myth of Eros and Psyche (thereby displacing, or at least complementing, Freud's Oedipus) at the center of his program to renew psychology by returning soul to its rightful place as the archetypal human concern. But it was Keats the poet who recognized the earth to be "the vale of soul making" and acknowledged that Psyche, a latecomer on Olympus, had no temples in the ancient world:

        Nor altar heaped with flowers;
      Nor virgin choir to make delicious moan
      Upon the midnight hours . . .
—and now deserved no less than the human heart for a home:
      Yes, I will be thy priest, and build a fane
        In some untrodden region of my mind . . .
     And in the midst of this wide quietness
        A rosy sanctuary will I dress

With the wreathed trellis of a working brain . . .
And there shall be for thee all soft delight
That shadowy thought can win,
A bright torch, and a casement ope at night,
To let the warm love in.

The initiatic tale of Eros and Psyche, told by Apuleius in "The Golden Ass" in incult Latin—the vernacular—is, as Hillman points out, the only real account of Psyche that we have. And it shows Psyche conjoined inevitably with Eros. They are a couple. Are they identical? Does their hierogamy celebrate the androgyne—the hermaphroditic consciousness—we are? The goal of Eros is Psyche, and conversely. Alone, each is destructive: the world falls apart, imagination dies, there is no creativity. For "the imaginal is entered primarily through interested love; it is the creation of faith, need, and desire" (Hillman).

The Troubadours

In a sense, Sappho was the first Troubadour. She was certainly the first to give individual, lyric voice to the singularity of human experience. She wrote, as she spoke, her own language: in the vernacular. The Troubadours were the first Western Europeans to do so. Thus the Troubadours were the original romantics, for they wrote in the romance language, their vernacular or mother-tongue. This was in Provence, in the South of France, and appropriately they sought to create a culture in which a profane theory of love, of the exaltation of the soul—a contextually feminine or soul theory, as would befit expression in the mother-tongue—influenced everything. Indeed, a case could be made that Troubadour culture and the "Troubadour" tradition constitute the only soul-based culture we know.

From this point of view, the Troubadour vision must be distinguished from the chivalric or courtly tradition—to which it was related and which it could be said to have feminized or ensouled. The chivalric tradition for its part rested on the primacy not of the feminine but of the more masculine or spiritual virtues. By which I mean that chivalry affirmed equality—the chivalric court was a community of equals, an ideal brotherhood; it was heroic (death in the service of one's lady was more than acceptable), virile, outward, open, realistic; it exalted courage, daring, generosity, loyalty, fidelity (but not continence); hence it valued marriage (it was not essentially adulterous), and rested upon desire as an end in itself. The Troubadours reframed these virtues: in lieu of equality, they proclaimed inequality; instead of superiority, they embraced a voluntary inferiority, humility, submission to, and distance from, the Lady, who was often married to someone else; hence the love they embodied was essentially adulterous on the moral plane and the Troubadour by definition was single (Nelli says he represented youth, the *joventus*); and therefore, instead of openness and outwardness, discretion or secrecy and interiority were valued; instead of communality, moral isolation, solitude; instead of desire, pleasure or joy.

The origins of the Troubadours, as all origins, are unknown. Arabic sources have been suggested, likewise Celtic sources, as well as women's songs and songs in women's voice. Neoplatonism and thereby the Greek Mysteries have also been invoked, particularly the Mysteries of Eleusis, part of which (according to this likely story, as trickling up through Erasmus Darwin and Sar Peladan to Ezra Pound) was reputedly the myth of Eros and Psyche, later told by Apuleius. For our part, we shall impute no historical source, but imagine this cultural flowering as the fruit of Love itself—as we may likewise take Sappho to be. This fruit of love was not limited to the Troubadours, however, for their age witnessed also both the School of Chartres with its great recovery of the goddess Natura—the world soul—and the flowering of devotion to the Virgin, sung by great mystics such as Bernard of Clairveaux.

Historically, the Troubadours begin with Guillem IX, Duke of Aquitaine (born in 1071), and end about two hundred years later with Giraut Riquier. Guillem is, as it were, transitional between the chivalric/heroic and true Troubadour vision. He is a mixture, an ambiguous figure, bursting onto the scene ready-made, without antecedents. Guillem is a wild man—one of the greatest knights of the world, and very unfaithful toward women, says his Life. Not a true Troubadour, Guillem nevertheless introduces certain essential themes.

Above all, he affirms that to sing love—which is joy—is as natural to the human being as leaves are to a tree in Spring or the bird's song is to the bird:

> When we see again the spring blossoming of the
>   world,
> orchards and meadows growing green one more time,
> brooks and springs clear-running, fresh-running
>   winds,
> then every living man should take full
>   measure
> of what gives him pleasure.
>   (tr. Blackburn)

Pleasure of course is joy: "I am gladdened through" he writes "by the love of / A joy that I want to delight in more, / And since I want to return to joy / I must, if I can, go to the best."

There are mysteries here. For in another sense these poems are about nothing(ness). "I shall make a verse about nothing, / downright nothing, not / about myself or youth or love / or anyone." They are made while asleep, and when walking and loafing. They are more folly than sense. But it makes no difference. What makes the difference is the authentic witness they bear to states of soul: to the experience of the great joy of life and love, to the perpetual fountain that is the imaginal self.

By 1150, the Troubadour movement was underway. The new Troubadours are inferiors, jongleurs, not aristocrats. "Marcabru was left outside a rich man's door, and no one ever knew who he was or where he was from." New elements are introduced, at first only hesitantly. A new element is the idea of the purification of love by love. This means the purification at once of the singer and song. "Love weeps to be differentiated from lechery." The lover must not be confused with the lecher. True love is "fine love" (*fins amor*) that "carries a medicine intended to heal his companion." At the same time love, while remaining profane, begins to play with a sacred aspect: "O noble love, source of all giving / by whom the whole world is illumined."

Another important idea is that of distance: the space necessary for desire to become joy. A celebrated expression of this is Jaufre Rudel's "When the Days are Long in May": "No other joy could mean so much / as that I have / my love afar." Jaufre was not a jongleur but a very noble man, the Prince of Blaie. He was a Troubadour. The story goes that he heard pilgrims returning from Antioch speak of the beauty of the Countess of Tripoli. And forthwith he gave his heart to this mistress he had never seen, and spoke of her in his poems. Yet he longed to see her. For years. One day the inspiration came upon him to make pilgrimage to Tripoli and he embarked upon the sea. On the journey, he became gravely ill; his companions thought he would die. Nevertheless, he reached Tripoli where he was taken to an inn. The Countess heard of his coming and went to see him at his bedside. She took him in her arms. He knew it was the Countess and came to life, praising God that he had been fulfilled. Then he died. The Countess buried him in the house of the Templars, and next day took the habit of a nun.

Between 1150 and 1250 is known as the classic age of the Troubadours. The chivalric, more masculine element has been eliminated or assimilated. And in its place we find an entire initiatory psychospiritual soul path of love articulated. Rene Nelli sees seven stages, moments or aspects to this:

1. Falling in love;
2. Joy;
3. Fins Amor;
4. The Perfect Lover;

5. The Perfect Lady;
6. The Rewards of Love;
7. The Exchange of Hearts.

ENAMOUREMENT (falling in love). This is the wound of love: a psychic, not a bodily wound. It is effected through the gates of the senses—the eyes or ears above all—and descends to the heart. "Love wounds in two places: the ears and the eyes." "I thank God and my eyes for this / that through their knowing / joy came to me," writes Dante Arnaut. And: "And if I see her not / No sight is worth the beauty / of my thought." But the ears, the hearing, too can play its part. Not only does the voice of the lady have a magic charm, but simply hearing about her can wound as well. This last indicates that it is the spirit or soul—the heart—of the Lady that is addressed. It is a friendship of hearts that is at stake. A mysterious magic substance, a fiery ray of desire, capable of action at a distance, moves in that look, in that hearing, to descend to depths of the lover's heart. It lights a fire in that heart that once lit, never goes out, but grows in intensity from day to day. This ray moves through the gates of the senses from heart to heart. "The flame, the fire, the conflagration of love are born in the heart, and give rise to reflection," writes Peire Vidal. In this way it can and will, if obeyed, make two hearts one. "With a single desire it unites two hearts." Thus, though perhaps glimpsed, the Lady is never seen—not with the physical eyes alone at any rate. She is seen, and sees, with eyes of fire and this union of hearts is an imaginal work, a magic work with images and a purification of the senses.

To be wounded by love is to feel, above all, the joy of desiring, and to benefit from the beneficent, exalting, ennobling influx (eros) that comes from joy.

JOY. Joy is an activity, an exalting game—the play of pure love, of psyche as such. Or of the heart: joy is the heart's desiring. Joy is to desire in one's heart; to enclose the other in one's heart—the image of the other. It is to serve the image of the other in one's heart. Thus joy has a quality of absolute interiority. It is the soul in its own realm, deliteralized from the body. "I would rather have the desire of you, than what a carnal lover has," writes one poet. It is said that, in the heart, desire is transformed into joy. The image of this joy is Spring, the song of birds: the sound of music. It is perpetually youthful. And indeed there is a connection between *joi* and *jovens*, between joy and youth. Such joy is the beginning and end of the virtues. Arnaut de Mareil writes: "Whoever has joy is given great honor, for all springs from joy: courtliness, pleasure, education, candor, measure, a loving heart, the desire to serve, mercy, knowledge, gnosis, and the capacity to speak well and reply pleasingly."

Now joy, though following the wound of love, and deriving from the look or hearing, is prior to loving itself. It is the precondition of loving. Without the hard-won freedom of joy, true love/loving is not attainable. It is hardwon because joy depends upon love held solely in the heart or soul, hence it is pure and simple.

FIN'AMORS (true, pure love) is the end of joy. It is the path of joy, which is the purification of desire, the experience of desire as such. This accounts for the mixture of the purest love and the most natural desires and language. One Troubadour wrote: "I am the most accomplished of lovers, because I neither say nor ask anything of my Lady. ... I am her friend, and I serve her occultly, discretely and silently. For she does not know the good she gives me, nor how I receive joy and value from her. I rejoice in my Lady's spirit and smile and I would be mad to ask for more." It is a stage in itself and in a way includes all the others. Giraut Riquier names five doors of love: desire, prayer, service, kiss, fact. Elsewhere the service of love is given four stages: sighing, supplication, understanding, bodily fulfillment.

This is love that is more than love. It is most precious in that it makes possible perfect human virtues. Without this mystery of love, conceived in joy, there would not be the possibility of youth, generosity, mercy, compassion, etc. Rene Nelli writes: "The effort of the Troubadours consisted not at all in celebrating continence for its own sake—for after all these ladies were married and they themselves had mistresses in the flesh—but in repeating tirelessly that love, whence all virtues proceed, presupposes spiritual bases which can only manifest to begin with in all their purity in their separation from sensuality, even though they derived from it and must in the end return to it and envelop it anew. This entire philosophy only proposes to create the idea of love, and the sole preoccupation of the lovers was to attain this reality in their hearts. This is why the comparison arises between this erotic work and the work of alchemy."

THE PERFECT LOVER. The duties of the perfect lover are to serve, praise, honor, and conceal. It is the painful practice, the real suffering (*sofrir*) of these, that makes possible certain virtues—virtues that, as compared to the virtues of the perfect lady, we may call feminine or of the anima: obedience, patience, hope, sincerity, fidelity, humility, timidity, discretion, vassalage. The first victory is over pride. "Such service was well suited to mortify male pride, and there was in this voluntary submission of the friend to the lady, a most profound truth: since the functional misogyny of the male had thus far impeded the development of love, this now had to begin in the symbolic humiliation of masculine power." One Troubadour, Arnaut de Mareil, cries out: "Love, permit nobility to bow down before you." There was a reciprocal relation between bowing down and being raised up, between the practice of humility, timidity, etc., and being perfected, ennobled by love.

The cardinal rule is to please; the cardinal virtue, patience in the practice of humility, sincerity, and fidelity. The experience of this was often a death experience. Arnaut de Mareil says that he dies every day. And every day he rises again in hope. The perfect lover is one who never ceases to hope.

Praise is another practice. This is to ever more see the Lady in terms of her moral graces. Here is a description: "Courteous and cultivated Lady, amiable towards all people, aware of everyone's needs in acts, words, and thoughts, your courtesy and your beauty, your gentle words, your agreeable company, your culture, your merit, your gracious body, the freshness of your complexion, your beautiful smile, your loving look, and all your other qualities, fine actions and fine words, make me dream night and day."

Discretion went without saying: it was the supreme practice of containment, interiority, the sealing of the vessel.

THE PERFECT LADY. The Lady was love from head to foot. She was the natural source of desire and the supernatural source of love. Her virtues/practices were innate nobility, merit, glory, power. All this for the exercise of joy. "Lady Maria," writes Bieris de Romans, "in you merit and distinction, / joy, intelligence, and perfect beauty, hospitality and honor and distinction, / your noble speech and pleasing company / your sweet face and merry disposition / the sweet look and loving expression / that exist in you without pretension, / cause me to turn toward you with a pure heart." And the joy? In the words of the Countess of Dia:

> I thrive on youth and joy
> and youth and joy keep me alive,
> for my friend's the very gayest
> which makes me gay and playful.

Finally, then, there are the rewards of love.

CONTEMPLATION OF THE LADY NAKED and the TEST OF LOVE. This unmediated, direct vision is both image and reality. In alchemical language it is the naked truth. The contemplation is given by the lady, received in the spirit of service by the Troubadour. "She will call me into her chamber where she undresses, and by her command I shall be near her by her bed, and on my knees, humbly, if she offers me her foot, I shall pull off her slippers," writes Bernart de Ventadour.

Whatever is contained in this contemplation could lead to the *asag* or TEST: a test imposed on the masculine by the feminine. This is the alchemical Immersion in the Bath. It is very little described. Nelli quotes Fabre d'Olivet: "To enjoy (to have), without possessing, is the instinct of the man; to possess before having is the instinct of the woman." In this sense, the test tries whether the Troubadour has perfected his feminine nature to the point that it has become nature to him also. But this is not a test to pass or fail: rather it is an exercise in the very heart or interiority of love. It has nothing to do with resisting temptation, or continence in a literal sense. The Countess of Dia, a woman Troubadour, gives a clue perhaps: "How much I would give to hold in my arms one night my Lord, provided he thinks himself happy enough to receive what I would give him—only my breast as a pillow. I am more taken with him than Flor with Blancheflor. I give him my heart and my love, my spirit, my eyes, and my life. Handsome friend, charming and kind, when shall I have you in my power? If only I could lie beside you for an hour and embrace you lovingly—know this, I would give anything to have you in my husband's place, but only under the condition that you do my bidding." And Azalais de Porcairages, another woman Troubadour:

> I have a friend of great repute
> who towers above all other men,
> and his heart toward me is not un-
> true, for he offers me his love.
> And I tell you I reciprocate,
> and whoever says I don't,
> God curse his luck—
> as for myself I'm safe.

> Handsome friend, I'd gladly stay
> forever in your service—
> such noble mien and such fine looks—
> so long as you don't ask too much;
> we'll soon come to the final test,
> for I'll put myself in your hands:

you swore me your fidelity,
now don't ask me to transgress.

Finally, there is THE EXCHANGE OF HEARTS, the Conjunctio. The center of Troubadour imagery is this "almost chemical combination," the exchange of hearts, the communion—the fusion—of hearts. "Love with a single desire unites two hearts." The Troubadour's heart is where his lady is. But it is also "the mirror in which he sees his lady." "Love inscribes her beauty at the bottom of the heart." It is the heart which is the vessel of the practices. The mutuality of the lovers resides in their opening their hearts to each other: contemplating each other's heart. This is an imaginal act, the union is an imaginal union—the Troubadour lovers' coitus, as that of the alchemical lovers, takes place in water.

For this to happen, the lovers must rest breast upon breast, as equals. The exchange of hearts makes absolute equals. I = not-I = Thou: this is the ring that unites them as one.

Inconclusion: The Thinking Heart

A lady asks me
I speak in season
She seeks reason for an affect, wild often
That is so proud he hath Love for a name
    —Cavalcanti (Ezra Pound)

The story by no means conludes with the Troubadours. Subsequent chapters unfold in Italy, with Dante, Guido Cavalcanti, and their friends. Then the Renaissance Platonists and magicians—above all, Pico della Mirandola and Giordano Bruno—raise the stakes to include a fullblown gnosticism of love. But almost before they have done so, another movement unfurls, focusing (let us say) on Shakespeare—especially the Shakespeare of the Sonnets, as Joel Fineman's marvelous book *Shakespeare's Perjur'd Eye* recounts. Finally, Romanticism proper—above all, Goethe, Novalis, Hoelderlin, Keats—prepares our present moment, the work we have to do. But these are other stories.

Perhaps we may ask concerning the Troubadours, What pedagogic function did they perform? How does their teaching transform? For it is important to recall that consciousness evolves (if it does) through individuals. Whether it is the incarnation of the Logos, or Descartes' "Cogito ergo Sum," or Newton's mechanics, something enters the stream of human consciousness through an individual or a group of individuals and assimilated and digested it becomes the province—the faculty—of humanity as such.

What faculties, then, entered through the Troubadours? What movement or faculty began in the Mysteries of Eleusis and with Plato and Sappho and passed on through the Troubadours and Dante to the Renaissance and Shakespeare, Goethe, Novalis, Freud, Jung and countless others? May we call it perhaps "the thinking heart"?

Selected Bibliography

Barnard, Mary. *Sappho: A New Translation*. Berkeley: University of California Press, 1958

Barnstone, Willis, trans. *Sappho*. Garden City: Anchor Books, 1965.

Blackburn, Paul. *Proensa: An Anthology of Troubadour Poetry*. New York: Paragon House, 1986.

Bogin, Meg. *The Women Toubadours*. New York: W. W. Norton, 1980.

Carson, Anne. *Eros, the Bittersweet*. Princeton: Princeton University Press, 1986.

Dronke, Peter. *Medieval Latin and the Rise of the European Love-Lyric*. Cambridge: Cambridge University Press, 1966.

Ellenberger, Henri F. *The Discovery of the Unconscious*. New York: Basic Books, 1970.

Graves, Robert, trans. *The Golden Ass* by Apuleius. New York: Farrar, Strauss, and Giroux, 1973.

Hillman, James. *The Myth of Analysis*. New York: Harper and Row, 1978.

Lot-Borodine, Myrrha. *De l'Amour Profane a l'Amour Sacre*. Paris: Librairie Nizet, 1961.

Nelli, Rene. *L'Erotique des Troubadours*. Toulouse: Edouard Privat, 1963.

Pound, Ezra. *The Spirit of Romance*. New York: New Directions, 1968.

Press, Alan R. *Anthology of Troubadour Lyric Poetry*. Austin: University of Texas Press, 1971.

Steiner, Rudolf. *Wonders of the World, Ordeals of the Soul, Revelations of the Spirit*. London: Rudolf Steiner Press, 1963

Seating Arrangements in Plato's Symposium

ROBIN WATERFIELD

PLATO'S *Symposium* is, as even a casual reading reveals, a work to which Plato devoted the greatest care. Here is a curiosity which arises in the dialogue, which I am tempted to believe is an example of that care.

Throughout the dialogue, considerable play is made over the seating arrangements and the consequent order of the speeches which constitute the bulk of the work (see passages 175A, 175C–E, 177D, 185C–E, 213B, 222E–223A). The passage at 185C–E is the one I want to home in on—the famous interlude of Aristophanes' hiccups.

There are six chief speakers—remembering that the seventh speech, that of Acibiades, is an unexpected bonus, since he burst into the symposium late in the day (212D). The order of the six speakers, according to the seating arrangement, is: Phaedrus, Pausanius, Aristophanes, Eryximachus, Agathon, and Socrates. Suppose we place them round a circle as follows:

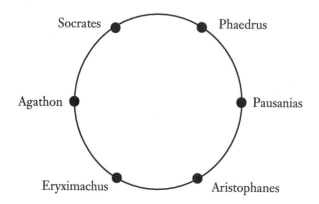

At 185C–E, for reasons which are obscure (apart from the light relief the episode affords), Plato alters the sequence of speakers (though not the seating arrangement) by having Aristophanes so overcome by a bout of hiccups that he is unable to deliver his speech in its proper place. He swaps with the next person, who is Eryximachus. Suppose we map this exchange onto the seating arrangement already depicted:

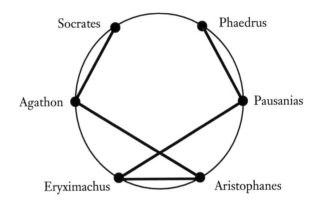

Lo and behold—a stylized cup! What could be more appropriate for a symposium, whose chief activity was normally the consumption of large quantities of alcohol?

Coincidence? I doubt it. It is true that the form of the cup is not that of any of the common ancient Greek kinds, but it is still unmistakably a cup. I prefer to see it as deliberate, then, and as another example of Plato's artistry.

ALL RELIGIONS are ONE
The Voice of one crying in the Wilderness

William Blake

The Argument   As the true method of knowledge is experiment the true faculty of knowing must be the faculty which experiences. This faculty I treat of.

PRINCIPLE 1st   That the Poetic Genius is the true Man and that the body or outward form of Man is derived from the Poetic Genius. Likewise that the forms of all things are derived from their Genius, which by the Ancients was call'd an Angel & Spirit & Demon.

PRINCIPLE 2d   As all men are alike in outward form, so (and with the same infinite variety) all are alike in the Poetic Genius.

PRINCIPLE 3d   No man can think write or speak from his heart, but he must intend truth. Thus all sects of Philosophy are from the Poetic Genius adapted to the weaknesses of every individual.

PRINCIPLE 4.   As none by traveling over known lands can find out the unknown, so from already acquired knowledge Man could not acquire more. Therefore an universal Poetic Genius exists.

PRINCIPLE 5.   The Religions of all Nations are derived from each Nation's different reception of the Poetic Genius which is every where call'd the Spirit of Prophecy.

PRINCIPLE 6.   The Jewish & Christian Testaments are An original derivation from the Poetic Genius. This is necessary from the confined nature of bodily sensation.

Apollo Delphinios

Apollo is here shown with his lyre and quiver seated upon a winged mantic tripod, representing the Tripod at Delphi. According to A. B. Cook, "The tripod itself, for those that know its history, is tantamount to a celestial seat. The god seated upon it is for the time being in heaven, released from the limitations of terrestrial life and free to range in thought over land and sea." Here, the diving dolphins identify him as *Apollôn Delphinios*.

The Dolphin in Greek Legend and Myth

MELITTA RABINOVITCH

ANYONE who has lived on the shores of southerly seas, or who has taken long voyages there, will treasure a certain image: that of the dolphin, suddenly springing out of the gently-moving waves, then mysteriously returning to the deep—a creature at home in both elements, water and air.

The rhythm of the dolphin's movements is willful and unpredictable. One scans the surface of the sea, excitedly wondering when and where the creature will reappear. Usually neither the moment nor the place are what one expects.

Several species of dolphin were already known to antiquity; Aristotle and later Pliny described their differences. Since the ancient zoologists (i.e., probably since Aristotle), it has been classified with the whales, making a middle term between mammals and fishes. In the popular imagination, it passes as a fish.

The dolphin of Greek legend is tame, smallish, and blue-black in color. It almost seems as if the deep violet-blue sea has been concentrated in dolphin form, especially when one sees it against the background of the bright-green evening sky of the South. The leaping and diving dolphin is like a rising and dissolving wave.

In ancient art, one often sees dolphin-heads poking out of the waves. They are carved thus in relief on Roman sarcophagi.[1] There are vase-paintings in which the dolphin is even used in place of waves to indicate the sea.[2] The dolphin loves the sea as the Greeks love it, and like them it also loves music, which always tempts it out of the waveless depths. Pindar sings of how it loves especially the sound of the flute, but also that of the lyre.

It is most wonderful to see the play of shining and shimmering rainbow colors, when the dolphins go leaping out of the waves in the sunlight, making great arches as they somersault in water and air. They swim fast, and can leap into the air higher than a ship's sail.[3] Pindar makes the telling comparison of the champion jumper Melesias with a dolphin.[4]

The dolphin is at home in almost all the temperate seas of the northern hemisphere. It is especially numerous in the Black Sea, and in the waters that wash around the Greek mainland, the isles, and the Ionian coast. One also finds it in the Mediterranean.

No other animal was so honored in myth and legend, art and poetry. No other sea-creature interested the naturalists of antiquity to the same degree. The dolphin is the most celebrated of creatures, the king of the Hellenic seas.

This music-loving sea-dweller is intertwined in the perils and trials of the poets.

It is also close to the everyday life of the seaman, who recognizes it as a friend and helper. It is a good omen for the sailor, for its appearance promises a calm sea and a prosperous and speedy voyage. No land-animal exceeds it in speed, so say Aristotle and Pliny.[5]

Only Zeus can outdo the dolphin on the waters.

The dolphin is a fine predictor of wind, for it swims in the direction from which the wind will come. It also heralds storms, and warns seafarers and fishermen of imminent danger. If it makes especially bold and extravagant leaps, hopping wildly and boisterously over the surface, that is a sure sign of an approaching storm.

The Greeks also regarded the dolphin as a sacred animal. If one was caught in a fishing net, it was freed. To capture and especially to kill one was disgraceful and criminal. The miscreant was hated by the gods, suffered their punishment, and was banned from their altars. Oppian, a poet of the second century C.E., says "There is no beast holier than the dolphin."[6]

The Greeks were rich in creative imagination. They made up countless legends about the manifold qualities of the dolphin, its fidelity, loyalty, and gratitude for good deeds. They valued most of all

Picture on a Cup, *circa* 500 B.C.E.

its selfless readiness to rescue. Plutarch says: "Of all beasts, only the dolphin is endowed by nature with that which the noblest philosophers crave: altruistic love of humanity."[7] For it owes nothing to man, and has never been taught by him, yet it helps him even at the cost of its own life.

In Friedrich Creuzer's eloquent words, the dolphin is "a symbol of humanity in the depth of the sea, which otherwise shelters only monsters."[8] For the act of rescue is the basic motive of all the Greek dolphin-legends, whether Ionian or Dorian. Many of these have been preserved for us by Plutarch,[9] most of them having several variants.

The poet Stesichoros, reported by Plutarch, says that Odysseus bore the image of a dolphin on his shield. The inhabitants of the island of

Zakynthos can supply the reason for this, for they knew it well: When Odysseus' son Telemachus was a child, he fell from the shore into deep water. Dolphins hurried up and rescued him, catching him and bringing him to land unhurt. Out of gratitude to the animals, Odysseus took the dolphin as his heraldic image and used it as his seal. His nickname was *delphinosêmos.*

But didn't Odysseus himself need the dolphin's help on his many hazardous voyages?

On vase-paintings, one often sees one or two dolphins on the hero's shield.[10] That of the great hero Herakles also had two silver dolphins.[11] We even find a winged dolphin on one warrior's shield. The dolphin's image symbolizes the shield's protective and defensive power.

A Lesbian legend tells of how the first founders of the colony on the island of Lesbos received an oracle: On arriving at the island, they were to sacrifice a bull on a rock to Poseidon, god of the sea, and a young maiden to Amphitrite and the Nereids. The lot fell on the daughter of Smintheus. Dressed in costly raiment and decked with gold, she was to be drowned in the sea to the accompaniment of prayers. Then the noble youth Enalos hastened up to share her fate, for love of her, and plunged with her into the waters. Soon the rumor was spreading around the fleet that they had been rescued by dolphins. Later Enalos appeared on Lesbos, washed up by a giant wave, with a golden cup in his hands. He told of how dolphins had carried them through the sea on their backs, and brought them to the island.[12]

A Parian legend bears witness to the gratitude of dolphins. Koiranos, a native of the island of Paros, while on a voyage to Byzantium, bought the freedom of a pod of dolphins caught by fishermen, and let them go back to the water. Soon afterwards, Koiranos was crossing the sea in a ship of fifty oars. The ship foundered in a storm while passing the narrows between Paros and Naxos, and all hands were lost. Koiranos alone was saved by a dolphin, carried to the island of Sikynthos, and set down there at a cavern which is now called "Koiraneion." Koiranos died at a great age. When his funeral pyre was built close to the sea, a great crowd of dolphins came up to the beach and remained there during the cremation, as if they wanted to pay their last respects and gratitude to their benefactor.

Many legends tell of the fidelity and loyalty of dolphins. A Iasian story describes the friendship of a dolphin for a boy who lived in the town of Iasus in Caria. In one version, he is called *Hermias*. He played with the animal, rode on it, and it went wherever its rider steered it. During a sudden hailstorm, the boy slipped from its back and drowned in the waves. The animal gathered him up, threw itself with him on the beach, and out of self-reproach did not stir from his side until the dolphin itself died. In memory of this devotion, the town of Iasus put the image of the boy riding a dolphin on their coinage. The inhabitants also erected a statue of the dolphin-rider as a memorial.

This story was later altered and embellished in various forms. A boy befriended by a dolphin, called *Dionysios*, is supposed to have been summoned by Alexander the Great. In another version, Alexander appointed him as a priest of Poseidon in Babylon.[13]

The rescued boy seemed to have had a divine aura about him, as shown by the names given him. Thus he was consecrated as a priest of the god associated with dolphins.

The dolphin is not only eager to help mortals, but also to serve the gods.

On the island of Naxos, the sea-god Poseidon spied the beautiful Amphitrite dancing with the Nereids and fell in love with her. But Amphitrite fled to the World's End, in the depth of Ocean, where Atlas bears up his burden of the sky. Poseidon sent his messengers everywhere to seek her, but none could find her. Only the nimble dolphin succeeded, and even talked Amphitrite into following him, then brought her in triumph on his back to the delighted god. Out of gratitude, Poseidon set his faithful helper among the stars. Thus arose the constellation Delphinus.

The story was well known in Megara and Corinth of Ino (or Leukothea) and her son Melikertes (or Palaimon): a story full of deep significance.

A human event turns here into a divine event.

Ino, originally a mortal (though no ordinary one, being a daughter of Cadmus) and her husband, King Athamas, were driven mad by the jealous Hera.[14] Pursued by the raging Athamas, Ino fled from Boeotia with her little son in her arms. From the Molurian Rock, between Megara and Corinth, she plunged with Melikertes into the sea. Here again, the dolphins rescued mother and child, and brought them to land at the Isthmus. Thereafter they were worshipped as gods, protectors of seafarers; a cult was founded, and they were given other names. Melikertes became Palaimon, and Ino was renamed Leukothea.

On the shore, at the place where Melikertes was set down after his rescue by the dolphin, an altar consecrated to Melikertes-Palaimon stood near the sacred pine-tree.[15] The Isthmian games were also founded in his honor, of which Plutarch says: "The games which were instituted in honor of Melikertes-Palaimon begin at night, and have the character of a mystery, not a popular festival."[16] In Euripides, the blessed son of Leucothea is addressed as divine protector of sailors.[17]

Ino-Leucothea became a sea-goddess. She was raised to immortality by Dionysus in return for her nursing him as an infant. Hermes prophesied this, as the messenger of the gods placed the child in her care. According to Nonnos, she holds the key that stills the sea.[18] When the brave seafarer is in danger, she stands by him. Leukothea is well known from Homer, for she helped Odysseus through the peril of the storm, handing him for protection her *kredemnon* or sacred veil.[19]

The dolphin is sacred to many gods and goddesses, and especially to those whose protection is invoked during perils on the sea.

For example, the goddess Artemis, Apollo's sister, is addressed as ruler of the sea and protector of sailors with the epithet *Delphinia*. One can see the goddess's head surrounded by dolphins on many Syracusan coins.

The dolphin is especially connected with Poseidon. The ruler of the stormy deep is usually represented with a dolphin.

Poseidon gave Theseus dolphins as guards and companions on his journey to the bottom of the sea, where he had to find the ring of King Minos, and on his successful return from this labor.[20]

The dolphin is also sacred to foam-born Aphrodite, and is often depicted with her. When the goddess was born, a dolphin carried her from Paphos to Cyprus. This island has the shape of a dolphin, given it by the sea-god Nereus when he sketched out its coasts with his sharp trident.[21]

There are innumerable tales of the dolphin, and innnumerable pictures in which this most celebrated of animals appears. However, we never find the motif of taming it, despite the many occurrences of the dolphin-rider. For the dolphin is naturally tame.[22]

The stories often tell of the leap into the sea, caused by mortal or immortal power: of the plunge into an element where the candidate suddenly finds himself bereft of all earthly support. Such stories come out of cultic practices. But the origin of the public cult is the sanctuary where one strove to grow in fearlessness, presence of mind, and courage. The leap into the sea is the exoteric representation of the trial that took place in the *Mysteries*.

The legends also tell of rescue by self-sacrificing dolphins from the peril of the water-trial. Many of the people rescued by dolphins are raised to the status of gods, and thereafter bestow their own powers of aid and salvation. The dolphin-rescuer helps in the divine ascent of the person tried by the waves and who bravely overcomes them.

The spiritual life of Greece was divided into two major streams. Emerging from the sanctuaries of the Mysteries and oracles, they entered Hellenic culture and dominated it: the well-known Mysteries of Apollo and of Dionysus, in which the neophytes strove, respectively, for knowledge of world and for self-knowledge. These twin streams have been treated often and thoroughly, yet they remain as inexhaustible as the outer world and the inner man. When the *mystes* in the Apollonian mysteries thrust through the barriers of the visible world, he beheld the gods of the higher world. The gods of the depths were revealed to him who crossed the threshold of his own inner world in the Dionysian mysteries.[23]

The Apollonian singer plucks the lyre-strings from the outside, molding the element of air. But the Dionysian depths of the soul sound through the flute on the inner stream of the breath.

The dolphin is connected with the central figures of both these mysteries, the gods Apollo and Dionysus.

The Greek gods possessed countless epithets, each one expressing a different aspect of the godhead, often reflected in a local cult. Some of these diverse epithets portray the gods' development and their changing forms over time. The long list of these epithets, rounded off into a garland, would reveal to the synthetic gaze the rich complexity of the godhead, bringing to view the totality of its being. One would sense its divine presence.

One of the oldest epithets of the god Apollo is *Delphinios*. Many scholars assume that prior to Apollo, and older than him, there must have been a god called Delphinios. Under this epithet, Apollo was the god of seafarers, who called him by this name. (Epiklesis of Apollo.) Many places, especially harbor towns, bear witness to the cult of Apollo Delphinios.[24] The most famous one in Asia Minor was at Didyma, in Caria.[25] We know from a votive offering of the Milesian philosopher Thales that he sacrificed to the god in the Didymaion. Thales, who regarded water or fluidity as the original material of the universe, dedicated his offering to the god associated with the sea, for the inscription reads "To Apollo Delphinios."[26]

In Athens there was a temple called the *Delphinion*, a court and place of atonement.[27] According to Attic legend, the temple was built by Aegeus, the father of Theseus. Here Theseus made atonement after the murder of the Pallantids.[28] Here he offered the Marathonian bull which he had vanquished.[29]

Theseus visited the Athenian Delphinion before sailing to Crete to overcome the Minotaur and thereby free the Athenian citizens of their terrible tribute—the seven youths and seven maidens who had to be sent every year to the monster. There Theseus offered to the god a branch of the sacred olive-tree wound about with white wool, for himself and the fourteen victims. Then he prayed, and took ship for Crete with the condemned men and women.[30] There, in the Cretan Labyrinth, he slew the Minotaur. The Athenian seafarers reenacted this rite before venturing onto the wide and rolling sea.

One month of spring, probably April, was called Delphinion. We also know of Delphinion-feasts, connected with the cult of the dead, in which the departed were remembered.[31] The god Delphinios must also have guided and guarded souls, on the spiritual sea of the after-life.

The dolphin is interwoven with the foundation of the mystery-and oracle-sanctuary of Delphi, that place of unrivalled importance in the life of Greece. That life had been molded by, and linked with Delphi from time immemorial: the founding of colonies and cities, laws, wars, religions, and all personal matters. In any difficult situation, one would make a pilgrimage to Delphi, consult the oracle, and follow its advice.

The original foundation of the ancient sanctuary of Delphi is lost in the mists of antiquity. The first giver of oracles was the earth-goddesss Gaia. Themis followed her, on whose sage advice cities were founded, then Phoebe. Poseidon holds an especially important place in this series, related to Apollo Delphinios from the earliest times, through their common element.

Aegeus, the father of Theseus, once made a pilgrimage to Delphi to consult the oracle about his childlessness. From the inscription on the picture of a bowl which represents this consultation, we can tell that the goddess Themis was then ruling in Delphi.[32]

Several scholars derive the name of Delphi from the dolphin (*delphis*). They assume that there was a founding god, Delphinios, and connect him with the god Delphos, a son of Poseidon. The words

Delphoi and *Delphis* also resemble *delphys*, meaning uterus. This word points to the fruitful deep, the primordial source from which the oracle's wise sayings come.

Fragments of older traditions make it certain that the Pythian Apollo, conqueror of the Python, was not the first hero and lord of Delphi; also perhaps not the oldest, earthbound aspect of this god. Nevertheless, the decisive aspect of Apollo is that of the dragon-slayer, the liberator and savior.

The Homeric Hymn to Pythian Apollo describes in hieratic images how the Cretans wished to sail from Knossos to Pylos, and met Phoibos Apollo there on the sea. He leaped onto the Cretan ship in the form of a giant dolphin, and settled on the deck. The sailors sat terrified, not daring to set their hands to rope or sail. The ship glided, quick as an arrow, without any human assistance. The presence of the god alone guided it, as a wind sent by Kronion blew it onwards. It sped past Pylos, rounded the Peloponnese, and landed in Krisa, the harbor of Delphi. Then the god sprang from the deck onto the shore; like a star in broad daylight, a host of sparks flew from him, and a light blazed up to the sky. Apollo walked between the tripods to the Adytum, and there he kindled a flame. Then he leaped back onto the ship and spoke with the men of Crete. The Cretans recognized the god. They were to set up an altar to him on the shore, in the foam, and there light the fire—so Apollo commanded them. He installed the Cretans as his priests. Since he had jumped onto their sailing ship as a dolphin, they were to call him "Dolphin-like."

So Apollo, in dolphin form, showed the Cretans the way to the sanctuary, which would be a center for centuries to come, and not for Greece alone.

According to other traditions, it was the god Apollo himself in dolphin-form, or a dolphin sent by Apollo, who hastened the Cretan ship and guided it to Krisa.

Another legend of the foundation of Delphi goes as follows. *Eikadios*, the son of Apollo and the nymph Lykia, was shipwrecked in a storm on the way from Lykia from Italy. A dolphin rescued him, took him on its back, and set him down near Parnassus. There Eikadios dedicated a temple to his father Apollo, calling the place Delphi in honor and gratitude to the dolphin which had saved him.[33]

There are mysterious relations between the god and the dolphin. The pilgrims who crossed the sea to the sanctuary of Apollo on the island of Delos, his birthplace, regarded the dolphins that played around their ship as a sign that the god himself was leading them.

On a vase-painting, we see the god Apollo with the attributes of his sacred power: Apollo with the quiver, on a winged tripod, a lyre in his hands. The tripod glides over the waves, a dolphin at each side.

The dolphin is also related to the god Dionysus, known for his connection with the watery element. The god stays in the depths of the sea for part of the year, preceding his epiphany. When he was pursued by the Thracian king Lykurgos, Dionysus plunged into the sea and escaped to the sea-goddess Thetis.[34] *Pelagios* is one of his epithets associating him with the sea and its winds. And the attribute of Dionysus Pelagios is the dolphin.

On a coin of Eurymenae (Magnesian Peninsula), one sees the head of the young god Dionysus on one side, and on the obverse, the vine, cup, and *dolphin*. A gold plate of the post-Christian era, found in Syria, shows Dionysus garlanded and clothed in panther-skin, strolling over the waves with a torch in either hand.[35]

The connection of Dionysus with the dolphin is enigmatic, as shown in the surviving fragments of the Homeric Hymn to Dionysus.

One day, when the young god was standing on the shore in his purple cloak, he was seen by pirates. They captured him and forced him aboard their ship, thinking him to be a king's son. The Tyrrhenian robbers tried to fetter the god, but the ropes fell from his hands and feet. Ignoring the helmsman's warnings, they hoisted the sail. Thereupon the strangest sign appeared: wine ran all over the ship, sweet breezes filled the air. Suddenly a giant vine grew right up to the sail, spreading out overhead and laden with delicious grapes. Dark ivy, the sacred plant of the god, entwined the mast. Dionysus, in the shape of a lion, seized the pirate-chief. To avoid a similar fate, the Tyrrhenians leaped into the sea and were turned into dolphins.

Many legends hold that dolphins are transformed men, and even today the fishermen of South Italy (in Capri and Sicily, for instance) tell of the human-like cry of the dolphins: the animals weep and sing.

They also sigh like humans, says Pliny.[36] Perhaps in dark remembrance of their ancient guilt, the kidnapping of a god—the cause of their expiation in selfless sacrifice, as tireless servants of gods and men. It was as a warning that the seer Tiresias told Pentheus the story of the metamorphosis of the Tyrrhenians into dolphins.[37]

A black-figured bowl by Exekias (sixth century B.C.E.) shows the god Dionysus on a dolphin-shaped sailboat, easy and relaxed as if after the dramatic adventure on the same ship, from which the Tyrrhenian pirates dove into the sea in panic terror. By the mast is the miraculous vine. Around the speeding ship seven dolphins are at play.

Apollo and Dionysus are protectors of sea-voyages. They also protect the founders of colonies who go overseas. But this is only one of their many realms of action. The dolphin is connected with both of these gods, as shown in the Corinthian and Lesbian legend of Arion.

Arion lived in Methymna on Lesbos as an Apollonian poet and singer, and one of the best cithara-players of his time. The ruler Periander (*circa* 652–585 B.C.E.), one of the Seven Wise Men of Greece, invited him—doubtless advised by the Delphic clergy—to Corinth, in order to be the poet of a cultic reform within the Dionysian religion.[38] A step had to be taken, corresponding to the new age that was dawning: the spiritual event of the Dionysian Mysteries had to emerge from its concealment (even though not yet to its full extent) and be placed at the disposal of all. This could only be done in artistic form: tragedy had to be born.

This required preparation. Several traditions credit Arion with inventing the *dithyramb*, the special cult-song of the god Dionysus, which, turned into an art-form and given a new content, now sounded loud in the worldly life of the Greeks.

Dionysus on the Ship (sixth century B.C.E.)

Aristotle says that tragedy arose from the artistic germ of the dithyramb.[39]

The dithyramb juxtaposed with the chorus the free and individual voice of one person, the Exarchon. His solo rose above the mass of the responding chorus and contrasted with it. Aristotle depicted the genesis of tragedy. It began in the first simple attempts of the solo dithyrambist, then after many stages of development culminated in the complete creation of a *single* poetic individual. One result was the beginning of dialogue. This contained the germ of the later capability of tragedy to present the workings of destiny. The foundation of tragic dialogue is the dithyramb. The voices of destiny become audible.

It is said that Arion cooperated with the decisive event of spiritual history that became a reality in the sixth century B.C.E.: the uniting of the Apollonian and Dionysian cults.[40] Until then they had striven in rivalry.

The destiny of Hellas was molded from the Apollonian oracular sanctuary of Delphi outwards. *But there was no corresponding Dionysian sanctuary in Greece.* Dionysus brought about the destined event as the god of the inner man that was then stirring. Later he became visible to the audience in the art-form of tragedy. Two central streams of world-changing energy, the inner one of Dionysus and the outer one of Apollo, joined their divine forces in the Attic *Dionysus Melpomenos.* The Apollonian Muse Melpomene entered the Dionysian realm, and the god Dionysus, who lives in the depths of man, in his very self, as the *exciter* of destiny, becomes as Dionysus Melpomenos the *depictor* of destiny.

As inventor of the dithyramb, the poet Arion prepares the way for tragedy.

On his journeys, Arion gained costly gifts and great wealth through his art. As he was intending to sail from Tarento to Periander in Corinth, he hired a Corinthian vessel. Once on the high seas, the sailors plotted to kill him and help themselves to his possessions. The helmsman disclosed this to him. Then Arion asked the rowers to let him sing and play his lyre one last time. They consented. The poet put

Dolphin Coins

A) Tarentum (380–345 B.C.E.)
B) Iasus (600–500 B.C.E.)

on his finest clothes and wrapped himself in his purple cloak, to serve him as a winding-sheet. Solemnly plucking the strings of his lyre, he called out to the protecting sea-gods and sang a Pythian song. Scarcely had he ended, than the singer threw himself into the waves. Dolphins hurried up and took him: a host of the creatures collected and, as if it were an honor for them, took turns in carrying Arion over the still and

Dolphin Coins

A) Corinth (192–180 B.C.E.)
B) Iasus (250–290 B.C.E.)
C) Methymna (330–240 B.C.E.)

moonlit sea, setting him ashore at Cape Tanairon.[41]

At Tanairon they erected a monument with the dolphin-rider, said to be Arion's thanks-offering. On their coins they stamped the picture of a dolphin-rider holding a lyre in his hands.

The poet Arion was rescued because he served the gods with his poetry. Here, too, the legend tells of a leap into the sea, and here too the man of courage and decision is saved. The sea-gods summoned by the singer evidently sent the dolphins to his rescue. The purple wrapping also points to trials in unsafe and moving elements. Theseus, when in danger, also used a purple cloak for his protection, when he had to fetch from the bottom of the sea the ring thrown there by King Minos. According to Bakchylides, the cloak was lent him by Amphitrite.[42]

The *tainia* was also purple-red. This was the sash or sacred veil which the initiated seafarers received in Samothrace.[43] It was supposed to protect them through perils and trials on the seas, evidently as the material image of the protective spiritual forces. Those who knew and practiced the Mysteries were more strongly protected than others.

The Arion legend is interwoven with this significant event of spiritual history: the rise of the dithyramb as an art-form, and the birth of tragedy.

The source of tragedy is the cultic mystery-play (of which the Eleusinian is usually given as an example), which the mystes were only permitted to see under the vow of silence. The dithyramb is its precursor.

The step taken by Arion in Corinth was to bring the form of the mystery-event out of its protective tradition into the unconsciously surging life-element, by allowing the free improvisation of the soloist in the dithyramb, as opposed to the tradition-bound words of the hierophant. Did not this bold deed call for a trial, a rehearsal, in his courageous leap into the stormy waves of the sea?

Outside Greece and in later times, we find many legends of the dolphin, and a boundless host of dolphin-representations. These occur among the Etruscans, and especially among the Romans.

The Romans regarded the dolphin as sacred. Servius says that even in his time, its statue was set up in the highest honor beside the tripods of the Quindecimviri. On the eve of the sacrifice, it was ceremoniously carried round by the priestly college of the Quindecimviri—the custodians of the Sibylline Books—as the creature sacred to Apollo.[44]

It is surprising to encounter the dolphin again in the texts and images

Winged Ephebe on a Dolphin (Hellenistic period)

of Christian times. Gregory of Nyssa, the famous Church Father of the fourth century, calls it the "king of fish."[45]

One can trace the dolphin legends up to the tenth century, now peopled by Christian heroes, saints, and martyrs.

The best-known is the legend of the saint and martyr Lukianos,[46] Presbyter of Antioch, noted for his close relations with Arianism. He is mentioned as Arian's teacher. At the end of the year 311 C.E., hence before the Edict of Tolerance for the Christians, Lukianos was imprisoned on the orders of Maximinus Daza and brought before the judgment seat of the Emperor Constantine. The Emperor wanted to make him renounce Christianity. He offered Lukianos great rewards if he would sacrifice to the gods. But Lukianos would not be persuaded. He was thrown into prison and tortured. He remained steadfast through all his sufferings, and with his last breath cried out three times "I am a Christian!" and died. His body was sunk in the sea.

(In another version he was thrown in while still alive.) For fourteen days it remained on the sea-bed. His disciples waited on the shore, hoping that the rough seas of winter would give back the body of their master. In the night before the fifteenth day, the saint appeared in a dream to one of his disciples, Glykerios, and told him the place where the body would be found. Glykerios and the others went immediately to the appointed place. The moment they arrived, they saw a huge dolphin leap out of the waves and come to shore. It carried the martyr's corpse, lying stretched out with marvelous serenity on the animal's smooth back. Near the beach, a high wave lifted the dolphin and brought it to land. Scarcely had the faithful beast laid down its holy burden, than it too gave up the ghost.

The dolphin brought the saint's body back from the depths of the sea to dry land so that it could be buried with religious rites. In just the same way, a dolphin brought to shore the body of the poet Hesiod, thrown in the sea by his murderers, and also the unknown man of Naupaktos, and then breathed its last.

Here again, the dolphin is involved in an important event in spiritual history: that of Arianism, which had a successful influence on the history of both East and West. For Saint Lukianos was closely linked with Arianism.

Thus in both antiquity and Christendom, the divine dolphin accompanies man in life and death, on the journey over the as yet unknown spiritual sea. It is thus shown in many representations on sarcophagus reliefs, grave steles, and cremation urns. For example, on the handle of one bronze vessel used for preserving the ashes of the dead, there is an ephebe with mighty wings. One arm slung around the neck of a dolphin, already freed from earth, he trusts to his guide as he glides over to the other world. The image shows simultaneously peace and movement. Perhaps he is the genius, the immortal psyche of the deceased whose ashes rest in the vessel.[47]

The Christians also recognized the dolphin as sacred.[48] One finds it even in the depth of the Catacombs, drawn by skillful hands and associated with the sacred image of the Fish.

The fish symbol is rare in pre-Christian cultures. But its few traces are pregnant with its divine meaning, as if in anticipation.

One example is in the Indian flood legend. The "Hundred-pathed" Brahmana tells of how Manu, a son of the sun-god *Vivasvat*, found in his ablution water a tiny fish which begged him to protect and keep it. It promised him that, in return, it would save him from the coming flood. When the fish had grown large, it told Manu to build a ship, and to embark on it when the flood began to rise. Then he was to wait for the fish. As the waters rose, Manu got onto the ship and the fish swam up to it. He attached his hawser to its horn. Drawn through the waters in this way, he was brought to a mountain, where he escaped the flood unhurt. In one episode of the *Mahabharata*, "Matsyopakhana," which contains the same story, *the fish sacrifices itself at the end as the highest god, Brahman.*[49]

The fish is equally rarely met with in Greece, in contrast to the wealth of dolphin legends. The fish myth was not yet cultivated there. But the fish was held sacred by the wise seer, Homer.[50]

If tradition is silent on the matter, many a picture speaks clearly about this. The tuna fish is the heraldic badge of the town of Kyzikos in Mysia. One sees it on their coins, held in the hand of a god. A tuna is also shown on one of the oldest electrum coins, placed upright so that its tail-fins serve to support it. *A tainia hangs on it.*[51]

The fish is also sacred here, as the worthy bearer of the divine protective powers. We meet again these divine helpful forces which were given to the initiates of Samothrace, as it were woven into the *tainia*, the sacred purple-red veil of the Mysteries.

So *one* of the motives of the Christian fish-symbol, that of salvation, appears in pre-Christian cultures, and the myth of the dolphin-savior echoes on through the Christian centuries.

* * *

Spirit and matter encounter each other again and again in different ways.

This encounter was accomplished in a unique way during the

flowering of humanity under the Greeks. The spirit seized earthly matter and penetrated it. In the early period, especially, not only the temples but all art-forms became dwellings of the gods.

The original images were incarnated in earthly form through the god-like creative powers of the artist. Through him, the will of the gods penetrated the earth.

One is perpetually amazed at this most beautiful of all cultures. But understanding of what was special and unique in the Greek epoch is only achieved in retrospect, looking back from that event which is the greatest and most unique of all world history: the descent of the Christ into the earthly body of Jesus. We see this fusion of spirit and matter anticipated by the Greeks. Christ has been drawn into the inner man, and the power of the Resurrection penetrates the whole material world. What was felt formerly as the Apollonian-Dionysian contradiction is here resolved and elevated.

There is a vase-painting that shows Apollo and Dionysus extending their hands to one another over the Delphic Omphalos.[52] The Greeks were also aware of the union of their cults. The cleft between the outer and the inner is bridged.

The dolphin is connected with both gods, the light Phoibos Apollo and the god of dark depths, Dionysus. With their opposition, as well as with their agreement, it leaps up into the sunlit world, then slides down to the hidden depths.

The dolphin fulfilled its purpose for the Greek epoch, given it by the heights and the depths, by uniting them in the rhythm of its movement. In its power to use the sunny heights to master the dark depths, it is the very picture of Greece.

It lives in words and pictures as a tremendous Imagination, which for centuries inspired the greatest works of art, as a preparation and model for the Christian fish-symbol.

The saving dolphin was succeeded by the saving, healing, and nourishing fish.

Both dolphin and fish fulfill the goal of the great stream, each according to time, the ruler of all things.

Translated by Richard M. Brown from *Der Delphin in Sage und Mythos der Griechen* (Dornach: Hybernia-Verlag, 1947).

Notes

1. See H. Dütschke, *Antike Bildwerke in Oberitalien* (Leipzig, 1874), Roman sarcophagi: I, 98, 111; III, 85.

2. E.g., *Monumenti del'Instituto*, VII, 77.

3. Pliny, *Natural History* 9.7.

4. Pindar, *Pythian Ode* 4.29; cf. *Nemean* 6.72–74. Significantly, a dolphin was also excavated in the Hippodrome of Olympia. Pausanius 6.20.7.10.

5. Aristotle, *History of Animals* 4.241; Pliny, *Natural History* 9.7.

6. Oppian, *Halieutica* 1.

7. Plutarch, *De sollertia animalium* 36.

8. F. Creuzer, *Symbolik und Mythologie*, 3rd ed. (Leipzig and Darmstadt, 1841), vol. 3, p. 269.

9. Plutarch, *De sollertia animalium*; *Septem sapientium convivium*.

10. E. Pfuhl, *Mahlerei und Zeichnung der Griechen* (Munich, 1923), vol. 3, fig. 312.

11. Hesiod, *The Shield of Herakles* 211; cf. also 210.

12. There are several variants of this legend. See H. Usener, *Die Sintflutsagen* (Bonn, 1899), p. 161.

13. Pliny, *Natural History* 9.8. Cf. Usener, p. 166.

14. The preceding events of this legend are omitted here. See Plutarch, *Septem sapientium convivium* 19; Pausanias 1.44.7; 2.1.3; 2.3.4; 2.7.8.

15. Pausanias 2.1.3. In the Isthmian Games, the victor was crowned with pine branches. See Usener, pp. 153f. The pine is also sacred to Dionysus (Plutarch, *Symposium* 5.3.1). The thyrsus-staff still carried a pinecone in Roman times. The images on Corinthian coins also point to the Dionysian connection: the dolphin-riding Palaimon is shown with the thyrsus in his hands. Another Corinthian coin points to Samothrace: the thyrsus carries *tainias*, the sacred veils of the initiated seafarers in the Samothracian Mysteries. See Usener, Münztafel 13; also p. 154, 3.

16. Plutarch, *Theseus* 25.

17. Euripides, *Iphigenia in Tauris* 270.

18. Nonnos, *Dionysiaca* 9.86; cf. also 60–85.

19. Homer, *Odyssey* 5.330ff.

20. Hyginus, *Astronomica* 2.5.

21. Nonnos, *Dionysiaca* 13.436ff.

22. The description of one of the oldest depictions is in Plato, *Kritias* 116.

23. On the Apollonian and Dionysian Mysteries, see the important and conclusive treatments by Rudolf Steiner, *Orient im Lichte des Okzidentes* (Dornach: Phil. Anthr. Verlag am Goetheanum, 1942), especially Lectures 5 and 6.

24. Plutarch, *De sollertia animalium* 36. W. Aly, *Der kretische Apollonkult* (1909).

25. See Pausanias 7.2.6; Strabo 14.634.

26. A bowl that Thales himself received as a presentation. Diogenes Laertius 1.29.

27. Plutarch, *Theseus* 12; Pausanias 1.19.1.

28. Pausanias 1.28.10.

29. Plutarch, *Theseus* 14.

30. Plutarch, *Theseus* 18.

31. Delphic months, see Pindar, *Nemean Ode* 5.44. Delphic festivals, see Pindar, *Pythian Ode* 8.88. According to the decree in the Testament of Epicteta, on the island of Thera the male relatives of the departed were to hold a commemorative reunion on three days of the month Delphinion. See Usener, p. 148.

32. Ed. Gerhard, *Das Orakel der Themis* (Berlin, 1846).

33. Servius, *Commentary on Virgil, Aeneid* 3.332.

34. Homer, *Iliad* 6.130ff.

35. E. Maass, "Dionysios pelagios," in *Hermes* 23 (1888), pp. 73, 78.

36. Pliny, *Natural History* 9.7.

37. Nonnos, *Dionysiaca* 45.104ff. cf. also Ovid, *Metamorphoses 3.670ff.*

38. Cf. W. Schmidt and O. Stählin, *Geschichte der griechischen Literatur* (Munich, 1929), in *Handbuch der Altertumswissenschaft*, ed. J.Müller, pp. 406ff.

39. Aristotle, *Poetics* 4. Cf. A. Lesky, *Die griechische Tragödie* (1938), pp. 9ff.

40. Plutarch, *On the E at Delphi* 9; *Isis and Osiris* 35. Cf. W. Schmidt and O.

Stählin, *Geschichte der griechischen Literatur*. M. P. Nilsson, *Geschichte der griechischen Religion* (Munich, 1941), in *Handbuch der Altertumswissenschaft*, ed. W. Otto. E. Rohde, *Psyche* (Tübingen, 1921), vol. 2, pp. 44, 52ff.

41. The Arion legend has different versions, e.g. Herodotus 1.23ff.; Plutarch, *Septem sapientium convivium* 18; *De sollertia animalium* 36.

42. Cf. S. Wide, "Theseus und der Meeressprung bei Bakchylides 17," in *Festschrift für O.Benndorf*, 1898.

43. O. Kern, *Mysterien der klassischen Zeit* (1927), pp. 30ff. Cf. O. Gruppe, *Griechische Mythologie und Religionsgeschichte* (Munich, 1906), vol. 1, p. 229; vol. 2, pp. 891, 1349.

44. Servius, *Commentary on Virgil, Aeneid* 3.332.

45. In *Patrologia Graeca*, ed. Migne, vol. 44, in verba Faciamus Hominem, vol. 1, p. 265.

46. Symeon Metaphrastes, in *Patrologia Graeca*, ed. Migne, vol. 114, pp. 413–5. K. Heussi, *Kompendium der Kirchengeschichte* (Tübingen, 1928), pp. 53–4, para. 17 t., p. 74, para 24, b, c.

47. Pictured in E. Pottier and S. Reinach, "Appliqués de bronze appartenant à des vases de Myrina," in *Bulletin de Correspondance Hellénique* 7 (1883), Plate 5. The authors interpret the figure as Eros. K. Dilthey has made the important observation that "in certain typical contexts and decorative uses, the Eros figures have the meaning of the genii who reign in the happy regions of the Blest, and sometimes flow together with the image of the blessed souls, exactly like the angels of Christian mythology..." *Jenaer Literaturzeitung* 28 (1878), p. 420b.

48. V. Schultze, *Die Katakomben* (Leipzig, 1882). F. Becker, *Die Darstellungen Jesu Christi unter dem Bilde des Fisches augf den Monumenten der Kirche der Katakomben* (Breslau, 1866), pp. 13, 15, 17, 67, 82. Dolphin as denoting Christ: pp. 30, 85. Many dolphin representations on sarcophagus reliefs in J. Ficker, *Die altchristilichen Bildwerke im christlichen Museum des Lateran* (Leipzig, 1890). J. Wilpert, *Die Malereien der Katakomben Roms* (Freiburg im Breisgau, 1903). G. Wilpert, *I sarcofagi christiani antichi* (Rome, 1929–1936). Fr. Gerke, *Die christlichen Sarkophage der vorkonstantinischen Zeit* (Berlin, 1940).

49. H. Jakobi (formerly F. Bopp), *Die Sündflut, nebst drei anderen Episoden des Mahabharat* (Berlin, 1829). A. Höfer, *Indische Geschichte in deutscher*

Übertragung (Leipzig, 1841).
50. Homer, *Iliad* 16.407.
51. *Numism. chron.* Ser. 2, vol. 7 (1887), pl. 1, no. 1; cf. Usener, p. 229.
52. Late red-figured vase in the Hermitage, Saint Petersburg.

Note: It is not the intention of this work to deal exhaustively with *all* the countless legends and representations of the dolphin. We indicate only a few characteristic traits of this wonderful creature, as they shine forth from word and image.

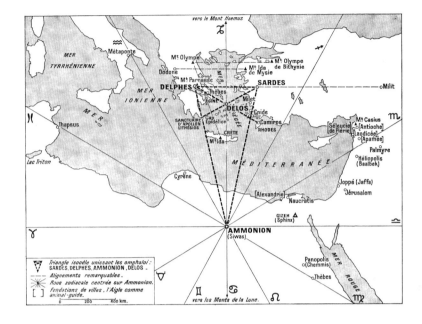

Isosceles triangle joining the oracle centers of
Delphi, Sardis, and Ammon.

Sacred Geography of the Ancient Greeks

CHRISTINE RHONE

Sacred Geography of the Ancient Greeks by Jean Richer, the late French scholar and writer, was first published in 1967. It is an important work on symbolism and geomancy, part of a study in three volumes, two of which earned the author awards from the Académie française. The triptych is, to the best of my knowledge, the only work that incorporates evidence of ancient alignments of temples and sacred sites ever to have been so honored by an academic body. In Great Britain, more so than in the United States or even in France, many academics view the very suggestion of significant alignments with overwhelming suspicion. To have the work recognized in France, and then to have the first English translation published by a university press in the United States, may provide some support for the defensive position taken by some researchers in Britain, where Richer's term "sacred geography" has already spread.

Even so, nowhere have the vision and the interpretative keys given in his work been integrated either into general archeology or into the history of art and architecture. The work provides a far-reaching and original contribution to these fields. The short and long distance axial alignments of which Richer finds evidence clarify unresolved questions of temple orientation and the selection of the artistic themes employed in temple decoration, which were never arbitrarily chosen. Since the system may be used predictively, and is supported by all the artefacts analyzed by Richer, it could be used to pinpoint sites where archeological excavations would very probably yield interesting results. In terms of the history of art, the symbolic themes discussed in *Sacred Geography of the Ancient Greeks* are, with some modification, applicable to Roman and Byzantine art, and in some cases, may even be traced through to post-Renaissance Europe, thus encompassing a period of millenia and adding a new layer of meaning to the entire study of sacred art.

Perhaps its most important contribution is to provide a unifying approach to the study of geomancy in the ancient world as a whole. This overview is in harmony with the archetypal city-state as described by Plato in the *Laws* and in the *Republic*. The structure of the city, according to the philosopher, should mirror the face of the heavens, and repeat the pattern of the stars and planets, which were the eternal gods. Pre-existent to human life, the celestial pattern was an ideal, to be understood and applied on many levels, but ultimately beyond ordinary human knowledge.

The city was to be located, insofar as possible, in the country's center, which symbolized alternatively the pole star, the *axis mundi*, and the navel of the pregnant Gaea. From the center, which contained a walled citadel, the country was to be divided into twelve equal parts. Each territorial section corresponded to a portion of the celestial zodiac. The name of a ruling zodiacal deity was given to each portion and to the tribe that inhabited it. Inside the sectors, everything from temples to place-names, from local myths and legends to painted vases and shields reflected a zodiacal meaning appropriate to its position on the stellar wheel. Astral beliefs were all-pervasive, the foundation of a unity that made possible such a vast coordination among widely distant places. In the words of Michel Butor, "All of Greek religion could be described as a great metaphor of the marriage of heaven and earth."

Richer rediscovered several twelve-part divisions of the Greek territories, the main ones centered on Delphi, Delos, Sardis in Asia Minor, and the desert oasis of Ammoneion or Siwa, in ancient Libya, west of Egypt. Seen together on the map, the sites define an isosceles triangle, whose height, Richer says, is double the length of the base. Delphi and Sardis, both oracle sites, are on the same latitude. The height of the triangle intersects the island of Delos and finishes at the oracle of Ammon or Hamun, the ram-god, in Libya.

Plato states in *The Laws* (Book V) that the three most authoritative oracles were those of Delphi, Sardis, and Ammon, especially in questions relating to colonization or the founding of new cities. It would thus appear that Richer has found evidence of the pattern of Plato's ideal city around the most important oracular centers of the ancient Greek world. It is very probable that Plato's description was, at least in part, a later codification of what had been a far earlier practice, particularly as regards the division of the country into twelve regions under the patronage of the gods of the zodiac. My *Twelve-Tribe Nations and the Science of Enchanting the Landscape*, co-authored with John Michell (Phanes Press, 1991), gives many examples of ancient societies based on this model, in locations as diverse as Iceland and Madagascar.

Although it is the works of Plato that provide the best textual basis for Richer's research, Richer did not begin with Plato, but came upon these supporting texts later on. Richer's vision began with an intuitive perception, fuelled by intensive study of the poet Gérard de Nerval, on whom he had already written several books before beginning his study of sacred geography. Nerval, who took his own life in the winter of 1855, believed that dreams are a means of communication with the spirit world; he made no distinction between waking and sleeping dreams. The poet was steeped in the study of various occult traditions, obsessed with mythology, the tarot, numerology, alchemy, and Pythagoreanism. Nerval's *Aurélia*, considered the capstone symbolizing the poet's whole spiritual life, describes a process of initiation that begins with the vision of a star and cosmic circles opening in the heavens. One literary source for this work was Nerval's translation from the German of Klopstock's poem of 1830, "The Constellations." The very first line of *Aurélia* reads, "A dream is another life."

In the 1950s and 60s, Richer lived for several years in Greece and had a series of premonitory and divinatory dreams. His curiosity had been stimulated by the selection of sites of the Greek temples and the supposedly abnormal orientations of some of them. Having made several trips to Celtic Brittany, he became convinced that there was a deep analogy between what he was observing in Greece and the remains of megalithic civilization.

The key to this puzzle seemed to be the solar temples of Apollo. In 1958, Richer made a second visit to the oracle center of Delphi, where the sanctuaries of Apollo and Athena stand side by side. He returned to his home in Athens, situated on one of the highest points of the city, exactly on the western slope of Lycabettos, an ancient sacred hill formed mainly of a huge monolithic block of stone.

There he had a vivid dream. He saw the figure of a *kouros*, generally equated with Apollo, facing away from him and very slowly turning 120 degrees clockwise to face him. Awakening from this dream, while still half asleep, he took the first map of Greece he could find and drew a line joining Delphi and Athens. He continued the line and saw, to his surprise, that it intersected Delos, and further on, Camiros on the island of Rhodes. This line, after much subsequent research, turned out to be the zero degree Virgo line in the zodiacal wheel centered on Delphi. Years later, Richer's brother, Lucien, extended this same line through western Europe and found that it corresponded with a corridor of sites sacred to the Archangel Michael. Richer later found that the *kouros* figure that had appeared in his dream dated from about 550 B.C.E., the period when the system of zodiacal geography reached its point of perfection.

Delos is traditionally considered to have been the birthplace of Apollo, and Delphi was his main sanctuary. The fact that the line passed through Athens cast light on the relationship between Athena and Apollo at Delphi and explained the presence of a statue of Athena that faced the road coming from Athens to Delphi. Richer then noticed that a series of sites located along the meridian of Delphi, starting from Tempe in the north, corresponded with the legendary spread of the cult of Apollo. This in turn provided a geomantic key to certain ancient texts and legends, such as the legend of Zeus letting go of two eagles from the ends of the earth and the two birds crossing at Delphi.

He then followed a clue from the Homeric Hymn to Apollo, where it is mentioned that the priesthood who served at Delphi was originally from Crete. He drew a line joining two sacred mountains—Mount Ida in Crete and Mount Parnassus at Delphi—and saw that it passed through a third sacred mountain, that of Corinth, where there is yet another temple of Apollo.

It was this axis that was to prompt the next phase of his work. He wrote, "The Mount Ida to Delphi line, which represents the vital spirit of the country of Greece, intersects parallels of latitude at a 60 degree angle and can be considered a projection on part of the earth's surface, taken as a flat plane, of the Leo-Aquarius cosmic axis, which defines the same angle in relation to the line of the equinoxes. This axis is the cosmic signature of Greece and makes it a mirror of the celestial Harmony of the planets and of the zodiac."

He then realized that the Greeks, like the Mesopotamians and the Egyptians, wanted to make their country a living image of the heavens. Pieces of the puzzle began to fall into place, from temple orientations, artistic themes on temple pediments, imagery on coins and on vases, place names and legends, references in texts, and certain unexplained facts of Greek religion. Over the lines he had already found passing through Delphi, he superimposed a twelve-part zodiacal division, assuming that each 30 degree sector should correspond with an astrological sign. Because Leukas was the allegorical site of the death and rebirth of the sun-god, he took Leukas to represent spring, or the sign of Aries.

He found his hypothesis confirmed by hundreds of pieces of evidence. One major source was the iconography of coins, whose symbols referred to the position of the city where the coins were made in relationship to the center or *omphalos*. Richer's analysis of the evidence is sometimes complex, but to take a short example, the island of Cephallenia is the sign of Aries in relation to Delphi. The island's name means "head." This is usually taken to refer to the shape of the island. The island, however, does not look anything like a head, while that part of the body traditionally corresponds with the sign of Aries. The head of a ram is depicted on local coins. Cephallenia was the headquarters of Ulysses' island kingdom and a flourishing center of pre-Mycenaean culture. The names of two heroes associated with the history of the island are Helios, the sun, and Kephalos, "head." The Aries sector is where Leukas, marking the spring equinox, the beginning or "head" of the year, is located.

To take another example, the island of Kea, formerly Ceos, is in the Leo sector of the Delphic zodiacal wheel. Local coins bore the image of a leaping dog, a reference to the dog-days, which occurred when the risings and settings of the star Sirius, the dog-star, coincided with those of the sun, which was when the sun was in Leo. Other local coins bore images of bees, a solar insect. The inhabitants of Ceos held the star Sirius in great veneration, made sacrifices to it, and considered the conditions of its first appearance in the sky an oracular sign for the abundance of their crops.

At a short distance from Ioulis, a place name related to July and another reference to Leo, there is a colossal statue of a lion, six meters long, carved into the rock in a style reminscent of the Egyptian. Richer says that there were many of these ancient colossal statues. They were meant to place a whole province or region under the protection of a zodiacal divinity, and he cites the colossal statue of Castor and Pollux, symbol of Gemini, at Cape Sounion, and a colossal statue that symbolized Scorpio at Sinope.

A very interesting echo of these themes is found in Byzantine frescoes and icons, which regularly give the image of St. Christopher either the head of a lion or that of a dog. His feast day, both in the Catholic and Eastern churches, falls on July 25th, when the sun is in Leo.

For art lovers, *Sacred Geography of the Ancient Greeks* opens up a new level of appreciation of ancient art. This level does not necessarily depend on acceptance of Richer's rediscovery of the zodiacal wheels. A visit to any major museum of ancient Western art will reveal examples of what Richer calls the dynamic symbols of seasonal variations. The most common motifs are fighting animals, such as a lion attacking a stag, a lion attacking a bull, a serpent being snatched away by an eagle, or a dog chasing rabbits. The animals in question represent either particular seasons or months, and if more than one such motif is present on a piece, the piece will refer symbolically to a specific time span. This period of time may in turn be related to the use of the object, especially if it is a ritual object. Richer gives numerous illustrated examples of this. In the third volume of his triptych, *Iconologie et tradition*, Richer extends his studies of seasonal, zodiacal, and calendrical symbolism to Christian art from the fourth to the eighteenth centuries. Some of these symbols retained their meaning for four thousand years.

In *Sacred Geography of the Ancient Greeks*, Richer's breakthrough work, he expanded the inventory of astrological symbolism from the familiar bull for Taurus, lion for Leo, and so on, to include many other recurrent images, mythological characters, and both Olympian and pre-Olympian deities. This enabled him to interpret the time spans referred to on many Greek vases of the classical period, such as those of the great vase painter Exekias. Since the astrological symbolism referred in many cases not only to time, but also to space, Richer found that he could determine the location where the vase was painted in relation to one of the centers of the zodiacal wheels. He says that the city of Corinth played a prominent role in this tradition of esoteric vase painting.

On many Greek vases are paintings depicting battles with warriors who are bearing shields. Richer noticed that the motifs that appeared on the shields extended the symbolic meaning of the vases. The shield motifs often showed to the enemy a symbol that had a magical protective value to the fighter in terms of astrology.

This in turn led Richer to examine the armlets of shields, which were made of metal, and which have thus survived better than the shields themselves. The side of the armlet that faced the body of the warrior was decorated with several registers, each containing a symbolic scene. The scenes were repeated in sequence on the upper and lower halves of the armlet, with an unrepeated register at the level of the warrior's heart. The symbolic interpretation of these scenes and the key register enabled Richer to determine whether the armlet had been designed for general use by any member of a given troop, or for the use of a chieftain, whose individual birth season was sometimes indicated. It also enabled Richer to determine the place of origin of the armlets. Through the use of zodiacal symbolism, the outer surface of a warrior's shield became an image of the celestial vault, while the inner armlet established the link between the cosmos and the individual.

This sacred and magical approach to art goes counter to the widespread assumption that aesthetic or plastic considerations were the primary concern of ancient craftsmen and artists. This assumption is modern and insufficient for the art of traditional societies. As Richer puts it, "Does anyone really believe that, in a society of the traditional type, the priesthood could have been subordinate to the artisans and sculptors? In reality, religious considerations, and especially the importance of sacred geography, were never forgotten, and often outweighed questions of aesthetics and plastic values."

The aesthetic approach is most inadequate in the interpretation of temple art, whose motifs obviously must have been deeply meaningful. The juxtapositon of apparently unrelated themes on one or two pediments of a temple can be baffling, if the themes are not seen from a symbolic viewpoint. Analyses of the pediments of many archaic and classical Greek temples are given by Richer, and a very interesting interpretation of the temple of Athena at Assos in the Troad. He finds that the underlying unity is astral rather than aesthetic, and that orientations and motifs contribute to a concerted unity in relation to sacred geography, referring to the omphalos and placing the individual temple within the zodiacal landscape.

In his second volume, on the sacred geography of the Romans, Richer shows that astrology was the common denominator of the religions of the ancient world. The association of astral beliefs with zodiacal geography profoundly influenced the customs and institutions of Greco-Roman civilization, thus uniting them with the basic beliefs common to all the peoples of antiquity and perhaps even earlier.

The first translation into English of Richer's work is forthcoming from the State University of New York Press, which will be publishing *Sacred Geography of the Ancient Greeks: Astrological Symbolism in Art, Architecture, and Landscape* in 1994.

A Fish Pictogram

This gently and beautifully swirled "dolphin" is one of a series of gigantic "fish" shapes which marked the fields around Silbury Hill during the summer of 1991.

The Cosmological Rorschach

DAVID FIDELER

IN THE FIRST issue of ALEXANDRIA we presented two lengthy reviews of books relating to the crop circle phenomenon, a topic which had been gaining a fair amount of media attention at the time. Over the last fifteen years or so, unusual circular markings have been appearing in wheat fields around the world. The season before my own review was written, the phenomenon had escalated in England with the appearance of mysterious "pictogram" formations. As of that writing, there had been approximately 2,000 crop circle formations around the world, most having occurred in southern England.

Whatever may actually produce the formations, crop circles can accurately be seen as "a cosmological Rorschach test," based on the number of theories which have been projected upon them. As C. G. Jung noted, anything that is unknown acts as a magnet for unconscious projections. Crop circles, as one of the most mysterious unexplained phenomena of modern times, have given rise to myriad mythologies, cosmologies, and prophecies, and thus are of interest to students of cosmology, culture, and human behavior. As I wrote, "crop circles may represent the ultimate cosmological Rorschach test, and it is at least as instructive to study the investigators, their theories, and mythologies, as it is to study the actual phenomenon itself. It is also enlightening to study the effect that crop circles have on human behavior."

Since many individuals were attempting to predict how the phenomenon would evolve over time, I concluded the review with my own mythological prophecy, "Crop Circles: A Prediction for the Coming Year." This prediction, written in a state of far-seeing enthusiasm on May 17, 1991, was based on a number of sources. Strangely enough, as we will see in this article, many aspects of the prediction later came to pass! Naturally, as one would expect of a mythological prediction, the prophecy was not fulfilled in a *literal* sense; but the events which transpired in the summer of 1991 were so closely related to the prediction that it was impossible to ignore the resemblances.

At the very end of the 1991 growing season, two men named Doug Bower and Dave Chorley came forward and claimed that they were responsible for the crop circles, and that they had personally made all of the formations.[1] As the phenomenon evolved, it had become increasingly clear that there was some type of intelligence behind the formations, which had become increasingly difficult to explain in terms of meteorological phenomena. This, naturally, had the effect of making some people anxious and eager to solve the mystery; the British civil authorities, too, must have been made uncomfortable by the presence of an unknown, undetectable intelligence, creating massive pictographic formations in the midst of the most heavily secured area of southern England. Given these circumstances, it is fortunate that Doug and Dave came forward and admitted that they had cooked the whole thing up, thus putting people's minds to rest. Moreover, the media was relieved of covering crop circles, and thus allowed to return to the more important business of reporting on crime statistics, the economy, and providing weather forecasts.

The problem, however, with the Doug and Dave story is that, while they may have made some formations, they surely were not responsible for all 2,000 crop markings. On some nights, several formations appeared in different parts of the country. And when Doug and Dave demonstrated their crop circle making technique to the news media to "close the whole thing down" as they put it, they produced a trampled mess of wheat which bore little relation to the delicately formed pictograms.[2] This does not mean that people haven't produced crop formations—crop circle researchers know better than that—but there are some serious flaws in the Doug and Dave confession. Moreover, the level of Intelligence reflected in some of the formations indicates that—if they were created by humans—they certainly were not constructed by the likes of Doug and Dave.

Since crop circle formations have continued to appear for two years since the Doug and Dave confession, the only route left is for scientists and cereologists to continue gathering data. We particularly like the approach of the well-known astronomer and mathematician Dr. Gerald Hawkins, who subscribes to no particular theory about crop circle formation, but conducts mathematical analyses of the data to arrive at what he calls an "intellectual profile" of the circlemakers.[3] This seems like a worthwhile method and is also supported by an axiom of traditional metaphysics: namely, that it is possible to infer something about the cause of a thing from the produced effect.

After reviewing the crop circle prediction, reproduced below, we will explore some aspects of the prediction that were later confirmed by the events of 1991.

Crop Circles: A Prediction for the Coming Year Revisited

The phenomenon will start manifesting much slower than this year, but will greatly pick up by mid-season, and far surpass the formations of last year both in terms of quantity and complexity of design. We will see many designs based upon the pure forms of geometry and the quadrature of the circle.

Cereologists will begin to investigate the ratios and dimensions of the figures, both in terms of the English foot and other ancient standards of measure.

There will be an entirely new dimension to the phenomenon. The familiar warbling sound will be heard by many and lights will be seen in the sky, playing down upon the fields. The new aspect will be the manifestation of "musical" tones. People in the fields will hear tones coming from a variety of directions. The tones will be impossible for witnesses to describe, but all will agree that they are celestial in nature. Most tones will sound like single notes but will resonate to a previously unheard pattern of modulation. Other tones will be more complex: They will develop from a single tone, which will be maintained, but bloom forth into the harmonic spectrum as though someone were tapping out the overtone series on a monochord.

There will also be reports of music. Some will propose that it is the harmony of angels; others will suggest that it is a faery orchestra. People will be entranced by the strange, unearthly tones. As the harmonies are heard, colored lights will dance in the skies and wash across the tips of the wheat in waves, like a localized manifestation of the *aurora borealis*.

Animals will be especially affected by the harmonies. People walking in the fields will witness small congregations of rabbits, field mice and hedgehogs heading toward the source of the tones. There will be instances where boulders and large stones will be found to have moved in the night, seemingly on their own accord. Sensitive and alert farmers will be puzzled by the fact that certain trees have inexplicably wandered a few feet from where they previously stood, without having been uprooted in any way. In one remarkable instance, a band of cereologists will see multicolored lights streaming forth from the ground in the distance, as though coming from an aetherial fountain. The tones will be heard. In the morning will be discovered a crop circle surrounded by standing stones, where none had stood before.

One cereologist will plot out eight successive crop circles in the county of Wessex and discover that a line drawn connecting them in the order of their appearance will closely approximate the relative string lengths of the diatonic scale in Pythagorean tuning.

In some areas, where the tones are most commonly manifest, townspeople will be puzzled by something taking place in local ponds and streams. When the tones are heard, great numbers of fish will be seen jumping out of the water, into the air.

The phenomenon will have a remarkable effect upon the minds of many individuals. People will dream of interpenetrating and unfolding geometries bathed in the colors of the rainbow, and colors never before seen. They will be massaged by an unheard music in their sleep.

People from all walks of life will be drawn to the tones in the fields. There will be reports of healings from individuals who have pursued the lights and the tones. A well publicized incident will involve the case of a little girl who was in a car accident and has been in a coma ever since. After being carried into the fields by her parents she will awake and embrace her mother for the first time in three years.

Lights will dart above Glastonbury Tor and, for several days, silver water will bubble forth from Chalice Well. Healings will be reported in connection with the draught of silver water which will then be widely sought after. People will feel impelled, for an unknown reason, to sprinkle small quantities of the water on their favorite trees and on ancient sites of sanctity near their homes. Some will feel electrical fields near standing stones they visit, while others will say that certain stones have given off colored lights and tones.

Personalities will be transformed. People will let go of their fears and mental armoring; they will reach out toward others in love and in a common quest for knowledge. Teenage boys who previously spent most of their time torturing cats and listening to heavy metal will begin to read books and think about the nature of the universe. Many will take up the study of music, Plato, and geometrical harmonies. In the same way that makers of American flags could not keep up with demand during Operation Desert Storm, manufacturers of compasses will have their inventories of precision drawing instruments entirely depleted. Other individuals will study the movements of the planets and stars, setting up observatories in their backyards. Many will be moved to write poetry, recite long-forgotten tales, and compose songs of unusual beauty.

The season will reach a climax on August 12. Thousands of

people will see vast wheels of light rotating in the sky, throwing off prismatic beams in all directions. This light will cast no shadows, however, and some people will feel as though it is passing through their bodies, hearts, and souls. Also seen will be luminescent, undulating "jellyfish," composed entirely of light. As they pulsate and float across the sky in the orange and purple afterglow of dusk, the tones will be heard, keeping time with their graceful and hypnotic undulations. Many will be drawn into the fields and will see in the distance a figure with a lyre, sitting in a crop circle, surrounded by lions, giraffes, panthers, swans, and other animals, native, exotic, and fabulous.

An air of enchantment will descend upon the earth, and there will be light and music all around.

In the morning there will be discovered hundreds of new crop circles—and it will mark the end of the phenomenon in our lifetimes.

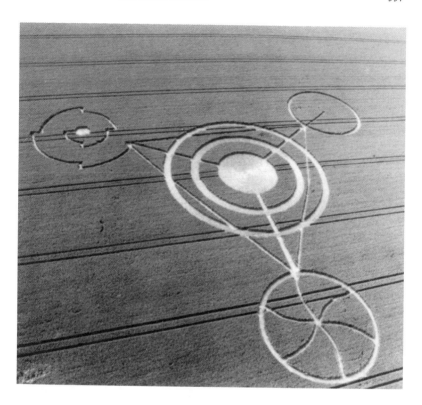

Figure 1. The Barbury Castle Formation

This colossal crop formation appeared next to the Iron Age hill-fort of Barbury Castle on the night of July 16, 1991. It was accompanied by unexplained aerial sounds and pulsating lights in the nighttime sky. (Photo: Richard Wintle)

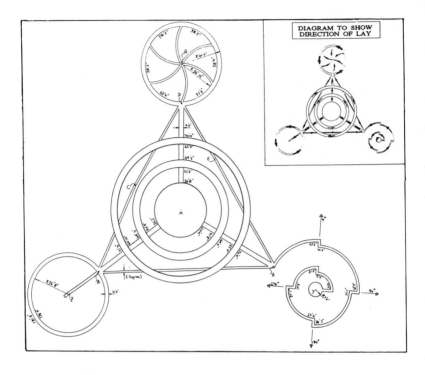

Figure 2. John Langrish's Survey of Barbury Castle

The flow of the crop in the ratchet spiral and the arcs in the topmost circle make it difficult to believe that this gigantic formation was created by human hands.

Analysis of the Prediction: Some Highlights

• **Crop circles and sacred geometry.** "We will see many designs based upon the pure forms of geometry and the quadrature of the circle. Cereologists will begin to investigate the ratios and dimensions of the figures, both in terms of the English foot and other ancient standards of measure."

As predicted, there was a quantum leap in the crop circle complexity, based on the forms of pure geometry, which was most clearly reflected in the stunning Barbury Castle formation. (See *Figure 1* and *2*).

This remarkable form appeared on the night of July 16th–17th 1991, beneath the slopes of Barbury Castle, an Iron Age hill-fort on the north edge of Wiltshire's Marlborough downs. On the night that it appeared, pulsating lights were seen in sky, and the warden of Barbury Castle was awakened by "a low throbbing sound" from above which "sounded like a hundred aircraft in formation, passing overhead."[4] Despite the noise and the appearance of the lights, we are unaware of any commentator who has suggested that the formation was the result of a tornado or an electrified vortex!

John Michell published an analysis of the Barbury Castle formation in *Cereologist* 4, based on the meticulous survey of John Langrish, in which he demonstrates how the figure is describing a type of ideal geometry.

Michell describes the construction shown in our *Figure 3a*:

Draw a circle and, with the compass opening unchanged, mark off six arcs from the center to the circumference.

Draw a line from the center of the circle mid-way between two of the points on its circumference and, with the same compass opening, divide the line into six lengths, each length equal to the radius of the circle.

Draw a circle equal to the first with its center on the last of the six division points on the line.

Form an equilateral triangle on the line between the centers of the two circles and draw a third equal circle centered upon the triangle's apex.[5]

Michell then demonstrates that if a circle is drawn inside the resulting triangle that *the area of the circle within the triangle is exactly equal to the sum of the areas of the three outer circles.* (See *Figure 3b.*)

If the triangle is removed as in *Figure 3c,* we are left with the geometry of the formation.

This geometry conforms *precisely* to the structure of the Barbury Castle formation, which was obviously not formed by Doug and Dave who claimed to create formations using a wire optical sight mounted on a baseball cap!

The outlying circles of the Barbury Castle formation measure about 41 feet in diameter, and the great inner circle measures about 71 feet in radius. This ratio, 71/41, is a very accurate whole number approximation of $\sqrt{3}$.

As I was discussing this formation with the astronomer Gerald Hawkins on the telephone, Dr. Hawkins described another way to define the geometry. It is, he said, created by ten circular discs, which form a perfect equilateral triangle, as is shown in *Figure 4.* As he described the image over the telephone, I immediately recognized it in my mind's eye as the famous Tetraktys symbol of the Pythagorean school. Dr. Hawkins was not familiar with the Tetraktys, but I had mailed him a copy of *The Pythagorean Sourcebook and Library* before we spoke, so he was able to confirm this identification after our conversation. In addition to incorporating the Tetraktys, Dr. Hawkins writes that the Barbury Castle pictogram also incorporates "*Euclid*-based theorems, a gear wheel whose cusps trace out the spiral of *Archimedes,* and a number theorem based on the work of *Gaus.* That is quite a galaxy of famous brains!"[6]

Both the schema outlined by John Michell and the Tetraktys pattern of Dr. Hawkins perfectly describe the geometry of the Barbury Castle formation. However, now that the geometry has been identified, are the dimensions of the figure in any way significant? This is, after all, another aspect of the prophecy.

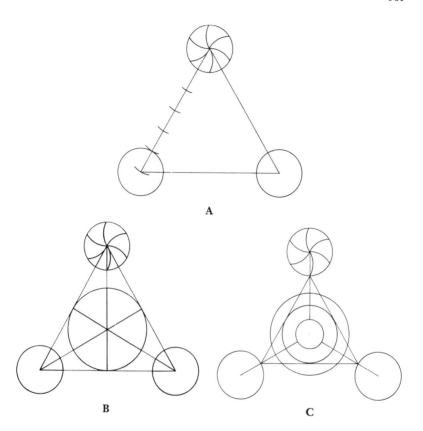

Figure 3. John Michell's Analysis of the Barbury Castle Geometry

Due to the construction of the underlying geometry, the great central circle shown in *Figure 3b* is precisely equivalent to the combined area of the three outer circles.

In his *Cereologist* article, John Michell suggests that the total area of the three-in-one geometry—the total area of the four circles in *Figure 3b*—amounts to 31680 square feet. This analysis is based on the premise that the radius of the great inner circle measures 71 feet, which, when squared, brings out the number 5041, one unit more than

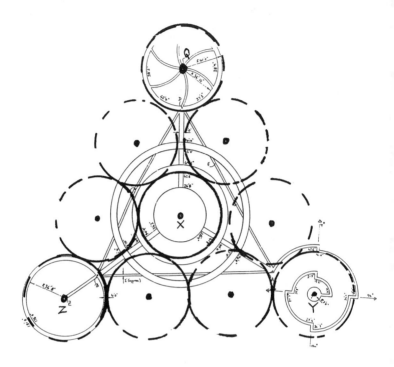

Figure 4. Barbury Castle and the Pythagorean Tetraktys

An alternate way to describe the geometry of the Barbury Castle formation, discovered by astronomer Gerald Hawkins, is that the geometry is based on a triangular pattern of ten closely packed circles. The pattern thus formed is the Tetraktys, a Pythagorean symbol of musical harmony and the four levels of reality.

5040, the number of citizens in Plato's ideal city Magnesia, described in the *Laws*. The number 3168 has been identified as a significant cosmological number from antiquity by Michell in his various writings on the ancient number canon.

While there is much to support the Michell hypothesis—and it is certainly as likely as any other—there is another interpretation of the Barbury Castle formation which also conforms with significant cosmological numbers from antiquity. According to the alternate interpretation, the radius of the great circle is not √5041 but represents the value of √5000, or approximately 70.7 feet. If this is the case, then the following results are obtained:

- The total area of the four circles is not 31680 square feet, but rather 31,415.927... square feet, exactly 10,000 times the value of π— certainly an important universal and cosmological number.

- The radius of the great circle is 70.7 feet, and 707 is the gematria value[7] of the Greek title THE GOD HERMES. Hermes, who was known to the Greeks as the Logos, was the inventor of the lyre, which he gave to his brother Apollo.

- The diameter of the great circle is 141.5 feet, and 1415 is the numerical value of THE GOD APOLLO, the Greek god of music, geometry, and celestial harmony.

- These two values, .707 and 1.415, represent the exact harmonic center of the octave in terms of string length and tonal frequency respectively, and are reciprocals of one another. (See my note on Ptolemy's polychord in this issue of ALEXANDRIA.)

- Finally, the great circle of the Barbury Castle formation *exactly* encompasses the underlying geometry of the New Testament allegory of the "miraculous feeding of the five thousand," which is also said to have taken place in a field, and is fully described in chapter five of my recently published book, *Jesus Christ, Sun of God: Ancient Cosmology and Early Christian Symbolism*.[8] (See *Figure 5*). This exact coincidence of the Barbury Castle formation with the ancient cosmological geometry is rather miraculous in itself, since there were only two individuals in England who were familiar with this New Testament geometry when the formation occurred, and neither one of them could have possibly created the formation. As is conclusively demonstrated in the book, the number values associated with this geometry are codifications of the primary harmonic ratios which were studied in antiquity by the Greeks and the Pythagorean school, and were later adapted by some of the first Christian writers to form the basis of their spiritual allegories.

Figure 5. Barbury Castle and the Feeding of the Five Thousand

The great inner circle of the Barbury Castle formation has a radius of 70.7 feet which is equivalent to √5000. Therefore, the central circle perfectly encompasses the underlying geometry of the New Testament allegory of the miraculous feeding of the five thousand, shown above. Moreover, if the radius of the inner circle is √5000, then the total area of all four circles amounts to exactly 31,415.927 square feet, the value of π multiplied by 10,000.

The Barbury Castle formation thus emerges as a potent cosmological symbol, regardless of whether one accepts the √5041 interpretation or the √5000 model. Because the geometry of Barbury Castle is inscribed on a field of wheat, it is impossible to know which interpretation is correct, for the three radius measures of John Langrish's survey—70'9", 70'10", and 71'4"—can be taken as representing either 71 feet or 70.7 feet. The difference is too close to call and, as someone suggested to this writer, perhaps the Intelligence behind the formation was pointing toward a reconciliation of the two models.

Another case of a geometrical crop formation is the Mandelbrot

Figure 6. The Mandelbrot Set and the Mandelbrot Pictogram

This illustration shows the close resemblance between the Mandelbrot set of chaos theory (left) and the crop marking which appeared near the village of Ickleton on August 12, 1991 (right).

set—the well-known self-recursive fractal design described by "chaos theory"—which appeared near the village of Ickleton in Cambridgeshire on August 12, 1991. This crop design, however, is not a pure Mandelbrot, but is, as John Martineau has shown, based on the Type A megalithic flattened circle geometry discovered by professor Alexander Thom.[9] This flattened circle geometry underlies the Castle Rig megalithic site, and the Mandelbrot pictogram itself closely approximates the size of this ancient megalithic structure.[10] Another peculiar feature of the Mandelbrot pictogram is that the placement of the detached circle on the main axis does not truly correspond with the placement of the circle on the fractal design. (See *Figure 6*.) Rather, as Wolfgang Schindler has shown,[11] it is proportionally placed in refer-

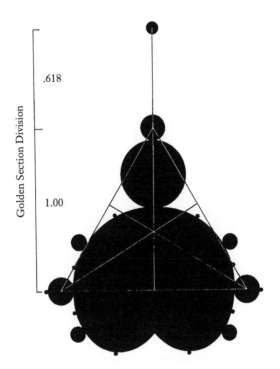

Figure 7. The Golden Section and the Mandelbrot Formation

This illustration shows how the circle on the axis of the formation is placed by reference to the Golden Section or phi proportion, an omnipresent mathematical ratio which controls the growth patterns of living systems.

ence to the phi ratio or "Golden Section." (See *Figure* 7.) Thus, in the same way that the Barbury Castle formation incorporates a number of different mathematical models and theorems, the Mandelbrot pictogram neatly synthesizes megalithic and contemporary mathematics, and incorporates the timeless forming principle of the phi ratio or Golden Section.

• **Musical harmonies and crop circles**. The prediction told that there would be reports of music and mysterious tones: "They will develop from a single tone, which will be maintained, but bloom forth into the harmonic spectrum as though someone were tapping out the overtone series on a monochord."

While I am not aware of anyone hearing such tones with their ears, there can be little doubt that the harmonic dimension of the prediction was neatly fulfilled via the manifestation of "unheard harmonies." As Joscelyn Godwin notes in his 1984 article on "The Golden Chain of Orpheus":

> Musical esotericism centres around the fact that not all music is heard with the ears. There is another music of the soul and of the spheres which gives to the actual music that is sung by voices and played on instruments its reason for existence. The idea has its roots in the unfathomable antiquity of mythical times: the times of the lyre-playing gods Hermes and Apollo, and their spiritual son Orpheus. Sometimes the idea has disappeared beneath the surface of history; at others it has burgeoned as an inspiration to poets and philosophers. Parallel to it at every point has been the exoteric activity of music making, with its own separate history. In every era there has been music which could act as a catalyst for experiences which lie beyond hearing; but since the experiences are of something timeless and ineffable, the style and period of the music that prompts them are immaterial . . . Truth, which is unchanging, is not to be sought in the protean changes of the incarnate sound, but in that to which the sound can sometimes lead.[12]

These "unheard harmonies" that Godwin describes are embodied in the Pythagorean symbol of the Tetraktys, which underlies the Barbury Castle formation. The Tetraktys has many meanings. It is a symbol of cosmic *harmonia*, it represents the four levels of being, and it denotes the Pythagorean philosophy of whole systems. (See *Figure 9*, "The Elemental Continuum of Hellenistic Cosmology," next two pages.) One of the primary meanings of the Tetraktys is musical, for

THE ELEMENTAL CONTINUUM

1

GEOMETRICAL STAGE	PLATONIC SOLID	STATE OF MATTER	PSYCHOLOGICAL FUNCTION
THE POINT • **OR MONAD** NONDIMENSIONALITY	**TETRAHEDRON**	Fire PLASMA	**INTUITION** The Soul's Relationship with the World of Divine Ideas

2

GEOMETRICAL STAGE	PLATONIC SOLID	STATE OF MATTER	PSYCHOLOGICAL FUNCTION
THE LINE •—• ONE DIMENSION	**OCTAHEDRON**	Air GAS	**THINKING** The Soul's Relationship with the Intellectual World

3

GEOMETRICAL STAGE	PLATONIC SOLID	STATE OF MATTER	PSYCHOLOGICAL FUNCTION
THE SURFACE TWO DIMENSIONS	**ICOSAHEDRON**	Water LIQUID	**FEELING** The Soul's Relationship with the Emotional World

4

GEOMETRICAL STAGE	PLATONIC SOLID	STATE OF MATTER	PSYCHOLOGICAL FUNCTION
THE SOLID THREE DIMENSIONS	**CUBE**	Earth SOLID	**SENSATION** The Soul's Relationship with the Physical World

OF HELLENISTIC COSMOLOGY

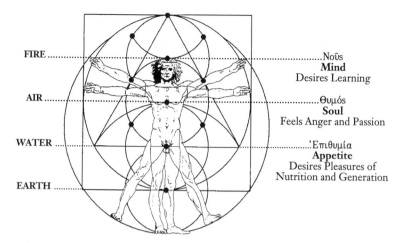

FIRE .... Noûs
Mind
Desires Learning

AIR ....Θυμός
Soul
Feels Anger and Passion

WATER ....Ἐπιθυμία
Appetite
Desires Pleasures of
Nutrition and Generation

EARTH ....

The Pythagorean and Platonic Division of the Soul: The Three Worlds in Man
"The soul is divided into reasoning power, anger, and desire. Reasoning power rules knowledge, anger deals with impulse, and desire bravely rules the soul's affections. When these three parts unite into one action, exhibiting a composite energy, then in the soul results concord and virtue. When sedition divides them, then discord and vice appear."

—Theages the Pythagorean, *On the Virtues*

The Tetraktys: A Symbol of Cosmic Wholeness
In Pythagorean thought, the so-called *Tetraktys* (Fourness) represents the four levels of reality, the four elements, the four states of matter, the four stages of geometrical existence, and so on. Symbolizing the Pythagorean philosophy of whole systems, the Tetraktys also expresses the perfect harmonies of music: 1:2 (the octave), 2:3 (the perfect fifth), and 3:4 (the perfect fourth).

The Tetraktys of Pythagoras

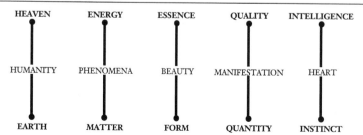

HEAVEN	ENERGY	ESSENCE	QUALITY	INTELLIGENCE
HUMANITY	PHENOMENA	BEAUTY	MANIFESTATION	HEART
EARTH	MATTER	FORM	QUANTITY	INSTINCT

The Symbolic Continuum: Including the Harmonic Offspring of Ideal Opposites

it represents the ratios of perfect harmony: 1:2 (octave), 2:3 (perfect fifth), and 3:4 (perfect fifth). This is exactly the sequence you follow and produce when "tapping out the overtone series on a monochord," and thus we can see how the harmonic "tones" did indeed appear during the summer of 1991.

- **The diatonic scale in Pythagorean tuning**. "One cereologist will plot out eight successive crop circles in the county of Wessex and discover that a line drawn connecting them in the order of their appearance will closely approximate the relative string lengths of the diatonic scale in Pythagorean tuning."

This little fancy was inspired by the research of the astronomer Gerald Hawkins who discovered (before the prophecy was written) that crop circles describe previously unknown Euclidean theorems. In his article which appears in *Cereologist* 3, Hawkins points out that these theorems, in terms of surface areas, also describe harmonic ratios such as the perfect fourth in music.[13] Based on this discovery, I arrived at the notion that the ratios of the entire scale would be discovered by crop circle researchers.

Needless to say, I was quite pleased to receive, after the prophecy was published, another paper by Dr. Hawkins which shows how the crop circles further conform to harmonic ratios.[14] The data set used by Hawkins involves crop circles with concentric rings and crop circles with satellites from the period 1981–88. This is considered by some to be the golden age of cereology before there was much hoaxing involved. What Hawkins discovered is that *the ratios described by the data set correspond with the ratios of the regular diatonic scale*. (See *Figure 9*.) This figure shows that

> the ratios are falling on or closest to rational notes. The 1981–88 crop circles give all the white notes of the piano (except A), but do not give the chromatic (black) notes, which have n-values 1, 3, 6, 8, or 10. If one postulates the target numbers to be limited to the above eight fractions of the major scale, then the Bernoulli confidence rises [from 95 percent] to better than 99 percent.

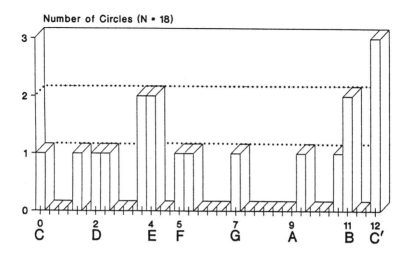

Figure 9. Crop Circle Ratios and the Major Diatonic Scale

This analysis by Gerald S. Hawkins demonstrates how the ratios generated by crop circles correlate with the ratios of the major diatonic scale.

As Hawkins concludes in his paper,

this report shows how the ratios within the crop circles share the same mathematical relationship as the intervals of the major diatonic scale of music. This "circle law" is seemingly a real effect, statistically established for the period 1981–88. It is unlikely that the results are an oddity of the selection process used by Delgado and Andrews in compiling the catalog. Futhermore, if, as some have suggested, the crop circles during that time period were made by various groups of hoaxers, then coordination was required, because Meaden finds clustering around diatonic ratios for the phenomenon as a whole. If David Chorley and Doug Bower were the masterminds behind the venture as they have claimed, then they were encoding astoundingly high brow information for self-styled jokers.

On the other hand, if the crop circles are produced by natural processes, then any physical theory for their cause must account for the occurrence of the concomitant mathematical relationships that have appeared in the 1981–88 time-frame.

• **Fish responding to music**. "In some areas, where the tones are most commonly manifest, townspeople will be puzzled by something taking place in local ponds and streams. When the tones are heard, great numbers of fish will be seen jumping out of the water, into the air."

This part of the prophecy was inspired by the sacred fish known as *orphoi*, which were kept in decorative fish ponds at some of Apollo's temples in antiquity. These fish were trained to respond to music, which signalled their feeding time. Similarly, fishes responded to the magical music of Orpheus, for when he played his lyre the fish jumped out of the sea to greet him. As the Greek poet Simonides writes,

> Above his head there hovered birds innumerable,
> and fishes leapt clean from the blue water because
> of his sweet music.[15]

While fishes were not literally seen responding to the harmonic tones of the crop circles, the most astonishing thing did occur, which may have some relation to the prophecy. In the summer of 1991, a new type of formation appeared, which was described by researchers as a giant "fish," "whale," or "dolphin." About a dozen of these giant fishes—all different from one another—covered the plains of England around the prehistoric earthwork of Silbury Hill, like vast creatures washed up from some cosmic sea. (See *Figure 10*). These beautiful and awe-inspiring fish pictograms had not been seen before the summer of 1991, nor have they appeared since.

• **Lyre-players in crop circles**. "Many will be drawn into the fields and will see in the distance a figure with a lyre, sitting in a crop circle, surrounded by lions, giraffes, panthers, swans, and other animals,

Figure 10. A Pictogram Belonging to the "Fish" Series

This photograph shows one of the many vast "fish," "whale," or "dolphin" pictograms that covered the fields of southern England around Avebury during the summer of 1991. Each one of the designs was slightly different but clearly belonged to the same family. This particular design appeared on the night of August 3, 1991, in a field which shows crop damage from the wind. Behind the pictogram looms the megalithic earthwork of Silbury Hill, part of the ancient Avebury ritual complex, which over the years has attracted crop formations like a magnet. Silbury Hill, whose exact function is unknown, is the largest megalithic structure in all of Europe.

native, exotic, and fabulous."

While we have received no reports of Orpheus being sighted in the wheatfields of England, there have been reports of Celtic harps appearing in crop circles. When *Cereologist* 4 from the summer of 1991 arrived, we were delighted to learn that "when Michael Omejer played his harp in the relatively unknown pictogram under Milk Hill, the [dowsable energy] circles and the spirals expanded greatly, as did parallel lines in the central avenue of the figure."[16]

When this writer purchased a Celtic harp in February of 1992, it merely reflected his musical interests; but during my telephone conversation with Dr. Gerald Hawkins, I was confessedly astonished to discover that both he and his wife are Celtic harp players too! Hawkins, as we have noted, discovered the presence of harmonic ratios in the crop circle data set from 1981–88.

What Inspired the Prediction?

While the prophecy of May 17, 1991 draws upon many sources, the central idea behind the prediction goes back to an earlier date when a young lady solicited my opinion regarding the origin of crop circles.

After making sure that she really wanted to hear my opinion on the matter, I explained my theory that crop circles were being sent to humanity, as a geometry lesson, by the god Apollo.

I then told her about a similar Apollonic geometry lesson from antiquity, the well-known story of "the doubling of the cube," one of the three special problems of Greek geometry.[17]

According to this traditional account, the people of the isle of Delos, the birthplace of Apollo, were experiencing a plague. The oracle of Apollo was consulted, in the hope that a solution for the malady would be found. The response from Apollo was that the situation would resolve itself if the Delians would simply construct a cubic altar that was exactly twice the volume of the existing one. However, the Delian craftsmen were confounded by the problem, which is far more complex than it initially seems; "they therefore went to ask Plato about it, and he replied that the oracle meant, not that the god wanted an altar of double the size, but that he wished, in setting them the task, to shame the Greeks for their neglect of mathematics and their contempt for geometry."[18]

I explained to the lady that geometry is similarly ignored today, and that Apollo is producing the crop circles in order to encourage this beneficial and therapeutic study. This leads us to one final aspect of the prediction, the "make geometry, not war" theme.

• **Make geometry, not war.** "Many will take up the study of music, Plato, and geometrical harmonies. In the same way that makers of American flags could not keep up with demand during Operation Desert Storm, manufacturers of compasses will have their inventories of precision drawing instruments entirely depleted."

Only recently did I discover how the "make geometry, not war" theme of the crop circle prediction also relates to Apollo's earlier geometry lesson, the doubling of the cube. My witness is Plutarch, a priest of Apollo at Delphi, who discusses the doubling of the cube in his essay *On the Sign of Socrates*, a piece that I hadn't read before transcribing the prophecy.

While Plato states that the oracle of Apollo was meant to shame the Greeks for their contempt of geometry, Plutarch explains that Apollo's geometry problem is rooted in a vision of universal harmony. According to Plutarch, Apollo exhorted the Greeks to "double the cube" and study geometry because

> he was ordering the entire Greek nation to give up war and its miseries and cultivate the Muses, and by calming their passions through the practice of discussion and study of mathematics, so to live with one another so that their intercourse should be not injurious, but profitable.[19]

Conclusion

This theory of the Apollonic origin of the crop circle formations is not advanced here as a definitive explanation. There may, after all, be other factors involved, and perhaps even other divinities. It is unlikely that one single answer to the enigma will ever be found, and it is unbecoming for any individual to proclaim that he possesses the one and only truth about crop circles. Nonetheless, it must be noted that this theory has as much in its favor as any other. In some respects, the Delphic hypothesis has shown its superiority to others, because it has successfully predicted aspects of the unfolding phenomenon in ways that other theories have not even approached.

One of the many theories advanced about the crop circles is that they might be the work of the army, testing out some type of particle beam weapon, based from a satellite in space. After seeing the Barbury Castle geometry, one esteemed scholar (and contributor to this journal) amusingly wondered if "Pythagorean military-men" might somehow be involved?

Despite its value as a source of entertainment, the military hypothesis can be rejected on the basis of the available evidence. As Plato states in the *Republic*, "geometry is the knowledge of the eternally existent" and its purpose is "to draw the soul towards truth and to direct upwards the philosophic intelligence which is now wrongly turned earthwards."[20] The ancients sharply differentiated between the study of *true mathematics*—the philosophical type described by Plato—and mere *logistics*, the type of calculations that are employed by merchants, shopkeepers, and accountants. Historically speaking, military-men have always been more interested in logistics than the Pythagorean study of mathematical harmony. From this perspective, if some type of particle beam was used to create the Barbury Castle pictogram, it is unlikely that it originated from the military establishment or from any human source.

As John Michell notes in his article about the Barbury Castle geometry,

> There is a world of symbolism in this Barbury Castle wheat impression, some of it already apparent and some still awaiting recognition. Neither physically nor intellectually does this figure give signs of being a human

creation. To identify its author seems therefore to be a problem for theology. One's rational mind shrinks away from the implication that this diagram constitutes a divine revelation. Yet in the traditional histories revelation is said to have been the source of all cultures and to have inspired successive renewals of the human spirit. It occurs, presumably, at times when it is most needed, and its content is always the same, being that cosmic Law, Canon, or compilation of numerical, musical and geometric harmonies which provided the ruling standard of every ancient civilization.[21]

These observations, as can be readily seen, accord very well with the themes of our crop circle prophecy.

While there is still no universally acceptable explanation for the crop circles, the phenomenon reached a dramatic peak in 1991 with the Barbury Castle formation, the fish swimming around Avebury, and the Mandelbrot set. To careful observers of the cereological landscape, it certainly seemed as though something was trying to "break through" into a wider sphere of public awareness. Whether this was some type of harmonic, auroral effluence from the Hyperborean regions we cannot say. But with the appearance of the Barbury Castle formation, it became clear, once and for all, that there is some type of Intelligence at work behind the crop circle phenomenon.

Regardless of whether Barbury Castle was made by human hands, particle beams, or was a direct emanation of the Logos itself, a careful study of geometry reveals the source of the formation. Expressed in Pythagorean terms, this geometry bears the imprint of an exalted form of Harmonic Intelligence. This pattern of Intelligence—known in antiquity as the Logos and personified by a number of ancient divinities—embodies the mathematical first principles of creation that were seen as underlying the structure and harmony of the manifest universe. Crop circles certainly possess a mythological dimension, yet, as the pagan theologian Sallustius observed in his treatise *Concerning the Gods and the Universe*, "even the universe can be called a myth, since bodies and material objects are apparent in it, while souls and intellects are concealed."[22]

What the future holds for crop circles, or anything else, no mortal can say for certain. Nonetheless, it seems best to be ever alert to all the wonderful possibilities of life, for as the Greek philosopher Heraclitus once noted, "The god whose oracle is at Delphi neither reveals nor conceals, but indicates through signs."

Notes

1. See George Wingfield, "The Doug 'n' Dave Scam," *Cereologist* 5 (Winter 1991/2), 3–6.

2. See photo in Wingfield, "The Doug 'n' Dave Scam," 6.

3. See Ivar's Peterson, "Euclid's Crop Circles," *Science News* 141 (February 1, 1992), 5, 76–77, and Gerald Hawkins, "Probing the Mystery of those Eerie Crop Circles," *Cosmos: A Journal of Emerging Issues* 2 (1992), 1, 23–27.

4. See Gary Hardwick's essay on "Pulsating Lights at Beckhampton" in the book *Ciphers in the Crops: The Fractal and Geometric Circles of 1991* (Bath: Gateway Books, 1992).

5. *Cereologist* 4 (Summer 1991), 24–25.

6. Letter from Gerald Hawkins dated July 10, 1992.

7. The letters of the Greek alphabet were used in antiquity to represent numbers, the values of which are given in every Greek lexicon. These numbers indicated here are the numerical sum of the letters making up the indicated title in ancient Greek.

8. The Barbury Castle geometry is thus also related to the New Testament allegory of the 153 fishes in the unbroken net; see Fideler, *Jesus Christ, Sun of God* (Wheaton: Quest, 1993), 304–06.

9. See B. L. van der Waerden, *Geometry and Algebra in Ancient Civilizations* (Berlin and New York: Springer-Verlag, 1983), 19.

10. For the geometry of Castle Rig, see Keith Critchlow, *Time Stands Still: New Light on Megalithic Science* (New York: St. Martin's, 1982), 34–35.

11. See Wolfgang Schindler's article on "Mathematische Harmonie" in Jürgen Krönig, editor, *Spuren im Korn* (Frankfurt: Zweitausendeins, 1992).

12. Joscelyn Godwin, "The Golden Chain of Orpheus: A Survey of Musical Esotericism in the West," *Temenos* 4 (1989), 7.

13. This isn't, in a sense, an entirely new discovery. Archimedes, for example, discovered that the relation of the volume of a sphere to an enclosing cylinder is 2:3, the ratio of the perfect fifth in music. To commemorate the discovery, he had it inscribed on his tombstone.

14. Gerald S. Hawkins, "Mathematical Properties of Crop Circles, 1981–88," in Donald Cyr, editor, *America's First Crop Circle* (Santa Barbara: Stonehenge Viewpoint, 1992).

15. For the source of this fragment and many other ancient examples of fish responding to music, see Fideler, *Jesus Christ, Sun of God*, 352.

16. Report by Colin Bloy on dowsing the crop circles in *Cereologist* 4 (Summer 1991), 18.

17. The two other problems are the squaring of the circle and the trisection of any angle.

18. Eratosthenes, quoted by Theon of Smyrna, in Heath, *A History of Greek Mathematics I: From Thales to Euclid* (New York: Dover, 1981), 245.

19. Plutarch, *On the Sign of Socrates* 579D.

20. Plato, *Republic* 527B.

21. John Michell, "Geometry and Symbolism at Barbury Castle," *Cereologist* 4 (Summer 1991), 24.

22. Sallustius, *Concerning the Gods and the Universe*, edited and translated by A. D. Nock (Cambridge: Cambridge University Press, 1926), 5.

Psalm

SING praise for ALL THAT IS
Extending everywhere, endlessly
Through Time and through Space.

Sing praise to the farthest
Outward reaches of the Cosmos
And to the subtlest inner reaches of Being.

Sing praise to the Galaxies,
With suns and stars and roving planets.

Sing praise to the miracle of matter and life,
To the dense rocks and waters,
To rooted green plants,
To earthbound creatures and winged ones,
To the tiny vastnesses in every atom.

Praise the Grand Universe
With harps and timbrels and flutes.
Praise all existence
With congas and gamelons,
Kotos and Gospel choirs.

Give praise with reggae and symphonies,
Oratorios and Flamenco guitars.
Strum strings and pipe on pennywhistles.
Strike up the band and let the trombones wail.

Belt out praise with grand Opera,
Steel bands, blues and Jazz.
Ring the bells and blow the bagpipes.
Beat the drums and sound the trumpets.

Let everything that has voice
Sing out praise.
To the end of breath, Sing!
With every single cell, Sing!
Body, mind and spirit, Sing!

Hallelujah!

Psalm 150
A version by CAROLYN NORTH

To Artemis

INCENSE: FRANKINCENSE POWDER

Many-named Maiden of Zeus, hear me, O Queen:
    You Titanic, Dionysiac, great-named one
    You, skilled archer, dreadful one,
    All-illuminating, divine torchbearer!
    Goddess of the Chase, you bring to birth,
    You ease the pain, yet are a stranger to it.
    You loosen the mother's belt, in love with hysteria!
    Huntress, running swiftly you banish worry,
    Showering down arrows, loving the wild, roaming the night.
    Bestowing renown, gracious, liberating, masculine,
    Orthis, you swift-born, godly matron of mortal children,
    Immortal, Chthonic, killer of beasts, destined to prosperity!
    You, whose keep is the oak grove in the mountains,
    Deer-huntress, dread Lady, Queen of everything!
    You, lovely blossom, She who is forever,
    You of the oak and hunting dog, Kudonian girl,
    You whose form can change so rapidly!
    Come, beloved Goddess of salvation,
    To the gathering of initiates who welcome you,
    Bringing the earth's choice fruit, and perfect bliss,
    And Health with her beauteous curls—
    Banish to the mountaintops affliction and pain!

Orphic Hymn to Artemis
Translated by SHAWN EYER

Apollo's Journey to Hyperborea

These Greek coins show Apollo's annual journey to Hyperborea on the back of a swan, or on a swan-drawn chariot. According to an account which dates from 600 B.C.E., when Apollo was born, "Zeus arrayed him with a golden *mitra* and a lyre, and giving him a chariot of swans to drive sent him to Delphi and the streams of Kastalia, there to utter justice for the Greeks. But Apollo, stepping onto the chariot, urged the swans to fly to the Hyperboreans. The Delphians, perceiving it, composed a paean and a song, and arranged dances of young men round the tripod, and called upon the god to come from the Hyperboreans. He, after he had spent a whole year in giving law to the men that were there, thought that the right time was come for the Delphic tripods too to be sounding, so bade his swans fly back again from the Hyperboreans. Now it was summer, indeed midsummer, when, according to [the poet] Alkaios, Apollo was brought from the Hyperboreans. Hence, at the time when summer shines forth and Apollo is here, the lyre too brightens into a summer strain concerning the god. Nightingales sing for him as one would expect birds to sing in Alkaios. Swallows also sing and cicadas, not telling of their own fortunes among men, but voicing all their songs about the god. Kastalia too in poetic wise rolls her silver streams, and Kephissos rises high with tossing waves after the likeness of Homer's Enipeus. For Alkaios, like Homer, does his utmost to make the very water able to feel the god's advent" (Himerios, *Oration* 14).

For more on Hyperborean traditions and the Northern Apollo, see Frederick M. Ahl, "Amber, Avallon, and Apollo's Singing Swan," *American Journal of Philology* 103 (1982), 373–411.

Reports from Hyperborea

JOHN HENRY

Editor's Introduction

JOHN HENRY wrote to us after being struck by the synaesthetic elements in the mythological crop circle prediction which appeared in ALEXANDRIA 1. He explained that he felt some type of connection with the piece. For example, he couldn't help but notice the parallel between the line "As the harmonies are heard, colored lights will dance in the skies and wash across the tips of the wheat in waves, like a localized manifestation of the *aurora borealis*" and his own poem "Auroral Transubstantiation," which was written the year before, in 1990.

John Henry's spiritual voyage began in 1976 after he walked down to the shore of a lake and had the experience of "being hit by a falling star." After this, Henry had additional experiences of synaesthetic phenomena, celestial harmonies, and the types of phenomena that some people would classify as "paranormal." After the initial experience, he started to explore, in chronological order, the following topics: Orpheus; Novalis; the poet AE (George W. Russel); Early German Romanticism; Gerard de Nervál; Alexander Scriabin; Vladimir Solovyov; intersense analogy (synaesthesia, chromaesthesia); Corybantes, Theurgy, and Hyperboreans; the Aeolian Harp; Nietzsche and Wagner; American Transcendentalism; Animism, Panpsychism, and Hylozoism (the philosophical doctrine that all matter has life); Charles Henry and psychophysical aesthetics; the German films of Werner Herzog; Neurosemantics; and the writings of Gaston Bachelard, James Hillman, Henry Corbin, and Thomas Moore. As they say, one thing leads to another!

In his prose poems, which conform to no known literary canon or genre, Henry tries to express experiences which cannot be depicted in conventional language. This tension gives form to all true poetic work which, if successful, transports the reader beyond words to the core experience which is the seed of the work itself. Based on a variety of considerations—not to mention the theme of auroral harmonics—we present these works under the rubric of "Reports from Hyperborea."

Being hit by a shooting star or a thunderstone is no small matter. In a traditional society, a person who experienced such a thing would receive recognition as a shaman, visionary, or healer; his gifts would be made use of for the benefit of the entire culture. Today, despite the archetypal and recurrent nature of such experiences, our society has little place for shamanic inspiration, which is the ultimate source of all true culture. Similarly, scholars of spiritual traditions usually prefer to study the ideas of people who are dead in a strictly historical context, rather than investigate the content of an idea itself. Therefore, we are publishing these reports in ALEXANDRIA as a reminder that visionary insight is an ever-present reality. True art, we think, while manifesting through the medium of the individual, ultimately comes from another source. The doorway to this transcendent source is always open to each individual, each in his or her own unique way, through the medium of the *mundus imaginalis* and the inner voice of the creative genius.

The journey into the Imaginal world is always an initiatory experience; it is a journey of recollection, a journey of remembering. In the process of recollection, the individual follows that unique "internal signature" which is truly his, and is led to explore topics and ideas with which he has a true, internal resonance. In the process, the individual learns not only to recognize his true self, but is also led to recognition and acknowledgement of those kindred spirits—both living and dead—who make up the "tribe" to which he belongs.

Based on these poems, it is clear that John Henry belongs to the tribe of the Hyperboreans. In classical Greek mythology, the Hyperboreans were a happy, immortal race of Apollo worshippers who lived beyond (hyper) the North Wind (Boreas). Once a year when Dionysus became the active divinity at Delphi, Apollo would return to the land of the Hyperboreans, either by flying on the back of a swan or being carried there on a swan-drawn chariot. Historically, there was a Hyperborean pilgrimage from some site in northern Europe, which carried votive offerings to Delos, the birthplace of Apollo and Artemis. Consequently, scholars have endlessly debated who the Hyperboreans actually were and where their homeland was once located. According to Pindar, however, "Never on foot or ship could you find the marvelous road to the feast of the Hyperboreans." Among the Hyperboreans, as he writes in the tenth *Pythian Ode,*

> Never the Muse is absent
> from their ways: lyres clash, and the flutes cry,
> and everywhere maiden choruses whirling.
> They bind their hair in golden laurel and take their holiday.
> Neither disease nor bitter old age is mixed
> in their sacred blood; far from labor and battle
> they live; they escape Nemesis,
> the overjust. . . .

As one would expect, the "Hyperborean realm" is represented differently in each tradition. But no matter how it is described—and regardless of the cultural context—one thing remains sure: if no physical road can lead to Hyperborea, the only remaining entry point is the gnostic faculty of visionary insight.

—DAVID FIDELER

Arrival of the Hyperboreans

Celebrants dance amidst thrushing lyres and citharas at Delos. In the cerulean skies above, sonic air-prisms flash from billowing, mauve-blushed cloud tufts. Gossammery, crystalline swans emerge from the cumuli, descending in a processional glissading annular orbit around Apollo's temple, purifying the temenos with a choral, fluvial chrome-yellow madder. From beyond the North Wind, Column of Dawn, Hyperoche and Laodice arrive with votive offerings of sacred objects bound in wheaten straw.

1990

Ortygia

Nature is an Aeolian Harp, a musical instrument whose tones are again keys of higher things within us.

—Novalis

SOUNDS and colors that transcend physical laws interfused in a dreaming garden of consciousness. Canorous whispers from hyacinths, angelicas, lilies, and other flowersouls trembled with fragile sounds. A pale, aquamarine vapor enveloped the soundcolor diapason. Souls from cherub statues hovered through the symphonic vibrations of light and sound. Mauve sighings verticulated from Aeolian harps that the cherubs held. Hylozoi lay sleeping on moonflower vines. His consciousness was suspended in the harmonic whorls of metasounds and metacolors. Amphion appeared in the garden next to Hylozoi, arrayed in a long, flowing purple robe. He strummed an ancient, yet futuristic invocation on a golden lyre. Every tone evoked laminar wakes in the garden's symphony of sound-color forms.

"Rise in your oneirospheric body of light," Amphion softly said.

Cherub souls wove moonflower vines, forming a small floating vessel.

"Out of the corporeal form we move in radiance," said Amphion, and they glided from the garden to an opening inside an effulgent mountain where all around was a vast cavernous space. Torches in the ground lit the dark and shadowy crevice.

A yawning cleft appeared in the ground from which issued a warm breeze. The abyss seemed to descend into the heart of the mountain. A pyre was glowing on an altar, filling the air with redolent aromas of rue and maythen. A silver sphinx was perched upon a tripod positioned over the yawning cleft.

"What *is* the cosmic significance of wheat?" inquired the sphinx.

Hylozoi responded: "It was seeded in the cosmic Wheat of the Virgin's Sheaf which She holds over Her shining mantle."

The sphinx and tripod disappeared and the two travellers descended into the abyss. The warm current breathed through them as they continued along a narrow, deep gorge, on either side of which rose cliffs of vibratory amethyst with towering peaks. Devas with violet eyes hovered above the peaks, flapping their huge, sail-like wings.

Amphion and Hylozoi came to an assembly room, a glowing grotto with walls of awarized mobile frescoes, evolving shapes, seeping tapestries, and petroglyphs. A silent group of souls adorned in white garments formed a circle around a sacred omphalos stone then slowly moved to the grotto walls and blew into variously arranged petroglyphic sequences of openings. Deep, resounding, resonant sounds reflected throughout the grotto and the vibrating walls.

A hidden door opened, admitting a flood of light into the grotto. Hylozoi moved toward the opening between two bluish agate pillars. Beyond, was an ethereal sea which emitted transcendental music, neither orchestral nor choral. The atmosphere shone with a liquescent, aurcolin light that encompassed the immense lightsound sea of space.

A floating island lay beyond in the sea of transcendental music. Meerschaum pillars slowly faded into visibility, and from these a beacon of celestial light, an emicating blaze, formed a bridge of air-prisms extending from the floating island to the grotto entrance.

Amphion spoke in a musical language: "The audible lifestream is the celestial light. Collectively, we have constructed these forms and patterns, arranging pure sound and light vibrations into dynamic constructs. It is by this theurgic art that we are the architects who plan and construct our physical forms. Light and sound are apports of the same source of consciousness."

When Hylozoi stepped onto the oscillating rainbow bridge his dream body modulated in frequency and form, transforming wavicles into rainbow sparks, entraining with the air-prisms of the rainbow bridge. Hylozoi became the bridge. The grotto and Amphion had dissolved into the all-encompassing light. The rainbow bridge and the island floated in the light-sound sea of space.

Materializing once again in his dream body, some unknown force within Hylozoi had fused with electrical, spherical tone colors of the island.

Once again he heard the musical voice of Amphion: "In the true symphony of your being you *are* sounds and colors; you are an ensouled instrument through which you orchestrate yourself."

Fountains materialized all around the island, each spray possessing its own metacolor and metasound. The spray from these wondrous fountains materialized a monumental lyre directly in front of Hylozoi. Shaped like an angel, the lyre's frame was constructed with gleaming myriads of ocean shells inlaid with radiating stones. The wings were strung with coruscating quartz crystal. The angel lyre's chromatic heart burned with a pulsating violet flame that penetrated through Hylozoi's dream body. Multitudes of Seraphim and Devas appeared streaming through the lyre's strings, all blazing with astral glories. Amphion appeared once more above the lyre's strings and blew into a conchshell. The angel lyre manifested eyes *poco a poco animato* which became fired with the purest gaze of Love, orbs that flushed waterfalls of light and a symphony of disembodied orchestral/choral energy personality essences. The harp cast its flushing eyes on Hylozoi. He felt a magnetic, syzygial force pulling at his chest. His dream body made warbling sounds, then he was propelled, as if from a celestial archer's bow, towards the harp. He was dissolved in the hydrobath of metasounds and metacolors within the chromatic heart of the lyre.

Hylozoi awoke in the garden on moonflower vines. The dreaming sound and light had waned into the silence of sound and invisibility of the higher octaves of color. A light veil of glistening moondew covered the tacit garden. He sat up on the vines and heard faint harmonic sequences from an Aeolian harp. Turning around, he saw a diaphanous cherub fading back into one of the statues. Hylozoi gazed upward at a falling star trailing across the twilight interval of dawn.

1988 (revised 1992)

Auroral Transubstantiation

Angel of the Celestial Earth, World Soul that sets musicopoeisic fire
to the polar heavens, I, an ardent acolyte imagine a recontre within the
interworld of ensouled Aurora: to arrive with symphonic senses, a
librating image-current bonded with Auroral harmonics; to envision
animate flame's weaving loom of sound-color, the bathysmal flaming
blossom of archetypal image-sound, that convoluting fresco of the
World Soul's flame-spun pulse in the region of the penumbral crown
where Auroral streams softly burn.

1990

Catechization for Orpheus

Zaotar Orpheus, will your advent from the Synesthetic Heart of the World Soul occur in a versicolored, interdimensional airship to confer your ecumenicity with transcendental jeweled music? Or, have you always been abiding among us in your asteriated chariot of soul? Are you concealed within multidimensional realities, composing eidolons of sonic astral atmospheres, holonomic imagescapes of harmonic woven brilliancy, quantumpuntal polychromatic soul-phasings of Uranian sound-lucence?

You, Orpheus, can create an entire universe by evoking a single sound.

Blessed Orpheus, your consortium here imagines immersion in your Cosmic Sound, as expressed to the prismal-like ones. Ardently, with aisthesis and gnosis we remain tribunal acolytes to your divinity. Perhaps by futuristic dream-art teletae and spiritual discernment we shall be vouchsafed a soul-alembic passage to your interdimensional threshold, resounding in your wondrous, theurgic Signature.

April 1992

Book Reviews

Modern Esoteric Spirituality. Edited by Antoine Faivre and Jacob Needleman. Associate Editor: Karen Voss. (World Spirituality: An Encyclopedic History of the Religious Quest, Volume 21.) New York: Crossroad, 1992. Cloth, pp. xxx + 413, $49.50.

WHILE THERE has never existed a grand, unified phenomenon suggested by the monolithic term "Western esoteric tradition," all of the *traditions* discussed in this anthology are united by common threads. Antoine Faivre notes that all esoteric traditions—whether Alexandrian Hermeticism, alchemy, Kabbalah, or Christian theosophy—hold several tenets in common. First, there exists a system of universal correspondences: humanity is a microcosm, a reflection of the entire universe, and is thus in sympathy with the cosmos. Second, Nature is a living entity: the cosmos is animated by a universal soul, which links all phenomena together, and of which manifest creation is a living image. Third, all esoteric traditions invoke the principles of imagination and "mediation": visionary insight enables the soul to penetrate to the heart of reality and read the secrets of Nature's Book. This faculty of visionary insight—sometimes personified as a spiritual Revealer (Hermes, Christ, angels, or other celestial messengers)— discloses to the philosopher, mystic, or theosopher the secrets of universal nature, thus acting as mediator between the spiritual and material levels of existence. Fourth, central to all esoteric traditions is the experience of personal transmutation: one cannot see into the heart of creation and remain untouched by the experience! Gnosis, or the direct experience of spiritual realities, always involves an existential and "alchemical" transformation of the human personality. Through this experience, we more fully realize our intrinsic nature and become aware of our role and central position within the universal scheme: "the contemplative brings all creation to God through himself," to quote from Faivre's essay.

The wide range of topics surveyed makes this book a valuable resource while the comprehensive bibliographies provide launching-off points for further exploration. Included here are essays by leading scholars on alchemical esotericism, Renaissance Kabbalah, Paracelsus, Rosicrucianism, Jacob Boehme and his followers, Freemasonry and esotericism, as well as the modern schools of Rudolf Steiner, Theosophy, René Guénon, and G. I. Gurdjieff. An excellent essay discusses the work of C. G. Jung within the context of Christian esotericism and cultural history. Arguably the most remarkable paper is Antoine Faivre's 70-page contribution on "Ancient and Medieval Sources of Modern Esoteric Movements," an unparalleled overview of esoteric thought and thinkers reaching from ancient Greece up to the end of the fifteenth century.

An irony involved in writing about these traditions is that language is incapable of fully expressing esoteric insight. Like the nature of a true symbol, our innermost, authentic perceptions can never be exhausted by mere description, for the gifts bestowed by meaning are inexhaustible. Nonetheless, in the hands of a master, the skillful use of words can lead us toward an experience of that primordial silence which underlies the genesis of art, language, and phenomenal reality.

The contemporary value of esoteric insight lies in the fundamental realization that the world in which we live—and the world we all create—is ultimately a manifestation of consciousness. Nature is "fallen" only insofar as we humans are asleep. All of our current crises—whether social, political or ecological—spring from perceptions and motivations that are out of harmony with authentic insight. However, by invoking the principles of awareness and vision within the fabric of our lives, we will participate in the alchemy of creation— and this alone can help the earth return to its essential, glorious state.

—DAVID FIDELER

The Harmony of the Spheres: A Sourcebook of the Pythagorean Tradition in Music. Edited by Joscelyn Godwin. Rochester, Vermont: Inner Traditions, 1993. Cloth, pp. xiii + 495, $29.95.

THE ACHIEVEMENTS of Pythagoras and Plato in the development of philosophical thought have been described often enough, but as Joscelyn Godwin makes evident in *The Harmony of the Spheres: A Sourcebook of the Pythagorean Tradition in Music*, they cannot be described too often. For in their theoretical significance the sum of these achievements marks a watershed in the history of philosophy, science, mathematics, and in that discipline in which all three participate, namely, harmonics. Among these achievements, one of the most profound and far-reaching has at its origin the discovery by Pythagoras that the hypotenuse of a right-angled triangle is equal to the sum of the squares of the two sides containing the right angle. Two conditions were involved in Pythagoras' proof: the acceptance of certain facts as self-evident, and the application of certain principles by means of which consequences are deduced from these facts. In the case of the right-angled triangle, the consequence of Pythagoras' reasoning was indisputable: no fraction m/n will measure the hypotenuse of any right-angled triangle. This conclusion was reached solely by rational inference—the deductive thought process of Pythagoras himself— and it has stood unchallenged ever since. It is a mathematical truth that is certain, incontrovertible, and of universal application. With a tool of thought that could produce so fundamental a conclusion, the Greeks were eventually able to transform arithmetic and geometry from disciplines whose practice had relied largely on rules of thumb into the rigorous science of mathematics. In the process they demonstrated that the science of mathematics is in fact the art of deductive reasoning.

On the basis of the success that they had achieved in proving various geometrical theorems, the Pythagoreans felt that reason, in the form of its most luminous product—mathematics—had disclosed to them the source of exact and eternal truth. As they saw it, the truth of the numbers embodied in their mathematical descriptions of circles, squares, triangles, etc., existed apart from time and place, apart, in fact, from the physical world. If anything, the mathematics descriptive of things in the physical world appeared to them to be the necessary conditions of all existent things. It was with this in mind that Pythagoras pronounced his celebrated dictum: "All things are numbers."

The influence of Pythagoras on all subsequent thinkers from Plato to Kant, and on most of the intermediate philosophers, has been immense. This influence derives largely from Pythagoras' having made mathematics the basis for a belief in exact and eternal truth, for a belief, consequently, in a super-sensible, intelligible universe. Of particular significance in the present context, however, was Pythagoras' momentous discovery of the fixed relation between numbers and musical pitches. For with this discovery he set into motion a revolution from which the world of ideas has never fully recovered. Indeed, Pythagoras' discovery meant that all existent things are not merely numbers, but that they are numbers standing in harmonious relations with one another (thus, the relationship between string lengths and musical pitches is expressible as 2:1 for the octave, 3:2 for the fifth, and 4:3 for the fourth). Numbers standing in such harmonious relations had then to be the *Urstoff* of which the whole universe is constructed. That being true, the universe, if reducible to numbers in harmonious relations, had to be accessible to human reason. Thus, if, as Pythagoras maintained, "The whole heaven is a harmony and number," it was by studying numbers in harmonious relations that one could see into the holy purity and harmony of the cosmic design. The importance of Godwin's book consists in his showing how Plato made this Pythagorean conception of numbers in universal harmony the basis for all subsequent speculative cosmology.

Plato, as Godwin explains, gave impetus in his *Timaeus* to a new discipline—Musica Speculativa—by arguing that the mathematical reality of Pythagoras' harmonic ratios mirrors and animates a World-Soul fashioned by the mind of a *Deus Absconditus* or, as Plato calls him, a *Demiurge*. It follows that for the Platonists, many of whose texts

Godwin has assembled here for the first time, mathematical realities like the right-angle theorem or the ratio of the musical whole-tone (9:8), had to have existed even before the universe came into being. Or, to put it another way, such mathematical realities seemed to them to have the power to exist independently of the universe itself.

By retrieving, translating, and assembling texts on the subject that would otherwise remain virtually inaccessible, Godwin has provided for the student of *Musica Speculativa* a unique resource. Indeed, many of these writings, such as those of Isaac Rice, Johann Friedrich Hugo Freiherr von Dalberg, and Louis-Claude de Saint-Martin, are quite possibly unfamiliar even to initiates in the field. Godwin has arranged the relevant passages in the chronological orders: Classical, Medieval, Renaissance, Baroque, Enlightenment and Romanticism. A brief biography precedes each text, and a learned commentary is appended in the Notes. The reader, guided thus through centuries of Pythagorean thought, is enabled to appreciate the concept of world harmony as a nature second only to nature itself, and is made to recognize that in exploring this concept we are vicariously contemplating our own universe. It might be mentioned in conclusion that given the richness and variety of the texts presented here, one misses the pertinent passages from Plutarch's critical work on the subject, the *De Animae Procreatione in Timaeo* (On the Creation of the World Soul in the Timaeus), a work to which Godwin refers only minimally. Also, on a matter of personal privilege, I may be permitted to observe that the passage in the commentary on Nicomachus (p. 408), which Godwin cites as "in which the orbital swing of the earth takes place" should read "in which the orbital swing of each takes place."

—FLORA R. LEVIN

Nature, Contemplation and the One: A Study in the Philosophy of Plotinus by John Deck. Foreword by Lawrence Dewan. Burdett, New York: Larson Publications, 1991. Paper, pp. 152, $14.95.

JOHN DECK taught in the philosophy department of The University of Windsor from 1955 to his death in 1979. If Ontario doesn't sound like a center of philosophical activity, one could respond that Deck wasn't exactly teaching academic "philosophy," and that consequently this book is not a typical academic treatise, despite showing a few traces of its origin as a dissertation submitted to the University of Toronto.

Instead, Deck uses Plotinus' extraordinary idea of Nature as a "contemplative producer," bringing about the world of trees, plants and earth by its own Contemplation, as a key providing access to the whole structure of Plotinus' universe: "Contemplative producing (is) a synthesizing principle (which) co-ordinates best Plotinus' picture of the world." As such, no student of Plotinus, or of consciousness generally, can ignore this systematic exploration of the West's most profound and influential metaphysician.

Deck takes this initially "dreamy" notion and brilliantly unpacks it as being the result of gradually introducing more and more duality or "otherness" into the "primary instances" of being and knowing: the super-Being and super-Knowing proper to the One. In this way Deck derives, chapter by chapter, the various levels of Plotinus' multi-storied universe. At the same time, our metaphysical "concepts" of non-dual Being and Knowledge are validated by showing how they can be "built-up" from their everyday counterparts by gradually strengthening the weak and incomplete grasp they ordinarily have of their objects.

Deck's book is also important as a kind of demonstration project. He shows the post-Enlightenment skeptic how the non-causal, "top-down" method of explanation, common to Idealism from Plato to Hegel to Whitehead, can provide substantive and spiritually useful results. Consistent with this perspective, the results are presented here in a way that mirrors Plotinus' own method, "adopt(ing) many perspectives and mov(ing) eventually to synthesis," in accordance with the intuitional, as opposed to "logical," nature of metaphysical doctrine. As Deck says of Plotinus, "he does not so much prove his propositions as accustom his readers to their truth" by circling around some initial metaphors and intuitions (such as the "playful" suggestion that Nature contemplates) until the reader suddenly finds himself already having a grasp of a whole doctrine.

Readers who come to the text with some background in Plotinian scholarship will also be interested in Deck's unique discussions of such issues as whether a kind of non-dual "super-Knowledge" can be truly predicated of the One (basing himself on the idea of "wakefulness" in *Enneads* 6.8.16), and whether the One's emanation of the Nous is a separate act from its own prior act of self-subsistence (where he draws on the distinction between the "act *of* the entity" and the "act *from* the entity" in *Enneads* 5.4.2).

Finally, all readers will be enriched by Deck's chapter "Is Nature Real for Plotinus?" where he shows that Nature, precisely by being Contemplation in its truest form, is actually *more* "real" than we ordinarily believe: "Plotinus does not have two worlds, but only one. His world of true being . . . *is* the everyday world . . . when the latter is known by the best knowing power (i.e., the *Nous* or Intellect)." The nature of Reality, in short, is Consciousness.

Larson has done a superb job in reissuing this book. The Greekless reader will benefit by the transliteration of Deck's copious Greek quotes. Lawrence Dewan's Foreword places Deck as a member of the "workshop of Plotinus," and the Publisher's Preface recalls the immense influence Deck had on the late Anthony Damiani. This is indeed a worthy addition to Larson's "Classic Reprint Series."

—JAMES O'MEARA

Performance: Revealing the Orpheus Within by Anthony Rooley. Rockport, Massachusetts: Element Books, 1990. Paper, pp. x + 142, $12.95.

ANTHONY ROOLEY has delighted and inspired the modern world with forgotten musical masterpieces of the Renaissance as founder of the famed *Consort of Musicke*, in his duo with the peerless Emma Kirkby and their sometime trio with soprano Evelyn Tubb or bass David Thomas, and as a lutenist and scholar.

Sharing his experiences as a musician, but also as a student, cook, sculptor, and family man, Mr. Rooley proves that "our entire 70-year span (or whatever is our alloted length) is nothing, but nothing, other than a play, a performance" and "performance contains such powerful things: heightened states of awareness, time seeming to stand still, moments of incredible clarity, moments of beautiful reverie, a sense of wonder, awesome beauty and love, profound admiration and respect."

In proving his point, Mr. Rooley guides us through a spectrum of topics including the myth of Orpheus, number symbolism, the philosophy of the musical Neoplatonist Ficino, the performance of famed lutenist Francesco da Milano, Castiglione's *Il Cortegiano* and Courtly Love, "Lute-songs on the theme of mutability and metamorphosis" by John Dowland and his contemporaries, the philosophy of melancholy, the art of masks as practiced by La Famiglia Carrara, the concept of temenos as sacred space, and Thomas Campion's "Songs of Mourning."

Music at its best, Mr. Rooley explains, is a reflection of the Divine: the performer reflects the Divine to the audience, often comprised of souls who have become alienated in the world of sensation. "Orpheus is really the archetypal performer, receiving his inspiration directly from the Divine, and through this gift, giving it out to all those with ears to hear." Orpheus has four main roles:

(1) the performer—in oratory, poetry, and music
(2) the priest—in ritual, revealing divine mysteries

(3) the healer—in restoring imbalance in body, mind, and soul

(4) the lover—in drawing Eros to the world and so bringing harmony

Mr. Rooley reminds us that Orpheus is within each of us, that any art or action in life can be a reflection and revelation of divinity.

Providing a cogent analysis of *Il Cortegiano* and other renaissance improvement manuals, Mr. Rooley divides the master performance into three elements. *Decoro* "embodies tradition, the laws or rules." Overemphasis of *decoro* "leads inevitably to rigidity, to dullness, to a shallow 'empty decorum.' " "The balancing principle to *decoro* is *sprezzatura*: courage, boldness, even rashness—a 'noble negligence,' a delighting in the moment, a love of improvisation." Too much *sprezzatura* results in what abounds on any AOR radio station or MTV. But there is a third principle above *decoro* and *sprezzatura*: this is *grazia*, "a quality from the Divine, uncontainable, unownable, without limit," perhaps noticed first "in the spaces between the notes." "Ficino regarded it as 'divine frenzy,' and yet also 'sublime tranquility.' It is, writers agree, a state of bliss."

This witty, enjoyable, and civilizing book is a modern entry in the noble series of improvement manuals that characterized the Renaissance. Fans of the *Consort of Musicke* will treasure this glimpse into the life and mind of one of the twentieth century's musical legends. Any reader will find *Performance: Revealing the Orpheus Within* a catalyst for personal and, one hopes, cultural renaissance.

—R. C. HOGART

We've Had a Hundred Years of Psychotherapy—And the World's Getting Worse by James Hillman and Michael Ventura. New York: HarperCollins, 1992; Cloth, pp. viii + 242 pp., $18.00.

THIS EXCITING BOOK by James Hillman and Michael Ventura has something of a deceptive title. That's because the book deals with the ideas and models of psychotherapy, it often seems, only in passing. Rather, this discussion is an incisive, furious look at our contemporary social, political and ecological malaise, which uses the notions of psychotherapy as launching-off points to question the fundamental premises of a world gone bad.

We've Had a Hundred Years of Psychotherapy and the World's Getting Worse grew out of an *L.A. Weekly* interview between writer Michael Ventura and archetypal psychologist James Hillman, reproduced in part one of the book, which starts off with the observation that "We've had a hundred years of analysis, and people are getting more and more sensitive, and the world is getting worse and worse. Maybe it's time to look at that." Part two of the book is comprised of passionate, well-crafted letters exchanged between Hillman and Ventura, each dealing with a particular subject, while part three consists of a concluding dialogue.

The problem with psychotherapy, the two contend, is that *the world* is left out of the equation. Psychotherapy, with Freud and Jung, started off in part dealing with the sickness of civilization, but today everything is reduced to the individual. The individual is supposed to cope, get in touch with his feelings, and, the two contend, become assimilated to a system that is itself pathological and dysfunctional. The effect of psychotherapy's underlying assumptions is to help the individual cope by focusing his energies inward and, in effect, anesthetizing the passions and discontent which could otherwise be directed at the problems of the world.

Hillman and Ventura don't have any quarrel with the idea of therapy itself; they argue, however, that the idea of therapy needs to be radically enlarged to a cultural level if it is to be meaningful. We must do therapy on the soul of the world itself. The soul reveals itself through pathology and, while our materialist cosmology would like us to forget the reality of the Neoplatonic *anima mundi*, the World Soul still speaks through its symptoms: "Alar on your apples; asbestos around your heating pipes; lead in the paint on the schoolroom ceiling; mercury in your fish; preservatives in your hot dogs; cigarette smoke in the diner; rays from the microwave; sprays, mothballs, radon, feathers, disinfectants, perfumes, exhaust gases; the glue and synthetics in your couch; antibiotics and hormones in your beef... You see what I am driving at: my suspicions and my precautionary rituals announce that I am living in an animated world. Things are no longer just dead materials, objects, stuff."

In this book the authors emerge as true warriors of the soul and provide the reader with a work where ideas pop off the pages like grasshoppers. They discuss such varied topics as love ("what does the madness want?"); the breakdown of marriages (there must be a collective cause for a collective phenomenon); the value of letter writing; the American cult of practicality; telephones (and answering machines); mediocrity; the modern mania of busyness (by staying busy all the time we keep our justifiable depression about the world at bay); conversation; and aesthetics ("suppose we are being harmed by the form of things . . . the predjudices against beauty expose our culture's actual preferences for ugliness disguised as the useful, the practical, the moral, the new, and the quick"). *We've Had a Hundred Years* is itself strong therapy for anyone who's ever been subjected to, in Ventura's words, "the destruction of imagination that this culture calls education, the destruction of autonomy it calls work, and the destruction of activity it calls entertainment."

James Hillman also takes a brilliant look at contemporary therapy's developmental fantasies of "growth," which is itself "a consumer attitude toward life." For the authors, when we experience insight we don't so much "grow" as "molt," giving up the parts that no longer work, so that we can become who we truly are.

"The goal of my therapy," Hillman writes, "is eccentricity, which grows out of the Jungian notion of individuation. Jung says, 'You become what you are.' And nobody is square. We all have, as the Swiss say, a corner knocked off." Elsewhere he writes, "Only the unconscious can save us: in your pathology is your salvation. Otherwise, the white bread ego rules and we will have Dan Quayle in the White House, the man without a quirk. I don't want psychotherapy working for Dan Quayle, normalizing and eliminating psychopathology, for I see our psychopathology as the 'rough beast' in Yeats' poem, who is actually the Second Coming, as the poem says in its very title."

Whether or not you agree with all of the ideas set forth in *We've Had a Hundred Years*, this compelling foray into cultural therapy will get your juices flowing; quite possibly, it will inspire conversation with others. At all events, it engages and invites us to step outside our self-imposed isolation and care for the ailing soul of the world.

"Our society offers places where you can let your feelings out," writes Hillman. "But where can you go to play with ideas? One of the great difficulties in our American life is that we don't have places for entertaining ideas. And that is precisely what we're supposed to do with an idea: entertain it."

In this work, James Hillman and Michael Ventura enter that living space, the Garden of Discourse, where all true philosophy is born, and invite the reader to enter, too. They may not have all the answers, nor is that their goal, their fantasy. But this penetrating dialogue certainly raises the right questions and presents many ideas worthy of being entertained—and seriously discussed.

—DAVID FIDELER

Books in Brief

DAVID FIDELER

Alchemy: A Comprehensive Bibliography of the Manly P. Hall Collection of Books and Manuscripts, Including Related Material on Rosicrucianism and the Writings of Jacob Boehme. Edited by R. C. Hogart; introduction by Manly P. Hall. Illustrated. Los Angeles: Philosophical Research Society, 1986. Cloth, pp. 314, $125.00.

This oversize cloth volume is a beautiful catalogue of the Manly P. Hall collection of alchemical works at the Philosophical Research Society in Los Angeles; it includes annotated entries, reproductions, and select color plates.

Autobiographies by Kathleen Raine. London: Skoob Books Publishing (11A–15 Sicilian Avenue, Southampton Row, London WC1A 2QH), 1991. Paper, pp. x+372, £12.99.

A very welcome paperback edition of Kathleen Raine's three volumes of autobiography—*Farewell Happy Fields*, *The Land Unknown*, and *The Lion's Mouth*—collected together here in one volume. Evocative, beautifully written, and highly recommended, from one of the most eminent literary figures of our time.

The City of the Moon God: Religious Traditions of Harran by Tamra Green. Leiden: E. J. Brill, 1992. Cloth, pp. 232, $63.00.

This valuable study treats the religious and intellectual history of the city of Harran (Eastern Turkey) from Biblical times down to the establishment of Islam. The author unravels strands of religious tradition in Harran that run from the old Semitic planetary cults through Hellenistic Hermeticism, gnosticism, Neopythagoreanism, and Christian cults to esoteric Islamic sects such as the Sufis and Shia, showing the city to be a collection point for Near Eastern and Hellenistic ideas.

The Elements of Native American Traditions by Arthur Versluis. Rockport, Maine: Element Books, 1993. Paper, pp. 122, $8.95.

A lucid study of cosmological patterns and symbolism in Native American spiritual traditions. Discusses Northern and Southern traditions, the warrior, hierophanic nature, spirits and ancestors, sacred sites, sacred art and myth, the visionary world, and much more. Comparisons with cosmological ideas from other traditions show that "the American Indian religious tradition has its place among the great spiritual and philosophical traditions of mankind," assuming that such traditions can be oral, emblematic, cosmological, and visionary. This beautifully written essay stands out as a valuable resource in a field that has recently become saturated by much new age fluff.

The Epic of Gilgamesh. Translated, with an introduction and notes by Maureen Gallery Kovacs. Illustrated. Stanford: Stanford University Press, 1989. Cloth, pp. 122, $29.50; paper, $4.95.

This new translation of the Epic of Gilgamesh is the first in English to take into account the new sources and linguistic research of the past twenty years. Newly found pieces of tablets have filled in gaps in the text, and the meanings of many words are better understood. It now makes the Epic accessible to the general reader in as clear and complete a form as possible. This is a definitive, beautifully produced translation, and contains much helpful background material.

The European Emblem: Selected Papers from the Glasgow Conference 11–14 August, 1987. Edited by Bernard Scholz, Michael Bath, and David Weston. (Symbola et Emblemata: Studies in Renaissance and Baroque Symbolism, 2.) Leiden: E. J. Brill, 1990. Cloth, pp. 190, 115 Dutch guilders.

This anthology of papers is full of historical details and analysis, but it does nothing to convey the atmosphere or ends of the emblematic tradition. These scholars appear as outsiders looking in; if they have any real feeling or appreciation for the tradition, it is not reflected in this anthology. For an antidote, see "Printing, Memory, and the Loss of the Celestial" in this issue of ALEXANDRIA.

Fez: City of Islam by Titus Burkhardt. Translated from the German by William Stoddart. Cambridge: Islamic Texts Society (5 Green Street, Cambridge, CB2 3JU, England), 1992. Cloth, pp. 175, $39.50.

This study of Fez, Morocco—a fabled center of Islamic learning— contains chapters on the Islamic mystical tradition and traditional science. This beautifully written volume also embodies the highest production values and is illustrated with 41 color and 17 monochrome plates. Remarkable!

The God of Socrates by Lucius Apuleius. Foreword by Daniel Driscoll. Seattle: Heptangle Books/Ars Obscura (PO Box 20695, Seattle, WA 98102), 1993. Cloth (limited to 1,000 handbound copies), pp. v+55, $15.00.

An essay on the Greek concept of the *daimôn* or "genius" of Socrates, by the Latin Platonist and novelist Apuleius (born *c.* C.E. 123), presented in a handsome edition. The title page does not tell us who the translator is, but the style and footnotes reveal it to be the work of Thomas Taylor. While speaking highly of his novel *The Golden Ass*— the only complete surviving Latin novel—the *Oxford Classical Dictionary* perhaps goes overboard when it amusingly observes that "The works of Apuleius are tinged throughout by his personality—a rhetorician posing as philosopher, peacock-proud and full of an immense store of undigested and superficial learning."

Greek Musical Writings: II, Harmonic and Acoustic Theory. translated by Andrew Barker. Cambridge: Cambridge University Press, 1989. Cloth, pp. 581, $94.95.

This anthology of ancient Greek texts in translation is indispensible for anyone interested in harmonics, Pythagorean philosophy, or

ancient Greek music theory. A full review will follow in the next
ALEXANDRIA.

*The Hermetic Museum, Restored and Enlarged: Most Faithfully
Instructing all Disciples of the Sopho-Spagyric Art how that Greatest
and Truest Medicine of the Philosopher's Stone may be Found and
Held, Containing Twenty-two most Celebrated Chemical Tracts.*
York Beach: Samuel Weiser, 1991. Paper, pp. 700, $29.95.

  This welcome reprint of a classic anthology presents in one volume
many primary texts of the alchemical tradition; an essential work for
anyone engaged in alchemical studies.

Magika Hiera: Ancient Greek Magic and Religion. Edited by
Christopher A. Faraone and Dirk Obbink. New York: Oxford University Press, 1991. Cloth, pp. 298, $44.50.

  Ten essays by American and European scholars. Disputing the
widely accepted notion that a clear dichotomy exists between magical
and religious ritual, the essays survey specific bodies of archaeological,
epigraphical, and papyrological evidence for magical practices in the
Greek works, determining in each case whether the traditional dichotomy between magic and religion helps in any way to conceptual-
ize the objective features of the evidence examined. Essays include
"Incantations and Prayers for Salvation on Inscribed Greek Amulets";
"the Pharmacology of Sacred Plants, Herbs, and Roots"; "Dreams and
Divination in Magical Ritual"; "Magic and Mystery in the Greek
Magical Papyri"; and more.

The Mystery of Numbers by Annemarie Schimmel. New York:
Oxford University Press, 1992. Paper, pp. 288. $19.95.

  A basic, popular introduction to arithmology and number symbolism from various epochs and cultures around the world. While not as
useful as Hopper's *Medieval Number Symbolism* in some respects,
Schimmel's excellent bibliography with many foreign language sources
is a valuable resource.

The Panarion of St. Epiphanius, Bishop of Salamis. Translated and edited by Philip R. Amidon. New York: Oxford University Press, 1990. Cloth, pp. 378, $49.95.

At long last, a welcome English translation of Epiphanius' polemical "Medicine Chest" directed against the gnostic schools and other Christian sects that were rejected by developing Christian orthodoxy. This book is a valuable resource for all students of early Christian heresiology.

Paul and Hellenism by Hyam Maccoby. Philadelphia: Trinity Press International, 1991. Paper, pp. 222, $17.95.

The apostle Paul has long been supposed to have been a rabbi, thinking in rabbinic style. This provocative book argues that such a picture is completely wrong. The truth, it claims, is that Paul was strongly influenced by both Gnosticism and the mystery religions, and his attitude towards the Jews and Judaism was chiefly influenced by Gnostic antisemitism. It was he, not Jesus, who was responsible for instituting the eucharist, the arguments for the Jewish origins of which are untenable.

Hyam Maccoby begins by examing who the Gnostics were and how they came to be antisemitic. He sees them as Hellenists on the verge of Judaism rather than rebellious Jews or deviant Christians. He then goes on to demonstrate the structural similarity between Paul's doctrines and those of the Gnostics. There was also a difference between them, namely Paul's sacrificial doctrine of salvation, derived from Hellenistic mystery religions. In this work Hyam Maccoby presents a compelling, well-documented argument which provides much food for thought.

Pherekydes of Syros by H. S. Schibli. Oxford: Clarendon Press, 1990. Cloth, pp. xiii+225, $59.00.

In the sixth century B.C.E., Pherekydes of Syros, the reputed teacher of Thales and Anaximander, wrote a book about the birth of the gods and the origin of the cosmos. Considered one of the first prose works

of Greek literature, Pherekydes' book only survives in fragments. On
the basis of these as well as the ancient testimony, the author attempts
to reconstruct his theo-cosmological schema. The theogonies of
Hesiod and the Orphic tradition, the cosmological speculations of
certain Presocratics, and the Pythagorean tenets on the soul, are all
profitably compared with the remnants of Pherekydes' book. Appen-
dix 2 contains all of his fragments in Greek with an accompanying
translation.

Pythagoras: An Annotated Bibliography by Luis E. Navia. New
York: Garland Publishing, 1990. Cloth, pp. xviii+381, $50.00.

This annotated bibliography of 1,197 items from many languages
describes each article, book, dissertation, etc. Not only does it alert the
scholar to a wide range of sources with excellent synopses, the
descriptions of less interesting works often could prevent one from
chasing down dead end trails. The bibliography is arranged by theme:
Journals and Periodicals; Bibliography; Source Collections; General
Works; Philosophical Studies; Socrates and Plato; The Testimony of
Aristotle; Mathematics—Astronomy—Natural Science; Music—Art—
Architecture; Pythagoreanism and Literature; and Miscellaneous
Works. This book is an invaluable resource for anyone doing serious
work in Pythagorean philosophy and the most extensive bibliography
of its type ever published.

Pythagoras Revived: Mathematics and Philosophy in Late Antiquity
by Dominic J. O'Meara. Oxford: Clarendon Press, 1990. Paper, pp.
251, $28.00.

An in-depth study of the revival of Pythagoreanism in the Neoplatonic
school and the influence of Iamblichean Pythagoreanism in the later
Athenian school. Contains new Greek fragments in translation from
Iamblichus' works *On Physical Number* and *On Ethical and Theological
Arithmetic*.

Religion, Science, and Magic: In Concert and In Conflict. Edited by Jacob Neusner, Ernest S. Frerichs, and Paul Virgil McCracken Flesher. New York: Oxford University Press, 1989. Paper, pp. 294, $16.95.

Essays by distinguished contributors on the relations and tensions which exist between religion, science, and magic. Essays include: Hans Penner: "Rationality, Ritual, and Science"; Jacob Neusner: "Science and Magic, Miracle and Magic in Formative Judaism: The System and the Difference"; Moshe Idel: "Jewish Magic from the Renaissance Period to Early Hasidism"; Howard Clark Kee: "Magic and Messiah"; Susan Garrett on "Magic and Magicians in the New Testament"; Karen Louise Jolly: "Magic, Miracle, and Popular Practice in the Early Medieval West: Early Anglo-Saxon England"; Georg Luck: "Theurgy and Forms of Worship in Neoplatonism"; Stephen Sharot: "Magic, Religion, Science, and Secularization"; and more.

The Secret of Secrets by 'Abd al-Qâdir al-Jîlânî (1077–1166 C.E.). Translated by Tosun Bayrak. Cambridge: Islamic Texts Society (5 Green Street, Cambridge, CB2 3JU, England), 1992. Paper, pp. 122, $17.95.

The chapter headings "Man's Return Home to the Original Source"; "On Islamic Mysticism and the Sufis"; "On the Pilgrimage to Mecca and the Inner Pilgrimage to the Essence of the Heart"; and "On Witnessing Divine Truth through the State of Peace Coming from Abandonment of the Worldly and through Ecstasy" give one a feel for the content of this work by a saint, scholar, and one of the most venerated figures in Sufism.

Sky Phenomena: A Guide to Naked-Eye Observation of the Stars by Norman Davidson. Hudson: Lindisfarne Press, 1993. Paper, pp. xiv+208, $19.95.

This nicely illustrated guide is an excellent introduction to observational astronomy and the motions of celestial phenomena. In addition to containing much material relating to the history of cosmological ideas, the book also contains practical exercises and experiments.

The Theoretic Arithmetic of the Pythagoreans by Thomas Taylor. York Beach: Samuel Weiser, 1991. Paper, pp. xxxv+248, $14.95.

A welcome reprint of Taylor's digest of Pythagorean number theory *"containing the substance of all that has been written on this subject by Theon of Smyrna, Nicomachus, Iamblichus, and Boethius—together with some remarkable particulars respecting perfect, amicable, and other numbers, which are not to be found in the writings of any ancient or modern mathematicians. Likewise, a specimen of the manner in which the Pythagoreans philosophized about numbers; and a development of their mystical and theological arithmetic."* The subtitle says it all!

The Works of Philo. Translated by C. D. Yonge. Peabody: Hendrickson, 1993. Cloth, pp. xx+918, $30.00.

A very useful edition of the works of Philo (20 B.C.E.–50 C.E.), the Platonizing and Pythagoreanizing Jewish theologian of ancient Alexandria, complete in one volume. This is the only one-volume Philo available; the Loeb Classical Library edition, with the facing Greek, is twelve volumes. Since Philo thought like a Greek (and knew the Jewish scriptures only in Greek translation), serious scholars will occasionally need to refer to the Loeb edition to discover the Greek terms hiding behind the translation. Nonetheless, this is a very useful edition.

Notices

Contemporary Neoplatonism Conference

Plan now to attend the "Contemporary Neoplatonism" conference which is being co-sponsored by the International Conference for Neoplatonic Studies (ISNS) and the Center for Neoplatonic Studies at Vanderbilt University. The conference will be held at Vanderbilt, in Nashville, Tennessee, May 18–21, 1995.

It is anticipated that all the papers will be critical and creative studies of Neoplatonic themes as they may now be significant in our present century. In short, the conference will focus on "What is alive and what is dead in Neoplatonism?" Some place on the program will be provided for strong critics of Neoplatonism, so long as it is evident that they understand what they are criticizing, as well as for exposition of the views of contemporary philosophers, writers, and artists, who hold essentially Neoplatonic views.

This could be the largest Neoplatonic conference ever held in the history of the world and presents an excellent opportunity to visit Nashville's exact replica of the Parthenon, all in the same trip.

Individuals interested in attending this conference should write to: Professor John Lach, Department of Philosophy, Vanderbilt University, Nashville, Tennessee 37235 for information about registration and housing.

Call for Papers: ALEXANDRIA 3

We are always on the lookout for quality contributions for ALEXANDRIA: The Journal of the Western Cosmological Traditions. If you have been researching a particular topic or have something brewing in the alchemical stew, we'd like to hear from you. We are especially interested in work that is scholarly, but not boring; learned, yet not "academic" (in the post-modern, semiotic, deconstructionist sense of the term). If you are doing work in the spiritual, philosophical, or cosmological traditions of the Western world, feel that there is more to scholarship than just writing about dead people, and want your work to actually be read, please contact us. Together, perhaps we can make a difference.

About the Contributors

Christopher Bamford is a publisher, editor, translator, and writer. He is the co-director of both Lindisfarne and Anthroposophic Press. His publications include *Celtic Christianity*; *The Noble Traveller: The Life and Work of O. V. de L. Milosz*; *The Voice of the Eagle*; and an introduction to C. G. Harrison's *The Transcendental Universe*. Christopher Bamford recently delivered a paper of Gemistius Pletho at the Villa Carregi near Florence (the site of Marsilio Ficino's Renaissance Platonic Academy), at a conference sponsored by the London Convivium for Archetypal Studies.

Richard N. Brown, translator of Melitta Rabinovitch's *The Dolphin in Greek Legend and Myth*, is a writer and translator who lives in New York. He has contributed to A.R.I.E.S. (the journal of the Association for Research and Information on Esotericism) and to other foreign journals.

Peter Cawley, author of "The Castle of Heroes," works in the field of library science and studies the history of modern occult and esoteric orders. He lives in Lantzville, British Columbia, Canada.

Shawn Eyer is a scholar of Hellenistic religions and part-time archaeologist who lives in Defiance, Ohio. He was a guest speaker at the Nashville Panathenaia Festival which was recently convened around the full-scale replica of the Parthenon in that city's Centennial Park. He has produced translations from Greek and Latin authors, including Catullus, Sappho, Horace, and Tiberianus, as well as selections from the Homeric and Orphic Hymns and the New Testament.

David Fideler studied Hellenistic religions and philosophies at the University of Pennsylvania. He is the editor of *The Pythagorean Sourcebook and Library* and the author of a recently published interdisciplinary study, *Jesus Christ, Sun of God: Ancient Cosmology and Early Christian Symbolism* (Quest Books, 1993), which deals with the cosmological and harmonic symbolism of the Logos in both early Christian and pre-Christian sources. In addition to his scholarly work, his interests include musical composition, astronomy, and cultural therapy. At the moment, he's trying to figure out how to hook his polychord up via modem to the Internet.

Joscelyn Godwin was born in England and educated as a musicologist at Cambridge and Cornell universities. Since 1971 he has taught at Colgate University. His most recent books are *Harmony of the Spheres: A Sourcebook of the Pythagorean Tradition in Music* (Inner Traditions International) and *Arktos: The Polar Myth in Science, Symbolism, and Nazi Survival* (Phanes Press). He has also edited (with Paul Cash and Timothy Smith) a tribute to the philosopher who has most influenced him, *Paul Brunton: Essential Readings* (Crucible Books/HarperCollins). A new book, *The Theosophical Enlightenment*, is forthcoming from the State University of New York Press.

John Henry's interests include Novalis, early German Romanticism, Alexander Scriabin, American Transcendentalism, archetypal psychology, and much else. He makes his home in Danville, Illinois, where he is a jazz percussionist and music instructor.

R. C. Hogart is a poet, musician, and the translator of *The Hymns of Orpheus: Mutations*, published by Phanes Press in 1993. He lives in Los Angeles.

Michael Hornum, educated at the University of Pennsylvania (Oriental Studies, B.A. 1985) and Bryn Mawr College (Classical and Near Eastern Archaeology, M.A. 1987; Ph.D. 1991), is an archaeologist with a special interest in ancient religion and philosophy. He recently published an analysis of the role of Nemesis in the Roman Empire, *Nemesis, the Roman State, and the Games* (E. J. Brill, 1993). His major philosophical interests revolve around Neoplatonism, in particular the ethical implications of Plotinian metaphysics, and the relevance of Neoplatonic thought for the modern world. He contributed to the introduction to the Phanes Press edition of *Porphyry's Launching-Points to the Realm of Mind* (1988).

Flora Levin is a musician, classicist, and scholar of ancient Greek music and Pythagorean harmonics. Her translation of *The Manual of Harmonics of Nichomachus the Pythagorean*, complete with a chapter-by-chapter commentary, has just been published by Phanes Press. Her article on "Aspects of Ancient Greek Music" appeared in ALEXANDRIA 1. She lives in New York City.

Adam McLean is editor of the Magnum Opus Hermetic Sourceworks series published by Phanes Press. For the past several years, he has been cataloging alchemical books, manuscripts, and artwork in European libraries. His "Note on the Muses" is extracted from *The Triple Goddess: An Exploration of the Archetypal Feminine* (Phanes Press, 1989). He lives in Scotland.

Eric Mueller was educated at the University of Chicago, the Islamic University in al-Madîna, Saudi Arabia, and the University of Texas. At the University of Texas he obtained an M.A. in political science on the basis of research into the political philosophy of Abû Nasr Muhammad al-Fârâbî, the medieval cosmologist. He is interested in the ancient traditions of cosmological speculation of the Middle East and Mediterranean region, Neoplatonism, Arab-Islamic philosophy, and Sufism, and currently works in the editorial department of a trade publisher in Hong Kong.

James J. O'Meara studied philosophy at the University of Windsor, Ontario, mainly in the "workshop of Plotinus" presided over by John N. Deck. He has also studied at the University of Colorado, the Naropa Institute, and Rensselaer Polytechnic Institute. He is Corporate Librarian at a law firm in New York City, as well as a free-lance writer and book reviewer. His current interests, in addition to Neoplatonism, include Eric Voegelin, the Southern Agrarians and other anti-Modernist movements in America, and the *sophia perennis*.

Nancy Nietupski, who contributed the article on Hypatia, has a background in electronics and works in the field of telecommunications. She developed an interest in Hypatia, which led to this article, after watching an episode of Carl Sagan's *Cosmos* series which mentioned the ancient Alexandrian philosopher. Nancy Nietupski lives in Grand Rapids, Michigan and, when looking for someone to translate "The Life of Hypatia" from the *Suda*, stumbled—quite by accident—onto the existence of this journal.

Carolyn North is the author of *The Musicians and the Servants: A Novel of India* and *Seven Movements, One Song*. She lives in Berkeley, California and teaches dance as healing.

Jerry Reedy, who translated the "Life of Hypatia" from the *Suda*, is professor of classical studies at Macalester College in St. Paul. His translation of *The Platonic Doctrines of Albinus* was published by Phanes Press in 1991.

Christine Rhone is a writer, translator, and artist interested in landscape symbolism. She is the author, with John Michell, of *Twelve-Tribe Nations and the Science of Enchanting the Landscape* (Phanes Press, 1991), a study of amphictyonies in the ancient world. Her translation of Jean Richer's *Géographie sacrée du monde grec* will be published in 1994 by the State University of New York Press.

Therese Schroeder-Sheker is a singer, harpist, and international concert and recording artist. She publishes frequently on the women mystics, contemplative spirituality, and monastic medicine, and is a pioneer in the palliative-medical field of music-thanatology. She may be reached at The Chalice of Repose Project, St. Patrick Hospital, 554 West Broadway, Missoula, Montana 59802. The editor of this journal highly recommends her recordings *Rosa Mystica* (Celestial Harmonies, PO Box 30122, Tucson, Arizona 85751) and *The Queen's Minstrel* (Windham Hill).

Siemen Terpstra is a musician and musicologist with a degree in philosophy who has been conducting research into harmonics for many years. His writings include *The Matrix Model of Musical Harmony*; *Studies in the Transition from Medieval to Renaissance Tuning Paradigms*; *Tuning Practica*; *Means and Music*; *Musical Metaphors in Pythagorean Philosophy*; *A Short List of Musical-Cosmological Monochords*; *Five-Limit Monochord Divisions*; and many other works. A recent solo bicycle trip took Siemen, a mandolin, and some recorders from the Netherlands to Morocco. In Morocco, he was enthusiastically embraced by villagers who enjoyed his music and took him to view ancient megalithic stone circles high in the mountains.

Jane Thigpen, author of "The Fish Bride," is a writer with an interest in mythology, folklore, and fairy tales. She is a Ph.D. candidate in classical studies and is currently completing her dissertation on Roman epitaphs from Spain and Portugal. She lives in Grand Rapids, Michigan.

Hugh Urban is a graduate student in religious studies at the University of Chicago. His articles have also appeared in *Temenos* and *Avaloka*.

Arthur Versluis, who holds a doctorate in American literature from the University of Michigan, is currently a Fulbright Professor of literature at the University of Düsseldorf, Germany, and is author of various books and articles, including *American Transcendentalism and Asian Religions* (Oxford University Press, 1993) and *Theosophia: Hidden Dimensions of Christianity* (Lindisfarne, 1994). When possible, he returns to Grand Rapids, Michigan, where his family has a fruit and vegetable farm.

Robin Waterfield, author of "Seating Arrangements in the Symposium," is a distinguished translator of Plato. His versions of the *Philebus*, *Theatetus*, and other dialogues have been published by Penguin Books, and Oxford University Press recently commissioned him to produce a new translation of *The Republic*. His translation of *The Theology of Arithmetic*, attributed to Iamblichus, was published by Phanes Press in 1988.

Daniel Willens is a freelance writer and translator living in northern California. He has studied at the Sorbonne and at the Friedrich Wilhems Universitaet, Bonn, receiving his degree in Modern Languages from Ripon College in 1978.

List of Subscribers

THE FOLLOWING INDIVIDUALS have made the publication of ALEX-ANDRIA 2 possible by joining THE ALEXANDRIA SOCIETY. Without their generous support of our publications program, this journal would never have seen the light of day. We thank these individuals for making this forum possible.

Semi-Divinities ($500)
Carole M. O'Connor

Ann Grocott
William R. Laudahn

Benefactors ($100)
J. H. Bruening
Neil Bull
Kimbal R. Clark
F. P. Cruikshank
Joseph Cuda
Doss McDavid
John Deveney
Kenneth G. Field
Bernard Gauthier
Daniel A. S. Loureiro
Lorna D. Mohr
James Burnell Robinson
R. H. Weeks
Walter Wehrle
Tom Whiteside

Supporters ($50)
Anonymous (2)
Eiler Anderson
Robert Armon
Prof. A. V. Askew
Ralph Bellantoni
Randy F. Buchanan
Roland Carter
Michael Castelli
Ralph Cizmar
Armand Courtois, Sr.
Joseph Coyle
Francis Paul Czawlytko
Kathleen Damiani
Frederick A. De Armas
Rob DeLoof
Edward C. Deveney
Katia Anne Dich
Harry Doumas
Gertrude Drake

Sustainers ($75)
Anonymous (1)
A. Jay Damon

Harold Eberle
David A. England
Kimberly A. Evert
Antoine Faivre
Robert Firth
John Fogarty
Anthony Fuller
Virginia Gaines
William D. Geoghegan
Carlos Godo
Joscelyn Godwin
Rick Goldman
Federico González
Ignacio L. Götz
Geoffrey Gough
Sara & John Michael Greer
Mark D. Grover
James Haberland
Dr. H. T. Hakl
Meredith Hardin
Michael Hattwick
Helen Henry
R. M. S. and S. C. Hershey
R. Nemo Hill
Denis Hines
Karl F. Hollenbach
John F. Horan, III
Paul Huson
Evangelyn D. Johnson
John R. Johnson, Jr.
Clarke E. Johnston
Marie-Louise Kagan
William J. Karkut
Ordo Lux Kethri
Brace I. Knapp, M.D.
Dr. Maurice Krasnow
Melvin Land

Huguette Lapierre Lanoue
Rev. James Lassen-Willems
J. S. Lemmon
Ray Manzarek
Chris Marr
Forest McIlwain
Ruth McMahon
Jeffrey G. Mead
Ralph Metheny
Patricia J. Middleton, M.D.
David Mitchell
Dr. John Mizenko
Frank Modica
Dr. John L. Moffat
Joseph Mohacsi
Frederick Morgan
Alexander Moshos
Thomas Nary
Raymond G. Newak
Dan Noreen
Paul V. O'Leary
Charles Obert
G. M. Onslow-Ford
Einar Pálsson
Willie Mae Parker
Laura Peterson
Steven Petrin
Richard Pickrell
John G. Pladel
Randall N. Pratt
Karen Prince
Val Savenko
J. Scott Sawyer
Barry M. Scheben
Michael Schneider
James Skinner
Patrick J. Smith

William Smith
Jeffrey Snyder
John Soto
Louis Spiegel
Chuck St. John
Jesse Stanowski
Robert G. Steffel
Timothy J. Stough
Michael Strom-Tejsen
Terrence M. Sullivan
Göran Svarvell
A. H. Thelander
Erol Torun
John R. Urban
John T. Walker
David Hale Whitlock
Elinor Williams

Members ($35)
Anonymous (3)
Shawn Abbott
Marc Adamchek
Robert Adams
John Alwill
Annjohnna C. Andrews-Hunt
Anton A. Armbruster
H. Scott Armstrong
Steven G. Ayre, M.D.
William R. Bacher
Diane Bagchi
Iris G. Ball
Eleanor J. Barnes
Chester L. Behnke
Brian and Carolyn Bender
John F. Berglund
Seymour Bernstein
Joanne Stroud Bilby

R. A. Binnewies
Robert E. Birdsong
Dr. R. Bolton
David Booth
Jane Boyce
Rex Boyer
Robert Boyer
Carolyn Brafford
Prof. J. Bregman
Robert V. Broughton
Francis P. Broussard
Dean Brown
Dennis Brown
Richard Brzustowicz, Jr.
William Buchanan
Susan Buchanan
Hall C. Burbage
Tom Cabot
Jeffrey P. Cain
James L. Capots
Toni Cardona
John Carey
Jim Carpenter
Amy Opperman Cash
Peter and Micheline Cawley
Lawrence J. Chisholm
David Ciarlo
Ann B. Claflin
James H. Clark
Leroy Clark
Chas S. Clifton
Arthur Cohen
John Robert Colombo
Kirk Crady
Bill Cranstoun
Ralph W. Crawford
Dr. James C. Cutsinger

José Jorge de Carvalleo
Ronald Decker
Bro. Cecil Elroy Deeg
Dennis Delorme
Nancy Denton
John Deveney
Anne de Vore
Suzanne B. Diamond
John Di Gravio
David C. Dodge
Thomas J. Dooley
Bill Downey
Patrick W. Dugan
Peter Dussik
Bruce L. Eaton
Doug Eblen
Charles Edgerton
Harry Eighmey
Robert S. Ellwood
William Elmhirst
Cecilia Englert
Jacques H. Etienne
Nancy Fairhurst
Robert Ferguson
Dr. Dian Fetter
V. H. Flach
Stephen Flowers
Karl C. Folkes, Ph.D.
Brett Forray
Farida Fox
Dolores Freckmann
Elisabeth Furbush
Diane Gaboriault
Michele Gagnon
Robert Galbreath
Brenda Galindo
David J. Gazarian

Mikael W. Gejel
Henry Genowa
S. T. Georgiou
Derek Gilman
Sarah Gilmer
Sallie Ann Glassman
William Gohlman
João Varela Gomes
Liesel Gras
Joseph Groell
Linda Gromlich
Glen Grosjean
Marilyn Gustin, Ph.D.
Mrs. Yvonne Hack
Maxwell Hammersmyth
Clara Hancox
Robert S. Hand
Leo Hansberry
Craig A. Hanson
M. S. Hanson
Robert Haralick
Jeff Hardee
Suzanne Harmon
Carol Harrison
Ruth-Mary Harrop
Janet Hartley
John R. Haule
Russell Heiman
Fritz Heinegg, M.D.
Chuck Henry
Michael Hergoth
Dr. W. R. Hetrick
Delbert Highlands
Jane Hill
Frederick M. Hoagland
John Hodgson
Paul Evans Holbrook

Michael Honea
Richard Hornaday
Gisela G. Ibrahim
Albert Jacobbe
Kenneth W. James
Dr. Herta H. Jogland
Larry Johnson
Dr. Roger W. Jung
Sylvia Kalb
Stephen L. Karcher
Patti Karger
Marianna Kaul-Connolly
Elizabeth Kelley
Bonnie and Joe Kelly
Scot Kelly
Jeane Glens Kennedy
Bob Kilthau
Noel Q. King
R. Russell Kinter
Richard M. Kline
Laura Louise Klohn
James Koehnline
Amy Krupski, L.C.S.W.
William M. Kuhn
Lorene Kuimelis
Alberto I. La Cava
Sandy LaForge
Enrique R. Larde
John A. Leaman
Allen R. LeCours
J. Douglas Lee
Chris Lemoine
Gerald F. Leska
Flora Levin
Monica R. Lewis
Juan and Doris Lorca
Bruce MacLennan

James J. Malpas
Perry Manac
Scott E. Mann
Stanton Marlan
Anne E. Marshall
Jon Marshall
Mario Matas
Carla Mathews
Robert Mathiesen
David E. Mathieson
Dorothy Mayer
Robert Mc Gahey
Rosa McGehee
Owen McKinney
Rev. Malcolm McLeod
Dr. J. McNamara
Sean McNiff
Ronald P. Mieir
Virginia L. Miller
Patrick Miner
Robert Miner
Mark Mirabello
Steve Mitchell
Janet Moffett
Blair A. Moffett
Doris and Thomas Mooney
Thomas Moore
James R. Morgan
Gary Moring
Seth Morrison
Robert Morse
Jim Moyers
Eric Mueller
Lorraine Muns
Raymond R. Mytko
Deanna J. Neider
Bruce Nelson

D. D. Nelson
Stephen Neuville
Frank Neves
Katherine Neville
Charles Newlin
Katherine O'Brien
G. Antoinette O'Heeron
Timothy O'Neill
Joe Otte
Richard Palcanis
Edward Paolella
Charles E. Pasley
David Perkins
Anthony N. Perovich, Jr.
Dr. Joseph M. Perry
Sandra L. Pitts
Barry Popik
Michael Praetorius
Todd Pratum
John A. Price
Ramon Jun Quitales, II
Rose Marie Raccioppi
John Raithel
Rebecca Reath
Chris and Paul Rechten
Geoffrey Redmond
Christine Rhone
David Richards
Paul Robinson
Rolf D. Rockliff
Philip J. Romei
Franklin Romero
Steve Ronan
Joseph F. Rorke, M.D.
Sherri Rose-Walker
Elisabeth Zinck Rothenberger
Andrew E. Rothovius

Raimund Rueger
Carl W. Ruppert
Sharon R. Sailer
Mark Sanders
Andrew D. Schmith
Shirley Self
Karen Sen
James Sesame
Elizabeth Sewell
Stephen J. Shartran
Rev. Milton R. Shaw
David Siddall
Carole Silver
Carolyn Sims
John F. Smith
John L. Smith
Laura Smith
Walter B. Smith
Robert Snow
Alvin Souzis
Jackson Spielvogel
Richard A. Sprott
David B. Spurgeon
Willard Stackhouse
Barton Stanley
Robert Stein
Helga Stern
John Stevens
Ted Stimpfle
David Stobbs
Audrey M. Stone
Jon T. Strehlow
James Strickler
Bill Sturner
Ray Styles
Margaret R. Sullo
Linda Sussman

Sondra Ford Swift
Florian Sydow
Toby Symington
Frank Tarala
Deloris Tarzan
Siemen Terpstra
Holly P. Thomas
Gretchen Thometz
Carol A. Thompson
Robert F. Thompson
Shawn Tillman
Mary M. Tius
James Togeas
Kenneth C. Turner
Harold Tynan
Marcia Van Horn
Jean-Pierre Vila
Thomas V. Vitale
Jaromir Vonka

Rod Wallbank
Dennis Walton
John Warner
Donald Weiser
Joseph Weitner
Luiz Weksler
Bruce R. Welton
David Wemple
J. C. Whitacre II
Eugene M. White
Ralph White
Thomas Willard
Dr. Terry Williams
Ruth G. Wiskind
Clifford P. Wolfsehr
Lorraine Yee
Dave Yount
Tobi Zausner
Robert S. Zelenka

Guido monochul   Theodal dulcis

F A B C D E F G a b c d e f g d

The Monochord Shoppe

NOW THAT you have read Siemen Terpstra's article "An Introduction to the Monochord," you have all the knowledge needed to build your own polychord and start researching the principles of harmonic science.

However, if you would rather purchase a professionally made polychord instead of designing your own, please contact us. If there is sufficient interest, we will have some made; we would also like to make available tuning templates and other related monochord reference materials such as diagrams, charts, posters, and software.

Regardless of your interests—whether they be cultural, scientific, cosmological, therapeutic, transformative, mystical, or just because you feel like it—please write to us if you would like to receive further information on polychords and our other services.

The Monochord Shoppe
c/o Phanes Press
PO Box 6114
Grand Rapids, MI 49516

Sophia Perennis
et Universalis

*Publishers and Distributors of Books on the
Wisdom Traditions of Humanity*

IN AN AGE compounded of skepticism and credulity, we
look to traditional philosophy and religion as the provi-
dential expression of the perennial wisdom, but recognize
that these must, in our day, be shorn of the inessential.
This implies neither syncretism nor shallow ecumenicism,
but synthesis—which postulates a common esoteric source
without violating the integrity of exoteric religious forms.

Sophia Perennis et Universalis is based on the premise
that the truth which underlies the great religions and
ancient philosophies—Pythagoreanism, Platonism, Hinduism, Buddhism, Taoism, North American Native Traditions, Judaism, Christianity, Islam, and others—is the sole
basis, in this age as in earlier ages, of inward peace and
outward equilibrium, and for this reason it emphasizes
"traditionalist" authors especially concerned with this
perspective. We offter primary texts, commentaries,
hagiographies, and studies of traditional arts and sciences.

You are warmly invited to participate in our book service
and ongoing translation and publishing program.

Sophia Perennis et Universalis
RD 2, Box 223P
Ghent, New York 12075
Telephone (518) 672–4323

Free catalogue upon request.

ALEXANDRIA
ON THE INTERNET

IF YOU ARE INTERESTED in the types of subjects covered in this journal and have a computer, modem, and electronic mail address, you will soon be able to travel to Alexandria electronically by subscribing to our free ALEXANDRIA mailing list on the Internet. By posting a message to the central address, it will automatically be distributed to everyone else on the list. This is a great way to initiate roundtable discussions, learn more about the Western cosmological traditions, connect with others, discover new lines of inquiry, and find answers to your obscure questions. No matter where you live in the terrestrial matrix of time and space, you may now join our virtual community in the Garden of Discourse.

For further information, visit our web site at:
http://www.cosmopolis.com

We look forward to meeting you in cyberspace.

Jesus Christ, Sun of God

Ancient Cosmology and Early Christian Symbolism

A superb marriage of daring spiritual metaphysics and careful, painstaking scholarship.

—Jacob Needleman
Author of *Lost Christianity*

David Fideler has given us a book of enormous importance. As a culture we've lost the wisdom and imagination that a traditionally symbolic view of religion provides. We are left with moralism, platitude, and a disturbing hunger for spirit. This elegantly written book is full of images that can draw us deep into religion as such and give our very idea of Christianity much needed depth.

—Thomas Moore
Author of *Care of the Soul*

Jesus Christ, Sun of God by David Fideler is a labyrinth of treasures. Scholarly, literate, fascinating, Fideler has offered us a Chinese wisdom book, based on his knowledge and intuition of the spaces that connect Pythagorean numbers to visual speculations of late Alexandrian mathematicians, philosophers, gnostics, and mystics. I am very grateful to have his lucid and handsomely made sourcebook.

—Willis Barnstone
Editor of *The Other Bible*

This work is clearly an advance towards better understanding about the wide range of possibilities available to interpreters in the ancient Mediterranean worlds.

—Robert A. Kraft
University of Pennsylvania

The most convincing argument I have ever read for the historical significance of gematria as the literary embodiment of geometric formulas. This study is comprehensive, articulate, and beautifully illustrated.

—Ernest G. McClain
Author of *The Pythagorean Plato*

Like an archeologist, Fideler digs beneath the surface of the Christian story to uncover the universal myths on which it is based. Then he goes further, into the bedrock of culture, by showing that these universal myths are themselves founded on a system of musically significant numbers.

—Joscelyn Godwin
Author of *Harmony of the Spheres*

This book makes a convincing case for the continuity of the European tradition, from Greek Orphism and Hellenistic Hermeticism to early Christianity, through detailed and original research on Pythagorean number theory and Hellenistic gematria. It is a brilliant achievement, literally thrilling, and a definitive text on Greek and Christian gematria and sacred geometry.

—Ralph Abraham
Professor of Mathematics
University of California

David Fideler sheds new light into the cave where Plato's historians of religion and students of intellectual history have been laboring with the shadows of the past. It is about time someone synthesized the astronomical and cosmological traditions of Hellenistic religion. Christianity's symbolic vocabulary is rooted in that tradition, and *Jesus Christ, Sun of God* propels us into an inquiry about the full function of astronomy, mathematics, and cosmology in ancient thought.

—Dr. E. C. Krupp

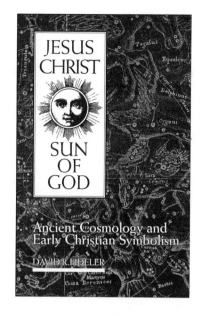

JESUS CHRIST ☉ **SUN OF GOD**

Ancient Cosmology and Early Christian Symbolism

DAVID R. FIDELER

Author of *Beyond the Blue Horizon: Myths and Legends of the Sun, Moon, Stars, and Planets* and *Echoes of the Ancient Skies: The Astronomy of Lost Civilizations*

This work is an extraordinary contribution to our knowledge of the rich tradition of thought and symbols of hierarchy and harmony.

—Paul G. Kuntz
Professor Emeritus of Philosophy
Emory University

A fully documented, highly illustrated, multi-disciplinary study

Cloth, 450 pages, $24.00 • Paper, $16.00
Published by Quest Books

Available through your local bookseller

The Manual of Harmonics of Nicomachus the Pythagorean. Translation and commentary by Flora R. Levin.

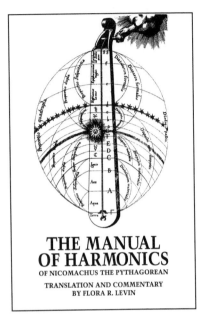

THE MANUAL OF HARMONICS
OF NICOMACHUS THE PYTHAGOREAN
TRANSLATION AND COMMENTARY
BY FLORA R. LEVIN

IN ANCIENT Greek thought, the musical scale discovered by the philosopher Pythagoras was seen as a utopian model of the harmonic order behind the structure of the cosmos and human existence. Through proportion and harmony, the musical scale bridges the gap between two extremes. It encapsulates the most fundamental pattern of harmonic symmetry and demonstrates how the phenomena of nature are inseparably related to one another through the principle of reciprocity. Because of these relationships embodied in its structure, the musical scale was seen as an ideal metaphor of human society by Plato and other Pythagorean thinkers, for it is based on the cosmic principles of harmony, reciprocity, and proportion, whereby each part of the whole receives its just and proper share.

This book is the first ever complete translation of *The Manual of Harmonics* by the Pythagorean philosopher Nicomachus of Gerasa (second century C.E.) published with a comprehensive, chapter-by-chapter commetary. It is a concise and well organized introduction to the study of harmonics, the universal principles of relation embodied in the musical scale. Also included is a remarkable chapter-by-chapter commentary of the translator, Flora Levin, which makes this work easily accessible to the reader today. Dr. Levin explains the principles of Pythagorean harmony, provides extensive background information, and helps to situate Nicomachus' thought in the history of ideas. This important work constitutes a valuable resource for all students of ancient philosophy, Western cosmology, and the history of music.

Limited cloth edition, ISBN 0-933999-42-9, $35.00; Quality paperback with sewn binding, ISBN 0-933999-43-7, $18.00. *Published by Phanes Press.*

What some scholars are saying about this book . . .

Flora Levin's way of working with this text is an inspiration. She takes the dry sentences of a notebook and, with her commentaries, turns them into living words, exchanged between living people. One can see from this why harmonics was so important to the Greeks: like modern physics, it gave entrance to the mystery of the world's construction, and to the intelligence latent therein.

—Joscelyn Godwin
Professor of Music, Colgate University

Thanks to Flora Levin's lucid commentaries, this work is the best introduction to Greek tuning theory available, including its philosophical, scientific, and cosmological implications. Coming from one of the most acute writers in the world on harmonics, this is a book that many readers have been waiting for.

—David Fideler
Editor, *The Pythagorean Sourcebook and Library*

For decades Flora Levin has been producing studies about the most sensitive and far-reaching topics in the theory of ancient Greek music. Convincingly and gracefully written, this expansive commentary handles with impressive tact the complications of what can be derived about Pythagoras not only in the light of ancient testimony, but also in the light of the major doctrines of both Plato and Aristotle, as well as their followers. Musical theory, enlightened by Levin's stereophonic command of both Greek and modern music, serves as a prism for the whole range of philosophical speculation about the relation of music to human thinking generally, as it comes through this long, multiple, major philosophical tradition.

—Albert Cook
Professor of Comparative Literature, Brown University

After a long underground existence, the Pythagorean tradition is experiencing a significant and healthy renaissance. This new edition and translation of Nicomachus testifies to the growing awareness in our society of timeless values.

—Siegmund Levarie
Professor Emeritus of Music, City University of New York

Saturn Castration ; Ourano

Maieutic
Multiplicitous
division
Pinion
vale
lane

Lydia's armored hoplites
Anaktoria

Hegel Revolution ? Consciousness
Schelling